Also by Paul Schneider

Brutal Journey

The Adirondacks

The Enduring Shore

BONNIE
AND
CLYDE

BONNIE AND CLYDE

THE LIVES
BEHIND THE LEGEND

PAUL SCHNEIDER

A John Macrae Book
Henry Holt and Company
New York

Henry Holt and Company, LLC
Publishers since 1866
175 Fifth Avenue
New York, New York 10010
www.henryholt.com

Henry Holt® and ⊞® are registered trademarks of Henry Holt and Company, LLC

Distributed in Canada by H. B. Fenn and Company Ltd.

Library of Congress Cataloging-in-Publication Data

Schneider, Paul.
    Bonnie and Clyde : the lives behind the legend / Paul Schneider. —1st ed.
        p. cm.
    "A John Macrae Book."
    Includes bibliographical references.
    ISBN-13: 978-0-8050-8672-0
    ISBN-10: 0-8050-8672-2
    1. Parker, Bonnie, 1910–1934.   2. Barrow, Clyde, 1909–1934.   3. Criminals—United States—
Biography.   I. Title.
    HV6785.S36 2009b
    364.15'52092273—dc22
    [B]   2008050296

Henry Holt books are available for special promotions and premiums.
For details contact: Director, Special Markets.

First Edition 2009

Designed by Meryl Sussman Levavi

Printed in the United States of America

1 3 5 7 9 10 8 6 4 2

For Nina

and Nathaniel

I'm going to tell the truth about these rats. I'm going to tell the truth about their dirty, filthy, diseased women. I'm going to tell the truth about the miserable politicians who protect them and the slimy, silly, or sob-sister convict lovers who let them out on sentimental or ill-advised paroles.

—J. Edgar Hoover

People only live happily ever after in fairy tales.

—Blanche Barrow

CONTENTS

A Note About Sources

The following is a work of nonfiction in which nothing has been created out of whole cloth by the author and everything has a reasonably acceptable pedigree as a "fact." That said, some sources are better than others, a situation that is true for every work of nonfiction and is even more unavoidable in stories as rife with rumor and lacquered with legend as that of Bonnie Parker and Clyde Barrow.

For now, all the reader needs to know is that no dialogue has been made up: all statements surrounded by quotation marks are direct quotes from the sources identified (and often qualified!) in the endnotes.

BONNIE AND CLYDE

CHAPTER 1

EASTHAM

Fog rolls off the Trinity River in East Texas in the hours before dawn, especially in winter, and lies on the land like Vaseline. It's thick and calm and quiet and peaceful in the fog, there where the piney woods that stretch on east into Louisiana give way somewhat abruptly to blackland prairies that spread west all the way to Dallas and beyond. She almost can't see her hand held out of the open car door in front of her own face. It's that thick.

And even better, surely no one can see her sitting here in this car on this dirt side road off another dirt side road, not far from the river bottoms. Sure, her leg that was burned badly a few months back still hurts and the other hip hurts even more from the rheumatism that flared up only recently. Rheumatism, at only twenty-three years old, no less. Too much sitting in cold cars. Too much sleeping in cold cars! But even with the pain, it's a comfort to know she can't be seen parked here in a cloud at daybreak, like a ghost in heaven. It's chilly, this cloud on the ground, but it's safe, and if death is like this fog it might not be so bad.

Only it's not worth thinking about death. That's the rule. "Let's don't be sad," she said to her mother only a few months before when the subject came up. We're here now. We're alive.

"Let's don't be sad" is what she said.

It's like thinking about air, for God's sake. And why think about air? Death and air. Fog, though, is good. Thick and quiet, except for now and then an occasional *tick ticka tick* of the steel in the car that says the sun has risen, even if she can't see it rising.

❀

When you're standing in a cold ditch in fog so thick you can't even see the car only a few yards away it's amazing where your mind will want to wander. Standing there with a fat automatic rifle in your hand waiting, what has it been now, ten minutes, an hour? Could be either. But you don't let your mind wander for the same reason you don't drink much moonshine even when everyone else does. Or, rather, you don't drink it *especially* when everyone else does. Even when Bonnie does. She likes it sometimes, but you know it dulls the senses, slows you down, gets you caught, gets you killed. So you don't drink much moonshine and you don't let your mind wander through the fog.

Where are they? Should be any minute now.

Eastham Farm, burnin' Eastham, bloody burnin' Eastham Prison Farm. This breakout was your idea in the first place, you and Fults thought it up together. But that was back a few years, back when you were still a prisoner on the inside. Not out here and free. Ha! FREE! As much as being on the run from the laws is freedom. Yeah, what a wonderful freedom this is: being wanted, being wounded, being hot as hell in three states, four, five states, whatever. Feels like you and Bonnie are hot as hell everywhere. Hot right in this ditch in the chilly fog a mile from the burnin' hell. Oh they'd love to find you here, for sure.

But you weren't thinking how it would feel to get this close to this place again when you said let's do it. No way. And you weren't thinking you would be here with this pathetic drug addict Mullins instead of Fults or Raymond or someone you don't have to watch every second, someone who's likely to turn rat just for another hit of dope.

It's amazing what a man can force himself not to remember most days and nights, except when it creeps up. And standing here in a ditch so close to it all, to where most of it all happened anyway, some of it does creep up no matter how you fight it. Burnin' Eastham. Burnin' hell.

Sure, you have killed a few men, more than a few, but you're not a killer at heart. Not according to your friends, anyway. This is not to say that you're afraid to pull the trigger when it has to be pulled. And not to say that you don't like the look of fear in big cops' faces when a gun's pointing their way. (If they'd look a little more afraid and not be reaching for their own guns all the time, you tell your friend, the trigger might not need pulling so often.) You pull the trigger, sure. It's just that there's no pleasure in it, even when it has to happen. So you're not a killer, right?

But when those memories do creep up, you start to think about those guards and their finks, their chains and their bats. And their "trusties" who will sit on your head while the man—the "captain"—whips you with the strap. And even worse sometimes is what goes on when the guards aren't around.

When those memories creep up. . . . Those guys, well, they deserve whatever comes their way. At least as much as you do.

❋

The guards at Eastham Prison Farm, some thirty miles north of the main Texas State Penitentiary at Huntsville, hate that fog but are pretty well used to it. Running the boys out the two miles or so to the work site from the building in dim dawn light and fog means riding closer to the jogging squad than the guards want to ride, just so they can see the boys clearly. Closer to the convicts means the convicts are closer to the guards, closer to their reins and closer to their bridles. Closer to the loaded Smith & Wesson .38s in their holsters. Closer to the shotguns, though with those right in a guard's lap all day, he is damned well likely to get a blast off if a prisoner is stupid enough to try to come near it.

Or not. Trouble comes fast in fog. On a foggy morning just like this, in fact, an Eastham guard named John Greer rides into the middle of his squad, all fired up to give the lazy bastards a piece of his mind, and maybe a piece of the bat for milling around instead of chopping weeds. Only instead of pistol-whipping some sorry two-time loser across the side of the head as planned, it's suddenly Greer who is pulled off his horse and passed around a circle of convicts, like some Julius Caesar, to be stabbed one at a time with homemade dirk knives. Greer doesn't even get a single shot off and he winds up dead with no witnesses as to who exactly did it. Funny how you can have lots of killers but no witnesses at all. Not that someone at burnin' Eastham won't be made to pay hell for the killing of a guard.

This foggy morning another guard, whose name is Olin Bozeman, isn't going to make that particular mistake. He'll make a different one, which he'll live to regret, and one of his fellow guards, Major Crowson, will make an even dumber move that he won't live to regret because he won't live. No, as a general rule the guards don't ever want to be too close to a squad of felons armed with hoes and other tools, not to mention guns snuck in from outside. Guns that the guards know nothing about until the cold barrel is pointed straight at them by a man who may hate them enough to kill them or may not, but who is desperate to get out by whatever means necessary.

But Eastham guards still have to be able to count the boys as they jog along. So the thicker the fog, the closer they have to stay.

❋

§eems like counting is most of a guard's job most of the days. Over and over again, for fourteen or sixteen hours a day, for a few bucks' pay to feed a family they only get to see every other night at best, and an occasional Sunday. A guard gets his breakfast before dawn in the guards' dining room, gets his horse after breakfast from the lot boy, who has the animal all saddled up and waiting, gets his shotgun from the picket, and just about the first words he hears spoken is the trusty yelling out the number of men coming out of the tank for their squad.

"Eighteen, Boss," he says, or whatever the number of the day is, and they count them coming out of the door in their white suits for those that haven't tried to run in the past and their striped suits for those that have run off and been caught.

"One, two, three, four, five, six . . ." until they get them all and can yell back "Eighteen," to let them know inside the building they got the same number outside, as if someone could get lost in the doorway. Then all day on the horse with that shotgun in one hand and the reins in another, come hot sun or come thick fog, they count those boys over and over until lunch.

The only reason the guards might run in sooner than lunch is come hail or rain. They got hail around here can kill a man once in a while, and lightning: an Eastham guard named Sye Fulsom once saw a convict get zapped right off the water wagon. Scared the shit out of the mules, literally.

On a normal day, though, it's work the squad hard until lunch and then run them back to the building, yell "Eighteen coming in" and hear the voice come out "Eighteen, Boss" when the men are in the door again. Lunch is usually ham and beans, but it's better than the squad is getting, and for that a guard in these times can be thankful. And maybe there's a moment for a catnap or at least a few minutes of horizontal in the guards' bunkhouse before it's time to get the horse and get the shotgun. (The pistol never leaves his side. "Goes to bed with you, gets up with you, and goes to the long table with you," says a guard who was there. "Boy, it damn near grows into you.") Then it's back to "Eighteen, Boss" out the door and "Eighteen" called back in. Back out to fields in summer or the woodlots in winter for the afternoon's work session.

That would be the afternoon and evening's work. "Can to can't" is what the prisoners call the workday on burnin' Eastham, meaning the work goes "from the time they can see until they cannot."

And for the guards, from can to can't, it's counting. Trotting the boys out, counting them, counting them as they hoe, counting them as they chop and pick, trotting them back in and counting them as they run. Maybe a little discipline now and then. Some guards are more inclined toward that part of the work than others, but even the ones that don't like seeing men beat up aren't going to say anything about it. Not with jobs as scarce as they are. Not with unemployment running 30, 40 percent. It's the Depression. It's the drought. It's hard times in a hard place to make a living even in good times. Even if they haven't lost the farm yet, farming won't pay. Maybe they got a sick kid, and a doctor to pay off. So who are they going to say anything to about some bastard convict getting hurt out in a field?

"See nothing, hear nothing, tell nothing," says a guard from those years. "That was the way it was. That's why those old big captains could treat the guards like they did. It's also why some of the little captains and guards were brutal to the convicts. No one dared to tell what was really going on."

There is plenty going on. But mostly, just counting men hoeing cotton all summer and chopping wood all winter. That's all anyone sees anyway, right? If anyone asks, which nobody does.

❀

Except this particular morning work doesn't get started right off because Raymond Hamilton, bank robber, ladies' man, and general pain-in-the-ass braggart, is not in the right squad jogging out to the woodlot, and guard Bozeman knows it. Hamilton's running out last in line with Bozeman's number one squad and he's supposed to be in the number two squad under a guard named Bishop.

It should make Bozeman nervous, this switch, and no doubt it does somewhat, though apparently not as nervous as it turns out he ought to be. There are a lot of squads, after all, not just his. Two hundred or two hundred fifty men jogging out on any given morning, and the convicts are always pulling this kind of stunt for whatever pathetic reasons they may have. And Hamilton's a wiseacre anyway.

Maybe Bozeman figures he'll take care of it as soon as they get to the woodlot. Perhaps not incidentally, the woodlot means out of sight of the building, so if there's some punishing that needs to happen it's out of sight, too. (Not saying that's his thinking, just a possibility.) But the fact that it's Raymond Hamilton in the wrong squad and not just some two- or three-time loser should make Bozeman more nervous then he is. Should WAKE HIM UP. Pretty much since the minute Hamilton arrived at Eastham from the main prison at Huntsville—"the Walls"—he's been talking about how he won't be staying long.

"I'm Clyde Barrow's buddy, Captain," he says one day not long after he gets there. Says it right to the face of the boss of the farm, no less. That's

Captain B. B. Monzingo, the Big Captain, as everyone calls him. "Clyde is coming down here and take me out and I won't be here long."

It's always that way with Hamilton, no matter how much the guards rough him up or whatnot. Clyde this, Clyde that, Clyde and Bonnie, yeah, yeah, yeah, until no one pays attention anymore.

Yeah, yeah, yeah, maybe, but Bozeman and everyone else knows, or should know, that Hamilton is, in fact, an old friend of Clyde and Bonnie's. More than a friend—Raymond was a member of the gang back in West Dallas. A Dallas detective named J. W. Fritz even warned the Texas prison officials about Hamilton when he turned the prisoner over to them, saying they "were asking for trouble if they sent Hamilton outside the Walls to work." But the warden just laughed at Fritz.

So when Hamilton turns up running out in the wrong squad on a foggy morning, a person might think guard Bozeman will take the time to stop and get Hamilton out of squad one and back to squad two as soon as he notices the switch. But Bozeman doesn't do it. He figures instead he'll wave to his fellow guard Crowson to come over once they're already out at the woodlot. Crowson can help take care of Hamilton. He's the kind of guard who is good at discipline.

❀

In the ditch about a hundred yards away, you and the drug addict can hear the twenty men huffing as they jog up to the woodlot. Shut up now, Mullins, that's them trottin' out now. Shut up now and keep quiet and keep ready with that gun if you ever want your lousy money from Raymond, Mullins. Whose damn idea was this coming right here to the very edge of burnin' Eastham.

Quiet now, quiet.

Get ready.

❀

> Mr. Simmons said there have been 27 escapes in three years from the two farms where "backfield" men are used. For the two years before that there were 172 escapes.
>
> —*The Houston Press*

It's completely against regulations for Major Crowson—that's his name, not his title—to come anywhere near squad one, even though his fellow guard Bozeman is waving him over. Crowson's job that day is to be the "long arm," the man with the steady aim and the long-barreled rifle who stays far enough away from the activity of the work gang to see the big picture and shoot a runner from afar. He's a sniper, you might say, only not hidden but there on his horse, moving around in the distance at the edge of the field, occasionally in but mostly out of sight. Something for the convicts to think about every time they consider doing something stupid like running off or causing trouble.

It's Prison Commissioner Lee Simmons's special idea to always have this "long arm," or "backfield man," as he sometimes calls it. Simmons says he's going to stop all these escapes that have been going on. His explicit rule is that the long arm should never come near the work gangs and has "no duty except to stay well clear of the convicts and to be in the background ready with his Winchester in case of any excitement."

Crowson, however, routinely ignores the regulation because who wants to sit out there on a horse all day, waiting for excitement? He's got a reputation among the prisoners for violence, and he carries in addition to his guns a rubber hose with a piece of wood in it that he swings around and cracks on the back of the convicts' necks.

Crowson is "a crack shot with both revolver and Winchester," says Simmons about what happened next, and "had he kept his post on the edge of the timber, things would have turned out differently."

Maybe the commissioner knows what he's talking about, even though he wasn't there on the day of the break. But one way or another there is going to be trouble this morning. Raymond Hamilton jumping squads is only the start. Both he and Joe Palmer, another dangerous convict and proven escape artist, have guns smuggled in from somewhere. And they haven't got much to lose: Hamilton's in for 245 years and Palmer's in for life.

So either someone is going to get away from burnin' Eastham this morning or somebody is going to get shot; or both. Crowson supposedly knows better than to ride up to a squad of men, but he reins his horse toward the clearing where Bozeman has told the squad to stop.

"It was about 7:15 A.M. when Bozeman called me and said, Raymond Hamilton has jumped in my squad," says Crowson. "I said, 'Boy, that is for something.'"

"Yes, it is," Bozeman says back to Crowson.

Both guards know enough to be nervous, but all the same Crowson, perhaps with his attention only on Hamilton, rides right on up to Joe Palmer. Palmer's got his back turned, and Crowson rides up to him not knowing he also has a gun in his hand.

"It all happened so quickly," says Bozeman. "I saw Palmer walking up to me as if he wanted to ask me something. Our rules do not allow the men to come too close to us in the field and I was just going to stop him when he came out with an automatic pistol."

"Throw up your hands," Palmer says. "Don't move and there won't be no shooting."

He does shoot, though. "He didn't give us time to do anything but fired point-blank into Crowson's stomach. He was shot through and through, from side to side," says Bozeman, who manages to get off a blast with his shotgun before he, too, is hit by a bullet from Palmer's automatic pistol.

"My God," says Crowson softly when the bullet hits him. Then he howls.

"They both screamed," says Britt Matthews, another guard on duty that day. "They both screamed and said, 'I'm shot.' "

❀

*P*op! *Pop!*

You hear the handguns go.

Blam!

There's a shotgun. That would be the guard.

That's it. That's them. Either Ray's shot them now or they got him, but it doesn't matter. Here we go. You stand up in the ditch and see Raymond running toward you. Palmer too, though he's coming a bit slower since he's trying to take off his stripes as he runs.

"Give us something else," Hamilton yells. "Let 'em have it, Clyde."

Sure, Ray. Sure, buddy.

"Clyde started to shooting," says Mullins—*rata rata rata . . . rata rata rata*—"and asked him what more he wanted."

You're just shooting the trees to pieces over the guard's heads with your Browning automatic rifle—your BAR. You're not aiming to hit anyone, just laying down cover for the boys on the run toward you in the fog.

God, that gun feels good.

Rata rata rat.

If you've got to be back here at burnin' Eastham, it's going to be back on your own terms at least. In a brand-new suit with a loaded Browning in your hands and a girl in a brand-new car behind you.

It's too long in the sleeves, the suit, a bit of poor tailoring that had you fit to be tied a few days ago when you first got out of the car and looked at yourself in it in the headlights with all the family gathered around for a secret visit in a cornfield outside Dallas. "I might as well bought an overcoat and been done with it," you yelled, making everybody laugh.

But nobody's looking at your coat sleeves when you're firing a flaming-hot BAR that with the giant double clip you had specially welded together can empty forty rounds in a couple of seconds.

Rata rata rata.

Remember me, Mr. Monzingo? Remember me, Big Captain of burnin' Eastham? I bet you do. And if you don't, it don't matter—I remember you.

Rata rata rata rata.

Ha!

Come on, Ray, run, you lazy bastard.

❅

Bozeman's on the ground, but he'll live. The other guards but one, meanwhile, are running away as fast as they can.* The guard who stayed, a brave fellow named Bobbie Bullard, who's in charge of squad six, fires his shotgun at Palmer and then turns back to make sure his own convicts don't take advantage of the mayhem and make a run for the river. He points his shotgun at a squad of men lying flat on their stomachs.

"The first man to raise his head," he yells, "will have it blown clear off." None test him on that.

The bullet Palmer puts through Crowson, however, tears his stomach up good. It puts four holes in his intestines, the lead expanding as it passes through the soft tissue before ripping out through Crowson's abdomen on the other side. He should be lying in the dust writhing in agony, but unbelievably, or maybe just out of fear of what will happen next, Crowson stays in his saddle, slumped over, and his horse takes him off first in the direction of the woods, then eventually back toward the main building.

And Palmer shoots him again.

"After Joe Palmer shot me in the stomach he shot at me once while I was riding away," Crowson says on his deathbed. "When Joe Palmer pulled his gun on me, Joe Palmer said, 'Don't you boys try to do anything.' I never did get my hand on my gun and I never did shoot at Joe Palmer, who shot me."

For a long time after the escape Palmer says he never meant to shoot Crowson, that he expected the guards to put up no resistance and that it was all an accident. But years later, when all his appeals have failed and he knows he can't escape Old Sparky, as the Texas electric chair is known, Palmer says, "It wasn't necessary for Crowson to be killed."

"But I hated Crowson and I killed him because I hated him," he says. "That's the truth and I'm ready to die."

---

* "I never left," one of them later protested in a hearing. "I just didn't stay."

❀

Back at the car in the fog, Bonnie hears it all beginning too. The sound of the guns, a Colt .45's firecracker bang. Distant shouts. A horse screaming madly. A shotgun's duller blast. Then *rataratararatarata.* The Browning automatic rifles. *Rata rata rat.* The crack of tree branches breaking, crashing. More distant shouts. And more shots. And again the familiar, faithful BARs. Clyde sure loves those BARs, steals them from National Guard armories every chance he gets.

She leans on the horn. *Beeeeeeeeeeeeeeeep* with that sort of tinny, thinny, wavering old-timey bleat. *Beep beep beep beeeeeeeeeeeeeeep.* That's the plan. Hear the guns, lean on the horn so the boys can find their way back to the car. Might as well start the engine now, too, what with all this noise. *Rata rata rata beeeeeeeeeeeeeeep.*

Where are they? Come on already! Come *on*! A girl can get bored of adrenaline it turns out, even when it's just about all there is left. That and cigarettes. *Rata rata rata rata . . .* not bored, that's not it. Just weary. Bone weary. C'mon, dammit, where are you now? C'mon, honey. C'mon now, sugar. Don't make this the day.

Beeeeeeeeeeeeeeeeeeeeep.

❀

You and the dope fiend, Mullins, get to the car first. The ditch is pretty close, after all, and you know exactly where to run. But even as you get there, the outlines of the other men appear out of the mist. Bonnie lays off the horn and slides over in the front seat, opens the door.

Here's Hamilton and Palmer, who's bleeding all over his stripes from the shotgun pellets someone managed to put in his head. Here's Henry Methvin, too, the Louisiana kid in for attempted murder. You knew him a little, back when you were on the inside. And a thief named Hilton Bybee.

All of a sudden Mullins, for some reason, thinks he's in a position to have an opinion about things and says, "Nobody but Raymond and Palmer going," meaning that Methvin and Bybee are just going to be left there to try and outrun the hounds that they can all hear baying in the not too big a distance. Hamilton also says, "We don't want that old boy," meaning Methvin, to which you reply, "Yes we do, come on, son."

Not while you're in charge. "Shut your damn mouth, Mullins," you say. "This is my car—I'm handling this. Three of you can ride back there."

You point to the turtleback of the car. Bybee and Methvin and Hamilton climb in. It's a tight fit, but no one's complaining.

"Guess four of us can make it up here," you say.

Up here, in a 1934 Ford V-8 coupe, is a space not exactly designed for four adults to sit comfortably. It's a two-door car with a single seat and some room behind that's stuffed with clothes and on-the-run necessities. But you don't take up too much room at only five feet five inches tall and not much more than 125 pounds. Bonnie's even smaller, four feet ten. She's tiny. So there's room for Palmer, who's sick and bleeding but has changed into one of the two suits of street clothes you brought, and for Mullin, too, though part of you would like to just leave *him* behind to face the dogs.

"Nobody but Raymond and Palmer going!" That's Mullins for you, all right. As if you might leave anyone behind in hell if they've got the guts to run and you've got the wheels to help. At least help them get past the dogs and the river. "You've got to get off the ground" is the first rule of getting away from the dogs.

Oh sure, sorry, boys, you go on back and see if Crowson's going to live and come back to work and find you. Oh he'll be overjoyed to see you! And if he's dead? Don't worry, the rest of the guards and their trusties will be happy to see you coming too.

No. No one's going back. Not as long as Clyde Barrow is driving and there's room in the car.

"Get in, son," you say to Methvin, who is only a few years younger than you.

"Everybody hang on," you say. "I'll take you out."

And then the accelerator is to the floorboards and you're gone.

❋

"I went to Governor Miriam A. Ferguson and former governor Jim Ferguson," says Prison Commissioner Lee Simmons. It's a month after the break at Eastham. "I told of my need for a special investigator and that I was considering Frank Hamer."

A lot of meetings with Governor Miriam include her husband, Jim. After Jim was impeached, convicted, and tossed out of his own term in office a few years back, Miriam ran and won in 1932 on a platform of "two governors for the price of one." It wasn't just lip service, so former governor "Big Jim" is sitting there with current governor "Ma" when Simmons comes in and explains that he wants to hire someone to track down the people who raided Eastham Farm, killing one of his guards and wounding another.

The creation of the position isn't a problem. The Fergusons have already said they'll do whatever they can to help Simmons catch Clyde

Barrow and his lover, Bonnie Parker, who everyone believes are responsible for the raid. The problem is the man Simmons thinks he wants for the job. Frank Hamer quit the Texas Rangers force in a huff when Miriam Ferguson was elected, saying he could never work for a woman. Simmons doesn't even want to ask Hamer if he's interested in hunting down Clyde and Bonnie without clearing it first in Austin, but it turns out Ma Ferguson isn't the type to hold a grudge.

"Frank's all right with us," she says to Simmons without batting an eye. "We don't hold anything against him."

CHAPTER 2

TELICO, TEXAS

In many country homes, where screens are not used on the houses, people sit down to meals with flies fairly swarming about and the children are seen sleeping while these loathsome insects gather in their faces and infect them with the filth and disease germs they may carry.

—*The Dallas Morning News*

It's 1909, and Shackleton is near the South Pole while Peary is near the North Pole. Closer to home, people are complaining about the new penny minted to celebrate Abe Lincoln's hundredth birthday. It's the first coin with a president's face on it, which smacks, some say, of imperialism. Others say the emancipator deserves at least a nickel or a half-dollar. In New York, DuBois founds the NAACP. In Boston, the Red Sox trade Cy Young. In Washington, the Wright Brothers deliver the world's first military airplane to the army. In Arizona, Barry Goldwater is born. In Oklahoma, Geronimo, the "last Indian to surrender," dies.

And in a three-room house in Telico, Texas, a small farm town some twenty-five miles south of Dallas, after a long warm rain that the paper says "made a rapid swelling of the buds on those trees not already in bloom," Cumie Barrow is giving birth to a baby boy. There are no screens on the windows, and there is no running water, no electricity, and not much in the larder. Most likely there's a woman from up the road—a midwife—helping her push this infant out of herself. But maybe not. Maybe just a neighbor or her husband, Henry. Birthing can kill a woman, but Cumie knows what to expect, this being her fifth child and all.

Or at least she thinks she knows what to expect from bringing children into this world.

It's March 24, and she and Henry plan to name their new boy Clyde Chestnut for no reason that anyone remembers other than they like the sound of the names together. Clyde Chestnut Barrow. Only later will Clyde Barrow let the police believe that his middle name is Champion.

❋

Cumie and Henry don't own the place where Clyde's being born. Not by a long shot. Henry, a hardworking man of not too many words, came to Texas around 1890 from the Florida panhandle. It's tempting to believe that one of his ancestors may have been the John Barrow who ran a boat across the Yellow River at Barrow's Ferry, Florida, a place that turns up only on ancient maps. This John Barrow came to northwest Florida around 1818 with Andrew Jackson, hunting Seminoles who had the dangerous habit of telling runaway Negroes they could be free Indians. Once that first Seminole war was over, this John Barrow set up running the boat across the river. But the lines of genealogy are tangled, leaving no clear line from Henry Barrow to that particular early Barrow of the Florida panhandle; what's certain is that by the time Clyde's father was born, in 1874, there were Barrows all over that part of Florida and in neighboring Alabama. Some were doing okay for themselves—the "wealthy Barrows." Others, including Henry's parents, Jim and Marie Jones Barrow, were not exactly getting rich, either quick or slow.

Starting when Henry was eleven or so, the family drifted west, following whatever harvest was hiring hands until they got all the way to Texas. There, in a farm field in the vicinity of Nacogdoches, surrounded by the puffy white balls of cotton busting out of their thorny burrs, Henry Barrow comes across Cumie Walker. She pronounces her name "Keemie," and later some members of her family will say it comes from Indian ancestry somewhere along the line. That could be, as there are Choctaw connections in the Texas Walker genealogy, though it isn't the kind of thing white folks are likely to admit and talk about in the 1890s. She was born the same year as him, about ten months younger, and is a tiny thing, under five feet tall and less than a hundred pounds, and in Henry Barrow's estimation she is worth running into again as soon as possible.

Courting among blackland prairie farmers traditionally goes on in cotton fields, at community sings, on occasional buggy rides, and, naturally, at church. Henry thinks Cumie is beautiful; she figures she's ready to get out from under her parents' roof. Cumie's father, William Walker, meanwhile, is thinking Henry's a bit young, only seventeen going on eighteen. What's more, given that Henry's been following the harvest most of his life, he's got no education to speak of: can't read, can't write, and never will learn to do either one. But he's a hard worker with a friendly face.

Henry Barrow is the right man at the right time for their daughter, figure William and Mahaley Walker. They're both a little on the young side, but not all that much by local standards. Nineteen's the average marrying age for girls, and Cumie's sixteen going on seventeen. But there's also girls getting married at twelve, even less. In December of 1891, after the cotton harvest is all in, the teenagers get married in a small ceremony at the Walkers' place with everyone hoping they'll be happy forever.

❋

The new couple set themselves up renting the farm next door to Cumie's parents. It's an arrangement made easier, no doubt, by the connections to the Walkers, a family that's been in the county for half a century. But however it comes about for Henry Barrow to lease his own farm to work himself, it's a big step up from being a migrant day laborer. A day laborer on a cotton farm is about the bottom of the barrel for a white man in Texas in 1891.

This isn't to say there aren't plenty of white day laborers around. A black man has to be pretty brave or stupid to show up in a Texas town where no one knows him. Nor is it easy for a dark-colored family to rent a farm, not with what the paper calls "night riders" showing up in some counties, warning landowners not to even think of renting to "negro tenants" and posting notices warning they'll be back around to burn the harvests and cotton gins of any man, white or black, who doesn't take heed. They'll sow Johnson grass on cultivated fields, they promise.

As for Mexicans, they aren't yet around in great numbers, and those who are have been in Texas longer than the Anglos and have their own ranches to show for it.

"We didn't have any Mexicans and just a few blacks," says Bernice Weir, whose family had a typical cotton farm around that time. "But we did have some white people that was transient that way, that had their wagons and teams. Just go from place to place. [They camped out] down close to the creek under trees, and they'd get their water out of the creek. There'd be plenty of wood they could pick up to cook with and everything. They cooked on a campfire. It'd be families. There'd usually be a family to a wagon and maybe there'd be a couple of wagons. They usually went in couples that way."

Henry knows that transient life too well, and to be renting a farm of his own, with or without help from the new in-laws, is a big step up. It puts him on a level with Cumie's people, or at least close. It's something to be proud of. It's a new start.

A decade later, when Clyde and the 1910 census arrive, about the only thing that will have changed is the number of mouths to feed and the address of the farm. Henry and Cumie have moved at least once and probably more times in the intervening years before winding up in Telico; the average blackland tenancy lasts only two crop cycles or so. Sometimes a family just grows out of a place. Sometimes the landlord backs out without having to give a reason. The deals are strictly year to year and both sides are always looking for greener pastures.

By 1909 Henry and Cumie have four children, not including the baby Clyde just making his appearance. Their first boy, Elvin Wilson, is three months shy of fifteen already and no doubt pulling his weight by now. His little sister Artie Adell is eleven and able to work hard as well. Marvin Ivan is six, and Nellie May is four. There's also a cousin listed in the census, Dave, who's seventeen, making him, too, a valuable adult. Clyde Chestnut will make eight mouths to feed off the farm. Eight mouths so far, that is.

Measured by nose count, that's pretty good progress. Most families in the Barrows' situation have lost a child or two by now. Generally speaking, one in five doesn't make it past the first few years. But there's no evidence that cholera or any of the other usual sorrows struck the Barrows in this period. Still, the land they're farming is not their own. The house is theirs only for as long as the landlord says it is. It's a place to live, but it isn't quite what you call a home.

"My dad [was] a tenant farmer," says Henry and Cumie's oldest girl, Artie. "We lived all over Texas."

❋

A million and one farmers have tried it a million and one times and finished the experiment in debt. Why, in view of the innumerable disasters, should any farmer still think he can win where failure has been the uniform experience? The one grave danger that confronts the South today is the danger that twelve-cent cotton will seduce Southern farmers into a new alliance with the deceitful cotton devil.

—*The Dallas Morning News*

If Henry and Cumie are still hoping to get ahead, they haven't yet figured out how to break through to the next level. Nineteen years since leaving Florida, and he's still farming another man's land. She's still pushing
babies out in a house that's not hers, and she's still got a couple more to go.
Not that this perpetual stuck-in-the-dirt is necessarily their own fault. In
1910 more than half the farms in the Lone Star State are owned by absentee landlords and farmed by tenants. In the blackland prairie belt, where
the Barrows are, the percentage is even higher, up to 70 percent in some
counties. And it's going up every year, which is another way of saying it's
getting harder and harder to become an owner. Land of the free small righ-
teous independent American farmer Texas isn't, and never really was.

What this blackland prairie is, intersected here and there with oaks and
pecans in the river bottoms, is good land for cotton. It's some of the best
in the world, dark, rich, and hot. And it's famous for its cotton pickers,
too. No joke. In 1896, nine-year-old Texas girls were picking two hundred
pounds of cotton a day. The best adults were picking about five hundred
pounds; they were picking a bale a day.

It doesn't much matter how good the land or how fast a man and a
woman and their children can pick a bale of cotton when the landlord is
skimming the cream year after year. A tenant farmer with a good landlord
generally works on what's called "thirds and fourths," meaning the tenant
supplies the labor, tools, and seed and he hands over a third of the corn crop
and a fourth of the cotton as rent. Maybe he gets a bit of meat and milk from
the absentee owner's herd to help feed his family, maybe gets a little land to
grow a few vegetables. Maybe he has permission to raise a few hogs, and almost certainly the woman has a mess of gangly chickens around.

Life is not made easier by the fact that the landlord decides what crops
the tenants will grow, an arrangement that always means cotton and more
cotton even when the price of a bale is falling year after year. There's more
than just plain greed making landlords more interested in cash crops than
fresh milk for the tenants' youngsters; even generous owners usually have
the bank breathing down their necks. So it is that a landlord might show up
on any given day and say, "I'm thinking we should put cotton in there in
that pasture where you been keeping that cow," and what he means is get
rid of the cow or plan to feed it out of your share of the corn. The word is
that the landlord usually even decides whom his tenants are going to vote
for, which is another way of saying which Democrat they will elect.

For Henry and Cumie and their growing brood, every year is a gamble
as to whether the price they're going to get for their share of the bales will
come close to covering the costs of seed and labor and tools.

"Way back yonder, when them cotton prices dropped, you just wouldn't make much of a living," says another tenant farmer from that place and time. "It'd sure be hard living. In other words, if you didn't raise your own living yourself back in those days, you wouldn't get by."

It's not the Depression yet and it's already a tough life, and that's not even mentioning weevils and other evils. The price of land keeps rising, the price of cotton keeps falling, the Barrows' chance of getting their own farm keeps seeming further and further away.

Still, Cumie's not complaining. There may not be screens to keep the mosquitoes out of the room where she's pushing Clyde out of herself, but at least there's a real roof over her head to keep that warm spring rain out. There's a floor between her and the black mud. Those aren't things to take for granted when a person could very easily be following the harvest, picking cotton, living in a tent and a wagon.

Most likely Henry and Cumie aren't even thinking about the possibility of owning a farm anymore. All they're thinking about, day in and day out, year in and year out, is young mouths.

"Rarely ever had enough to eat," remembers Clyde's older sister by four years, Nellie May. She goes by Nell. "Scanty clothes, and very few pleasures."

"I suppose," she says, "we weren't a very happy family. I remember that all my good times were connected with my little brother, Clyde."

❀

Good times. Living in a tent or even a shack isn't all that bad when you're a little kid out in the country being pretty much raised by your favorite big sister. Or, at least, you don't know it's bad yet. Your ma has another baby now, little L.C., born when you are four. Funny name for a boy, L.C. No one even knows really what it stands for or if it's even initials, as if your ma and pa just ran out of ideas for real names. They just like it. Anyway, Ma's got her hands full with L.C. when she's not doing farmwork.

As for your daddy, he's always doing farmwork, and pretty much has all the older kids with him. Even Marvin Ivan, who's going on ten now and everyone calls "Buck" because he's so fast, is off in the fields. Buck is fast like a deer and you want to be just like him, but he isn't around much because he's working. The times when your old man's a tenant farmer, he needs the help around the place himself; times the family is migrant working, anyone old enough to drag a cotton sack up to the wagon to get it weighed and marked down has to work. That's the normal situation in cotton country, especially in the fall, when a family working together might make five dollars a day.

"My daddy would carry us early fall when the cotton opened," says Julia Hardeman, a girl who lives the same kind of life as you, only maybe her life is even worse in that she's got eight brothers and sisters and a dead mom. "We wouldn't really get going to school just like we should till, say, after Christmas."

Still, there's plenty of fun to be had when it's not harvesttime. Or when you're still so small that you're just as likely to slow everyone down as you are to add any cotton to the family total, and just as likely to chop your toe off with a razor-sharp hoe as you are to turn a weed. There are places to make hideouts, and Indians to shoot. Not real ones, of course, but plenty of them everywhere you look. When you're Jesse James—you're usually Jesse James, unless you're the equally honorable and heroic bandit Cole Younger—there are banks to rob and cowards to shoot. You don't miss very often.

"Clyde loved guns from the time I remember," says Nell. "Toy guns if he could get them; if not, he'd use a stick for a gun."

Of course you love guns. Who doesn't? And Nell's a pretty good Indian, except when she doesn't want to play. To heck with her then.

"It was up to me to be the cowards and the redskins," she says. "And if I kicked about it, we didn't play."

❈

Nell loves her little brother, even if he's a bossy cuss sometimes. So cute, she thinks, how he always comes back begging to be forgiven after getting so mad right off the handle that he can't even talk for his sputtering. Steam coming out of both his ears one minute, all sweetness the next. Funny and sweet and a pain in the' you-know-what all at the same time. That's little Clyde.

She never knows with him. One day he's tagging along like a puppy when she might rather be alone with cousins and neighbors more her age. Next day he's wandering off when she's supposed to be watching him. Or he's wandering off when she's not supposed to be watching, which is better for her sake, but still worrisome. Clyde takes off for a whole day at a time when he's only about five and hitches a ride into town to see a movie with a nickel he got from who knows where. He just leaves the whole family worried sick and looking all over the place, thinking he's fallen into a well or been bitten by a snake or God only knows. Then he comes back in the afternoon as if nothing special is going on. Been to the movies, he says. He's got no fear and only slightly more sense.

Nell is of the opinion that her little brother's fearlessness may have come from his almost dying not just once but twice, and both times at her own hands. When he is tiny, just six months old, she nearly squeezes him to death with love. She squeezes him so hard and so long he stops breathing, turns blue, and lies there on the floor not moving.

"I didn't go to do it, Mama, I didn't go to do it," she yells when Cumie comes running and picks the lifeless infant off the ground and starts running with him up the hill toward the neighbors' house some half mile away.

"I didn't go to do it, Mama." She's crying real tears now. Clyde comes to eventually, after a few hours of no breathing, Nell says, which seems like an exaggeration or the funny way memory works as a child grows into an adult. Anyway, Clyde is blacked out long enough for it to be an Event in his young life that everyone remembers. After a few days, he's completely back to being a normal six-month-old. He's crying, crawling, pooping, peeing, and life goes on and nothing much changes except Nell doesn't hug him as hard.

Next time Nell almost kills him is a few years later and is more his own fault. She's supposed to be keeping an eye, sure, but she doesn't hardly know that the four-year-old is following down the path she and her cousins are taking from the hot cotton fields to the cooler shade of the creek. Swimming holes in that part of Texas aren't plentiful and they aren't particularly great in midsummer, when the water level drops and green slime creeps out from the edges. But kids don't care: wet is wet, and everyone is having fun until it seems like all of a sudden everybody notices at the exact same time that there's a bit of commotion at the other end and they look up and see his pathetic floundering and him slipping below the surface, and a few bubbles coming up.

Clyde! Clyde? CLYDE!!!

They're all slapping his face now, the three older kids. Rolling him around on the ground, moving his arms, and generally out-of-control panicking until he comes out of this one, too. Okay, he says to Nell when he can talk again, okay, he won't tell anyone about it. And he doesn't. Nell loves him for that. She can trust Clyde, and it's a good thing he didn't die.

There he is chasing the chickens around the yard again. Or trying to jump up on the calves in the pasture for a free ride. Brother Buck probably taught him that trick. Jumps on the milk cow, too, and the pigs. Buck only makes it worse when he's around, helping Clyde up on the semiwild ponies they find. And other people's cattle even. Clyde's got no fear, not much sense either. No fear in that child from the get-go. No fear at all.

❄

The younger cock gained the ascendancy, several feet above the ground, and administered a lick that sent a thin trickle of blood down the side of the old cock's head, without, however, seriously wounding him. As they struck the ground they whirled almost simultaneously, the old cock going over the other this time, but in a lower flight. The young cock rushed the battle to close quarters and the two became a ball of rolling, kicking feathers and clicking, flashing steel. The old cock gave out a steady, dangerous shuffle when not fought off his feet, but the younger bird shuffled equally well on his feet or off, on his side or his back; always his steel was flying, frequently cutting.

—The Dallas Morning News

God, Buck loves the cockfights. Six years older than Clyde, and there's something about the danger, the blood, the excitement that gets inside of him like nothing else going on in this dirt-poor cotton-town tenant-farm life. Maybe throw in a little corn liquor, a little side action. Makes a boy feel like a man. Makes him feel alive. Positively wakes him up and makes him forget cotton farming.

And of course there's the money. Big money, a hundred bucks on a single fight maybe. Everybody shouting their bets all at once, changing odds with each lick administered by one bird or the other, chicken blood on the ground, taking new bets while the cocks in the pit are slicing into each other with their metal claws. Those claws are two inches long unless it's what's known as a Mexican slasher fight, when they might be wearing a blade on their left leg as long as a man's palm is wide.

" 'Even money on the young cock!' shouted one. And, 'Ten to nine on him!' from another," says a Dallas newspaperman.

" 'You're on!' a loyal supporter of the old favorite accepted, adding: 'We still got a show and that's all Barnum & Bailey had.' "

The money is real, that's for sure. At the big cock mains up toward Dallas, with birds coming from all over, even St. Louis and Mexico, a big fight can carry even more than a hundred dollars. Even a thousand dollars, it's been said. Not that Buck's been up there to the big mains much, or ever. Yet. But he'll get there someday. Someday.

Not that he's got the big money to bet, either. Or the cocks to fight. Or even the claws to put on them, which might run twenty dollars a pair.

Still, it's fun just being in the know. For whatever reason, fights are illegal in Texas, so Buck can't just read about them in the paper or on a poster.

(He can't read anyway, even if the fights were on a poster. Clyde can read a bit, but not Buck.) So Buck's got to know someone who knows where it is all going to happen, and he likes knowing that bit of inside information. It's all part of the fun. Getting in a car with a friend who drives to the house of a guy who gets in the car and leads the way to, say, another guy. And that guy gets in his car, or maybe even has some birds to fight, and leads the way to the clearing off the road somewhere.

There might be ten cars already there, or fifteen, twenty-five. Plus a few wagons and horses. A crowd, and not just men either. Women, and even some kids like Clyde. The gamecocks in their cases are sticking their necks out, listening, looking out. Looking to fight. Waiting their turn to get dropped into the pit, to get put on their starting scores. They can't wait to fight, can't wait to hear the referee yell, "Pit your cocks" for them.

Illegal! What is that about? It's just fun. Like whiskey is just fun and illegal. It's not as if anyone's making or even really training those birds to fight. Shit, they'll peck each other's eyes out straight out of the egg sometimes. Illegal! Still, even the bit with scrambling off when the sheriff shows up is kind of fun. After it's all over, that is.

"Cheese it! The cops," yells someone, and everyone takes off in different directions, says Howard Hampton, a Dallas man who went to out-of-town cockfights in the 1920s. "It was every man for himself in case of a raid, and devil take the hindmost and even a few of those in front."

Just too bad Buck doesn't have a good supply of cocks to fight. He thinks about that pretty much all the time, say some. "Buck had one problem and it was that he was crazy about cockfights," says Boots Hinton. Boots doesn't know Buck, never met him, but his father, Ted Hinton, knew the whole family. "Cockfights is what got Buck into trouble in the first place."

The story is that Buck pretty much runs through the cocks that are available on Cumie and Henry's farm and starts eyeing a tough-looking rooster a few farms down the way. He could just borrow it maybe. Win a few fights, make some money. If it returns cut up a little, how's that old farmer going to know what happened? If it doesn't return, well, a dog got it. Or a chicken hawk. Chances are he won't miss that racket every morning. Cock-a-doodle-do! Ha!

Hey, Clyde, Buck supposedly says, how about I keep my eye out here on the road and you jump right quick over that fence and get me that rooster. He'll make us some money. You won't get caught, and if you do you're just a kid. We're going to have fun, Clyde. But we need that bird.

Nell says it isn't quite like that. Sure, she says, Buck "was always getting chickens and starting something." And, she says, "If there weren't any good

fighters on our farm, Buck wasn't against lifting good fighters from surrounding farms, which is where, I suppose, the story got started that Clyde's
first offense against the law was stealing chickens."

But that was Buck, she insists, not her little brother. "Clyde never stole a
chicken in his life," she says.

❀

> Farmers have kept their families in poorly constructed houses
> that have no conveniences: they have isolated them from their
> fellows: they have worked them too hard: then the boys go to the
> cities to be mechanics or clerks or doctors: the girls study to be
> teachers or stenographers or clerks. Their early environments
> have been such that they do not care to marry farmers, for that,
> as a farm girl said, would be stepping from the frying pan into
> the fire.
>
> —*The Dallas Morning News*

It's starting to wear on Henry and Cumie, this cotton-farming life. He's
getting a look of perpetual weariness from years of hard labor in the hot
sun, a resigned look that shows up in the few family pictures of him. It
breaks a body down. Cotton does that to you.

The life is wearing even faster on the older children, Elvin, Artie, and
even Buck. They don't see any future in it, and who can really argue with
them? All they see is endless work and getting nowhere on a plow behind
a stubborn pair of farting ox asses while cars from the city to the north occasionally go by on their way to the city to the south. Or just as likely, the
cars are going to the latest oil-patch boomtown to make a gushing of greasy
money. It doesn't matter which, or where: cars are going somewhere, while
the plow is just going back and forth in the dirt. Same as ever.

From the look of things, farm labor is getting on to not even being white
man's work anymore. When Henry was a teenager, migrant harvesters were
mostly whites like himself who drifted west out of the more devastated
parts of the Old South after the War Between the States ended. Ever since
the revolution broke out in Mexico in 1910, however, brown-skinned work-
ers have been coming over in droves to get away from the mayhem at home.
They want a piece of the wages that are five and six times higher on Texas
farms than on ranches south of the border. A poor Anglo can still get a job
or a place to rent, but, well, the wage is dropping and it's getting less ap-
pealing. It's becoming Mexican kind of work.

Those Mexicans must really want to come over the river with the Texas Rangers killing them by the twos, threes, and sometimes tens out in lonesome canyons with no judge or jury in sight. A "Ranger conviction" it's called in some quarters, and no one seems to care much except one uppity Tejano legislator from Brownsville named José Thomas Canales. He keeps making noise in Austin about reforms and rights, but he's been warned to watch his mouth by none other than Frank Hamer, probably the most famous Ranger of them all. Hamer is said to have killed a pile of Mexicans in the line of duty down on the border, and though he's a man of few words who prefers to let his badge and bullets do the persuading, he gives the uppity Canales a piece of his mind.

"You are hot-footing it here," he says. Standing well over six feet tall, he towers over the much shorter and dapperly unarmed lawyer. "And I'm going to tell you if you don't stop it you're going to get hurt."

Not that it matters in the bigger scheme. Canales keeps talking and doesn't get hurt. The Rangers keep ranging and don't get reformed. The Mexicans keep coming over the border and winding up either dead or employed. Henry and Cumie aren't keeping up on what's going on down south. All they know is it's not getting any easier to make ends meet on the blackland prairie. Big Jim Ferguson—a rich farmer but a friend of the poor one—promised that he was going to fix the tenant farmer problem if he was made governor, but he got thrown out by the legislature before he could deliver, impeached for corruption in 1917.

With or without Big Jim in office, there's no good argument to make to the kids that this cotton farming on other men's land is some kind of way of life that's worth hanging on to. Henry and Cumie are shipping Clyde and Nell off to various uncles' farms for months at a time as often as they can swing it. A few months at Uncle Frank's place in Corsicana, then back home, then a few more months over at another uncle's, and so on. In 1921, when Clyde's eleven, he's got a job as a night lookout in the oil rigs near Mexia, playing his Jew's harp and singing for the roughnecks. Then back home.

Henry and Cumie do whatever it takes to keep the young stomachs fed and young hands busy at a time when there's not enough work or food at home and there's no wages to be had by hiring them onto neighbors' places. But the ends, in the end, don't meet. Elvin, whom everyone calls Jack, is the oldest and the first to go. He wanders up to Dallas around 1919 and doesn't come back. Sends word that he's fixing cars out of his home, building a business that isn't making him rich but isn't breaking his back either. (At least not breaking it as fast as cotton picking will.) Artie follows him and eventually opens a beauty parlor.

Buck gets to Dallas as soon as he can swing it, probably around 1920, where at seventeen he falls in love with a girl named Margaret Henegan. Their marriage lasts just long enough to produce twin boys and then lose one at five months. Buck's eye wanders, and she takes the remaining boy and is gone.

Finally, in 1922, Henry and Cumie have had enough. It's not just the financial stress of farming that drives the decision to leave: Henry's not well. "He couldn't farm," says the oldest girl, Artie. "His health got bad."

They sell whatever farm equipment they have for whatever they can get, pack everything else, including the remaining children, into the wagon, hitch up the old cart horse, and set off to follow the cars heading in the direction of Dallas. Clyde and Nell, who are living with an uncle in Kerens, Texas, who works them from dawn to dusk, let it be known that they want to join the rest of the family in Dallas.

It's the Big D, the city at the three forks of the Trinity River, where Mrs. Emma Parker, a single working mother of three, has also made her way from the hinterlands and is struggling to make ends meet and bring her children up right.

CHAPTER 3

CEMENT CITY

The following industries are needed here: A weekly news-
paper, a cotton warehouse, a cotton factory, a woolen mill, a
creamery and cheese factory, a waterworks system and a can-
ning and pickle factory. Rowena is an excellent farming and
truck farming country . . . the people are social and anxious
to welcome newcomers.

—PROMOTIONAL PAMPHLET, 1908

What else is there for Emma Parker to do once her husband, Charles, up and dies all of a sudden on the last day of 1914, leaving her there in Rowena, Texas, with three children under the age of seven?

It should have been four children, but the oldest, Coley, died in the crib. That is a small persistent sadness for Emma, to be sure, but not an uncommon one by any means for those days and those parts of Texas. Just before Christmas of 1908 the birth of a boy, who is given the name Hubert and the nickname Buster, eases that pain. And then the girls, Bonnie on October 1, 1910, and Billie Jean in December of 1912, fill Emma Parker's time with happy labors. But the death of her husband comes out of the winter sky like a howling blue norther.

Life until that point is steady, and if the Parkers aren't getting rich, they are at least comfortable. It's reliable, and they are on their way to a solid, middle-class life on the prairie. Charles Parker is a skilled craftsman, a bricklayer in a growing town that's only ten years old and putting up banks, schools, storefronts, bowling alleys, and—hopefully soon—cheese factories.

"The only knocks that can be heard in Rowena these days is the rap of the carpenter's hammers," says the local paper gleefully.

There are plenty of bricks to lay with three brick buildings under construction and more planned. Bonnie's father is the kind of man who brings home a steady salary and laughs when his brother teaches little Bonnie to cuss like a sailor at the age of four.

Emma's not laughing, though. She's getting out the hairbrush, and not to use on the girl's pretty yellow curls but rather, she says, "where it would do the most good."

Rowena, way out at the western edge of Central Texas, near San Angelo, is higher, drier, flatter, and occasionally pricklier than the rolling lands south of Dallas that the Barrows left behind. But it's still cotton country, or becoming cotton country as fast as the Czech and German immigrant farmers can wrest the prairie back from the low brushy mesquite that is the product of a half century of overgrazing by immense herds of longhorns let loose by absentee ranchers where there had once been waist-high grass all the way to the horizon. Could almost be the Midwest, this country, except that in the distance a few low mesas keep a person cognizant that she's in Texas.

"The old stock ranches are giving place to agricultural farms," says a real estate ad for the county in 1908. "There are few that cannot be bought."

Mostly, the giant spreads that belonged to distant speculators are being carved up into smaller pieces and sold to hardworking people who call themselves Moravians and Bohemians. And lots and lots of Germans, like Emma's own parents, the Krauses, are living in the area around the time Bonnie is born. They're all a part of the great migration from central Europe in the decades around the turn of the century, a sea of people that fills parts of Wisconsin and Minnesota, Nebraska and Oklahoma. They are drawn to Rowena by slick promotions promising that "this county is as good as any Texas lands for growing cotton" and "the pear, fruit men say, never blights" and "nowhere do they raise better meated melons and cantaloupes than here."

They are good sturdy yeomanly people, mostly Roman Catholics, pulling out mesquite all day, planting cotton, digging wells. They are breaking their backs to make it pay, and see nothing wrong with having a glass or two of Lone Star beer at the end of the day at Zetner's Saloon to wash the dust down. Sometimes they might even have more than a glass or two: when the one-room town jail was built in 1910, its first prisoner was the man who built it.

"After he completed the job, he went out and had a little too much to drink," says the town constable, A. A. Fisher. "So in he went."

When Runnels County goes dry as part of the wave of prohibition sweeping the country in 1911, P. J. Barron, the man who originally laid out the six city blocks of Rowena alongside the Gulf Colorado & Santa Fe railroad tracks in 1898, is astounded. (The town voted "wet" by a margin of 169 to 13 but was overridden by the rest of the county.) The founding father of Rowena gets together a committee and buries a bottle of beer and one of whiskey under a granite monument in the center of town.

"Here lies our liberty," the gravestone reads, though someone digs the bottles up that very same night.

It's not all fun and games in Rowena. Not long after the prohibition vote someone burns down the little Baptist meetinghouse, whose congregation was presumably the source of the thirteen "dry" votes. There's also a sign at the town line that reads, "Nigger don't let the sun set on you in Rowena." It's been there since 1906, when a black migrant cotton harvester whose name is long forgotten by the town decided that he had finally had enough of being hit with a stick by a white farmer named Rudolf Turek and shot him dead in the street with Turek's own gun. The collective memory in town on what happened next is hazy: the cotton picker was either lynched in an oak tree down by the river by as big a mob as a town of several hundred could muster or he got away. But the sign went up.

The death of Emma Parker's husband is nothing so dramatic, though the details are similarly hazy. "In 1914, my husband died suddenly and I was left with three small children" is pretty much all Emma has to say on the subject.

Her fellow worshippers in the Rowena Baptist congregation are full of condolence. "Outside of church activities, socials, box suppers, and the like, we had very little social life," Emma says. Maybe they offer to take care of the older two children, Buster and Bonnie, for an afternoon here and there. They're good kids, after all, even if that Bonnie's a bit of a prankster, standing up in Sunday school one morning and singing "He's a Devil in His Own Home Town" rather than the hymn she is supposed to perform. But the Baptists are a dwindling band of ascetic believers who no longer even have a church building in which to hold such a service. (No one today can find Charlie Parker's grave in Rowena's Protestant or Catholic cemeteries.)

There's not much they can do for the young widow and her three children, and sympathy is no replacement for a salary. Emma can't lay bricks, and even if she could find work in the little town she can't leave three kids under the age of ten at home alone. It might be another thing if her mother and father still lived in the area, or if any of her nine brothers and sisters were nearby. Or if she owned a farm. But they're not around and she doesn't own a thing.

By the time Bonnie's father dies, Emma's parents, like the Barrows and waves of other farmers, have already moved up toward Dallas County, following their older children. Emma's mother has a job in a factory making overalls, and her dad is working a farm in the still-rural parts of the county. They've got a farmhouse on the Eagle Ford Road that's not big by any stretch but can temporarily fit three grandkids who have lost their daddy and one daughter who's trying to figure out where her happy life went. Houses in the nearby company town of Cement City rent for two dollars a room per month; maybe in time she can get one of those.

Come on up to the city, Mary Krause tells her twenty-seven-year-old daughter. You'll find work here, Emma, and maybe another man. Grandma can help with Bonnie and Buster and little Billie. It will work out, child. Come to Dallas.

Emma packs up her children and leaves Rowena behind.

❋

> To the west the smoking funnels of Cement City intrude upon the panorama, its belching stacks debauching the breaths of the furnaces of commerce upon the green reaches of the headwaters of the Trinity.
>
> *—The Dallas Morning News*

The school on Chalk Hill Road seems enormous to a six-year-old girl from Rowena, even though it's not. But it sure feels that way going up the dozen steep steps to the front door on that first day of first grade. The entryway is set into a false front—a style common in Texas—to give the building the feel of having an additional story. There are fancy, deco-inflected Tudor arches, a big one over the door and smaller ones above the windows. Along the top is a row of battlements, reminiscent of a fairy-tale castle, and there's plenty of other trim meant to suggest both the wondrous dexterity of concrete as a building material and the generosity of Trinity Portland Cement Company toward the families of its employees.

The cement company built the school. It built the baseball diamond and stands, where the town team does regular battle with teams from West Dallas and other neighborhoods. The cement company built the lighted tennis court—the new national craze. It built and stocked the fishing pond that is strictly for employees' use, and the wrestling venue, where contenders from across the river in Dallas proper sweat and groan for the amusement of the rock crushers' families. It runs the twenty-room hotel, and the grocery store and the meat market, both of which operate largely on company scrip, called food stamps. But they also take cash from members of the neighborhood who are not technically employed in the ongoing process of scraping million-year-old limestone and shale out of the hillside, pulverizing it into powder, cooking it into cement, packing it into bags, and loading it onto trains.

Most of all, of course, the company built itself out of concrete and corrugated steel. There are five great kilns, each a hundred and twenty-five feet long and eight feet around. There are seven rough mills that grind the rock into gravel, and five that crush it further. There are silos and half-ton bucket conveyor belts, coolers, dryers, and finish grinders. There are offices and repair shops of all types—electrical, machine, welding, carpentry—to keep it all running smoothly. There's a mule barn and mules, as there is still plenty of work for animals among the marvelous machines. And all of it is fed constantly by the great quarry, which is slowly migrating farther away as the phalanx of steam shovels bites into it, tears it down, and loads it onto train cars that haul it the quarter mile to the crushers.

Everything is basically brand-new; construction of the cement plant started in 1907. Three years before Emma Parker and her children arrived, in 1915, livestock still roamed in the streets, and the newly incorporated town of Cement, Texas, had to ask a judge if it had the legal authority to get the beef out of the roads. Forty years before, there was nothing but beef in the roads: the area was then still part of the town of Eagle Ford, which, as the western terminus of the Southern Pacific railway, was a bustling cow town with a shot to end up bigger and bolder than Dallas itself. Twenty years before that it was a colony of wacky French socialists come to build a utopia, and before that it was grass.

Now, though, it's America in fast action. Progress is under way, with smoking funnels and clanging steel. Down the road is an equally titanic oil refinery belonging to the Texas Company. And a rival cement plant, the Texas Portland Cement company, is nearby, too. Together the two plants churn out nearly two million barrels of cement a year, more than enough to build the longest concrete structure in the world: the Houston Street Viaduct, which stretches across the floodplain of the Trinity to Dallas proper.

Everybody from everywhere in the world, it seems, is here in Cement City, or in neighboring Eagle Ford, or just across the tracks in the grid of dirt streets and shotgun houses called West Dallas. Everybody is here, that is, who can't afford, isn't welcome, or otherwise just plain doesn't make the grade across the river in Dallas.

Blacks and Hispanics make up much of the workforce at the plants, living in their own neighborhoods and playing on their own ball teams. The blacks keep to themselves as best they can, with good reason. One night in downtown Dallas, the year Bonnie is ten years old, the city lights are dimmed at precisely nine o'clock and 789 citizens in cone hats and white sheets march single-file out of the Majestic Theatre. The first conehead carries an American flag. Ten feet behind him, the second carries a burning cross, as do many of the others all spaced precisely ten feet apart. And then begin the banners: "The Invisible Empire," "Here Yesterday," "Here Today," "Here Forever," "White Supremacy," "Pure Womanhood," "100 Per Cent American," "All Native Born," "All Pure White," "Dallas Must Be Clean," "For Our Sisters," "For Our Mothers," "For Our Daughters," "Parasites Go," "Grafters Go," "Gamblers Go," "Thieves Go," "Degenerates Go," "Our Little Girls Must Be Protected," "The Guilty Must Pay," "Right Will Prevail."

In total silence the mile-long line marches between crowded sidewalks in a rectangular route that eventually returns them to the theater. "The signs," says a reporter, "brought loud cheers and handclapping from many of the groups along the route. And then again silence."

The next day the Klan releases a statement. The organization stands for law and order, but "situations frequently arise where no existing law offers a remedy." In the breach is Klan law: "You can not deceive us and we will not be mocked. This warning will not be repeated." So the blacks of Deep Ellum, in Dallas itself, and of Cement City and other scrappier suburbs do their best to keep to themselves.

There are Italians and Germans and Moravians in Cement City and West Dallas, and a few old Frenchmen who have given up on socialism and are selling land. There are even, at times, a band of "Brazilian Gypsies" camping in their caravans, come from wherever gypsies in America come from, going wherever they go. They are feuding in a grand and theatrical manner over a hoard of $3,000 that a young husband named Lovell Mitchell supposedly stole along with his brother Joe from his father-in-law, Zulka Thompson.

"The money is alleged to have been in $20 gold pieces, which were fastened in a belt and the belt was hidden in the bed of Ruby Mitchell," says a reporter for the *Dallas Morning News* who is impressed with Ruby's appearance as a witness at the district attorney's office only three days after giving birth. "The woman, who is seventeen years old and strikingly beautiful, was married in accordance with the gypsy custom about a year ago to Lovell Mitchell. They have not lived together lately."

Salacious stuff for the readers of Dallas, but before the matter can go to trial "the iron hand of King Steve Frank was placed upon the belligerent factions and the trouble quelled." The money reappears, the charges are suddenly dropped. Gypsy law for the gypsies.

Occasionally Chinese laborers wander into town and are rounded up and promptly turned over to the Southern Pacific Railroad for prompt extradition. "So many Chinamen are handled," says the *Dallas Morning News,* "that the Southern Pacific has built special cars with barred windows and doors that can be securely locked." Southern Pacific law.

There are plenty of working-poor Anglos, too, with names like Parker and Barrow and Thornton and Hamilton. From the front door of the school a girl can turn around and gaze out over the immensity of it all. The new America is taking shape right there below Chalk Hill on a scale that dwarfs the schoolhouse, with its boys' wing to the right and its girls' wing to the left. But first grade is first grade, and the school still feels big to any smallish six-year-old on the first day. By all accounts, though, the little blond-haired girl is ready for whatever comes her way.

A girl named Flo Stewart, who is crippled from polio or some other childhood disease, says Bonnie is the nicest girl at the school, one who always stops to help her climb the stairs if she is having trouble. What her mother remembers, however, are the fights.

"When Bonnie was six she entered Cement City school," says Emma, "and proceeded to fight her way through it."

Usually it's just school-yard scraps with bullies and mean girls. Pencil thieves and the like, and Bonnie's cousin Bess is usually there to back Bonnie up. Not always, though. When she is about ten, says Bess, a boy named Noel, whom Bonnie kind of has a sneaker for, does something Bonnie doesn't like, so she follows him to the drugstore and starts beating the stuffing out of him.

"When a passing neighbor woman separated them, Bonnie had a piece of razor blade in her hand threatening to cut Noel's throat for him if he ever made her mad again," says Bess.

"And he was fairly blubbering, he was so scared."

❋

An opera star, that's what she'll be. That's what she is, in fact, on summer evenings with cousin Bess, serenading Grandpa's hogs and anyone else within earshot of the pigsty roof. It is a grand stage, Bess and Bonnie think, and they sing their hearts out until they nearly split their sides laughing, up there on center stage with all the fancy pigs in the front row.

"This went on night after night during that summer," says Bess. Whether the pigs are impressed or not goes unsaid, but Bonnie does have an ear for music, and some talent as well.

"She had musical aspirations. She could play piano," says her younger sister, Billie Jean, pronouncing the word more like "piana," with an easy and not unpleasant twang. "My mother gave us all piana lessons."

The lessons go well enough for a while, both Bonnie and Billie Jean practicing their scales dutifully. But ultimately the teacher is too slow and formulaic for Bonnie's taste, and Emma decides the lessons aren't worth the money for her older daughter.

"She just finally stopped givin', uh, stopped lettin' Bonnie take them because she'd play by ear and not by note," says Billie Jean.

"She could hear a song and she'd go home and play it."

❀

She'll be a circus star, that's what she'll be. That's what she and Bess are, in fact, up in the rafters all alone in Grandpa's barn. Hanging, swinging, doing tricks for the benefit of the spiders and swallows. Caught once by an aunt who kicked them out of the barn and told them never to go back in. Kicked out, but not stopped. Not when there's a hole in the back wall to squeeze through. They're back in, hiding out in the hay. Swinging from the rafters. Making trouble, practicing for the big center ring. Talking boys, laughing at girl things, and then stuffing it all up when they remember that Auntie might be within hearing distance.

Once, in a school play on a Friday afternoon, she's playing a black slave child, with soot on her face and a stocking cap. In the middle of the show, another kid pulls her hat off, letting her blond hair tumble out.

"Bonnie was so outraged," says her mother, "that she began weeping tears of anger. The smut ran down onto her dress, and the tears made white streaks."

When the boy who had yanked the hat makes the mistake of laughing out loud, Bonnie goes at him with both fists flying. She's tearing into him like a songbird into a crow and the audience is loving it. They're cracking up, laughing out loud at the spectacle.

"Bonnie stopped at the sound of the laughter," says her mother. "Things weren't so bad after all, apparently. People were being amused. She would amuse them further. She backed off and started turning somersaults and cartwheels right down the middle of the stage, and the program broke up in a riot."

She's a clown and an acrobat and a pistol and a half, and loving it. When she's nine years old her mother takes out a life insurance policy on her that costs a nickel a week.

❈

An actress on Broadway, that's what she is. Or better yet, in the movies, which have recently begun to talk.

"I knew Bonnie real well 'cause I attended the same school," says a classmate, Floyd Hamilton. "Bonnie was the type of girl that took parts in all sports, dances, and was what you call an all-around American girl."

She was, he says at another time, "a kind of fun-loving girl."

"Yeah she acted in all the plays in school," says her little sister, Billie Jean. "And I know so many times that, uh, a lot of times we'd go fishin' on Saturdays and I've always been a fishermen and she didn't care anything about it.

"She'd be all over acting. You know. All over that river acting and singing, and everything."

Bonnie is making a racket, jumping around elocutioning. She's scaring the fish, and what's more, it's dangerous. The year Bonnie is eleven a six-year-old kid who is fishing with his father and brother falls in the sluice-way, and when the father goes to save him he falls in, too. The poor little eight-year-old brother is left on the bank watching his daddy and little brother floundering until, finally, he runs for help. Too late.

"I'd tell her, be quiet!" says Billie Jean. "I couldn't catch any fish."

"Oh you'll be sorry when I'm on Broadway and I have my name in lights," Bonnie says back to her little sister and goes on acting and singing all up and down the river.

"You'll be sorry," Bonnie says, that "you talked to me like this."

"Was she a good actress?" someone asks Billie Jean.

"She was," says Bonnie's sister. "She was."

❈

> Cement City won the annual Dallas County interscholastic literary contest in Dallas Saturday.
>
> —*The Dallas Morning News*

There it is on March 28, 1922, her own name in print. "Cement City winners are as follows: Emma Emmons, first in senior spelling; Bonnie Parker, first in subjunior spelling . . ."

It's kind of a big deal for the whole school. Thanks to Bonnie and Emma taking first place in their divisions, Cement City actually wins the whole contest, edging out that farm town Lancaster, which at first tries to dispute the totals. Lancaster's teachers want to take the trophy back to their school on the grounds that they had more first-place finishers, but the rules are checked, and humble Cement City has won on points. Best of all about the day, probably, is that fancy Highland Park came in third.

Literary contest winner! Maybe she'll be a writer. Or a poet.

❀

Roy Thornton thinks he's in love with that short, kooky girl Bonnie Parker. He doesn't care at all how well she spells, or even that she's in all the school plays. What sixteen-year-old Roy Thornton likes is her good smile, and her curly hair cut in a sort of saucy bob and parted in the middle. He likes the way she barely comes up to his bicep, so that he can crook his own long arm completely over her shoulder and clear down her back around her waist. He likes the way her fifteen-year-old body, less than five feet tall, is nonetheless getting curvy in the right places, the way his palm is pretty much big enough that his thumb can sense the swell of the side of her breast through her dress, even while his little fingers are on her hip. He likes the way she puts her own arm around his slim waist, and hooks her hand onto his wide leather belt.

Most of all, though, it's her sassy, flapper style that catches attention. She's got the kind of grin that says, I know how to have fun, sure, but I'll fight you if I have to. And that's a useful quality in the neighborhoods they are both from.

As for Roy, he's not bad to look at himself, and he kind of knows it. Almost six feet tall, with a movie-star chin and a strong forehead, straight nose. Green eyes. Brown hair, combed back, and a big smile. And if he hangs around occasionally with a somewhat dicey West Dallas crowd of boys, kids like Buddy and Fred Mace, Floyd and Raymond Hamilton, Frank Clause, and Buck Barrow and his little brother Clyde, well, it's not as if Roy Thornton has no plan. He's learning to be a welder, a very good job in a boom economy.

Still, there is something a bit sad around the edges about Roy Thornton that's hard to put a finger on, as if he's just an accident waiting to happen. Or at least trouble.

"Death seemed to cling to Roy like smoke to a flannel suit," says Floyd Hamilton, but that's not until years later, by which time all manner of fast growing up has happened to the kids from Cement City and West Dallas.

In 1926, when he meets Bonnie Parker, Roy Thornton is just a fun-loving, shit-kicking, good-looking sixteen-year-old kid who seems to have a little money in his pocket from somewhere. Bonnie, meanwhile, has had childhood crushes, but she's never before been on a date. She's never been loved or in love. Bonnie falls fast and hard.

❋

> On March 22, following "What Price Glory?" the Circle company will produce "The Demi-Virgin," an A. H. Woods bedroom farce in which there takes place a poker game that caused New York to gasp a few seasons ago. However, New York has since then stopped gasping at a lot worse.
>
> —*The Dallas Morning News*

"When Bonnie loved, she loved with all her heart, and that was the way she loved Roy," says her cousin Bess.

There are walks home from school, and maybe on weekend evenings along the fancy sidewalks of Dallas. The jitneys go from Cement City and West Dallas across the viaduct over the Trinity River to downtown, where odd entertainments play the vaudeville theaters on Elm Street: Fred Lindsay and his "unusual act of Australian sports pastimes" at the Pantages, or "Striker and Fuller, prima donna and contortionist." There are also plays put on by stock theater companies, with cheap tickets for seats at the back.

There is even, if Bonnie and Roy dare, Deep Ellum, the Negro neighborhood at the far end of Elm, a remnant of the old "freedmen's town," where everything is for sale on the street and the music is lively at night. It's the Roaring Twenties, and there is a roof garden with dancing for the swells at the top of the fabulous twenty-one-story Adolphus Hotel, "the most elegant building west of Venice." Of course Roy and Bonnie can never afford it, but they can walk the street below and dream.

Mostly, from Bonnie's point of view, there are the picture shows. She loves those, and will for the rest of her life. Who doesn't? Particularly in the depths of summer, when the theaters have figured out marvelous new ways of piping cool, clean air into the darkened auditoriums. It's like heaven, that cool, dim space, with a cute boy in the seat beside you, nobody knowing who you are or why you're there, and the dream of fame up on the screen. There are plenty of theaters to choose from, with the Capitol, the Palace, the Melba, the Rex, the Old Mill. In June at the Capitol, for instance, there's Laura La Plante in *The Beautiful Cheat,* which, according to the paper, "is said to be the true story of a certain imported actress in Hollywood, whose antics are more or less public knowledge." In July at the Old Mill theater there's James Kirkwood in *The Wise Guy.*

It doesn't really matter what they see, as long as they see it together, and by September, Bonnie and Roy are ready for more than snuggles in the cool darkness of the movie theater. She gets his name tattooed on her thigh, a place not likely to be seen by many in 1926.

"Naturally, I didn't want Bonnie getting married when she was only sixteen," says her mother. "But she and Roy seemed so much in love and so determined that I gave my consent."

To be entirely accurate, though, Bonnie is still only fifteen on September 25, 1926, when she and Roy exchange vows. They promise each other everything forever. Roy smiles his good smile and slips onto her finger a ring that, like the tattoo, she'll wear for the rest of her life.

CHAPTER 4

UNDER THE VIADUCT

There are seventy-five families in what is generally known as the West Dallas Squatters' Camp. There are 275 people in the camp and 289 dogs! There are big dogs, little dogs, middle sized dogs—blacks, brindle and spotted. One family living in an old army tent, ragged and badly torn, has eight dogs. They are of the flea-bitten variety—long, hungry looking and apparently are throwbacks to the days when the wolf and the dog were one. The crimson cliffs of Mongolia would have little on the squatters' camp when it comes to dogs.

—Dallas Evening Journal

R olling through town on the back of some hayseed horse wagon from down Telico way, it doesn't matter if you're just barely a teenager—you know that you're not where you want to be. Not with the fancy cars coming and going, and the Adolphus Hotel towering, and the lights along the top of the viaduct twinkling. In the back of that wagon you're feeling like a, like a—well, you're feeling like a sharecropper. Or worse.

And when your pa and ma take up living in a tent under the great arches of the viaduct—not even in a tent, just camping out of the wagon, really— and your pa starts on to dealing in junk out of the back of that wagon to try and make a little cash. . . . Well, it just gets worse.

"I first saw Clyde Barrow under the Oak Cliff Viaduct in Dallas when I was five years old," says your neighbor William Daniel "W.D." Jones, whose own parents have also given up on trying to grow a living out of other men's soil and moved to the city. Jones and his four brothers and sister bumped around farms in the vicinity of Henderson County, Texas, before arriving under the viaduct, like your parents, with no cash and few plans.

"His family and my family was camped out there because we had nowhere else," says W.D., who is sometimes called "Dub" and sometimes called "Deacon." "Times was hard."

It's not just you and the Joneses camped out there, either. Fifty-one arches support this "longest concrete bridge in the world," and sprawling under various of them is a full-on neighborhood of sorts, with a fluctuating population of dozens of families. There's another, similar squatters' camp under the other end of the viaduct, in West Dallas, and eventually the Barrows migrate to that side of the river, perhaps to be closer to the jobs at Cement City, where Henry Barrow works for a time.

Most of the families are trying to figure out what their next move is, trying to figure out how to get out of the corrugated tin shack and into a shotgun house on land they can reasonably claim as their own. Others are single men resigned to waiting for whatever is next to be imposed upon them by fate or the city fathers.

"I've traveled pretty well over the old sphere," says an old-timer named simply Red who lives in the West Dallas camp. "Yep, I've been in Shanghai, Manila, and a few other places. Once belonged to the army, and I've been a few places. Well I got tired of roaming around."

And like any down-and-out neighborhood, the camps are places with their own miniature dramas of the sort that interest twelve-year-old boys like you and W. D. Jones's older brother Clyde. The year you arrive, Mrs. Alice Heron, fifty-six years old, jumps from the middle of the viaduct. Someone manages to grab her foot as she goes over the rail, but they can't hold on and she falls seventy feet headfirst into the seven or eight feet of muddy water of the Trinity. Amazingly enough, though, she lives, fished out of the river by a passing bank clerk who is lowered to the water by rope. It is something to look at.

Also in 1922, a live electric wire breaks loose from its mooring in the poles and falls across the neck of T. P. Dorman's horse. Dorman, who lives in the camp, is single and thirty-nine and apparently has nothing else in his life worth a damn but that horse. He runs up and tries to save the animal but only manages to get himself tangled in the wire, which sparks and sputters as it sends electricity surging through his body. Dorman's neck and head are getting severely burned as a crowd gathers. It is really something to see, smoking and smelling like the left wing on the day of judgment. But

Dorman, too, almost miraculously survives, ultimately being thrown free of the wire and taken away to the hospital. The horse, on the other hand, is left there, still tied to the tree, its charred and smoldering corpse sniffed at by the countless dogs.

One family story has it that the untimely death of your pa's own cart horse is what finally eases the family's way out of the squatters' camp. Old man Barrow's been using the horse cart to collect scrap metal, which he sells to the small foundries. In fact, everybody in the family is pretty much on the lookout for scrap and otherwise portable metal. That means you and Buck, too. Dallas Deputy Sheriff Bill Decker, who will later become sheriff, says the first time he ever ran into you and Buck was when he caught you swiping brass from a company yard.

"Their daddy didn't have any work," says Floyd Hamilton, who is about Buck's age and is a friend of the family. "I think some of the boys started picking things up to help out a little bit."

"Money was tight and times were hard and they did have to chip in to help and all," says the youngest Barrow girl, Marie.

❋

What Henry Barrow knows about the provenance of the scrap in his wagon only Henry Barrow knows, but he's using every bit of money he can come by from every member of the family to build a proper roof over their heads. He found an empty piece of land over near the Texas and Pacific Railway track and is slowly but surely putting together a three-room house there.

Almost all of West Dallas within a half dozen blocks of the river bottom is a squatters' camp of one sort or another: a sloppy grid of dirt and mud streets along the railroad tracks where folks from the hinterlands can pretty much throw up a building today and worry about legal title to the land sometime tomorrow. There is no running water, except in the streets when the river floods. No electricity, no sewage. Not yet incorporated, and not a part of the city of Dallas, so the only law is the county sheriff. It's known locally as "the bog," or "the devil's back porch," or, more kindly, "the back door to Dallas."

An exception, though only by a matter of degree, is the Eagle Ford Road, which starts at the western end of the Lamar Street Viaduct and runs parallel to the railroad tracks. It's such a relative thoroughfare out of Dallas proper, heading toward Fort Worth, that the county has seen fit to gravel it, though not yet to pave. There's nothing pretty about it, though. Coming west from the river are the massive tanks of the Dallas Power & Light Company; then, in short order, the Oriental Oil Refinery, the Simms Oil Refinery, a handful of foundries, and other industries facing the railroad on one side and the Eagle Ford Road on the other. In other words, it's a hardworking and strong-smelling road, but one that's busy enough for the owners of property along it to pay some attention to who is building on it. Unlike in the rabbit warren of the squatters' camp, a person has to buy or lease his lot along the Eagle Ford Road.

Buck, Clyde, and Henry's other children are occasionally bringing in more honest earnings than lifted brass. Buck works for a time, it seems, up at the cement plant, which isn't easy money by any means.

"I got a job working at the Trinity Portland cement company," says Floyd Hamilton. "I was getting six cents a hundred for tying bars around the top of the cloth cement bags. And you know at six cents a hundred you had to tie a lot of them to make any money."

"I'd work thirteen hours a night seven nights a week," he goes on, and "in that kiln the floor was just steaming hot cause they was burning rock . . . and it just killed me and my feet. Usually you had to tie grass sacks around your feet to walk on that floor."

Buck doesn't last too long. Most of the income for the house, therefore, is coming from junk, one wagonful at a time. Until the old trusty cart horse is hit by an automobile driving too fast and has to be put down.

It's a bad day: that horse brought the family up from the cotton fields and was doing more than her share of the work. For his part, Henry Barrow, farmer turned junk man, has owned a horse for just about as long as he can remember, and now this last one is gone. But the old nag has not gone without leaving behind one last gift: a lawyer convinces Henry he's got a case against the lush in the newfangled machine.

The settlement is not enough for the Barrows to start living the high life, not by a long shot. It's not even enough to get them across the viaduct to Dallas. But it gets Henry an old Model T, and with some help from Artie, whose beauty parlor is doing sufficiently well to keep both herself and her younger sister Nell employed, there's enough money to get a small piece of the Eagle Ford Road.* It's just a little plot on a nondescript corner, but it's theirs.

"I bought him a service station with living quarters," says Artie, with no mention of either the accident or the house already being built near the squatters' camp. But others remember the house being jacked up and moved to the site. It wasn't a big deal to do, as the house was just sitting on bricks or rocks anyway. That was the good thing about building in the long, thin shotgun style: people were slipping axles under and moving houses all the time.

---

* Now called Singleton Boulevard.

The Barrow family filling station on the Eagle Ford Road in West Dallas.
(From the collections of the Texas/Dallas History and Archives Division, Dallas Public Library.)

However it is that the building and land are bought and paid for, once the family's in the new location, Henry and the boys set to adding a gable to the front and building a roof the width of a car. Two gas pumps of the tall, round sort where a customer can see the gas through the glass cylinder at the top are installed at the end of the awning; this way they can service two cars at once, one under the roof and the other on the outside. At the peak of the roof is a proud sign: "Star Service Station, Gas, Oil, Gro," which is soon overshadowed by a pair of larger, brighter signs that also say "Star Service Sta." but mostly say "Drink Coca-Cola." Under the lip of the roof, carefully painted in block letters, it says "H. B. Barrow."

The address is 1620 Eagle Ford, and it's as good a location as any for a new beginning.

❂

"Clyde was kind of, I guess you'd call him backwards as far as playing games," says Floyd Hamilton. "He didn't take part in any school activities."

Floyd doesn't really know what he's talking about firsthand as far as Clyde at school is concerned. He's just the older brother of Clyde's real good buddy Raymond Hamilton. Like almost everyone who winds up in West Dallas, the Hamilton boys have moved around a lot. First they moved because of their father's comings and goings, and then, when he finally up and went away for good with some prostitute and what there was of the family's net worth, the Hamiltons moved around some more due to their new stepdad's comings and goings. By the mid-1920s the Hamiltons are settled around the corner from the Barrows' gas station.

"You see, I moved to Dallas about 1920," says Floyd. "Then Clyde Barrow moved into West Dallas about 1922. We all knew each other and lived in the same neighborhood."

With shotgun houses packed cheek by jowl in the blocks off the Eagle Ford Road, West Dallas is the kind of place where everyone knows everyone else's business, and Floyd, as something of a surrogate father to his younger brother, Raymond, has got a pretty good read on his little brother's pals. Besides, Floyd's new wife is only fourteen (she's the daughter of his family's landlord). That's a lot closer to Clyde's age, and she does go to school with him.

"My wife said he'd stand up against the school building and watch the other kids play," says Floyd, "or over by the fence and watch everyone else."

Floyd's not saying Clyde is some kind of an outcast, exactly, only that he is a bit shy about getting involved in the pickup baseball games or other organized activities. Maybe it's his size: he's a tiny kid—got it from his mom—who looks younger than his age. He's the type who's liable to get picked on or picked last in lineups to choose teams. It may also be that even in a humble school like Cedar Valley Elementary, in a ramshackle neighborhood like West Dallas, Clyde can't shake the feeling of inadequacy and humiliation.

"One of Clyde's problems," says his older sister Artie, "was that he was ashamed of being poor."

So he stands outside the fence or against the wall and watches the other children have their fun.

"He didn't take part in any school activities," says Floyd. "But still, he was a friendly kid and he'd go out of his way to make friends. Wasn't a bully or anything like that. He was nice to get along with."

❀

Truth is, you just don't much take to school. Never really have, even back on the farm.

"Neither of us ever liked school, but until Clyde came along to take the lead, I'd gone to school because I thought I had to," says Nell. The lead you take is called playing hooky. Still, in the years of bouncing around various farm towns, living sometimes with your parents and sometimes with your aunts and uncles but almost always with your big sister, you manage to go to enough farm schools to get through about the fifth or sixth grade. Unlike your dad, you can read and write if you have to.

Now, here in West Dallas, you show up in school at first. At least you're there in a group picture of twelve children from the early 1920s that looks to have been taken at a school, or maybe a church. You're sitting in the center of the front row with one hand clinched tightly around the other, like a double fist. Your elbows are locked to your sides, your knees together, your toes almost touching. Your round face, under a strictly parted thick head of black hair, is turned slightly away from the camera. But your eyes are staring straight into the lens.

You look a little wound up, but to be fair, none of the other children in the picture look particularly comfortable. The exception is your little brother, L.C. Sitting between two kids with positively grouchy visages, he's leaning back, legs out, arms relaxed, with a goofy grin between two big ears. His hair, in contrast to yours, is a mop. And though he's four years younger he looks to be about your size. L.C.'s a good buddy, mostly for marbles.

"All the time, Clyde and L.C. were playing marbles," says little sister Marie. "They carried their marbles around in tobacco sacks. They never would let me play with them."

Marie is not in the picture. She's too little. But Nell's there, looking kind of homespun and bored in the back row. Getting on now to be sixteen or seventeen, Nell is ready to quit school altogether and soon does.

"I found a job and went to live in town with a friend," she says simply.

For the first time you're living apart from your closest sister, though the two of you have lived away from the rest of your immediate family off and on for years. Nell was never your surrogate mom, but with her gone it's more and more difficult to remember why a person might attend school at all. You go when it suits you. You're not winning any spelling bees.

Who needs to spell anyway when you're going to make it rich blowing the saxophone in a big-time orchestra? Maybe you'll sing a bit too, like you did when you were just eleven and your family lived near the oil boomtowns of Mexia and Corsicana. You had your Jew's harp then: *twang twanga twang twang,* while the bored oily men with gusher wages in their pockets threw change at the cute kid who knew a mess of songs. You got real good at it, too, and that was before your voice deepened into a nice rich baritone that people don't always expect out of a little guy. You can really sing. Pluck a little ukulele, too, now that the ukulele craze is going strong.

When Nell gets married to Leon Hale, a professional musician, you've got access to a saxophone and a few lessons. You pretty much move in with Nell and Leon for a time, and though the honking is almost unbearable at first, after a few weeks you figure out how to pinch the reed between your lips to generate a sweet tone that wafts through the neighborhood. An uncle has a café out in Corsicana, near the oil fields, and once or twice you even sit in with the band down there. Artie is your big sister, it's true, but if she's any judge you've got what it takes.

"Clyde was one of the most talented musicians I've ever listened to," she says. "Everyone said Clyde belonged in one of those big name bands."

Nell, who, after all, is married to a professional musician, is a bit less glowing but nonetheless supportive. "Clyde still wanted to be a musician when he came to live with us," she says. "Clyde loved his saxophone playing and kept it up."

You love your sisters. You love music. You don't love school.

CHAPTER 5

WEST DALLAS

Juvenile bicycle thieves who operate much after the fashion of automobile thieves, save that they do not use "fences," are working constantly in Dallas, according to Chief of Detectives J. C. Gunning.

Twelve bicycles were recovered Tuesday by City Detectives Phillips and Simmons. About fifty have been recovered by these two officers in the last two weeks.

—THE DALLAS MORNING NEWS

The older Barrow girls are a little worried about Clyde and Buck. "My brothers didn't get into bad trouble until we moved to Dallas," says Artie.

Dallas, like a lot of cities in the twenties and thirties, is rife with boy gangs; no fewer than 196 different gangs, says a researcher from Southern Methodist University, and that is without even daring to come across the river into West Dallas and Cement City and Oak Cliff. There are harmless posses of young boys who are into harassing bees wherever they can find them, and slightly older gangs who fancy themselves explorers and pioneers and prowl around the riverbanks looking for high adventure.

A group called the Royal Order of the Fleas has a clubhouse near a quarry, where they specialize in skinny-dipping parties and "sex delinquencies." Tougher groups of older boys, like the Dirty Dozen, the Big Ten, and the Night Shadow, pretty much just roam their turf looking for trouble with rival gangs. One gang that makes a specialty of stealing slot machines whips new members with a leather belt just "to see if they could take it."

"We would steal beer from a beer joint, then take it to our club room (a hay loft over an ice company barn) and drink it," says Jerry S., a member in good standing.

In other words, in this city, it's not easy for a kid from the wrong side of the tracks to stay on the straight and narrow.

"Living in the West Dallas slums," Artie Barrow says simply and sadly, "was a bad environment."

There's at least one gang that specializes in stealing bicycles. According to Officers Phillips and Simmons of the Dallas Police Department, its members' method is to quickly disassemble the bikes and put them back together with different parts so that no one can definitively identify them. The chop shops are under culverts or in ditches; one on Pacific Avenue is found with more than a dozen bikes in various pieces.

With Buck, Clyde, and little L.C., plus a few friends from the block, the Barrow boys are almost a gang unto themselves.

"They were in scrapes a lot of the time," says Ted Hinton, a kid from the neighborhood who is a few years older than Clyde. "And there were enough of them that only a fool would dare to cross any member of the family." They are known locally, he says, as "that Barrow Bunch" or "the Barrow Boys."

It's not clear that Clyde and Buck are involved in the bike-stealing business. Buck, for one, is more interested in his old pastime. "Buck did fight them chickens, you know," says Marie. "Cockfighting. I remember him putting them spurs on them. And he had an old pit bulldog he used to fight. Mama made him get rid of it. It tore out the whole seat of my dress when I was playing ball."

But Clyde's pal Raymond Hamilton, whose house backs up on the Barrow garage, apparently is in the bicycle business. He's been picked up a couple of times by Deputy Sheriff Bud Walker for stealing car tires and various other accessories. Rumor has it as well that he might be selling hot bikes to Smoot Schmid, a giant man almost seven feet tall who has a bike shop in Dallas. Smoot Schmid is a Dallas character of sorts who is thinking of someday running for sheriff. He has a soft spot for the less fortunate boys of West Dallas, a bunch of whom hang out near his cycle shop on North Akard Street.* Ted

---

* "Where did you hear that?" Ted's son Boots asks, referring to Schmid selling stolen bikes. "That wouldn't be the Smoot Schmid I knew at all. Or that Ted knew. The Smoot Schmid I knew was nothing but a straight shooter," says Boots.

Hinton, for instance, whose father died when he was very young, says Smoot "practically raised me."

Doesn't matter really if Schmid's bike shop is knowingly or unknowingly moving hot bikes, there's always a market for them on the street. According to police, one of the main reasons kids steal bikes, in fact, is because they can't get a job as a messenger without one. Jobs as newsboys and telegraph messengers are the big opportunities for boys like Clyde and Raymond, both as ways to make a little money and, it seems, as a school for petty crime. Clyde works awhile with Western Union. So does Ted Hinton, whose mother, in fact, is the office coordinator for the Dallas branch.

"The other street urchins who took those jobs could get a fellow into a mess of trouble," Hinton says. "When they'd pair off, one kid would knock on a front door to deliver a wire or ask a direction while his buddy was ransacking something out back that could be peddled for pocket change." Hinton remembers a class picture of sorts from those days, showing thirty-seven Western Union messengers. "Twelve were to go to prison," he says, "and four would be electrocuted."

Clyde may have come by his bicycle honestly, bought it at Smoot Schmid's, or he may have gotten it from Raymond Hamilton. Or he may have stolen it in order to get the job at Western Union. But his sisters know that not everything their brothers are coming home with has a good pedigree. A sheriff's deputy named Ed Caster thinks he remembers arresting Clyde as early as 1923 for supposedly taking off on somebody else's motorcycle, though no charges apparently came of it. Clyde's sisters know as well that not everyone he hangs out with is a good influence.

"Buck and Clyde got in with some tough young people," says big sister Artie.

"Clyde was a . . . I think he was a tenderhearted boy," says little sister Marie. "I loved him very much and he was very good to me. He bought me—" She pauses and starts over: "I don't know if he bought it or what, but he got me the first bicycle I ever owned."

Marie pauses again.

"I kep' that bicycle until I was grown."

❋

There was a time, and not so many years ago, when the young man who invested his hard-earned cash in what was known as a best-girl buggy, got some attention in the home paper. His purchase was chronicled with the advice to "look out, girls!"

With red running gears, rubber tires, a tassel on the horse's bridle and a whip that cost at least $1.25, this young man was so well equipped that he was a force to reckon with when love-making was going on.

He has passed, and in his stead has come the long, low, rakish motor car. It burns gasoline and leaves an unpleasant odor in its wake, but it represents speed and exclusiveness.

—*The Dallas Morning News*

You love your sisters. By the time you're sixteen, you're out of school for good, working what jobs you can find. Not as a messenger boy anymore, but real positions at the NuGrape soda company, at a glass factory, at Procter & Gamble. You never get fired but you are always ready to quit and change if something better comes along.

And you don't want a bicycle. "Wheels," as they're called, are for kids. No, you want a "machine." You want an automobile. You want speed. You love speed more than almost anything else, except maybe your sisters and a few other girls you've had your eye on. You crave speed.

The first thing you buy with your earnings is a stripped-down old speedster, a Pontiac. You pay fifty dollars for it, and race around town for as long as you can keep it running. You even outrun the cops one night after they whistle at you for speeding, and when Nell hears about it she says, "Clyde, you should have stopped."

"It's easier to run away," you tell her.

Then you're seventeen, making more money at the A & K Auto Top Works, dressing fine, slicking your hair, chasing girls, especially the one named Eleanor Williams who's still going to high school in Dallas. Eleanor— or Ebbie, as you call her—is the most beautiful thing you've ever seen, and what's more, she says she will marry you as soon as she gets out of school.

Eleanor's family seems to like you, which is good, too, though they cannot be serious about this business of you waiting a few years to get married. You are just about dying for Eleanor, driving Nell nuts with the talk about her day and night. Nothing but Eleanor this and Eleanor that. You buy some rings. You go to a tattoo artist and ask for a heart with a dagger through it and her initials, EBW. The needles prick a little, but when you're done there it is, on the outside of your left forearm. Forever.

Of course you and the girl have a fight of some sort. Eleanor gets mad about some dumb thing and you get madder about her being mad and say stuff you wish you hadn't, or maybe it's the other way around. However it begins both of you are real mad, mad as heck, and next thing you know, Eleanor just up and leaves. You go looking for her and find out she's in Broaddus, Texas, way over near San Augustine. She just takes off for East Texas, supposedly to visit some aunt there, but basically to get away from you and think about things.

You have to see her. The problem is, your stinking car won't go that far. Even in the 1920s, fifty bucks doesn't get you much of a machine, and by the fall of 1926 the speedster is by all accounts a thing of the past. So you rent a nice new car and head off to make amends. You round up Eleanor's mother for good measure and offer to drive her out to visit her sister in Broaddus.

What a charming boy. What a charming idea. Yes, Eleanor's mama says, she'll go with you. You'll get Eleanor back. You have no choice.

And of course you do succeed. Eleanor can't resist that you've come all this way, and brought her mother along, too. You're in love again. It's on again. You stay the night, and another night. You are going to be married after all. Even Eleanor's mother is happy.

It's all so beautiful with Eleanor in Broaddus that you totally forget all about having told the Nichols Brothers car-rental service back in Dallas that you would only be needing the car for a half a day.

Or, more likely, you do remember—after all, the car is sitting there right in front of the aunt's house in Broaddus. You remember with a knot in your gut each time you see it, or every time you offer to drive Eleanor and her mom and whoever else might want to go out for the air. You remember. But somehow, you can't manage to figure out how to tell everybody that you were too poor to rent a car overnight, let alone for half a week.

It's too good. Eleanor's too beautiful. You're too happy. A new car, a beautiful girl—you feel almost rich.

So you don't say anything about the rental-car business to Eleanor or her mother; it will work out when you get back to Dallas. But you definitely remember that you were supposed to return the car, because as soon as local deputies arrive in front of the house and start looking at the tag on the machine, you take off out the back door and into a cornfield as fast as you can run. You might be charming, but you have a real stupid streak.

The sheriff takes the car back to Dallas. After you're sure he's gone you sneak back into the house, and you hide in the attic when he returns for another look. Eleanor thinks she's still in love, but her mom has had enough. She doesn't turn you in, at least, but she's not listening to either you or Eleanor. It's good-bye, Clyde.

She's a stubborn woman. Even when the whole thing blows over back in Dallas, the damn woman won't be moved. Soon as you thumb your way back home, the sheriff's deputies pick you up and take you down to the big red-brick courthouse and jail at the corner of Houston and Main and charge you with stealing the car. It looks grim for a few hours there on December 3, 1926, with the deputies shoving you around, talking tough, taking finger-prints and mug shots.

It turns out, however, that the owners of Nichols Brothers are reason-able businessmen. A pretty big operator in town, with a large fleet of taxis and "driverless cars" available, they hope that "Watch for a Nichols Bros. Cab" will become a slogan that catches in the minds of the car-needing Dallas public. What they don't need are news stories in the crime-obsessed dailies about how the big, bad Nichols Brothers is sending some love-struck local puppy off to jail for borrowing a car to romance his girl. That is not going to do anybody any good. With their car back in good condition, they drop the charges.

As soon as you're out, you're back at Eleanor's front door, trying to rea-son with her mom. One of her friends says she remembers you hanging around the block, hoping for a chance encounter.

Clyde, she says, "was just a kid then, and very much in love with Eleanor."

But Eleanor's mom will not be moved, and any hope that time will soften her up again is made less likely by the Dallas County Sheriff's Of-fice. They had to let you out of the Dallas County jail, thanks to the Nichols Brothers, but that doesn't mean they have to take you off their list of usual suspects. Not when you were already almost on it by virtue of where you live, who you hang around with, and who your brother Buck hangs around with, staging cock- and dogfights and the like. Now it's just official.

"After the ordeal with the rent car, he was fired from his job because the police kept picking him up," says this friend of Eleanor's. "Whenever a car was stolen, or a house was burglarized, the police would drag him down-town. Of course he was never charged with anything, but they'd beat him up and try to make him confess to things he'd never done."

It's a refrain picked up by almost everyone who knows you, including your little sister, Marie.

"After Clyde got in trouble, well, it seemed that every time that any-thing happened they always tried to lay it off on Clyde," she says. "And they would question him, and come out and, you know, always thought it was Clyde or Buck that done something."

Being jailed for seventy-two hours without any charges is known in the neighborhood as a "Decker hold," named for Deputy Sheriff Bill Decker. "They could also let you go and then pick you up again on the way home and hold you for another seventy-two hours," says your pal Floyd Hamilton. "I know, because it happened to me."

To the police, rounding up riffraff and bringing them in to headquarters is just the standard procedure for solving crimes. Something happens anywhere in the county and out they go to round up the usual suspects and check out their alibis. Between May 18 and June 26, 1926, for instance, more than six hundred arrests are made by Dallas police on "suspicion."

Your older sister Nell doesn't dispute that the police won't leave you alone after the rental business, but she points out that it doesn't help your situation any when you and Buck get caught just a few weeks later with a car full of stolen turkeys. Buck takes the fall and goes to jail for a week, while you, looking small and young, as usual, say you had no idea the birds were hot.

The result is the same: job gone; Eleanor gone. Damn the laws.

Engagement over.

❋

Roy Thornton loves his tiny wife, Bonnie, but sometimes she just about drives him nutty with her neediness for her mother. Always begging to go back and visit her and the like, even though they live only a couple of blocks away. Okay, she's only fifteen, or just turned sixteen, but still, she seemed all woman when they got married, so how come every night she's whining like a little girl for mama? She's such a mama's girl that even her own little sister, Billie Jean, ribs her about it.

"Bonnie was very superstitious," says Billie Jean, "and she loved her mother so much. We'd tease her about that—sometimes she'd just go in and kiss the hems of Mother's dresses."

Even Mrs. Parker has sympathy for her new son-in-law. "It really became a joke with us," she says, "and we felt sorry for Roy, who was having a lot of difficulty with his honeymoon."

Finally, though, enough is enough for Roy Thornton and they just move in with Emma. This saves the newlyweds money on rent and saves Roy having to trudge back and forth between two places. And to his surprise it's a great arrangement.

"That suited them exactly, especially Roy," says Emma.

Roy comes and goes pretty much as he pleases now, knowing that Bonnie will always have her mama around to take care of her. It's like having all the privileges of marriage without actually being tied down. He doesn't even have to come home at all if something, uh, comes up. His career as a welder has taken a new turn that's keeping him out late at night and, ultimately, away for pretty good stretches of time. Along with his pals Fred and Bud Mace, whose family has one of the remaining farms out on the outskirts of Oak Cliff, Roy is starting to put his skills with an acetylene torch to use on store strongboxes. They're dreaming of maybe even burning into bank safes one day. Put simply, Bonnie's husband has become a burglar, and not a particularly gifted one.

Sometimes he brings his pals the Mace brothers home to Mrs. Parker's house, where they're made to feel quite welcome. Little Billie Jean, especially, shines right up in the cheeks when Fred Mace appears. She's getting on toward fifteen now that Bonnie's almost seventeen. Billie Jean is getting pretty, too. There are some double dates, no doubt, some happy evenings out in the streets of Dallas with Roy and Fred and Bonnie and Billie. They go to the shows, or drive out somewhere to sip a little moonshine and moonlight. There is happy laughing and such.

But more and more, during that second year of Thornton's marriage to Bonnie Parker, Roy is simply spending long periods away from her. Weeks at a time, Bonnie is left alone with her mama, wondering where in the world her husband is. Starting on December 5, 1927, Roy Thornton is gone altogether.

"He treats you like a dishrag," her mother tells her.

"He was an alcoholic," says Ralph Fults, a friend from the neighborhood.

"I want him back, Mama," says Bonnie.

❋

"Dear Diary," Bonnie writes by way of an introduction on the first day of 1928. "Before opening this diary I wish to tell you I have a roaming husband with a roaming mind. We are separated again for the third and last time."

JANUARY 1

The bells are ringing, the old year has gone, and my heart has gone with it. I have been the happiest and most miserable woman this last year. I wish the old year would have taken my "past" with it. I mean all my memories, but I can't forget Roy. I am very blue tonight. No word from him. I feel he has gone for good.

This is New Year's Day, Jan 1. I went to a show. Saw Ken Maynard in The Overland Stage. Am very blue. Well, I must confess

this New Years nite I got drunk. Trying to forget. Drowning my
sorrows in bottled hell!

It's a miserable start to the new year, but at least there are the movies.
Bonnie goes almost every other night to the picture shows with one friend
or another, and for the few weeks she keeps it she takes care to write the
names of the stars and the titles in her diary.

"Met Rosa Mary today and we went to a show. Saw Ronald Colman and
Vilmma Banky in A Night of Love. Sure was a good show," she writes one
day. "Well, I went down town today and saw a picture. Milton Sills in
'Framed.' Sure was a good picture," she writes a few days later. Florence
Vidor and Clive Brook in *Afraid to Love* "sure was good," she says.

Mostly, though, Bonnie writes about how lonely and bored she is, like
any teenager whose love has gone away might do. There are other boys who
want to go out with her, a detective named Raymond, someone named Scot-
tie. But none of them break her mopey mood. "Sure am lonesome," she
says. "Blue as usual. Not a darn thing to do. Don't know a darn thing."

She can't find a job. She doesn't like the boys she knows. "I wonder
what tomorrow will bring," she writes. "Why don't something happen?" Two
nights later she writes it again: "Why don't something happen? What a life."

Finally, around the middle of the month, she stops writing in her journal.
The last lines are "Sure am blue tonight. Have been crying. I wish I could
see Roy." She manages to write the date of the next day—"Tuesday, Jan. 17,
1928"—but no entry. Part of the reason she stops may be that she finally finds
a job, as a waitress at Hargraves Café, on a winding little street called Swiss
Circle. It's a modest place with a short-order kitchen in the back, a wrap-
around counter, and a couple of booths. But it's a job. It's something to do.

She is a favorite of the women who work at the big Yates Laundry company, which is across the alley behind the café. They can't come in and sit
down, as their breaks aren't long enough, but Bonnie brings them food. If
there aren't too many customers back at the café she stays awhile and chats.
The laundry women like that. They like that she is always clean and tidy,
her hair just so, her uniform pressed. Presumably the ladies at Yates Laundry also like it that Bonnie is smiling a bit more as time passes.

Months go by with no sign of Roy Thornton, though his buddy Fred
Mace is still hanging around the Parker residence as much as he can. He
and Billie Jean are a definite number, now, and on September 8, 1928, they
get married. It's a happy day, even though Roy doesn't make the party for
his old friend and new brother-in-law. By then, though, Bonnie has at last
gotten over her husband.

When Roy does show up out of the blue, sometime in 1929, she tells him it's over and sends him away. She doesn't divorce him, though. Before she can manage to put the legal paperwork together, he gets caught in a bungled bank job south of Dallas and is sent to jail. She can't dump him now.

"It looks sort of dirty to file for one now," she tells her mother.

❋

You can't get married to Grace Donegan on account of her still having a husband up in Wichita Falls. But that doesn't mean you can't fall hard and deep for her in a way that makes you forget all about that schoolgirl Eleanor and her pushy old mama who thinks her daughter is way too good to marry you. Who needs marriage when you can just move in with Grace and pretend you are married?

She's a couple of years older than you, but great looking. Grace Donegan is even prettier than Eleanor, can you believe it? Even Nell says so. You meet her in Kate's Sandwich Shop on Swiss Avenue, right near United Glass & Mirror, where you work when the company has enough business to keep you employed. You are hugely in love with Grace and get her first name tattooed on your other arm, with a picture of a girl over it. But it only lasts long enough for you to move in together for a while and then she starts in about all the things she wants you to get her. That and she won't shut up about the tattoo for Eleanor, even though the GRACE tattoo is bigger.

"There were lots of scenes between them," your sister Nell says. "The fur would fly." Nell knows because she has to move in with you and Grace after her marriage to the saxophone player goes on the rocks.

Flying fur, that about describes it. Whatever. It doesn't last. Grace goes back to Wichita Falls. But by God is she beautiful.

❋

Prices of Stocks Collapse During Wild Selling Orgy:

Bankers Minimize Danger

—*The Dallas Morning News*

The lawmen and lawyers who come into Marco's Café sure do appreciate the new petite blond waitress. They like her even more than the washerwomen back at Swiss Avenue did. Marco's is right up near the big red county jail and courthouse; she starts working as a waitress there in early 1929, having switched jobs presumably for the better clientele and tips.

"She was perky, with good looks and taffy-colored hair that showed a trace of red, and she had some freckles," says Ted Hinton, who is not a lawman yet but will be soon. He's a few years older than Bonnie and has a good job as a special-delivery man for the U.S. Postal Service. "She always had a ready quip, too."

She looks like a piece of candy to tall men like Hinton and his mentor, Smoot Schmid, the nearly seven-foot cycle dealer who is thinking of running for sheriff of Dallas. "Photographs made with the little box cameras failed to do justice to her looks," says Hinton. They don't capture her style, he says, "the clothes she wore, the sparkle she had when I knew her, when she was waiting tables at the restaurant where I used to take my meals."

Her eyes and lips are painted up; her hair is in a perfect and saucy little cut. She's dressed in a funny uniform with enormous lapels, like some cross between a French maid and Raggedy Ann, and she's barely taller than the big brass cash register on the counter. The fact that she's said to be married but living apart from her husband just makes her, at eighteen, only more intriguing, in a flapper, been-around-the-block-already kind of way. She seems like a good girl at heart, a girl who is probably just waiting for a better roll of the dice, some of the men think. Maybe it's me, some of them think to themselves.

"Several of the men my age flirted with her," says Hinton, "and Bonnie could turn off the advances or lead a customer on with her easy conversation."

"Bonnie," he says, "could turn heads."

The streets outside Marco's Café are a complete mess, as the city has finally decided to do something about the perennial flooding of the Trinity River and is busy building levees, eliminating whole blocks of lowland, constructing new viaducts and underpasses. It's a marvel of engineering, and the area in the vicinity of the courthouse will eventually be called Dealey Plaza. Boom times in a boom town: there are plenty of customers among the foremen and supervisors who, added to the people with county business, should keep Marco's cash register ringing and Bonnie's apron pocket full of tips for the foreseeable future.

But in New York at the end of October the market crashes, not just the one big day but day after day, with implications that ripple west. By the end of November 1929, Marco's Café is closing its doors for good, throwing everyone out of work. Whether the failure of the restaurant is directly connected to national economic events or just a coincidence doesn't really matter to Bonnie and the other waitresses. What matters is that they are suddenly looking for new jobs when the vast majority of businesses are trying desperately to avoid laying people off. If she goes back around to Swiss Avenue, her old job is gone. It's the same story everywhere. No one knows it yet, but it's the end of the Roaring Twenties and the beginning of the Great Depression.

The only opportunities Bonnie can find aren't really jobs at all but situations: babysitting, housecleaning, and the like. One of the more steady of these starts in mid-January of 1930, when she moves into a house on the Eagle Ford Road, not far from the West Dallas end of the Lamar Street Viaduct. The house belongs to Clarence Clay, the father of a friend of hers. The girl has a broken arm, so Bonnie gets room and board in exchange for doing some light housework and cooking. It's not as good or as much fun as being a waitress making actual dollars and cents, flirting with the handsome customers. But it's not hard work, either, and Bonnie can keep looking for a better job and doesn't have to move back in with her mother, who already has Billie Jean and Fred Mace there, along with their adorable new twins. It's not bad.

Plus, this friend with the broken arm, whose first name no one remembers, seems to know everybody in the neighborhood. People are always dropping by to see how she's doing. Some of them are old friends of Bonnie's from around town, and some of them she can't believe she hasn't met before since they know so many people in common. One of these is a nice-looking guy, well dressed, neatly combed, with a smile that makes a little dimple on his left cheek. He shows up one day, puts on an apron, and says funny things while he makes everyone his favorite drink, hot chocolate. A little more sugar—there, that's it, perfect. Here you go, ladies.

He's a charmer, all right. His name is Clyde Barrow.

❀

It happens fast between the two of them, almost immediately, as if Clyde and Bonnie are meant for each other. Both of them can feel it, both of them know it and believe it. It's not puppy stuff, though: they've both seen love go by before, and both are veterans of happiness and heartbreak. No, even Roy and Eleanor weren't quite like this. And everybody around them can see it, too, since they can't seem to keep their hands off each other.

"They were very much in love with each other, and would reach over and either smack each other on the cheek or something, and were always calling each other sweet names or something," says Clyde's little sister, Marie. "He loved her and she loved him."

Billie Jean, Bonnie's sister, says the same thing. "Bonnie was in love with Clyde," she says. "They were in love with each other." When someone asks Billie Jean, "Was this a serious love affair?" she replies, "It was, it was."

Clyde and Bonnie together in the country. "They were very much in love with each other," says Clyde's sister Marie Barrow. *(From the collections of the Texas/Dallas History and Archives Division, Dallas Public Library.)*

And when they ask, "It wasn't just a physical attraction?" she answers, "No, it wasn't."

Bonnie's mother, Emma, naturally, has the best intuition about her daughter. "I knew there was something between them the minute Bonnie introduced him to me," she says. "I could tell it in Bonnie's eyes and her voice, and the way she kept touching his sleeve as she talked."

CHAPTER 6

ROOT SQUARE, HOUSTON

Life was desperate enough in West Dallas before the Great Depression, but after 1929, it was almost impossible to stay honest.

—Floyd Hamilton

You have to get out of town and you have to find a way to tell Bonnie. You have to tell her, right? If you didn't love her you could just go, but you do love her, so you have to tell her. But what are you going to say? Oh, hey, Bonnie, these past couple of months have been wonderful, but I just have to go away for a few weeks, nothing big, nothing important, I'll be back. I love you. . . .

That doesn't sound too good. Maybe you can say you have a job up in Oklahoma and if it works out you'll send for her to come and join you there, and if it doesn't work out, well, you'll come back to Dallas and see her then. And you love her.

But you have to leave town. And you have to tell Bonnie.

Soon, too, because the laws are on to you. The truth is that not necessarily all those times you got hauled downtown after the car-rental business were for things you didn't do or didn't know about. Along with your big brother Buck, and a pal named Frenchy Clause, and a couple of guys from Waco and Houston, you've kind of eased into a bit of the life of a burglar. And a car thief.

These past three months with Bonnie have been the sweetest of your life—better than Eleanor and Grace put together—but can you tell her everything? The question is, can you tell her and not lose her? You have to tell her something, though, because the cops are on to you and you have to get out of town. So what should you tell her about the past few years? Everything?

❋

"It was a bad situation over in West Dallas," says your pal Ralph Fults. "You gotta know the environment. They started off small, Buck and Clyde, stealing junk, things like that. They started off just like that."

Like that.

"Well, I guess at an early age they wanted things that they, uh, couldn't have," says your sister Marie. "And that seemed like the best way to get 'em: go out and take something or something another."

That's pretty much how it starts. Little stuff picked up here and there, and then eventually cars and money. It's going all right for the most part, largely because you and your pals are careful to move your business around. You don't work in Dallas, in other words, where everyone knows everyone and everyone might talk. You go over to Fort Worth at the very least or, better yet, to Waco. Once in a while you go all the way down to Houston, the other big city in Texas. You're living with your pal Frank Clause now. "Frenchy,"* as everyone calls him, spent his early years in Houston, and he still knows a bunch of guys down there who hang out in Root Square. They call themselves the Root Square Club, and are good guys like Dapper Dan and Johnny Dew, so you and Frenchy go down to Houston pretty regularly, looking as often for fun as for trouble. Maybe you borrow a car in Waco and sell it down there, then borrow another car there to bring back to Waco or Dallas.

"Clyde was just a wild eyed kid when one of the fellows brought him to the hangout one night and said he was alright," says a member of the Root Square Club who doesn't give his name. "The gang was mostly young kids, they stole automobile tires and sold them the next morning. With lots of money, the gang got women and dope and had a hot time getting drunk and hopped up on marijuana."

Harry McCormick remembers you down there, too. He's the muckraking police beat reporter for the *Houston Press* who wears his fedora cocked low over his left eyebrow and sometimes gets beat up by the police himself, apparently for telling things like he sees them. For this, and other reasons,

---

* The story is that his parents were vaudeville performers from France, named Champagne; Clause was his grandfather's name.

the boys on the wrong side of the law trust Harry McCormick to tell their side of the story.

"He was a little fellow and got his start down on Root Square in Houston," McCormick says about you. "I knew him, and Jimmie Arnold, and Frenchy Claus and Dapper Dan Black and all the boys pretty well."

The Root Square Club is mostly into small-time stuff, particularly on summer nights when the club boys head down to the beach near Morgan's Point to rifle through the cars of people who are cooling off in the water of Trinity Bay. The purses, clothes, jewelry, and watches in some of the cars make for easy pickings. Just imagining those stiffs and their girls coming out of the water all dripping wet to find their wheels gone is almost worth it for the laugh alone. The summer prowls are fun at least until the night of July 2, 1929, when someone in the club screws up and pulls a gun on a guy sitting by the beach with his girlfriend.

"I was sitting beside my stand when I heard the report of pistol shots—two of them in succession," says a root-beer seller, who follows the cries for help down to a car parked near some bushes. "A girl was standing beside the machine, moaning and crying. A man lay dead beside the car, his body half under the running board."

The girl, Lillian Bissett, is bleeding. "There's been an explosion" is all she can manage to say. One second she and her new boyfriend, Buster Gouge, were sitting side by side about twenty feet from the water, and next instant a bullet tore through Gouge's lungs and heart, leaving him just enough life to stand up, grab Lillian Bissett's hand, pull her to her feet, and say, "Let's get away from here," which was when the second bullet hit her.

"Then what happened?" someone asks Bissett.

"He walked toward the water and then turned around and came back to the car."

"And then what did he do?"

"Well, he fell," she says. Dead.

"What had become of you?"

"I had fell too. Then I got up—fell and got up by the side of the car and turned the lights on and put my hand on the horn and honked it to see if that would bring any help."

Beeeeeeeeeeeeeep beeeeeeeep.

"I had my hand on the horn, kept it there a long time," she says.

The Houston cops don't immediately suspect that the Root Square gang has anything to do with the killing; they're looking for a jealous lover who doesn't exist. And maybe, like you say, you and Frenchy weren't even in Houston that night. Regardless of who did it, for the rest of that summer the club lays off of beachcombing. This is fine with you, since rifling cars for beer money is getting a bit boring. You're not into drinking and getting hopped up, like most of them. What you want is real money you can carry around and spend.

"Clyde tired of petty stealing and convinced the gang it should go into the burglary and safe robbing business," says a member of the club. "Clyde knew how to use soup. We all learned later how to use the stuff."

Dapper Dan Black, who at about twenty-two is a little older than you and Frenchy and is sort of the "dean" of the Root Square crowd, has also moved on to bigger things. "I graduated from picking pockets to outside man in holdup jobs, then house prowling, then knob knocking," he says.

(Everybody loves the lingo: the boys in Root Square, Harry McCormick and the other reporters, the girlfriends, the detective magazines, the movies, even the detectives. "Yegg men" use homemade nitroglycerine "soup"; "knob knockers" break into safes by knocking the knobs off and sliding the tumblers back with a punch. "Knocking off" a safe is surprisingly easy once you know what you're doing. Just a couple of good whacks with a hammer and you're on your way. But soup, that's another story altogether. Just cooking the stuff is scary, let alone driving around with it in a car, hoping you don't end up getting chased.)

Dapper Dan is Frenchy Clause's best friend in Houston, and for the same reasons that you leave Dallas and go to Houston, Dapper Dan does some of his work up in your neighborhood. Not coincidentally, there's been a regular hailstorm of knob knocking going on in Waco and Dallas and Houston and the various smaller cities of Texas. You all help the other fellow out.

"Say, that boy Frenchy, he's a brick," says Dan. "He was with me for weeks while I was dodging officers and if it had not been for him I would have been captured several times."

You and Frenchy and Buck, and increasingly often Raymond Hamilton, have plenty of your own near misses, achieved both together and singly. In February of 1928 the Fort Worth police arrest you "for investigation," but as usual they don't come up with any charges and you're let go. Also that year a deputy in San Antonio sees Buck with his new infant girl in one arm going from car to car in broad daylight, trying to find one he can start up and drive off in. When Buck decides to get in a nice new machine and try the ignition, he's arrested, but no charges stick.

It's more of the same in 1929, getting picked up here and there "on suspicion." You get visited by cops all the time, some of whom even think they're doing you some kind of favor.

"I have from time to time visited him and his family," says Doug Walsh, the superintendent of the Dallas police bureau of identification. He starts up on you right after you keep the rental car too long. "In those early days of his career, a youth of nineteen, I thought that a good, persuasive talking would make him see the light and turn him from the path of crime toward which his actions were leading."

Yeah, right, Officer. Thanks. It might be easier if you cops would let a guy keep a job. Might be easier if most of these "persuasive" talkings down at the station didn't sometimes leave bruises.

"Even then, Clyde was a tough, unresponsive and stubborn character who believed every policeman to be his mortal enemy," says Walsh.

Walsh's colleague Detective Captain Leonard Pack isn't hoping to help anyone out with stern lectures when he shows up looking for you at your parents' filling station on the Eagle Ford Road with two backup officers sometime in 1929. He's got a request from the Houston police to collect the Barrow Bunch for "investigation." Pack's a tall guy who looks a little goofy in his round, thick-rimmed eyeglasses. But he lives in Oak Cliff, on the same tough side of the Trinity River as West Dallas, so he knows the Barrows and their neighbors reasonably well. What's more, he's tough as nails and everyone in the neighborhood knows it. He once ran down the street in his pajama pants, chasing a guy who broke in and stole his daytime pants right out of his bedroom in the middle of the night. That guy got away, but Pack doesn't plan to let young Clyde Barrow give him the slip.

"We'll hit the ground running," he says to his backup men, Dean Goss and Bob Abbott. "I go to the house. Bob goes to the right and Dean takes the left."

Around now Frenchy Clause, who's over for a perfectly innocent visit with Clyde's parents, figures out what's up and hops out a window and takes off across an empty field. He stops when he hears Goss firing his weapon in his general direction. Buck takes off in the other direction and runs right into the arms of Abbott, a big friendly cop with a yo-yo habit. That's it, though. No one else comes out of the house that the police see, though another pal— no one is saying who—manages to successfully hide under the house.

"Where's Clyde?" Walsh asks Buck and Frank, who just shrug. When the cops ask Cumie if they can come in and have a look around, what's she supposed to say? They aren't likely to take no for an answer, and sure enough, there you are hiding behind a closet door, mad as a cut snake.

"If I had a gun, I wouldn't go to town with these . . ." you yell to your mother as you're being led out to the car. (Either Captain Pack does not repeat your chosen epithet to the reporter or the *Dallas Dispatch* decides it is an unfit word to print.) Fortunately for everyone in the vicinity, you don't have a gun, and you and the other boys are hauled down to the station, with Nell tagging along to see if she can help. Detective Goss doesn't go into any details about his interrogation methods, but he says you "broke" and confessed to no fewer than eleven safe burglaries in the Houston area.

Your sister Nell doesn't remember you screaming anything about guns. She's there on the day of the raid and comes across you in the tiny room that passes for a kitchen saying good-bye to Cumie.*

"Gosh, Mama," she hears you say with tears in your eyes, "I can't go back down there—honest, I can't."

Nell's at the gas station that morning partly because she's worried sick about both of her brothers, especially you. The special relationship she's always had with you feels like it's slipping away as you move faster and faster into circles that take you further and further away from her. First there was that girl Grace, pushing you to give her more more more. And now, Nell thinks, the problem is mostly Frenchy Clause, who is nice to look at and all but who talks tall with what she calls "big ideas about how to get along in the world." Frenchy brings strange kids from Houston around to the apartment he and you share, and Nell doesn't like it. He's dragging you down.

Nell's losing her little brother; she knows it. The two of you fight about where you get the things you have, where you've been when you've gone for days on end. She calls you a thief. You call her names and say she's disloyal. You say she's dirty and other things that hurt her deep, but you'll always be her little brother and she knows—*knows*—she'll always stand by you even when others keep dragging you down.

So when the laws come to the filling station and take you from behind the closet door, or the kitchen, or wherever it is they find you this time, Nell's sure as sin getting in that car with you and going down to the station and waiting there, glowering, while the men with their badges go on and take you behind the doors and do whatever they do to make you confess to breaking safes. She's incredulous, in fact, that they have "broke" you, doesn't believe it at all when they come out of the back and say you've admitted to plenty of things. But the chief comes out and looks Nell in the eye and says, "You might as well stop trying to lie for him."

"I wouldn't believe him at first," she says, "but they kept hammering it into me. They said Clyde had been cracking safes for several months." There is nothing she can do, the police tell her.

"I was heartbroken," she says, "and the officers sent me on back home

---

* It's possible Goss and Nell are describing two separate raids, as they were regular occurrences, but so many of the details match that this seems unlikely.

to break the news to Mother that Clyde was definitely a criminal. It wasn't a happy day."

Just about the only bright side of the episode from Nell's perspective is that the charges, as usual, are dropped. Why, no one knows. Maybe Goss didn't break you quite as thoroughly as he thought. But Nell knows now that the reprieve is only temporary. They'll get you eventually. Her only longer-term hope of the moment for you is this new girlfriend.

"Bonnie was an adorable little thing, more like a doll than a girl," Nell says. "She had yellow hair that kinked all over her head like a baby's, the loveliest skin I've ever seen without a blemish on it, a regular cupid's bow of a mouth, and blue, blue eyes."

It's not how she looks that Nell really cares about, except to the degree that it might keep you in love. It's who Nell thinks Bonnie is that matters to your big sister.

"She worked hard, lived at home, stayed in nights and never ran around," she says. "She simply adored and worshipped her mother. All in all Bonnie Parker was the answer to a sister's prayer for a best loved brother. I hoped when she found out about it, she'd overlook Clyde's police record, make a good boy out of him and stick to him."

❁

Why do you have to tell Bonnie about all that if there were no charges filed? You don't, right? But you could, right? Bonnie's no dummy; she knows where money comes from and where it doesn't come from. Isn't her husband, Roy, in jail already for some dumb botched burglary? Isn't her little sister, Billie Jean, married to Fred Mace, who is as thick in the business as anyone else? Why do you have to tell her about all that if nothing sticks? Why can't your luck hold a little longer? Why do you have to get out of town now, when you've finally found the right girl? You love Bonnie. You love your sisters. You love your mama. You hate cops.

❁

Cumie struggles mightily inside, but somehow she'll bear it up. "My brothers' trouble with the law about run my mother insane," says her littlest girl, Marie. "She was crazy about her kids, but there was nothing she could do about it."

Nothing Cumie can do about it except worry herself sick night and day. Worry, that is, and haul herself over the viaduct to the sheriff's office to see her boys when they're behind bars, and talk to the men in suits and robes and badges who keep trying to say her sons are no good. Nothing she can do but tell them once again that no, they are good boys, will be good men if given half a chance. She hauls her tired bones over to Fort Worth for the same purpose, hauls herself and her old man and her littlest children all the way down to San Antonio and back that time Buck is charged with stealing a car.

"I remember Mama having fits with the police coming around all the time, coming to arrest one of her boys," says Marie. "She always believed they hadn't done nothing."

Cumie's not quite so woolly-eyed about Clyde as Marie thinks. This is no surprise, considering the girl is not yet ten in 1929. One small sweet thing, in fact, about the dismal situation in the beat-down house that is also a store and is also a gas station is to see how little Marie can just carry on being a little girl despite all the carrying on. As she herself says later, "I never paid much attention to it. It was just the way life was." Sweet to see that child there playing with her dollies while the police come and go. Sweet for a mother—or devastating, depending on the day, on the mood, on the temperature outside and whether anybody's actually bought any gas or sandwiches in these "hard times," this "great depression."

Cumie knows as well as anyone that Clyde is not entirely innocent. She is his mother, after all. And she knows better even than he does that the water is getting deeper every second, not shallower. Hotter, not cooler. She has her blind spots; what mother doesn't? But they are not about what her son does. They're about why he does them, because, as usual, Cumie knows what is bringing Clyde down: it's his new friends. It's not the neighbor kids— the Hamiltons, Sidney Moore, or even Frenchy Clause. She knows those boys. No, it's the boys from out of town.

"My son met Willie Turner and another, Frank Hardy, I believe, and maybe Pat Bewley, at the home of a girl friend, last winter," she says in March of 1930. "The Waco boys came to my house with Clyde, and I thought them very nice young men."

They are indeed nice young men, even if Hardy's a bit of a joker, with his funny question mark tattoo on his arm. All the boys have tattoos these days, and some of the girls, too. Mostly they're initials and anchors and hearts and girlies, though; it takes a different kind of mind to say, Let's put a question mark on my arm. Frank Hardy's got that ironic feel about him that makes a mother not know for sure if he's real smart and therefore good or just a guy with no spine. A question mark himself, he is. And Bewley has that odd burn scar on his face.

But Cumie's been on the poor side of the tracks with cousins on the other side long enough to be able to recognize that Willie Turner, at least, comes from what you might call a fancy family down in Waco.

"Turner is a Wacoan, of good family," says a reporter for the *Waco News-Tribune,* Turner's local paper. "He has blue eyes, blond hair, is slightly bald, height six feet one and one half inches, a native Texan."

It's hard to resist hoping that the "good family" attributes might slide over and stick to her boy Clyde, but the good feeling about the nice boys from Waco wears off on Cumie fast. "It was not long after this that I knew Clyde was in some sort of trouble," she says. "He seemed to be nervous, and afraid of the police. He didn't tell me what it was, but I know that he was mixed up in the robberies at Waco."

During November and December of 1929, the Waco boys Willie Turner, Pat Bewley, and Frank Hardy, along with Clyde whenever he can get down there, are on a regular spree of more than twenty car thefts and midnight burglaries. The usual routine is to steal a car in some other city, like San Antonio or Houston, and bring it back to Waco, something Frank Hardy has been doing off and on since at least 1926. The hot car makes good transportation during a week or more of prowling in Waco proper, or in surrounding towns like Hillsboro. Once they start to worry that the car might be getting too familiar, or that the laws might be catching up with it, they can abandon it, strip a few parts off it for resale, or pass it along to any of a number of fences they know up in Dallas or elsewhere.

The four men in this Waco gang are pretty good at their jobs, almost what you might call professionals. For a time they even have an old bread truck they can use to haul safes away from the small businesses they specialize in hitting. It's perfect, they love that truck, and they don't have to do the noisy work of knob knocking or blowing the door off until they're out in the middle of nowhere. Before they got the bread truck, they had to use Turner's mother's car, which was nerve-racking as all get-out since the only way to carry a safe was to lash it to the running board, where anyone could see it. Not likely a lawman who sees a car going by in the middle of the night with a safe strapped on the outside isn't going to think to himself, Huh? and turn on the siren. But a bread truck in the hours just before dawn, why, that's exactly when you expect to see one making deliveries.

Jobs don't always go smoothly, though. One time, says Turner, he "and his companions" broke into the Stolte grocery store. They were using a car they had stolen in San Antonio, which they parked out front, but while they were inside the store collecting their loot the Waco police came and hauled the suspicious vehicle to city hall. Job done, the burglars came outside to find their chariot had disappeared. It's funny in hindsight, sure, but at the time no one was laughing at having to walk home with bags of stolen cash.

Another time they think they might be able to get their revenge on

Sheriff Stegall of Waco. They still have the keys to one of their stolen cars he took from its hiding place in a gravel pit, but when the boys get to the courthouse parking lot the damn engine won't turn over.

Cumie doesn't know as much as she thinks she does, but she knows enough to be certain of what she thinks of Willie Turner, no matter how polite he is or how fancy his family down there is.

"Clyde was a good boy until he started running with Willie Turner and other boys from Waco last winter," she insists.

❋

You got to love your ma. The only problem with her blaming the Waco boys is they don't really have anything to do with how it is that you now have to find Bonnie and tell her something to make her understand why you have to say good-bye, at least temporarily. The year or so of feeling invincible—of having money, cars, girls, friends, nice clothes, fun . . . and no charges that ever stick—that year of lucky breaks starts to break down thanks to no one but you and Buck and a Dallas kid named Sidney Moore.

On a Friday night, November 29, you and Buck and Sidney make a run up toward the Oklahoma border in a stolen Buick to look for another car to steal. You find a nice new Ford in Henrietta and slip under the wheel and start her up. The car is probably the main grab of the night, and the house burglary that same night also goes off without a hitch. The owners aren't around, so it's just a matter of scoping it out, posting a lookout, getting in, and rifling around through the usual rooms. There's no cash, which is disappointing, but a couple of handfuls of jewelry are an easy grab. Then it's back out and on the road. Adrenaline buzzing, cigarettes burning, eyes open, hearts pumping, foot to the floor.

Without cash from either the car or the house job, and no telling how long it will take to fence the jewelry, on your way back toward Dallas somebody has the great idea to break into some business that closed its doors after the banks shut down for the weekend. Some business, in other words, that might still have its take for the day in the office. Nothing too big, as no one brought knob-knocking tools or soup mix, but maybe a gas station. You ease through Denton, Texas, on West Oak Street so as not to attract attention and there it is, the Motor Mark Garage. An office door is easily pried open with a pinch bar, and there is a safe that's small enough that a couple of you can simply heave it into the back of the Ford.

Just when you're about to set out for Dallas, though, a couple of nosy laws start blowing their stupid whistles for you to stop. Sure, buddy, and the accelerator slams to the floor and that new Ford just roars out of there like a thoroughbred out of the box, taking the corner of Piner Street on two wheels, one of which catches the curb, breaking the axle. Motherfucker! Get out and run!

Night patrolman Clint Starr sees it all playing out, sees you getting out of your wrecked car. He pulls his gun from its holster, yells for you to stop, takes aim, and squeezes the trigger.

Crack! Crack!

Buck, who is supposed to be so fast, goes down howling like a stuck pig and that's enough for Sidney, who just puts his hands up and turns himself in. Only you manage to slip through the dark streets and get yourself back to Dallas, thinking Buck is probably dead. Most likely you found whoever was still driving the Buick—no one is saying what ever happened to that car. But however you do it, you get back into Dallas, where even though you're supposed to be lying low, waiting for the mishap in Denton to blow over, you happen to go to visit a friend with a broken arm and fall madly in love with Bonnie Parker.

And she's in love with you. And Buck's alive after all, though he's gone to jail. And for a couple of months, January and part of February, you can't hardly remember being happier.

Except that now you have to tell her good-bye, because the word on the street is that the cops know there was a third man up in Denton and even though a couple of months have gone by they're looking to arrest you. So you have to get out of town as soon as you say something to Bonnie. Tonight.

❋

You find her.

She's moved back in with her mom, as the job helping the pal with the broken arm is over. You find her there at Mrs. Parker's and you're going to tell her everything.

It's all so sweet, you can't really stand up and leave. It grows late, and then later. You manage to get the words out of your mouth that you're going away, but not exactly why.

It gets later still, and you're sitting close to Bonnie's beautiful tiny self and you haven't said good-bye, and finally Mrs. Parker nicely says, Stay the night on the couch. She goes to get you some of Bonnie's brother Buster's pajamas and some sheets.

Just a few hours then, okay, you will sleep, thank you.

When the police arrive to arrest you they say with a sneer, "If you've got any rabbit in you, you'll run like Buck."

And they're right. But you know you're caught good.

"Buddy, I'd sure run if I could," you say.

CHAPTER 7

WACO

I met his old gal Sadie
She said, "Have you seen my baby"
I told her he was downtown in the can
She went down to the jail
Just to go his bail
She said, "I've come down here to get my man."

He's in the jailhouse now
He's in the jailhouse now
So you can understand
Why old kid Sadie's in the can
She's in the jailhouse now

—Jimmie Rodgers

After a month in the state prison system Clyde's older brother Buck figures he can probably make it through his four-year sentence and back out the other end to begin a new life with this new girl Blanche. He loves Blanche Caldwell, all right, even though he barely met her back in November, before heading up to Denton that stupid night and getting caught. She's beautiful, dark-haired and smoky-eyed, which maybe comes from her mom, who Blanche thinks is possibly half Cherokee or half Choctaw. Half whatever, Buck thinks, Blanche is heaven to look at and laughs at his jokes. He figures she's worth whatever it takes to get this life behind him and start over, just like she says to. They'll sure be happy then.

His life has been pretty much a waste up to here, and if he himself didn't know it before seeing his ma crying there while he was on trial, he's figured it out now. "My crookedness," he calls it in his first letter home from jail. Two wives he's had and left already, and now here he is lying in the Huntsville prison infirmary, wondering how long the bullet holes in his legs are going to hurt so bad. But Blanche says she'll wait for him, and they can start over. So he figures he can probably make it.

"Mother I am in the hospital now and my legs are hurting pretty bad," he gets someone to write for him in a letter home from Huntsville on January 16, 1930. (Reading and writing aren't his strong suits.) "It sure looks hard, but I'm going to take it."

He says, "Mother, try to get me a furlough and don't fail to write often and don't forget to tell Blanche to write me and to tell me all of the news that happens in the outside world."

And at the end of the letter he says, "I hope the outside world don't forget me because I'm in the walls.

"Good-bye mother and don't worry—

"PS: Don't send me any tobacco but send me some money. Because they won't let any tobacco in."

Back on the Eagle Ford Road in West Dallas, Cumie's actually not doing all that well. She's been sick. It's hard to say with what, exactly; she's just laid low. The wear and tear of seeing her boy Buck getting shot, shackled, tried, and carted off to jail has worn down her defenses. Cumie is a tough bird, the center of the family, but this is hard news, even for a woman who has been living a hard life for fifty-six years and counting.

Naturally, it gets worse. In February she learns that Buck's legs are healed up enough that the prison authorities want to ship him out to the Ferguson work farm. Healed-up legs is good news, but everyone in Texas knows those farms are fearsome places. Any natural-born mother would be worried sick to think of her offspring being worked and beaten like a, well, like an old-time slave.

She will bear this burden, too, of course. And Buck and Clyde's father, Henry, well, Henry is, as always, silent and bearing it in his own way. He'll pump gas for the customers, check their oil, nod at passersby, and listen to his radio, which runs all day and night. He'll get by okay. But sometimes it's hard to remember the reason for carrying on with it all. Cumie's body just lays her low now and then, as if to say, Enough, old woman.

When Buck hears she's feeling poorly he says, "Tell sister to send my shoes and send me some more pajamas because they burned mine up, but they will let me have some more now if you send them to me and tell her to help me all she can to get me out on a parole or a furlough while you are so sick."

Buck's such a good boy. He knows what his poor mother needs to hear. Or, at least, he knows what the best thing he can say to her is, given the circumstances.

"The guards and Captain down here treat me awfully good. So I see no reason why I should not get along," he says in a letter from the work farm. Because his legs are still not completely healed, he has a relatively easy job in the camp kitchen. "You ask me if I need anything," he says. "I am doing fine and don't need a thing, only lots of sweet letters from you, Mother dear."

That's a drink of water for Cumie, at least.

"You must write me often and with all of the good news," he says, and Cumie sure would like to believe she'll have some of that soon to share with him. She's not optimistic, though. The truth is, Cumie can't hardly stop to worry about Buck right now because suddenly Clyde's also been locked up and they aim to try him for the very same crime that put Buck away.

It's enough to make a woman . . . but she'll bear up somehow.

❋

Bonnie borrows a car to go across town and try to visit Clyde at the Dallas County jail. It's no fun, really. The jail is upstairs from the sheriff's office and she knows pretty much all the deputies there on the first floor, either from her waitressing days or maybe from the times old Roy Thornton got in trouble. And if they don't know her from those times, they know her now from coming in and asking to be let in to see Clyde Barrow even though she's not a relative. So somebody could have told her, maybe dropped her a line, called her up, saying, Hey, Bonnie, your boyfriend's getting moved.

But they didn't tell her, of course. She shows up at the jail trying to keep pride together while visiting yet another locked-up boyfriend and they just say, Sorry, sweetheart, he's gone. He's up in Denton to face charges in that slick job he and his brother pulled at that gas station. Buck got four years for that, she thinks. Four years! And here she's been telling Clyde that she wonders how she'll survive two or three weeks without seeing him.

She gets out of the jailhouse door with the pressure rising in her head, but thankfully without making a fool of herself.

"I was so blue and mad and discouraged, I just had to cry," she says, and once she gets in the car, well, the tears just start flowing down.

"I had maybelline on my eyes and it began to stream down my face and

I had to stop on Lamar street," she writes. "I laid my head down on the steering wheel and sure did boohoo."

Some policemen come by and see this car with a crying girl in it. They pause and tap politely. Can they help, they want to know. They're nice enough guys, gentlemen, but there's nothing they can do. Or nothing she wants from them.

"I imagine I surely looked funny with maybelline streaming down my face," she says. She tells the officers not to worry, says she just feels bad about something. When they offer to drive her home, she musters as close to a smile as she can get under the circumstances and says it's not necessary.

"I thanked them and dried my eyes and went on," she says.

✱

Bonnie's so sweet, the sweetest thing in the world. That morning you were arrested in her mother's house any other girl could have just up and said she doesn't need another convict in her life. Bonnie should have said that, in fact, but "should have" doesn't mean "could have," you guess, and if she feels for you the same way you feel for her then she couldn't have. And she says she does feel that way for you, and you believe her because it's got to be true from the look of her tears. And from her letters. Long letters.

"Honey, I sure wish I was with you tonight," she writes you on Valentine's Day. "Sugar, I never knew I really cared for you until you got in jail. And honey, if you get out o.k., please don't ever do anything to get locked up again. If you ever do I'll get me a railroad ticket fifty miles long and let them tear off an inch every thousand miles, because I never did want to love you and I didn't even try. You just made me. Now, I don't know what to do."

"And listen, honeyboy, you started this and somebody is sure going to finish it. Baby,—no, I didn't intend to call you that because you're not a baby. Well, darling, I'm going to have to close, as I can't seem to make this letter at all interesting. I have read it over and I can't seem to see any percentage in it at all. I'm so sorry, but I can't think of anything to say, only that I love you more than anything on earth, and I don't know if that is of any interest to you. When I find out for sure maybe I can write a sensible letter."

And on she goes for another couple of pages before finishing up with "I hate these long sleepless nights, but then time goes by as it always does, and maybe I can make it. Be sure to write me a long letter, honey, and think of me down here, thinking of you. I love you." She signs it "Just your baby,—Bonnie."

Yes, sir, that's your sweet baby Bonnie. Could turn her back and never shine those beautiful blue, blue eyes over her shoulder at you again. But she doesn't, and she sends you letter after letter and visits as often as they let her. You never did get the chance to take her to meet your family before all this mess set in, but as soon as you're arrested she just goes right over to the garage on the Eagle Ford Road and introduces herself to Cumie and Henry and Marie and the rest. Soon enough she's staying overnight and such, almost a regular member of the family. How about that?

"She began going out to see his mother a lot," says her own mother, Emma. "It seemed to comfort her to be near anybody who was kin to Clyde."

"I liked Bonnie," says Clyde's sister Marie. "She was just, you know, she was a sweet little old girl. She was real tiny, and little, wore three and a half shoe, and was very tiny and was just real sweet."

"And she was very much in love with Clyde and he was very much in love with her."

❋

Ha! Maybe your old good luck isn't all gone after all. The case against you in Denton is falling apart, just like all the other times. They can't prove you were the third man on the job up there without Buck singing, which of course he's not going to do. So it looks for a while in mid-February of 1930 like, once again, you're going to walk out of jail no-billed.

Only not so fast, because all of a sudden here's a couple of detectives up from Waco around the end of the month who want to ask you some questions. It seems that right around the time you were arrested out of Bonnie's mother's house, your pals Bill Turner and Pat Bewley break into a couple of businesses in Mount Calm, Texas, not far from Waco. The jobs all go off fine, though the take at the bank is less than a dollar, which is funny only if it happens to someone else. Heading out of town, though, they get their car stuck in the mud and start making all manner of noise while trying to shove the machine back onto the road.

There's mud all over those dirt roads of Texas this time of year, and normally you might hope a truck might come by with a chain, or a tractor. The only thing on this back road in the middle of the night, though, is a couple of lovers parked in their own car far enough away that Turner and Bewley don't know it's there but close enough that the cuddling couple can hear them yelling like madmen. For reasons they keep to themselves the lovers decide not to go help whoever is making the racket, but when they learn the next morning that their little hometown has been worked over by a pair of crooks in a car, they tell the law that they remember hearing someone yelling the names "Pat" and "Bill."

It doesn't take the Waco police long to figure out which Bill and which Pat might be hanging around together in suspicious circumstances, and once Turner and Bewley confess to the Mount Calm burglaries, the detectives start wondering about a slew of similar crimes perpetrated over the past few months. On Sunday, February 23, Bewley and Turner take Detectives Huff and Buchanan of Waco on "an all-day automobile tour of the county and city." By the time the tour is over, they have confessed to about thirty crimes.

No one is saying outright that Turner or Bewley ratted you and your pal Frank Hardy out, but somehow your names came up. This is why the detectives from Waco are now spoiling your "no-bill" celebrations in Denton. Huff and Buchanan tell you that Turner's confessed. So has Bewley. (Frank Hardy must be getting the same treatment down in Houston, because he just turns himself in without even trying to run.) Your only chance, they say, is to plead guilty and hope for leniency from the judge. They didn't come to Denton just to ask you questions; they came to take you with them back to Waco.

"After he had been involved by Bewley and Turner in the string of robberies to which they confessed, he was located in the Denton jail" is how the *Waco News-Tribune* tells the story.

You aren't walking out of the Denton branch of the Many Bars Hotel and back into Bonnie's arms after all. On Sunday, March 2, you're riding in handcuffs down the flat prairie lands from Denton, right past or even through Dallas, to Waco, to be reunited with the old gang at the McLennan County jail.

❈

In twenty-two years on the bench of the Fifty-fourth District court in the city of Waco in McLennan County in the great state of Texas, the Honorable R. I. Monroe has seen a little bit of everything come through his courthouse. Some of it has been exciting, some of it tragic, some of it political, and most of it just the run-of-the-mill civil cases of the sort that are supposed to keep small disputes from festering. That, and two-bit crimes.

He loves the bench, but sometimes it seems to him that the people of Texas just don't understand that the rule of law means there are processes that must be respected. His very first year on the bench, in 1909, no fewer than three "delegations" of locals come by the Waco jail demanding to collect Lockett Randall, a black man charged with criminal assault on Miss Ida Pratt. She's the daughter of a local white farmer. Three times Monroe tells them to go home, but things get so jumpy so fast that he and the sheriff decide to sneak the defendant out of town under cover of darkness. That works, but it's a damn disgrace when you can't trust your own town. An embarrassment, in fact, to this so-called civilization, and it happens pretty much any time some local Negro gets charged with a killing, attempted killing, or strange and sick violation toward some white woman or child.

It gets so bad in Waco in 1922 that Governor Pat Neff sends no less than Captain Frank Hamer of the Texas Rangers to the city to make sure three Negroes charged with murder make it into the McLennan County Courthouse alive and get their trial. The assignment is nothing new for Hamer; these days, it seems his number one job is shuttling from courthouse to courthouse making sure Negroes get to the noose through the proper channels.* The saying may be "One riot, one Ranger," but after considering Waco's reputation, Governor Neff sends four more Rangers to accompany Hamer and tells them to bring their machine guns. As usual, Hamer keeps the peace, stares down the crowd, and the case blows over. But Judge Monroe thinks it's a disgrace that the Rangers are needed at all in what is supposed to be a settled country.

"That negro may have deserved the punishment given him," he roars from the bench after one incident where the Rangers didn't get there in time to stop the defendant from being lynched. "But the mob that executed him was guilty of murder."

The judge is not soft on punishment; he's known in some quarters as the hanging judge. It's the lawlessness he can't abide. If it's not a lynch mob, it's the wife of some Klan member suing the sheriff for doing his job and stopping a mob. Suing the sheriff for enforcing the law! Or it's Miss Marcie Matthews, a seventeen-year-old white girl, who stands up right in the courtroom gallery and pulls an automatic pistol out of her coat pocket and points it at J. S. Crosslin, an older married man charged with assaulting her.

"He ruined my health, prevented me from getting an education and disgraced me," she says. *Bang!* The first bullet hits Crosslin in the stomach. *Bang!* A second blasts into his right forearm. Crosslin is trying to turn around when, *Bang!*, the third bullet goes into his heart. "But he will never ruin another girl," she says.

She's right about that. Crosslin is a dead man, and his wife arrives just in time to see his body carried out of Judge Monroe's courthouse. As the paper says, "An affecting scene occurred when she viewed the body."

It's all a disgrace, but the year the mob takes away a white man is beyond the pale. It's astonishing. Several hundred men just march to the jail, carry off

---

* "A colored man was the best friend I ever had," Hamer is quoted as saying. "A colored man pickt me up, while the Carr boys shot me down. Shot my guts out, and left me layin there. An a colored man come long, and my guts hangin out. An toted me . . . to a hospital. An let em wash that sand off a my guts and sewed me up, an I'm livin today. I want y'all ta surer than hell respect Em. That colored man cause me to be livin today."

Curley Hackney, and hang him from a tree and put a bullet through his chest for good measure. He'd been charged with assaulting a nine-year-old girl, a despicable crime, unforgivable, but where's the justice? Monroe thinks just maybe, this time, something can be done. This is not a Negro, after all.

"It's high time we should find out what this country thinks of mob law," Judge Monroe says sternly to a grand jury. "Mob law is no law at all, but anarchy, pure and simple, and it is high time that the question should be settled finally whether the mob shall rule or whether our Constitution and laws are supreme."

It's a good speech, and thunderously given, but after an investigation the grand jury finds no one to charge. That crowd that lynched Hackney must have all been strangers from outside of McLennan County, the grand jury reports back to the judge.

"I was born and reared in the South," he says resignedly. "I have been used to mob law—or mob outlaw—all my life."

After twenty-two years on the bench, Monroe takes what comfort he can from knowing he tried. In March of 1930, he's just a handful of months from retirement and the mob is, if anything, stronger than ever. Crime is on the rise. Youngsters who don't seem to care keep coming through. Sometimes all a man can do in a lifetime in the pursuit of justice is go to bed knowing he tried. Twenty-two years gone by, half a year more.

This month is nothing really different, except in volume. Business starts on the first Monday, which happens to be March 3, when the grand jury sends up a record one hundred and fifteen indictments. It sounds like a lot, but more than half of those are used up in multiple indictments against a handful of low-life petty criminals of the sort that come through the courthouse all the time and raise no hackles from either the crowd or the press. That's probably the one thing no one gets a burr in their boot about, poor white burglars.

There are ten indictments each for burglary and theft of over fifty dollars against Emory Abernathy and Monroe Routon, both of whom are already serving time for other crimes. Likewise, their partner Donald Sessions is coming from the state prison on a bench warrant, though he's charged only with eight counts. So that's twenty-eight indictments right there against one group of crooks.

Another sixty-nine indictments are against various members of a burglary gang led by a local good-for-nothing named William Turner. Twenty-five of those are against Turner himself. Sixteen—eight for theft over fifty dollars and eight for burglary—are against his sidekick Pat Bewley. The third member of the gang, Frank Hardy, who's on his way up from Houston in police custody, is charged with twenty-one counts. The last seven are against a Dallas punk named Clyde Barrow, who looks to the judge to be about twelve. Really. The *Waco Times-Herald* even calls him Clyde "schoolboy" Barrow.

So that's ninety-seven indictments right there, for all of which Judge Monroe expects the defendants to plead guilty. The rest of the docket includes the usual: L. C. Walker, two chicken thefts; Frank McCullugh, two chicken thefts; Eugene Gilbert, two chicken thefts; Walter Edwards, two chicken thefts . . .

There's always one oddball case, and this month it's a woman demanding that a one-legged twenty-four-year-old man named Otto Hardin be locked up and executed "for kidnapping my little girl, my only treasure in the world." The problem is that when the "little girl," who is five and a half feet tall and weighs 160 pounds, is brought before the judge she says, clear as day, "He kidnap me? Balogney!" "Balogney" it may be, but the girl is fifteen and the law is the law and the mother is adamant and Hardin has got to go to jail with the rest of them to await trial.

None of the cases in March of 1930, in other words, are likely to cause Judge Monroe any unwanted excitement. It's just the wheels of justice moving in hard times. Just the wheels of justice grinding along.

❋

You figure you'll probably take the deal. After all, they've got you fingered on all seven counts—two burglaries and five car thefts. The prosecutor says to just plead guilty, don't fight it, act sorry, and the likely sentence will be two years on each count. That sounds like a lot, but the sentences will almost certainly run concurrently, meaning you could be out in eighteen months. Maybe less.

Or you could fight it, and probably lose, and go in for longer. Who's going to pay for the kind of lawyers that might get you off? Not your ma and pa, though your ma has pretty much moved down here to Waco to be near you. She and Bonnie are staying at the house of one of Bonnie's cousins. Bonnie and your ma and pa are about all you've got on your side, and they can't get you off this time. So you figure to take the deal from Judge Monroe and maybe get through the sentence and do like Bonnie says and start clear.

"Sugar, when you do get out, I want to you go to work and for God's sake, don't get into any more trouble," she writes to you. "I am almost worried to death about this. Sugar, when you get clear and don't have to run, we can have some fun."

Fun. Wouldn't that be nice, and maybe even possible with her beside you.

"Dear I know you're going to be good and sweet when you get out. Aren't you honey?" she says. "They only think you are mean. I know you're not and I'm going to be the very one to show you that this outside world is a swell place, and we are young and should be happy like other boys and girls instead of being like we are."

So yes, you'll plead guilty on the seven counts and hope for the best. You might even get lucky and be with Buck, who says he's going to go clean, too. He's doing it for Blanche.

"And honey," says Bonnie in one of her letters,

> just remember I love you more than anything on earth, and be real real sweet and think of me, down here thinking of you.
>
> Your lonesome baby,
>
> Bonnie
>
> P.S. Don't worry, darling, because I'm going to do everything possible and if you do have to go down, I'll be good while you're gone, and be waiting—waiting—waiting for you. I love you.

❃

The day comes, Wednesday, March 5, for you to be led into Judge Monroe's courtroom in your shackles and tell him that yes, you plead guilty to all seven charges, and yes, you're sorry, and yes, you plan to turn your life around as soon as you can. Turner does the same thing with his twenty-five counts, as does Bewley with his sixteen and Hardy with his twenty-one. You all plead guilty. Maybe that makes it easier.

It makes things easier on the jurors, that's for sure. The cases are given to the jury in blocks, since the boys are pleading guilty, and they make quick work of it. Without much deliberation they recommend sentences of four years for Turner and Bewley and three years for Hardy. For you, "schoolboy" Barrow—no doubt because you successfully convinced them that you're only eighteen even though you are really twenty-one—they recommend only two years per crime. As promised, in every case, the jury recommends that the sentences run concurrently. It's now up to the judge.

The old man in his black robe looks down at you from his bench. He looks over at your sad mom and at Bonnie there in the gallery. He knows what he's going to do already. "I will sentence them as usual," he says, "and turn them over to Sheriff Leslie Stegall."

But there's no harm in letting you and your troublemaker friends sweat for a few more days. He'll announce his decision next week. The bailiff takes you back to your cell.

❁

No one in the cell is in much of a good mood, and why should they be. You and Turner and Bewley have just come back from pleading guilty and are waiting to hear how long you are going to be sent up for. But it's the one-legged guy, Otto Hardin, who is glummer than any of the others, and he hasn't pleaded guilty to anything. Okay, so he's got one leg from being run over by a streetcar, and a plate in his head from some mishap at work, and is in generally bad health from accidentally swallowing a tack or something like that. But all he is in for is a good time with a girl who says it's baloney that he kidnapped her, which means there's no way they're going to convict him of anything much. So what's his problem?

Cheer up, buddy, it's not like you just went in and accepted seven or twenty-one sentences without even putting up a fight. Buck up, man.

But the next morning, around nine-thirty on Thursday, Turner and Bewley are yelling for jailer Glenn Wright, telling him to come up quickly because it looks like the one-legged guy is sick. He's real sick, maybe dying. Then he does die. Right there in the cell there's a dead man and an empty bottle of carbolic acid. He told Bewley and Turner that he was in the habit of taking a drop in water for cough syrup, but he drank the whole thing sometime during the night, and now they're carrying him out dead. Damn.

"A note addressed to a Waco girl telling her he loved her and 'good-bye' was left in his cell," says the report.

Damn. Poor slob died in jail. To see the laws come and take a dead body out of the jail, that's the kind of thing to put thoughts in your head.

❁

What exactly Buck is thinking and how long he's been thinking it is anybody's guess. But chances are he's not pondering very far into the future when he decides, the very same week Clyde is sentenced, to take advantage of an unsupervised moment and walk away from his post in the kitchen at the Ferguson prison farm. He's not thinking of those promises "to do the best that is in me to lead a worthwhile life" he sent to his long-suffering mother only a few weeks before, that's for sure.

No. All Buck's apparently thinking is that no one's watching, that there's no fence around this place, that there's a car sitting there, and c'mon, buddy,

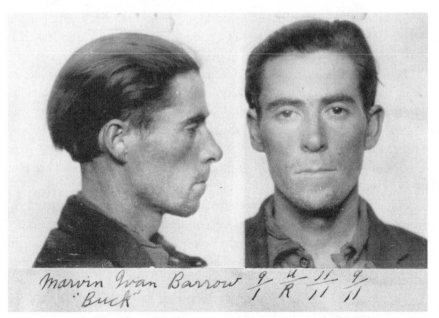

Mug shot of Clyde's older brother Buck Barrow. *(From the collections of the Texas/Dallas History and Archives Division, Dallas Public Library.)*

let's go. Next thing anyone knows, Buck and another "unapproved trusty," as the escape ledgers call someone in his position in the kitchen, are on the run. They haul as fast as that car will go, zigzagging on farm roads and by-ways all the way to Dallas, maybe stopping only long enough to steal the tags off another car and put them on the one they are driving so as to throw off anyone who might be looking for them.

Chances are they don't even stop that long anywhere, since Buck shows up at the gas station on Eagle Ford Road still wearing his prison whites. Cumie, Henry, and the little one, Marie, are sitting at home and he just walks on in the front door with a big smirk. He surprises everyone near to death for a second, and then scares them even worse once they figure out that he's actually on the lam.

The one at the house Buck is happiest to see, though, is Blanche. She moved in with the Barrows even though she only knew Buck for a few weeks before he got himself arrested up in Denton. Just a teenager, Blanche only recently came to Dallas, on the run herself from a bad marriage that wasn't of her own making. For most of her growing up she'd lived with her father up in Oklahoma, but at fifteen she'd moved in with her mother, who was remarried and living in Athens, Texas. She wasn't there long before her mother pretty much forced her to marry a middle-aged neighbor named John Calloway.

"Mother thought I'd have a good home," says Blanche, giving her the benefit of the doubt. Only it wasn't a good home at all, and after less than two years—"Oh I just got tired, I guess," she says.

Blanche and a girlfriend took off for Dallas. Not surprisingly, like so many others without money in their pockets who've come to the Big D for a fresh start, she winds up not in the city proper but in the jumble of shacks and shotguns on the poor side of the river. There, one happy afternoon, she catches Buck's eye.

"We met on Fort Worth Avenue in West Dallas," she says of her first encounter with Buck. "I wasn't divorced, I was just separated."

She also says, "I did not know Buck was in trouble when I met him," which was no doubt true for a few hours or days at least, since a twenty-nine-year-old man like Buck who's trying to impress a pretty nineteen-year-old girl he's met on a street corner is unlikely to announce that his primary occupation is burglary and car theft.

"But even if I had known it," says Blanche, "it wouldn't have kept me from loving him."

Buck is not a big man. At five feet four inches tall and 122 pounds he is even shorter than Clyde. But Buck has a ruddier complexion and more chiseled features than his little brother. Perhaps it's only because he's six years older, but there's nothing of the schoolboy about him. Plus, he has his smile; he has his jaunty way. Blanche is smitten.

"That's Buck," his dad supposedly says when Buck marches into the house out of the blue on March 8, 1930, announces that he just walked away from prison, and scoops up Blanche in his arms. It's not much of a family reunion, though, what with a stolen car out behind the house and a pair of brand-new escaped convicts changing clothes in the back room. There is just enough time for a hug, a request that Cumie burn the old prison uniforms, a pat on the head for little Marie, and then it's back out the door.

"When Buck escaped from the pen, he came by here and got Blanche," says Cumie. "And they went off someplace in a car. I think it was a rooming house someplace, where they hid for a while."

Blanche is thinking about Oklahoma, where her father still lives. Buck's thinking in the short run of his uncle Jim Muckleroy, who's married to Cumie's sister and has a place out in Martinsville, Texas, where they can hide out until the initial heat is off of them. In the longer run Buck's thinking about his cousins in Florida.

What Clyde's thinking when he hears about his big brother's escape is anybody's guess.

CHAPTER 8

MIDDLETOWN, OHIO

Jailer Glenn Wright, who has been getting nervous over his rambunctious charges, called attention several days ago to the condition of the cells, just before he was given a three months' leave of absence to recuperate from the strain of jail breaks and promised jail breaks. His blood pressure is 296, he reports, and he is going away to rest.

—Waco News-Tribune

If we had a gun . . .
Bill Turner and Clyde are in the same cell in the McLennan County jail in Waco, waiting to hear whether Judge Monroe will follow the suggestions of the jury. Unlike Clyde, however, Turner's got more than just Monroe to worry about. After getting nothing out of the bank at Mount Calm that night back in February, Turner went across town and broke into the post office and made off with about twelve dollars of the U.S. government's money. As a result, a few days after pleading guilty in Munroe's court, he's hauled over to the federal court, where his guilty plea gets him another three years, this time at the federal penitentiary in Leavenworth, Kansas.

As bad and crowded as the Huntsville and the Texas state prison farms are—and they are bad and crowded—the federal prisons are even worse. Thanks to a flood of narcotics convictions, prohibition convictions, and minimum-sentencing guidelines for car theft, there are twice as many prisoners in Leavenworth as the place was built to handle. Men are packed into that place like sardines, and not too many months back, in August of

1929, they rioted. It started in the mess hall and didn't stop until guards opened fire and killed a handful of inmates. So though Clyde is hoping to get out after eighteen months or so—even less if his parents can finagle a parole or a pardon—Turner knows he's looking at hard time.

The pardon business is important, because the relatively local and not exactly squeaky-clean politics of Texas make pardons and paroles somewhat easy to acquire. The populist Ma Ferguson is running for governor again, and her husband, also a former governor, is promising that "the first thing she'll do when she gets back in office will be to pardon those convicts who deserve freedom—2,000 of them." Turner himself has already been pardoned out of state prison twice in his twenty-one years, once by Ma Ferguson in her first term; when he wound up back in jail six months later, he got one from her successor, Dan Moody.

A pardon out of Leavenworth, on the other hand, is a horse of a different color. Washington is far away, and President Hoover's talking about building more prisons, not letting people out of them. So Turner isn't thinking about who his "good family" of Waco might know in the federal government; he's thinking about a gun he left hidden in his mom's house across town.

Turner's not planning on serving out his term, and he figures it's got to be easier to get out of this two-bit county jail, with its one guard and one turnkey, than out of Leavenworth. Or, for that matter, than getting over the walls at Huntsville, or across the fields at one of the farms, what with the dogs and all. If he only had that gun right now, it would be a relative cinch to get the drop on the guard when he opens the cell door to bring in food or . . .

Boy, it's hard to stop thinking about that gun.

It's possible that making a break out of the jail in Waco is not Turner's idea in the first place. Emory Abernathy, another man in the cell with him and Clyde, arrived a day or two before in the state paddy wagon to be sentenced for a couple of jobs he and his pal Monroe Routon committed five years back. That's going to add years to the sentence he is already serving at the penitentiary. It could even be Clyde who comes up with the talk of getting out, especially now that he hears Buck is out and free. That's Buck, as old Henry always says. Pretty smooth, just walking away like that.

It doesn't matter who it is that first has the idea of breaking out; for Emory Abernathy, William Turner, and Clyde Barrow, the problem is the same. They haven't got a gun. But Turner knows where one is.

❋

Bonnie is starting to worry about losing Clyde. It's funny, really, to think of a pretty girl worrying about losing a guy who's locked up in prison. Shouldn't it be the other way around? Him worrying about the girl outside fading away, finding someone else, deciding he's just not worth the bother. But that's the truth of it: Bonnie is worried.

"Darling," she asks him, "do you still love your baby?"

She also drops little bits into her letters, once in a while, about all the other boys who are paying attention to her now that he's gone. Nothing really overt—just enough, hopefully, to get his attention, make him think.

"One of the boys brought me box of candy," she says, "and the idiot tried to spend the day. . . . I did everything but tell him to leave, and he stayed and stayed and stayed."

Another time she tells Clyde that "someone told Bud I got my divorce on the 18th and he come out begging me not to get married again." It's all that kind of thing, designed to give Clyde a healthy moment of wondering, but she always follows it up with her sweet talk. She tells him she loves him and laughs about how those other boys sure "would like to meet the Lucky Dog that made me care."

Still, as the days go by, Bonnie is worrying more and more that her Lucky Dog might slip away. Like Roy slipped away—not that she cares about him anymore, but that's what happened to him and she loves Clyde even more. What if he gets out of prison and does not come back to her.

"Dear, promise me you won't go away when you get out," she says. "Honey if you should leave me I wouldn't know what to do."

Mostly it's that Frenchy Clause who's making her nervous, with all his talk about how the gang is everything to Clyde. Frenchy was locked up for a few days in Dallas around the same time as Clyde, but he was luckier and didn't get transferred down to Waco to face charges. Now he keeps telling Bonnie stories of how when Clyde gets out he and Clyde are going to go do this and go do that. Going to have to go off and carry on farther afield somewhere, and so on. She wouldn't put much stock in it, except that, after all, Frenchy has known Clyde so much longer than she has and they're such good friends.

"Frank says you are going far away," she tells Clyde. "I'm sure you wouldn't leave me for him, would you? Of course, he says if you care to have me go along, it'll be o.k. with him, but he says it in rather a disinterested way."

It's all incredibly stressful, trying to keep and figure out their relationship while Clyde is locked up and no one even knows yet for how long. He doesn't write back to her as much as she writes to him, though it hardly matters since she and her cousin Mary come visit him every day for as long as the guards will let them stay. They bring the boys in the cell cigarettes and other treats. Bonnie tells Clyde she's going to get a job and stay in Waco for as long as he's stuck there, and not to worry. But she can see he is all worked up about something, and she hopes it's just the natural nerves anyone in jail would have and not a sign of something worse.

"You didn't act like you were very glad to see me today," she says a day or two before he's meant to go in and plead guilty. "What's wrong? Don't you love me any more? I know how you feel honey. I guess you are awfully worried."

Inside, though, it's Bonnie who is trembling, feeling she needs to prove her love to him. Prove her worth. Her chance comes on Friday, March 7, when Clyde, now in a cozy, lovey tone, whispers to her that there is something big she can do for him. Really big. In fact, it's unbelievably, scarily huge what Clyde wants Bonnie to do, but only if she really wants to and loves him, of course.

He needs her to sneak into William Turner's mother's house and find a handgun that is hidden there. He wants her to find that gun and somehow hide it on her body and bring it back into the jail, to him.

He tells her it will be better this way, that they'll be together again and can get a fresh start in some new place far away. Doesn't he remember her letters saying, "I want you to be a man, honey, and not a thug?" Does she, for that matter, remember writing those things?

Yes, she tells him, she'll do it. Her heart is pumping.

Clyde slips a note into her hand. On it is a map of the house at 625 Turner Avenue, showing where the key can be found over the door, where the gun and the ammunition can be found. Turner drew the map, and he's certain there will be no trouble if she goes during the day, when his mother and sister are at work. But at the bottom, in Clyde's handwriting, is a personal note for her:

"You're the sweetest baby in the world to me—I love you."

She is going to keep that note forever if she can.

※

Mary thinks her cousin Bonnie is insane. Sure, her boyfriend, Clyde, is nice enough and cute enough, charming even. Maybe he's even worth waiting a prison term for, as Bonnie has said at least a thousand times. And it's been fun having Bonnie here in Waco these past few weeks, a bit of a change, even if she's understandably moody, given the circumstances. But this idea of sneaking into another person's house, even if you have the key, is crazy. And sneaking a gun into the county jail—what is Bonnie thinking?

Unfortunately for Mary, though, Bonnie doesn't tell her that this is her plan until they are already opening the door to the empty house and going inside.

"I was never so scared in my whole life," Mary says.

Bonnie, on the other hand, is as cool as a cucumber in icy brine. When the gun is not where the map says it should be, she sets about going through every cranny in the place looking for it, methodically pulling things out of drawers and closets. She dumps out boxes and moves furniture. Eventually, Mary figures she might as well pitch in and look too, since it's obvious they're not leaving the house until they find the gun. And they do find it, finally, under a window seat.

Then it's out the door as fast as they can get there. Put the key back, put the key back—which side of the door was it? Left? Right? Who cares, put it back, let's go.

As for the handgun, it goes down Bonnie's dress front, into a space between two belts she's wearing around her slip. Can you see it? she asks Mary. Are you sure you can't see it? Good.

Mary thinks her cousin is as crazy as a bird. Crazy as a bird and cool as a cucumber.

❋

Now here she is again, that friendly, flirty little blonde who's always wanting to visit "schoolboy Barrow" upstairs in his cell. Look, miss, you've already been up to see your boyfriend once today. I really shouldn't let you up again. But she's begging, looking sad, saying it's just for a minute this time, and that she is going away and won't be back to bother them again. She's too nice to be so in love with such a bum. That kid don't know how lucky he is.

Just this one last time, she promises, and the guard says, Okay, all right, make it quick, missy. Surprisingly enough, she does make it quick. Just a couple of minutes later Bonnie is back down the stairs, barely pausing to say thanks on her way out the door. She must be in a hurry to get somewhere, because she usually stops to make pleasant with the guards. Not this time, though. Poor sweet little old thing. What's she see in him?

Where Bonnie's in a hurry to is back to her cousin Mary's house to lock the doors, pull the shades, turn out the lights, and hide all through that day and the next day too, sneaking out only long enough to get the local paper and see if there's any news.

And sure enough, there it is in the *Waco Sunday Tribune-Herald,* right below an article about Bill Turner getting twenty-five guilty verdicts from Judge Monroe. "If William Turner were to live to serve out consecutively the prison terms given him by court and jury he would be by odds the oldest man in the United States," says the snarky reporter for the *Tribune-Herald.*

Those reporters sure think they're clever, but the story that makes Bonnie and Mary draw the shades and lie low another night is not about Turner's sentencing. It's a single paragraph titled "Waiting Life Sentence; Burglar Robs His Home."

> A burglary was committed Saturday night at the home of William Turner, while William was in jail waiting life sentence on burglary and theft charges. The intruder ransacked the Turner home, at 625 Turner Avenue in East Waco, while Mrs. L. Turner, William's mother, and the rest of the household were at work. When they returned at 10:30 p.m., they found beds torn up, boxes emptied, and the house generally upset, but only a .38-caliber Colt revolver was missing. When Mrs. Turner left the house Saturday morning she put the key in its accustomed place on the ledge above the door, on the right hand side. When she returned and reached up for the key, it wasn't in the proper place. She found it on the left side. Convinced that someone had entered the house, she unlocked the door, went in and found the condition described above, according to Motorcycle Officers Sam Fuller and Harry Robinson, who investigated.

When the boys break out, it's going to be obvious where they got the gun now, isn't it? There it is, in the paper: somebody knew where the key was and went in the house and only stole a handgun. How hard is that going to be to figure out? Mary's husband is out of town and the two women can't sleep. They lie there in bed with the shades drawn, and Bonnie talks endlessly about Clyde.

"He wasn't a bad boy," Mary remembers Bonnie saying over and over again. "If he got out of this mess and safely away, she'd get a divorce, go to him, and marry him. They would settle in some far off place and everything would be all right."

That night, after dark, two men come knocking on the front door. They bang on the door and won't go away for a long time; instead they sit across the street looking at Mary's dark house. Waiting for the girls to return home.

Inside, Mary and Bonnie are petrified, certain that the police have read the newspaper story, foiled the plan, and have now come to arrest the two of them. They peek out through the shades, but no way are they opening that door. Eventually, the men give up and go away.

❁

Can we get some milk up here, jailer? I need some milk. Hey, jailer.

It's about seven-ten in the evening on Tuesday, March 11, and Turner is putting the escape plan into motion by trying to get the night jailer, a man named J. P. Stanford, to come on down and deliver some milk. Between Turner's long history as a local troublemaker, the recent business of Hardin drinking acid and dying, and the people like Bonnie coming and going on visits, you and your cell mates all know the jailers and turnkeys by name now. You also know that Stanford's going to have to open the door to get a bottle of milk into the cell: the lattice of flat steel bars that make up the cage has square holes that are large enough to tip a small handgun through, but not big enough allow a quart jar of milk to pass.

Most importantly, you know that Stanford will almost certainly be following jail policy by coming unarmed. As head jailer Glenn Wright explains, "It is better to be beaten down unarmed by prisoners who would then escape also unarmed, than run the risk of their taking a pistol from an overpowered jailer and being thus in a position to do more mischief outside."

The one thing you don't know is whether Stanford will take the extra precaution of ordering you all into your bunks. The block is designed so that he can lock everyone into individual bunk cells before opening the door to the common area and putting down the milk. If that happens, you might have to wait for another opportunity, though you've been working to jimmy the locks on the inner cells so that they can open even when they appear fast to the jailer in the hall.

But for some reason he surely regrets, Stanford decides to just open the door to the cage—it pulls toward him—and put the milk on the floor. Turner is there, and he bends down as if to pick the milk up but instead hurls himself toward the door, jamming his head and shoulders far enough through to prevent Stanford from clanging it shut. Right behind Turner is Emory Abernathy, who has rushed over from a corner of the cell and is now pointing a pistol straight at the jailer's chest.*

"Stick 'em up," says Abernathy. Stanford hesitates. Where in the world did he get that?

---

* He's the gunman, no doubt, to throw the laws off the trail of Turner's local family and the ever-present Bonnie.

"I'll kill you if you holler," says Abernathy. "Stick your hands up now."

Stanford's hands go up. Someone tells him to just keep quiet and come on inside the cell, that no one needs to get hurt if he does what he's told. He's got no choice but to obey, really, what with three thugs with a gun against him. In he comes, hands over his head, and now it's his turn to hear the steel door clang shut and the lock click over. As soon as the three of you are out of the cell, the three remaining inmates in the cell—a counterfeiter, an embezzler, and a petty thief—rush over to Stanford.

"We are going to stay with you," they say.

Down the hall and down a flight of stairs is the only other man on the night crew, and he's sitting at his desk tucked in below a landing on the stairs. He's the turnkey, Huse Jones, and he's being kept company by a trusted prisoner. Neither of them heard anything of the doings upstairs, though, so the first they know of the trouble is when Abernathy appears on the landing with a gun.

"Stick 'em up," he says.

You and Turner leap down the rest of the stairs and start rifling the turnkey from both sides, looking for the keys to the outer door. He tries to hide them between his pants legs. What does he think you're gonna do? Say, Oh, no keys? Oh, okay. We'll just go back to our cell now, thanks for the milk. He's crazy. You and Turner twist his arms, and the keys appear. The door swings open. Abernathy is the last out, backing out of the room with the gun trained on Jones. At the last second he turns and takes off out of the building, down the stairs, and up Sixth Street.

POW!

The gun goes off accidentally, hurting no one. It just makes everyone run all the faster, which is a good thing since Jones is right behind you now with a gun of his own. By the time he gets out in front of the jailhouse he can see the three of you running across Columbus Avenue, passing the Episcopal church about a half a block away. He fires off a couple of rounds in your general direction, but it's too dark and you're too far ahead. You're nothing but crazed shadows. You run like hell.

Bang! Pow! Bang!

Jones fires off three shots into the darkness, but he doesn't think he's hit any of you and he hasn't. He's shooting to attract attention as much as anything else, but when you and the other two fleeing shadows take a right turn on Jefferson Avenue and are out of sight, he goes back in to check on Stanford and call the police. It's too late—you're in a car you find about two blocks away, and then in a faster car you find about twelve blocks away. You're gone.

Within hours you are hundreds of miles away, north and east, into Oklahoma. You're nervous as hell whenever there are headlights ahead, but you laugh together on the dark roads about how easy it turned out to be, and the look on that old boy Stanford's face when he put down the milk and saw the barrel of that pistol pointing at him. You laugh and sweat all the way into Missouri, changing cars whenever you see a likely candidate, pulling small stickups for cash along the way. You buy clothes and a suitcase in one town, safecracking tools in another.

In a strange sense, it's as if the three of you are still in a cell together, packed into cars, trading stories of close calls and payoffs as the miles go by. Compared to you and Turner, Abernathy seems like a real pro. Some of the jobs he has pulled make your gas station heists seem like punk stuff. His specialty is going through bank walls at night. He did that at Meridian, Texas, and at Abbott. In a bank in Riesel, he used a torch to cut a hole in a safe, and when it cooled off he reached in and pulled out something like $8,600. Now, that's the kind of money to get a boy thinking.

Abernathy is loaded with great stories. Right there in Waco, he and his partner, Routon (who got left behind in the escape because he was in another cell), sawed through the bars on the back window of a jewelry store one night and got out of there with $12,000 in diamonds. The best part is how Abernathy, once they were in the store, took his coat off, rolled up his sleeves, put a pencil behind his ear, and went up to the front window and pretended to be redesigning the display cases so that anyone walking by and looking in wouldn't be suspicious while Routon was scooping up the twelve thousand in rocks. That's hilarious!

Twelve thousand dollars! That's not the kind of change that turns up in two-bit gas station safes. No sir. That kind of money will buy you some smiles all around. Even if Abernathy ended up selling the batch for only eight hundred because diamonds are tricky to fence, it's still a great story.

Miles go by. You are on beyond Missouri now, across the big wide rolling Mississippi into Illinois. There, in the little town of Nokomis, you tell the other two to wait for you while you head into a Western Union office to send a telegram back to Bonnie in Dallas.

Everything is all right. Stop. Can she tell your mother the same? Stop. You will write to her soon. Stop. You love her. Stop.

❀

It's not the kind of thing a teenager living at home is likely to tell her mother, that she recently burgled a house with a cousin and snuck a gun into her boyfriend's jail cell to help him escape.

"Had I known about her part in the jail break," says Emma Parker, "I would have sent her away; I would have done anything rather than permit her to continue in a path which could have but one ending—death and dishonor."

Emma says that kind of thing periodically, as if the fact that Clyde has chosen to break out of jail and go on the lam isn't reason enough in itself for her to take drastic action with her daughter. She knows from experience that there's nothing she can do that will make much difference with Bonnie anyway. So when the girl returns from Waco, Emma Parker listens to Bonnie's silence and figures her new obsession with the newspapers, both morning and afternoon, is just to find out any news about Clyde.

Emma is half right. Bonnie positively scours the papers the second they arrive and breathes two sighs of relief with each sheet read. One sigh is for the fact that there's no word of Clyde, good or bad. The other—the one her mother has no inkling of—is for the fact that if the police are looking for the source of the gun, there's no mention of it.

"Bonnie was a dramatist, born so," says Emma later, "and above all else she wished to please Clyde. I'm sure that she was flattered to think that she had measured up to his standards with a daring and grit which even the famous bandit Belle Starr couldn't have surpassed."

❉

What the flying hell are the three of you doing back in Middletown, Ohio? That's really the question. Jesus Christ!

In Middletown on the night of March 17, you, Turner, and big-time Abernathy (Mr. Twelve Thousand in Diamonds Here, Eighty-six Hundred in Cash There) collect a grand total of about sixty-seven dollars by breaking into three closed-up gas stations, one dry-cleaning works, and the B & O Railroad station. All in all, it's not a great night's work, but it's the best you can do, and a couple hours before dawn you ease out of town in the usual style and then hit the gas hard as soon as it won't attract attention. By morning you should be in another state.

But it's still dark, and nobody in the car knows the roads. Where the hell are you? Where do you turn now? Left? Right? Turner says go this way, Abernathy says that way. It's all goddamn winding out here, no lights, no signs, and you're driving like, well, like escaped convicts in a stolen car who've pulled a couple of jobs. You're driving fast. You must be putting a hundred miles or more between you and the laws, because you're putting those miles on the car, right? So you stop for an hour of rest, off the road somewhere, near a creek, and wait for dawn, when at least the sun will give you an idea of east and west.

Too bad it's too cold to get out and stretch, though. Damn, it's cold up here in the North, crazy cold. The best you can do is doze, smoke some cigarettes, a cigar maybe. Open a can of beans. It's too cold to get out and change the tags on the car over to the set from Oklahoma that are stashed under the seat in back.

"We didn't have time to change the license plates," says Turner. Besides, Oklahoma's too far away—those plates might attract attention more than throw it off. Plus, it's cold and dark. No, keep the Indiana plate, number 163-439. No one saw it, right?

Right?

So the question is, if you've put so many miles on the car, what are you doing back in the stinking middle of Middletown driving past the very stinking train station you burgled less than five hours before? Somewhere you took a wrong turn and here you are coming down a hill into West Middletown and the B & O station is right there. Not surprisingly, it's full of police investigating the break-in of the night before. It's ridiculous, really.

"We didn't know we were back in Middletown until we were nearly at the railroad station," says Abernathy. "We had worked the town all night long, until nearly four o'clock in the morning. It was about eight when we drove back into it thinking we were going away."

What is even more surprising is that Officer Harry Richardson of the Middletown police just happens to be standing in front of the B & O Railroad station holding a scrap of paper on which is written the Indiana plate number of a suspicious car seen in town the day before. He's standing there by his police vehicle thinking about that number when he happens to look up and see a coupe with three passengers in it and Indiana plates coming around a bend in the road in the bright clear light of morning.

As you pass, you see him jumping into his car. Damn. Hang on, boys, here we go, and the accelerator hits the floor.

❈

That's it, that's the car right there—well, what do you know? Indiana 163-439. Yes, 163-439. That's it. Talk about luck.

Officer Richardson and his partner, Woody, jump into their vehicle and pull out after the coupe. Immediately confirming their suspicions, the coupe suddenly accelerates on down the hill and across the Great Miami River, toward downtown Middletown. Richardson guns his own car for the bridge.

It has to be them. It sure would be nice if another police car happened to be coming the other way, but it's not as if there are radios in these vehicles. Richardson and Woody can hope that someone back at the train station saw them taking off and rang up the police station, but unless they get lucky it's going to be entirely up to them to catch this car, which has now gone across the bridge, banged over the railroad tracks, and is passing between the brick buildings of downtown.

Inside the bandit car there's no time for serious recriminations about whose fault it is that they're back in Middletown. Clyde is driving—he loves to drive and thinks he's pretty good at it. At the first intersection, figuring he can lose the police, he slams on the brakes and screeches the coupe into a hard left turn onto Tytus Avenue.

It's a nice try, but Richardson sees it and makes the turn too. Now, looking out the windows behind them, Abernathy and Turner can tell the police are gaining ground with every second. Their car must be better powered. They're gaining, gaining. Clyde's got the accelerator pushed to the floor as they roar out of downtown and into a more residential area.

It's hopeless, though. The police car is faster, and within about a mile Richardson and Woody are almost alongside the coupe. Woody signals them to pull over. But Clyde doesn't stop. Instead he slams on the brakes again and skids a sharp right turn onto a little residential street called Auburn. But once again, it's not quick enough to lose Richardson, who also makes the turn.

Woody decides the time has come to draw his weapon, and he leans out of the passenger-seat window and takes aim at the coupe.

Blam!

Nobody is hit. But inside the fleeing car, it's time to make a quick decision. They're obviously not going to lose the cops. They don't even have much gas, as they've been driving all night. Their only chance is to scatter and hope those laws are old and fat and slow on their feet.

Clyde suddenly screeches over to the curb at the corner of Henry Avenue and all three jump out and take off in three separate directions.

Blam!

Woody fires his handgun at one of the fleeing men, but once again his shot misses. The runner, who is either Clyde or Abernathy, dodges into an ally between two of the modest clapboard houses that line Henry Street and disappears. It isn't Turner, at any rate, because Richardson manages to chase him down Auburn Street for two blocks.

Pow!

Richardson fires and orders Turner to stop, but he, too, disappears around a corner. Yet when Officer Richardson rounds the corner himself there Turner is, hands up in the air.

❋

Down at the station, Turner won't talk. The policemen tell him it's no use, that they know he and his friends were the crooks who knocked over the town the night before. They know it because of the evidence left behind in the car.

"Their car was full of all sorts of stuff," says a lawman involved in the case. "Canned beans, burglar's tools, license plates from other states, and other things."

It doesn't matter. Turner's not talking. He says his name is Jack P. Jones and just shuts up. (As if anyone is going to believe a name like Jack P. Jones. Ahoy, matey!) For about an hour he toughs it out under stern questioning, then finally, around the time a couple of Middletown cops capture Abernathy, not far from the train station, Turner begins to sing.

Down at the Waco Police Department, where they haven't had a lead in days and are still operating on the assumption that the escapees headed south and west, as opposed to north and east, the police are surprised and pleased when the Western Union boy shows up with a telegram saying, "WILLIAM TURNER ALIAS JACK P. JONES ARRESTED HERE." The wire even mentions Turner's artsy tattoos—a butterfly and a bird—so it's definitely him.

Then, only a few minutes later, comes a similar telegram saying the Ohio police have got Abernathy, too. Both Abernathy and Turner are now talking, if not exactly telling the whole truth. They're not really clear about how many cars they may have stolen. Abernathy says he and Turner left Waco on a freight train, which they rode to Wichita Falls, Texas. There they stole a car and went to Joplin, Missouri, and then on to Middletown. And neither Abernathy nor Turner, perhaps by previous agreement or unspoken code, is identifying the missing Barrow.

"Just a fellow we picked up along the road," they say when pressed about the identity of the third man in the car.

❋

You have the gun Bonnie smuggled into the jail cell, but it's not doing you much good while you're hiding in a crawl space under a house on some back street of Middletown, Ohio, hoping the police will give up on looking for you. Damn. It's cold under there, and how unbelievably stupid is it that you are there and not somewhere far away, all because you didn't know what road to take out of town? Damn. That's a lesson to learn. Not that it helps you now.

Seems quiet out on the street. Maybe you should make a move. Or wait until dark?

*

Two cops and two detectives from the B & O Railroad sit looking out the open windows of a police car parked at the edge of the dried-up Miami-Erie Canal. The canal, which runs from the Ohio River in Cincinnati through more than a hundred locks and across nineteen aqueducts to Lake Erie at Toledo, 250 miles away, was finished in 1845. It cost $8 million to construct, and the barges that traveled up and down it towed by donkeys and horses played no small role in the rise of Middletown as a steel town. But that was before the railroad. Now, in 1930, the canal is dead. Drained in 1929, it's just a trench remembered by old-timers as something wondrous. In an industrial town at the beginning of the Great Depression, it's just a ditch from the past waiting to be filled in, paved over, and pretty much forgotten.

The four men sit in their car and watch the empty canal and the streets beyond. They wonder about the third bandit, and where he could have gotten to, and if they'll catch him, and if he'll be armed, and if someone will get shot, and if it will be one of them or him.

Finally, at around one o'clock, one of the lawmen, an officer named Tom Carmody, sees someone on the other side of the canal making his way across a field. Carmody opens his door and tells the others to take the car around to where there's a bridge across the dead canal, on Germantown Road. He'll follow the man on foot, he says, and drops down and across the old canal.

*

You see him coming and start to run. What you need now is a car, and sure enough there's one waiting for you in the driveway of a house on Erie Avenue. C'mon c'mon c'mon start. Come on. Start.

And she does. Ha! You're on wheels again. See you later, Officer. Gotta run.

POW! You hear Carmody fire his gun uselessly in the direction of your new machine as it speeds away. He's still chasing on foot. Good luck, buddy. Ha!

Ahead of you now, turning onto Erie Avenue, the police car with the other three officers suddenly appears. Okay, damn, here we go. Slam the brakes and swerve left, onto a smaller street. Gun that engine for all she will give. The other car is right behind you, and there's Officer Carmody hanging onto the running board, waving his pistol at your car.

When the road dead-ends it's almost over, but not quite. Into the space between the last two houses you steer your machine, heading for the back-yards, hoping for a clear path. But the way is blocked by another canal, this one full of freezing March water. Out of the car now, gun out of your vest, a quick look at the water, a quick look up at the four men appearing, two on each side of you from around the house. Four guns pointing at you with your one pissy little pistol.

"I had the gun we got out with," you say. "I threw it in the river when the cops pressed me too close."

❋

For a few minutes you try to obfuscate. Try to say you don't know what the police are talking about, that you are just a seventeen-year-old kid named Robert Thorn from Indianapolis. But it's really too late, given what the Middletown police have learned from their counterparts in Waco.

"When they brought me to the station a telegram had just arrived from Sheriff Stegall about Turner," you say. Leslie Stegall is the sheriff in Waco. "Right after that a wire came about Abernathy."

You stop lying, except about your age. Yes, you are Clyde Barrow and you broke out of jail with Emory Abernathy and Willie Turner.

Down in Waco, a reporter finds Judge Monroe in the majestically domed county courthouse and asks him about what he might do when Turner gets back to town.

"I don't know if I will sentence Willie to the full one hundred years or not," he says. "I'll have to think about that. But at any rate, I'm going to set aside the concurrent sentence and give him a heap longer time than he had when he broke out of jail."

Also in Waco, Sheriff Stegall and an assistant district attorney, Jimmy Stanford, pack extra handcuffs and catch the three-thirty train north for Middletown.

CHAPTER 9

WACO, AGAIN

Mrs. Barrow and a young woman with her, who said she was a friend of Clyde's, were much interested, and the girl appeared amused, at the story of the latest jail-break attempt which was frustrated Wednesday.

—*Waco News-Tribune*

So here they are again, the daring escape artists, back in his courtroom not even three weeks later. It's Monday morning, March 24, and Judge Monroe is looking down from his bench at "schoolboy Barrow" and his pals. Clyde is handcuffed to Abernathy, and Turner to Frank Hardy, who didn't escape but is charged with many of the same crimes. Bewley and another guilty man are also there to hear their sentences.

All the attention, of course, is on the three former escapees. The local papers aren't calling Clyde "schoolboy" anymore, though. The editors are having a heyday with headlines like "Waco's Dumbbell Bandits, Captured in Ohio, Back in McLennan County Jail" and "Baby Thugs Captured."

"Dumbbells?" asked the *Waco News-Tribune* rhetorically in the lead paragraph. "Yes. Because they lost their way on the broad highways of Ohio, and, attempting to drive away from the town they had just looted, circled around and drove into that same town again."

It's great fun, and everyone in town is getting a snicker or two at the crooks' expense. But Judge Monroe isn't in a mood to be amused.

"They're just as bad at eighteen as they are at eighty," he says, looking directly at Clyde Barrow, who is still successfully lying about his true age.

The judge is just warming up. "I have lost my patience trying to help these men who keep getting into trouble. They get on the sympathy of the juries, a suspended sentence or a long sentence to be run concurrently, is recommended, then they break jail."

He adds, "I think it would be a good thing to save you boys from the [electric] chair, eventually, to send you up for long terms. You are liable to go round here shooting a peace officer, if you can shoot straight."

Emory Abernathy doesn't like what he's hearing. He gets a bit defensive, tries to speak up to say he never shot at anyone. Which may be true, but the judge isn't having any of it and cuts him off and continues:

"You keep breaking into houses, and some of these days you're going to either get shot or shoot somebody else. With the records you've got, you'd probably get the chair, when you were tried."

Abernathy sinks to his knees under the withering storm of judicial verbiage. Maybe it's just the mention of the electric chair, Old Sparky; unlike Clyde, he's already been to Huntsville and seen that hallway. He's heard the stories from prisoners whose job it is to clean up after executions: about convicts who caught fire before they died, about the smell, about how the dead men's legs are so cramped up after the execution that the morticians have to cut their tendons just to straighten them out enough to put them in coffins. Abernathy is kneeling there, as if begging Monroe for mercy, still attached to Clyde by the wrist.

"Well, boy," he says to Clyde, "you've got pretty good feet to stand up under all that."

Yup. Clyde just stands there and listens while Judge Monroe sentences him to fourteen years in prison. That's the same seven two-year terms he had before the breakout, only now they're to run consecutively rather than concurrently. It's not as bad as Turner, who gets forty years instead of four. Abernathy, who still hasn't been tried, can only hope Monroe's temper will cool.

The bailiff leads them back to their cell, the "third-floor strong box," as it's known. There, as soon as the guards are out of earshot, they get back to work figuring out how to jimmy the locks of their inner cell doors so that they will appear to be locked when they actually are not.

✳

Later in the afternoon, the guards come back for Clyde and take him into an interrogation room. A Mr. Jimmy Wyatt and another fellow have come up all the way from Houston and want to talk with him. Wyatt's an investigator with the district attorney's office down there, and he has a whole load of questions. Who Clyde knows, who Clyde doesn't know. Johnny Dew, Frenchy Clause, Dan Black—the whole Houston gang.

What Clyde doesn't know is that Jimmy Wyatt's been obsessed with the Root Square Club for months, ever since he got a "tip" about the gang. "This information caused me to spend a good many nights in association with known police characters who congregated at night in a public park," Wyatt explains. "Several of them were involved in minor charges from time to time and each time I talked with them it would be about one of these less serious cases."

Wyatt wasn't really interested in the less serious cases, but being a seasoned detective he didn't push; nor did he tip his hand.

"Drop by drop, they gave information about this little incident and that little incident," he says. "When some members were in jail on other charges I got signed statements from them."

Just before coming to Waco, in fact, Wyatt was in Shreveport, Louisiana, talking to Johnny Dew. Dew is in prison there awaiting trial on federal charges, and under pressure from Wyatt he signed a statement regarding Clyde and Frenchy. It was the sort of statement the detective has been seeking for months, and though he's dancing around with all the other questions he asks this "baby dumbbell bandit" of Waco, there's only one thing that he wants to know: Where were Clyde and his buddy Frenchy Clause on the night of July 2 of last year, the night Buster Gouge was shot and killed out at the beach at Morgan's Point?

✻

Three weeks after Charles Howard "Buster" Gouge, 20, was shot to death on the beach at Morgan's Point, July 2, 1929, and Miss Lillian Bissett, 18, his companion, was dangerously wounded, many officers labeled the murder as an "unsolved killing."

Three officers held different ideas.

They were Jimmy Wyatt, investigator for District Attorney Stevens; Frank Williford, assistant district attorney, and Sheriff "T." Binford.

Tuesday Mr. Wyatt filed murder charges before Justice Overstreet against Frank Clause, 18, and Clyde Barrows, 18. They are accused of killing Gouge.

Eight months of constant work on the part of these three officials led them through a maze of false and misleading motives and clues. Time after time they followed the wrong path, but each time they did this they eliminated faulty information.

—Harry McCormick, *Houston Press*

"Horse feathers," you say when a reporter from the *Waco News-Tribune* shows up in the jail cell on Wednesday morning, March 26. He's got a newspaper from Houston, no doubt the *Houston Press,* with a big picture of you and Frank Clause on the cover and the full banner headline "Two Charged in Morgan's Point Murder."

Charged with murder? It's hard to believe. It can't be. It's just another example of the laws trying to frame you. You look again. It's your picture all right. The reporter notices your face filling with blood and your eyes "burning."

"I've never been to Houston but twice," you say, "and I didn't stay till after dark either time." This is likely a bit of an exaggeration, like being eighteen instead of twenty-one. If you've only been twice, you sure met a lot of people in those two short visits. But you're darn sure you weren't in Houston around the Fourth of July.

"I was working for the United Glass Company in Dallas in July last year," you say, "and I didn't take any trips that I remember. I never heard of this fellow Gouge. A couple of guys from Houston were up here Monday talking to me about the case, and I didn't know what it was all about."

"Horse feathers!" you say again after he lets you read the article through. Some of the other prisoners in the central cell are looking over your shoulder, trying to read the story, wondering about you in a new way. Others, like your pal Frank Hardy, are trying to get the attention of the newspaperman, hoping to have their stories told. Hardy wasn't a part of the jailbreak, but he got thirty years from Monroe, who was apparently fed up with repeat offenders.

"Why don't they give a fellow some time he can serve and still have a little bit left when he gets out?" Hardy asks, as if the guy from the newspaper is going to have an answer. Hearing Hardy, Abernathy starts piping in with his own complaints. (Willie Turner is already gone: the guards came earlier in the day and took him off "at the end of a three-foot chain" to the train for Leavenworth.) But the guy from the newspaper isn't all that interested in Frank Hardy or Emory Abernathy. He's working his big scoop with the kid on the front page of the *Houston Press,* and he starts asking questions as soon as you finish reading.

Clyde "schoolboy" Barrow and his friend Frank Hardy as they appeared in
March 1930 on the cover of the now defunct *Houston Press*.

"Do you reckon Clause told the police you did it?" he asks.

"Naw, he's got too much sense," you say. "Clause is a friend of mine. I
roomed with him in Dallas. He's in the Dallas jail, and has been for five or
six weeks on a burglary charge."

But if it wasn't Clause, then who? the reporter wonders. You think it's
no one, just the usual system of the laws looking around for a scapegoat.

"If the newspapers hadn't put all that stuff in the papers about me
shooting at the officers up in Middletown, and all that other stuff about me
breaking out of jail, those fellows in Houston never would have thought of
mixing me up in this thing."

It's a nice theory, though it doesn't explain how Frank Clause, who had
nothing to do with your escape and recapture, got implicated. "They'll have
a tough time proving anything," you say for good measure. "I can prove I was
in Dallas."

You better hope you can prove it. Wyatt is planning on coming back to
take you down to Houston on Friday. You better hope you can prove it, or
hope you escape and stay escaped. . . .

✳

JAIL BREAK PLOT FAILS

ENTRY TO CELL OF BABY THUGS FOUND BROKEN WITH BAR

WORKMEN CALLED TO REPAIR MARKS OF PREVIOUS JAILBREAKS DISCOVER DOOR TAMPERED WITH

PRISONERS REMOVED FROM BROKEN CELLS

CLYDE BARROW AND EMERY ABERNATHY ARE AMONG THOSE WHO WERE HELD IN "STRONG BOX"

Another jail-break was frustrated Wednesday when it was discovered that the inner cell doors of the north half of the third floor strong box in the county jail had been jimmied with a bar of steel torn from a bunk.

—Waco News-Tribune

❋

Sheriff Stegall of McLennan County can't wait to see the last of Clyde Barrow and the rest of the "baby thugs" who are inhabiting his so-called strongbox on the third floor. Normally, once a convicted felon is sentenced, the state's legendary transfer agent, Bud Russell, comes along pretty quickly in his cage on wheels to collect the men and take them, chained together by the neck, off to "the Walls" at Huntsville.

Unfortunately for the sheriff, however, Huntsville and the rest of the Texas prison facilities are filled past capacity with prisoners, and run-down to the point where a full-blown crisis of sorts is in process. There's plenty of political recrimination going around the Texas state capitol—which, incidentally, was built out of granite quarried by chain gangs—but not much in the way of progress toward a solution. It's gotten so bad, in fact, that Uncle Bud's not coming for the "baby bandits" anytime soon.

The problems in the Texas prison system aren't the result of no one paying attention. There has been study after study, inquest after inquest, hearing after hearing in the legislature down in Austin every decade or so since the end of slavery, and even before that. Everyone talks up a blue streak, but nothing much gets done. It's been slowly coming to a head over the past few years, in a kind of simmering political bean pot that's been on the fire in earnest since about 1925, when there was a major inquiry by the Texas legislature into conditions at the prisons.

"The investigation of 1925, I can safely say, had more scandal and more politics in it than any other prison inquiry held in our state," says Lee Simmons, who was a member of the citizens' advisory commission that testified at the hearings. "The scandal part of it had to do chiefly with whether or not a certain prison official had improper relations with the wife of a convict. . . . Aside from that, the evidence pointed to barbaric cruelty, theft, drunkenness, murder, and all-round loose dealing with property."

Just about the only good news in 1925 was that several traditional methods of Texas penal torture were officially ended. As Simmons's committee reported, "The following barbarous punishments have been abolished: hanging on chains, bodies placed in stretchers, hanging on windows and ladders, the dark cell, restricted diet and the horse."

Hanging on chains, windows, and ladders was just that. Prisoners were fastened to the bars of a window, the rungs of a ladder, or just the ceiling, usually with just their toes touching the ground, and left there until their muscles gave out and they let their weight pull on their joints.

"This was done by putting a small block and tackle in the ceiling of the building with a long rope running through it," says Bill Mills, a prisoner who saw it applied to his fellow inmates in the early 1920s. "It wasn't unusual to swing him clear off the floor. According to the rules he was supposed to hang there three or four hours. But that depended on whether or not he became unconscious."

The "horse," or pole, meanwhile, was a beam a few inches wide. In a particularly painful ordeal, a prisoner would be forced to sit on it for hours, until he fell off, after which he (it wasn't used with women) was forcefully encouraged to get back on for another ride. Mills remembers it, too.

"I have seen many a poor devil ride this pole from early in the evening until 12 o'clock at night, without a bite to eat or drink," says another prisoner from those years. "Some of these poor fellows could not put on their shoes the next morning for swollen feet."

As for the "dark cell," it was a room eight feet long, six feet wide, and only six feet high, with no bedding or other furnishings in it. "The prisoner was undressed and pushed in there without anything except a gown," Mills says. "They had to sleep on the floor unless there were too many to lie down. I have seen as many as eight men in a cell at one time for thirty-six hours."

"The guards," he says, "enjoy punishing the prisoner more than the law required."

The legislators of 1925 were confident that with the elimination of the worst tortures, the laws governing guards would be clear and clinical, regularized and regulated. The more fundamental problem of prison over-crowding, however, was unaffected by the big investigations of 1925. Every-one agreed that something had to be done, but no clear majority formed in the legislature: some wanted to fix up the old prison at Huntsville, others to build a new facility nearer to Austin. It was, after all, the biggest piece of pork in a generation.

Meanwhile, with prohibition and hard times, the prisoners keep com-ing in faster than they get out. By 1930, when Clyde is sentenced, prisoners are sleeping on the floor in Huntsville, packed into cells with no toilets. On the prison farms, convicts are escaping at a phenomenal rate, sometimes sixty or more in a month. It's not just a Texas problem, either. In 1929 there are major prison riots in New York, in Philadelphia, and at the federal penitentiary at Leavenworth, Kansas. In Colorado, rioting prisoners kill ten guards and toss the bodies from the windows. At Huntsville, the warden is looking around like a long-tailed cat in a room full of rocking chairs, just waiting for a riot. But, still, nothing happens in Austin.

Finally, on March 4, 1930, the commissioners of the Texas prison sys-tem, in order to force some kind of action, simply stop accepting new in-mates from the county jails. They go on strike, so to speak.

"We are afraid to take more prisoners," says the chairman of the state prison board, W. A. Paddock. "It would mean probable mutinies, riots, disas-trous epidemics and submission of all prisoners to inhuman discomforts."

The legislature howls, demanding the resignation of the prison board. The prison board can't force the hand of the legislature, lawmakers say, but Paddock doesn't budge. He laughs at the suggestion that the warden of Huntsville might be held in contempt. Most importantly, Governor Moody backs Paddock up, saying "What is the Prison Board to do? Continue to crowd them into the system beyond all reason? Crowded conditions have been responsible for outbreaks, mutinies and riots in other State peniten-tiaries, and we certainly do not want such things to happen in our state."

Sheriff Stegall, in Waco, is thinking, Why should all of this be my prob-lem? He calls up the chairman of the prison board.

"Listen, Mr. Paddock," he says. "I've got a bunch of bad hombres up here, lifers and things like that. They've already broken out once, and I've had to give my jailer a three months' leave of absence because his blood pressure got too high."

He's not exaggerating. Between the time Clyde Barrow and the other "dumbbell bandits" escaped and when they were brought back from Ohio, jailer Glenn Wright's blood pressure hit 296 and he asked if his assistant, J. P. Stanford—the one Clyde and company locked in the cell—could take over his duties temporarily. Wright's last act before "going away to rest" was to order the repairs to the strongbox that resulted in the discovery of the second escape plan.

On the phone to Huntsville, however, Sheriff Stegall isn't having any luck.

"Sorry," Paddock replies. "We've got a few lifers and bad hombres ourselves and the S.R.O. sign is out. You'll have to worry along as best you can till we get rid of a few boarders."

The best Stegall can hope for right now is that at least the accused murderer in the bunch, "schoolboy Barrow," will soon be on his way to Houston. Come to think of it, Stegall kind of expected to have heard from Detective Wyatt by now about his plans to pick Clyde up.

"Maybe Houston jails are crowded, too," he says.

❋

Oh, it's true, her son is damn thickheaded sometimes, but murder?

"It was foolish of Clyde to break out and try to get away from jail," says Cumie. "He would have got only two years, I'm sure, if it hadn't been for that jailbreak."

But murder?

She can't get right down to Waco the day Clyde gets brought back from Ohio. It all happens so quickly: first the recapture, then the sentencing to fourteen years, and now, worst of all, the murder charge. Murder? She knows her boy can be a damn fool, but it's just not true that he's a killer. She thinks she knows it in her heart and knows she knows it in her head because she remembers the Fourth of July.

"He was not in Houston at that time," she says. "I know he was in Dallas every day that week."

She can't get right down to Waco to see him because she's got to find the people and scraps of paper and anything that will help her prove to the policemen from Houston that they've got the wrong boy. She's got some receipts showing that he made some car payments in Dallas on the days he was supposed to have been in Houston.

She gets somebody over to the United Glass & Mirror Company to talk with Pat McCray, the manager who was Clyde's boss last summer. Sure, he says, he remembers the week, too, and is willing to say so for the record.

"Barrow was among several employees laid off the week of July 1, but he showed up every day that week asking about work," he says in a statement that gets out to the press. "He was on the job the week before that and the week after that. He was a good worker and well liked. I believe he is innocent."

Cumie will go all the way to Houston to fight this if she has to, just like she went to San Antonio for Buck. (Ah, Buck, also thickheaded and sweet, still out on the lam somewhere with Blanche, running and hiding. Hope he's safe. Hope he's happy.) "Clyde never drank, and never liked to be around anyone who did," Cumie says to anyone who will listen. "He worked hard."

By Thursday Cumie's back in Waco, hoping to get in to see Clyde before he's taken down to Houston to stand trial. And naturally Bonnie's with her. Sweet girl. Clyde's lucky. Lucky and foolish.

In Waco someone tells Cumie and Bonnie that when he was caught Clyde was waving the pistol that he and the other three used to get out of jail, but that he threw it in a river rather than use it. This is news, but it sounds right to Cumie, and she says what she must know is a flat-out lie: "He never had much to do with guns and I'm sure he isn't a good shot."

Then she adds, "I'm glad he isn't."

Old Cumie's sweet. Sweet as a lamb and wily as a serpent at the same time. She'll say the right thing at the right time most of the time. Even if she's a little crooked now and again with the exact truth, like announcing, when she gets to Waco, "Clyde was just eighteen last Monday," even though she of all people knows that her boy is twenty-one if he's a day.

In Waco, while she's waiting to see her boy, someone tells Cumie and Bonnie about the recent second escape attempt by Clyde and Frank Hardy and their other cellmates. The whole thing was set to go if the prisoners hadn't coincidentally been moved to a new cell for repairs, they tell her.

This, too, is news to Cumie, and for some reason Bonnie, who is sitting next to her, seems to think it's one of the funniest things she's heard in a while. The girl can't keep a smile off her face.

❀

> It was not until the filing of the Clause and Barrows charges and attendant publicity that the case rapidly grew to a climax. . . . After Clause and Barrows had been charged, presentation of the case to the grand jury was delayed purposely while Wyatt and Binford went deeper into the case.
>
> —*The Houston Press*

Down in Houston Harry McCormick and the other crime reporters in their fedoras and trench coats are dogging the district attorney and the sheriff about progress in the sensational murder case.

"Just when will the case go before the grand jury?" one asks.

"I don't know yet," comes the answer. They scribble in their pads.

"When will those men be brought to Houston?" another inquires.

"I don't know yet," comes the answer.

"Do you know whether your investigator is out of the city?" they shout.

"I don't know where he is," the DA replies.

The reporters want to know the details of the case. What kind of evidence is there on these two Dallas boys, really? And what about the alibis coming out of Barrow and Clause—they sound pretty solid, don't they? Anything the reporters can think of to ask the two lawmen, they do.

But they get nothing for their trouble.

"I don't care to be quoted on that," says the district attorney.

To the reporters, the murder case against Clyde and Frenchy Clause is starting to smell like fish. From the very beginning, it was built on circumstantial evidence, even Investigator Wyatt said as much, and now Barrow and his family have come up with pretty good evidence supporting his claim to have been in Dallas that week: letters from his employer, payment receipts, and the like.

Clause, too, seems to be able to account for himself and has witnesses and a telegraph receipt to corroborate his story that he was in San Antonio. He's even got an aggressive lawyer named Abe Wagner, who's releasing statements to the press from his client: "My accusers ought to be willing to lay their cards on the table. I'm ready to do so"—that kind of stuff.

"I have spent half a day with my client and I am sure that he has an airtight alibi," Wagner boasts. He demands an immediate trial, and threatens to initiate habeas corpus proceedings to get Frenchy out on bond.

The Houston city police, meanwhile, who were never very impressed with the theories of out-of-town murderers put forward by their county government colleagues at the sheriff's office, are chasing their own leads. They're closing in on the murder weapon. A woman called the homicide squad and said she knew where to find "the pistol that boy was killed with." The gun, a .25-caliber revolver, doesn't have much to tie it to either Clyde or Frenchy.

Just about all the DA and the sheriff really have to go on, in fact, are statements from Johnny Dew and Marion Stanley, a sometime vaudeville performer who is currently in the Houston jail. Both say they saw Clyde and Frenchy running away from the scene of the crime. In the DA's favor, it's really not like Johnny Dew to finger an innocent man. Just a few months before accusing Clyde and Frenchy of being at the murder scene, Dew confessed to stealing a Buick that he hadn't even been charged with taking because, he told the court, "I didn't want to see an innocent man sent to the penitentiary."

That time the innocent man was another Root Square regular, Jimmie Arnold. Of Arnold, Dew said in court, "He knows me intimately. I know him intimately. . . . I wore some of his clothes, and he would wear some of mine. I frequently wore his shirts, socks, and used his handkerchiefs."

Jimmie Arnold is Johnny Dew's best friend in the world. So when Investigator Wyatt starts pushing Dew for what he knows about the beach murder, he hems and haws, mumbles, and finally comes up with the names Barrow and Clause. He hates to stick it to a couple of guys he hardly knows, but what else can he do? The gun that killed Buster Gouge, the gun the police are hot on the trail of, belonged to Jimmie Arnold. Johnny Dew knows this because he was there, too. He and Marion Stanley and Jimmie Arnold were all at Morgan's Point on the night of the murder. So, to protect Jimmie, he says it was that kid Barrow and Frenchy Clause.

❀

In the Waco jail, Friday comes and goes and no one arrives to take you down to Houston to face the murder charges like they're supposed to. You don't go down to Houston, where you might get sent up for thirty, forty years, or maybe even get the electric chair, you don't know. It's a small relief, but they'll come soon enough.

They don't show up Saturday or Sunday, either. You have to be wondering what it means, though it can't really be bad news, right? Still, you hear they took Frenchy down from Dallas. So . . .

What?

In the meantime, it sure is a pleasure to see your ma and Bonnie—sweet funny beautiful little Bonnie—even if they wouldn't hardly let any kind of proper visit go on. The McLennan County jail is nearly in a complete lockdown, thanks largely to you.

It's all holy horsefeathers.

❀

"Friends?" says Frenchy Clause. "Sure I have got them, but there are only a few in Houston and there is no telling what can happen when man after man keeps insisting you are guilty."

Sometimes, though, one good friend is enough. The Harris County DA's case against Clyde Barrow and Frank Clause falls apart for good on Monday, March 31, just a week after it began, when Dapper Dan Black— the leader of the Root Square Club—decides to talk about who was and who was not at Morgan's Point on the night of the murder.

"I was afraid my friend 'Frenchy' had been framed and I couldn't stand it," Dapper Dan says. He tells the police that Clyde and Frank weren't at Morgan's Point that night at all and, more importantly, that he saw Jimmie Arnold trading for a pistol behind a root-beer stand. He tells them to ask Marion Stanley about that night, and when they do, Stanley all but says he saw the murder take place.

"Jimmie went toward Gouge's car and I heard two shots," Stanley testifies. "I ran toward our car and got there about the time Jimmie did. I said, 'What the hell was that?' and Jimmie said, 'I played hell.'"

Further confirming the new theory, Johnny Dew suddenly clams up. After the news breaks Sheriff Binford races up to Shreveport, getting there at three in the morning, in a desperate attempt to reinterview Dew before Jimmie Arnold's lawyer gets a chance. But when Dew hears that Arnold and Stanley have been added to the list of those charged with the murder, he just looks at them blankly. They work him over for almost four hours. No luck.

"I may be a fool," he says, "but I'm not going to talk anymore."

With four men now charged with a spur-of-the-moment crime involving two bullets fired from one gun, the district attorney lets it be known that while he's not officially dropping charges yet, it's pretty likely that Clyde and Frank will be "no-billed" by the grand jury. In other words, they're off the hook.

"You can't frame a man while I'm in on the racket," says Dapper Dan of the whole affair.

❈

> I cried the other night when they insisted that I committed this Morgan's Point murder. I knew that it wasn't the thing, but I couldn't help it. It wasn't in character—it wasn't the smart guy who thinks he can beat the game. It hurts, though, to be accused of murder when you are hundreds of miles from home.
>
> —Frenchy Clause

No one ever comes to Waco to take you down to Houston. You and Frenchy just drop off the pages of the Houston papers and eventually get "no-billed," just like the district attorney predicted. No one ever comes to apologize for the fright they put you through either (at least no one that anyone remembers), to say nothing of the tears of your ma and Bonnie.

Why would they come and apologize? You are convicted on seven counts already and ran away from jail to boot. You're just a "police character," as the papers call it, and you've been hauled in "on suspicion" so many times in

Dallas and Fort Worth—just to be roughed up and released—that you're almost used to it. Some of the Houston papers even suggest that you were just bait in the first place, that the cops held off of convening the grand jury so they could poke around for better suspects. Still, it was a close shave and who knows how it might have turned out if Dapper Dan hadn't come through.

If you're expected to look at it like a lesson in how the wheels of justice eventually end up with the right man, well, maybe you will decide to look at it that way and maybe you won't. Frenchy, for his part, says, "It makes you feel sometimes that the question of innocence or guilt doesn't enter into it. It makes you feel that the cards may be stacked against you."

And Dapper Dan, though he was never implicated in the Gouge business at all, is suddenly thinking of giving up the adventurous life and becoming a barber. It's the cops, he says: "If they don't get you today, they'll get you tomorrow."

As for you, all you have to say is "They just thought I would be a good man to hang it on."

❈

It's adorable how Clyde gets all worried up about other boys and writes her letters.

"Now honey you know darn well I didn't mean what I said in my last letter," Bonnie reads in one that's dated April 19, 1930, from the Waco jailhouse. He's there day to day now, expecting anytime to be taken on over to Huntsville, which is again accepting a few new prisoners from the most crowded county jails.

"I'm just jealous of you and can't help it," he says to her. "And why shouldn't I be? If I was as sweet to you as you are to me, you would be jealous too."

She's not coming to see him as much in the past few weeks as she did when he first got sent down. This isn't because of anything that should make him jealous but because she's finally landed another real job. What else was she supposed to do, with him looking like he was going to get stuck with a murder charge? Even when the case fizzles, it's not as if Clyde is coming back to get a job and take care of her. He's set to go away for fourteen years.

Fourteen years! She'll be what? Thirty-three? Does he think she can really wait that long? Does *she* think she can wait that long.

"Well, baby, how are you liking your job by now?" He has cramped, little-boy handwriting, with misspellings. "And have any of those hop-heads got smart with you? If they do, just remember the name, because I won't be in this joint all of my life."

Fourteen years? Till 1944?

"Say, Sugar, you ought to see me. I've got on Frank's suspenders, and I'm sure a darb of the season, no fooling."

The boy loves his clothes. He wants her to tell Cumie to bring him "some old kind of shirt," since the white one he's wearing is too nice to lose when he's transferred to Huntsville. Think of that, a shirt folded up and waiting for him for fourteen years. Think of a girl folded up and waiting that long.

But Clyde is not thinking such dark thoughts.

"Honey, if I could just spend one week with you, I'd be ready to die, for I love you and I don't see how I can live without you. Say, honey, when I get down yonder and get to thinking of you, I'll jump right up and start towards Big D. I may not get very far, but I'll sure get caught trying."

That would be about Clyde's speed, bless his heart: escape and not get far. But he is sweet, and his mother sure hopes she can get him out early, and maybe she can. Maybe Cumie can get it done.

"Well, old dear," Bonnie reads near the end of the letter, "here's Bud Russell. I don't know whether he's going to take us up or not, but I guess he will. If he does, be sure and come down as soon as you can. Honey, I don't know whether they're going to take me or not, but if they do, do what I told you. Come when you can."

CHAPTER 10

HUNTSVILLE, TEXAS

"The condition of the Texas prisons constitutes a crime against society, a crime against the taxpayer and a crime against humanity," State Senator Thomas B. Love, a candidate for the democratic gubernatorial nomination, said yesterday in endorsing Governor Moody's program of prison rehabilitation. . . . "With 5,500 inmates in Texas prisons, two new buildings are needed," Love said. "The Texas prison system as it is now breeds crime instead of suppressing it. It is making confirmed criminals out of youths."

—THE HOUSTON PRESS

Bud Russell—or "Uncle Bud," as both inmates and lawmen almost universally refer to him—is something of a legend in his own time.

"I suppose Uncle Bud was personally known to more enforcement officers in the United States than any other man," says Lee Simmons, who has recently become superintendent of the ailing prison system.

As the Texas state prison transfer agent, Uncle Bud brings convicted men and women from the various county jails to the Walls unit at Huntsville, and from there to the various prison farms that are spread around the state. In his early days—he's been at it since 1908—he generally transported his chained lines of convicted men on the railroads. Since 1922, however, he's mostly been driving a big flatbed truck with a metal cage welded onto it. It's got a lot of nicknames: the "chain-bus," the "one-way wagon," "Black

Mariah," "Black Bessie." Whether by train, truck, or, later, bus, Uncle Bud's comings and goings often bring a certain sort of curious townsfolk out to witness the spectacle of the latest group of men shackled together by the neck.

"The customary crowd," Simmons calls them, "gathered around Uncle Bud and his 'one-way bus.' "

"Boys, get ready, Uncle Bud is here" is how the horse thief Bill Mills remembers the morning he was transferred to state custody. Mills and thirteen others were chained together in pairs of neck irons—"It really looked like seven yoke of oxen," he recalls—and marched up the middle of the street. The crowd, another prisoner says, "walked around and gazed as though we were a lot of lions and tigers or some other strange beasts, instead of a lot of human beings."

Uncle Bud isn't particularly impressed with the gawkers, if only because they can't be trusted once they gather in sufficient numbers. It's human nature to want to see, but at some point, especially with Negro prisoners, a crowd can become a mob. Within just a few weeks of Clyde's transfer, in fact, a mob of thousands of citizens surrounds the county courthouse in Commissioner Simmons's hometown of Sherman, Texas, to demand the custody of George Hughes, a Negro accused of attacking a white woman.

"Roast him! Roast him! Roast him!" the townsfolk shout. "Burn him alive! Burn him alive!"

Even Captain Frank Hamer and three other Rangers can't control the situation. Hamer is in the second-floor courtroom with the judge and the accused man when the mob starts to congeal out in the square. He leads his men down the grand formal staircase to the courthouse door, where he confronts the crowd just now entering the building.

"I was surprised and worried to see women in the first group," he says. "I could tell they were agitating the men, urging them on to take the Negro from us."

Seeing the famous lawman in the foyer, the mob pauses. Hamer tells them that yes, the accused man is upstairs. "And there he stays," he says. "If you take him, you have to come up the stairs. Don't try it."

But they do try it, and Hamer and his men pistol-whip them back. "We swung our old-style frontier .45s, clubbing a man here and another there," he says. Upstairs, the judge clears the courthouse of everybody except himself, the Rangers, the sheriff, the county attorney, and the prisoner, Hughes, who is locked into the courthouse vault for his own protection.

A second and third assault by the townspeople end pretty much the same way, with help from a few smoke bombs that the sheriff finds stashed somewhere. But when, a few hours later, the grumble outside starts up again, Captain Hamer, now out of smoke bombs and out of patience, has had about enough.

"Inasmuch as I never had threatened to shoot I thought it was about time to stop these charges," he says. "As the mob started entering the door I told them to stop and leveled the shotgun at them. They stopped a minute and I explained that this time if the charge were continued I would shoot.

"They didn't believe me."

BLAM! Hamer fires a round of buckshot into the legs of the mob and they retreat again. They don't disperse, however. A brick through the court-house window is followed by torches that ignite gasoline poured into windows around the base of the building. They cut the hoses of the firemen who arrive to try to put the fire out, and only grudgingly allow them to put up ladders to rescue Judge Carter and the county attorney. In a rare defeat, Hamer and his Rangers escape through the doors with minor burns and move to the edge of the square, where there is nothing they can do now but watch the orgy.

Once the flames die down, the mob sends an emissary up the fire ladder. He blows a hole in the vault and tosses the body of Hughes down the ladder. He is dead either from cooking or from the explosion and lands eerily in a half-sitting, half-squatting position. His body is then chained to a car and dragged through the black neighborhoods to a tree, where it is hung and burned. Black-owned businesses and homes are also torched.

"The corpse, burned beyond description, dangled from the cottonwood limb, a horrible spectacle," says a reporter who is there. "Women and girls looked on."

It doesn't end until hours past midnight, when the rains set in. "We never dreamed of the gang doing that," says Hamer in his report to the governor on the courthouse burning, "until the building was enveloped in flames."

That's the way it is with crowds—and it's anybody's guess where the next mob will form. So Uncle Bud Russell, who almost always has a couple of blacks in the mix of prisoners he's got to transport, is ambivalent about the folks that gather to watch his comings and goings. He's got enough to do making sure no one escapes.

By design or chance there are no crowds when Uncle Bud arrives in Waco to collect Clyde, his knob-knocking pal Pat Bewley, and two others. It's April 21, 1930, and onlookers might well have been expected, given the front-page coverage over the previous six weeks devoted to Clyde's escape, recapture, murder charge, and exoneration. After all, the misadventures of the "baby bandit" and his comrades are the biggest local news of the year in Waco. But five o'clock on a Monday morning is not exactly conducive to ogling, and Sheriff Stegall's got them ready to go with no breakfast when Uncle Bud arrives. It's hardly even light out when the chains go around the four prisoners' necks and Uncle Bud leads the way to the same stairs Clyde had dashed down during his brief escape a month before.

In the one-way bus, waiting outside the courthouse, are about twenty other people whose lives have somehow gotten out of their own control and into the temporary custody of Uncle Bud. He makes sure Clyde and the other three are securely locked to the bar that runs down the middle of the bus, shakes the chains, pulls the padlocks. When all are secure he climbs in with the driver, his only assistant on most trips. The engine starts. Shifts. There's smoke, noise, and the wheels roll. Another truckload of the miserable and the mean, safely heading for Huntsville.

Safety is not the only reason Uncle Bud doesn't pander to onlookers or parade prisoners unnecessarily. What everybody says about Bud Russell, prisoners and fellow lawmen alike, is that while he's tough as nails— only ever lost one prisoner out of some fifteen thousand transported in his career—he's also sympathetic and fair.

"Mr. Russell is one of the finest men whom I have ever met and any prisoner will tell you that he will treat you right if you will let him," says inmate Mills in a typical testimonial. "Bud Russell," says another alumnus of his one-way bus service, "was a sincere friend of the unfortunate men in prison, and don't forget for a minute that they know their friends."

❁

Right around the time Uncle Bud delivers you to the Walls, Governor Moody of Texas delivers a radio address on prison reform. "If I had a dog that I thought anything of, I wouldn't want him kept in the Texas penitentiary under present conditions," he says. "I'd kill him before I'd put him down there to stay."

The governor is trying to stir up outrage and, with it, political will for reform. "I don't care if those men have committed crimes. It is not a fit place for human habitation and I tell you that if I was guilty of breaking a law and was sent to the penitentiary to serve a sentence I'd leave that place cursing the state that sent me there."

Just the fact that you and other prisoners are again being admitted to Huntsville means the worst of the political crisis has passed. The legislature has finally given up arguing over a new prison in favor of upgrading the facilities at Huntsville. There's even some money promised. These break-throughs convinced Lee Simmons, at the end of March 1930, to take the job as general manager that he'd previously turned down, and with the im-passe over he's allowing a trickle of new inmates into the system. You and Bewley and the rest of the boys on the one-way bus from Waco are among the first to arrive under the new regime, which is another way of saying that you get there before any of the promised reforms are actually in place.

"The conditions which confronted me were appalling," Commissioner Simmons says. "At the Walls fifteen hundred prisoners were confined in quar-ters designed for a maximum of twelve hundred. There was no sewerage ac-commodation and practically no fire protection. The three-story antiquated hospital building was infested by bedbugs and had no fire escapes. In the cell blocks men were sleeping on the floor, in the aisles—anywhere there was room for a blanket on the concrete floor."

The guards, meanwhile, are living in constant fear of a riot. "You've got to watch 'em all the time . . . whenever you get careless about that, you're heading toward trouble," Warden Herrel of Huntsville says the same week you arrive.

Before you even make it into the cell blocks and find yourself a piece of concrete to call home, you have to get through the three great front gates of the place. You exit Uncle Bud's cage with a chain around your neck, march in that oxen line up to the massive first iron gate of Huntsville for the first time, past what one inmate calls "the usual crowd around the entrance, a crowd that apparently never tires of seeing the unfortunates about to start the payment of their debt to society."

The first gate is open and your little chain gang stops in the narrow pas-sageway in front of the equally enormous bars of the second gate. That's not the moment reality hits you, though, so much as when, with a clang, they swing the first gate shut behind you.

"No one who never has experienced the closing of the gates of freedom upon him can imagine the utter feeling of desolation that descends when the great key that locks and unlocks Gate Number One at the entrance to 'The Walls' grates in the lock," says a fellow inmate named Gilkerson.

Once the gate behind is locked, the one in front of you is opened and, still under the command of Bud Russell, you and the rest of your class of inductees shuffle into the space they call the "bull ring." Here, finally, the heavy necklaces are loosened and removed, which is about the only good thing in a long, exhausting day.

"I felt I would never be able to lift my head again," says Gilkerson of the day he went through the bull ring. "I always will have a kindly feeling towards Uncle Bud Russell," he says, "because he was the one who relieved my neck of this strain."

Uncle Bud leaves to put his chains around the necks of some other losers, bound out of Huntsville for the prison farms. Or he goes with his empty irons to collect another load of unfortunates. You're not watching. You're giving the wardens your money and you're giving them your name, and going through the third gate, to the laundry, where you give them your clothes.

In exchange they give you a nice white suit, cotton duck pants, and a rough muslin shirt. They give you meals, served three hundred prisoners at a time at long pine counters. "At the clang of the gong we were seated and at the clang of the second gong we were permitted to eat," says Gilkerson. "In a very short time, perhaps five to eight minutes, the gong sounded again and we simultaneously arose from our seats and filed out."

They give you a place to try and get what sleep you can, in a cell roughly six feet by twelve feet with a pair of bunks, maybe a worn-out chair, a wash pan, and a galvanized bucket, which passes for all the sanitary facilities. If you're lucky, one of the bunks might be available, but there aren't enough to go around and you're new, you're young, you're small: you may end up on the floor.

And of course they give you a number. Yours is 63527; your pal Pat Bewley, right behind you in line, is 63528. They write it all down in their big ledger.

Congratulations, Clyde Barrow, alias Elvin Williams, age 18 (liar), height 5'5½", weight 127 lbs., complexion white med/fair, eyes brown, hair dk chest, no church, shoe 6, marital status yes (liar), tobacco use no (liar), habits, temperate (no lie), et cetera, et cetera.

Congratulations, boy, you're in. Watch yourself.

❊

"We kept up with Bonnie," says Marie Barrow. "She, uh, she come around the house, you know, to see Mama."

What with she and Cumie traveling to Denton and Waco together during the weeks Clyde was there, Bonnie has gotten along to be pretty good friends with Cumie. It gives Bonnie a sense of comfort to be with his mother, who, after all, might just love Clyde as much as she knows she does. It helps her feel maybe he's not so far off. The same goes in a lesser way for Clyde's pa, Henry, though he's a quiet old soul. And for Clyde's sisters.

"She lost her job, and she came to my beauty shop looking for work," says

Artie, who, unfortunately, doesn't have any work to give her little brother's girlfriend. "She was just another of those Depression kids like Clyde."

Bonnie is between jobs in an economy with unemployment at 20 percent and heading up. With the Barrows living at the filling station there on the Eagle Ford Road, and their kitchen being a place where folks walk right in any time of day to buy a bologna sandwich—a "South Dallas round steak," they call it—or a cold pop, it's pretty easy for Bonnie to drop in to say hi and set down to talking and just end up spending an afternoon.

"She'd stay all night with us and visit with us quite a bit," says Marie. At eleven, Marie is eight years younger than Bonnie and naturally looks up to her big brother's girlfriend, who is always friendly to her. Bonnie listens to Marie's stories, pays her attention. "She stayed all night with us several times, and she'd write to Clyde. Say, 'Your sister Marie is talking my ears off.' So I guess I was a chatterbox or something. . . . She'd write and tell him about it."

To hear Bonnie's own mother describe it, she's writing to Clyde pretty much all the time.

"Bonnie was inconsolable," says Emma. "She cried constantly and wrote letters to Clyde every night."

At least at first, that is.

CHAPTER 11

BURNIN' HELL

A week and a half after you get to Huntsville, you're back on Uncle Bud's truck, this time in the company of a gold-toothed murderer named Willis Herrin, who has a nasty scar across his nose; a fellow Dallas burglar named Buck Channing; and a handful of other unfortunates. You are on your way forty miles north to the Eastham Prison Farm, because when the medical staff checked your vitals, described your tattoos, and otherwise took the measure of you, they classed you as fit for work. So off you're going to Eastham, where you better remember how to chop and pick cotton or you'll be sorry.

Uncle Bud pulls up in front of the big white cement structure that sits unadorned in the middle of a flat expanse of cotton fields, and you file off the back of his truck. They take your irons off and you and the other prisoners rub your necks there in the sunlight while the paperwork of the transfer is completed. Eastham is a sorry place to end up. Prison Commissioner Simmons may think Huntsville is bad, but Eastham and the other farms, he says, are even worse.

"The slave camps of olden times could not have been more unsanitary," he says, which is not an inappropriate analogy since the farms are basically former cotton plantations with a different source of free labor. Ever since a court ruling after the end of the Civil War, a felon in Texas has been legally considered "a slave of the state." That's you now, one of five hundred slaves of the state at the Eastham Farm.

"Everywhere was filth and garbage," the commissioner says. More than the squalor, though, it is the hard labor and violence that make the Eastham and its sister camps known and feared among the convicted population.

Not for nothing is it called "the burning hell," "bloody Eastham," or, as you will later say, "that hellhole."

Your first day there is an education of sorts. It's May 1, 1930, a bright spring day, and at some point during it a prisoner named Jack Hollis is held down by a couple of other prisoners and given what they call in the record books "twenty lashes reg strap." Hollis isn't the only one to get it, either. A skinny eighteen-year-old from Dallas named W. C. Gallagher, a kid with a scar on his arm and a scar on his brow and a scar on his hand and a scar on his chin, gets "ten lashes reg strap," as does James Harris. A pudgy guy named Irvin Loggins, meanwhile, gets eleven lashes.

The "reg strap" is the official record keeper's shorthand for what is more commonly known as the "bat." Or, sometimes, the "Texas bat." Or, among prisoners, the "red heifer." There are a dozen other names. It is what it sounds like, a strap of leather precisely regulated by the legislature to be "not over two and one-half inches wide and twenty-four inches long, attached to a wooden handle." The more medieval-sounding tortures, such as hanging prisoners by their wrists from the rafters or the bars of a jailhouse window or "putting bodies on stretchers," may have been officially banned in the reforms of the 1920s, but no one, least of all the new reforming commissioner, believes the newfangled notion that prisoners should not be beaten with the bat.

"We whipped our hardened criminals when other means of persuasion failed," Simmons says without apology. "I am a firm believer in corporal punishment—in the home, in the schoolroom, in the reformatory, in the penitentiary."

Most stories about the Texas bat are variations on a theme, and often the beatings coincide with the arrival of new prisoners. "He made Smith pull off his pants and lie down on the floor, face downward, and then called four other big fellows and made them get on him and hold him down, while he hit him thirty licks on his naked hide with that murderous strap of leather," says J. S. Calvin in a typical inmate's account. The victim writhes and moans and begs for mercy but doesn't get any, and just in case the message is lost on Calvin and the other new prisoners, when the beating is done, the guard makes them all sniff and lick the bat.

Bill Mills is similarly made to sniff the bat after the beating of a prisoner called Doodlebug for the crime of not picking cotton fast enough for the captain's pleasure. "We laid him on his stomach, pulled his pants down to his knees, baring the skin, and his shirt was pulled up under his arms. Two men held each one of his legs, one man on each arm and one astraddle of his head, which happened to be I," Mills says.

"Old boy, you had better get his damned head down so he can't holler so loud," the captain tells Mills when Doodlebug starts screaming. "That scared me," says Mills, until I put all my weight down on his head. His face was almost buried in the loose sand and dirt. He was trying so hard to get his breath that sand began blowing from his nostrils up each side of his face."

Mills at first thinks it's a kind of perverse mercy when the captain changes sides and hits Doodlebug in a new spot. "But I soon learned that he did this in order that the other side might be getting sore so when he changed back again it would hurt worse," he says. When it's over, he and the other new prisoners are made to sniff the bat.

The prisoners call the beating "getting the Bones' OK put on your back," because the whole operation is supposed to be approved of and presided over by a medical officer. His job is to make sure no blood flows, but everyone knows it's more of a formality than anything else. Inmate Gilkerson says, "I've never heard of a whipping being stopped," and Mills says the doctors turn their backs on the process until the last licks are in, so that they can say they stopped it as soon as they saw blood.

There's plenty of hurt involved, with or without blood. Though the flat, wide bat was designed precisely to maximize pain while minimizing cutting, some of the guards have their own methods of customizing the implement.

"Sometime they soaked them—a half inch thick, and they'd crimp 'em. And they'd cut you when they crimp 'em," says Ralph Fults. "It'd cut you all to pieces if they crimp it and hit you with those corners. It'd cut you up. In fact, I slept on my stomach about three weeks before I healed up. I wasn't able to even do anything. So I got bitter; that's the stage that I started getting kind of bitter." Fults, who is not at Eastham the day you arrive but will be your best friend at the camp, says you eventually became even more bitter than him.

It's possible you get to Eastham too late in the day to see the actual beatings on May Day of 1930, but most likely the guards waited for the arrival of newcomers before laying the bat on. Putting the reg strap on the bare asses of four inmates is exactly the kind of thing that it does a new batch of prisoners good to see; it's the policy of some captains to save all officially recorded beatings with the bat until after dark, when the sound of the men crying out will travel to all the prisoners in their bunks. And the truth is, it doesn't much matter one way or the other whether Uncle Bud gets there in time for you to see and hear the four men beaten on May 1, or whether the captain that day makes you and the other greenhorns lick or sniff the bat when the whipping is done. You will see plenty of the Texas bat, and more, before you get out of bloody Eastham.

Not all of it will be at the hands of guards. Three of the four men beaten on your first day, in fact, are being punished for stabbing a fellow inmate. Stabbing fellow prisoners is rarer than refusing to work or giving lip, but it's not altogether uncommon either. What's rare is someone getting caught. More often the attack is just hushed over, like the time Hugh Kennedy, a prisoner at Eastham with you, wakes up in the middle of the night because warm blood is dripping down on his face through the thin mattress of the bunk above.

"Building Tender," he calls out to the trusty in charge of his section. (Unless you want trouble fast, you don't get out of your bunk without first calling the prisoner appointed by the guards as "building tender.") The tender comes over to Kennedy's bunk, and together the two of them look at the fresh corpse on the top bed.

"He's dead," says the tender. "Go back to sleep. We can't do nothing about it now." All Kennedy can do is get back in bed the other way around, so at least the last of the poor guy's blood is dripping on his feet instead of his face.

Building tenders are a notorious breed in the camps, nearly as widely hated by their fellow inmates as the guards are. Almost as a rule, the tenders are sadistic characters with long sentences and not much to lose. They get their position of authority from the guards not because they are better behaved—or even more trusted, usually—but because they can control the other inmates. The guards may run the day's work outside, with all their counting off, their dogs, and their bats, but the tenders rule the tanks, as the long, dank rows of bunks are known.

"They carried dirk knives and clubs similar to a policeman's billy and believe me they would certainly use them if the occasion arose," says Beecher Deason, who was a prisoner at Eastham just a handful of years before you. "I have seen them make all the men, except a chosen few, get on their bunks and stay there during a rainy day when we couldn't work. If you wanted to get off of your bunk for anything," he says, "you had to get permission from the tender."

The layout of the building at Eastham is fairly simple. There are two main wings: one for dining and one containing the inmates' bunks. Off the dining wing are smaller rooms: the kitchen, the guards' dining room, the colored prisoners' dining room, and the like. At the back, in the center, is the guards' dormitory, rising two stories. The warden and his family have their own house not far away.

Between the two main wings is a picket, a room for the guards with barred windows opening into both wings, through which they can shoot rifles or shotguns into either wing to restore order as need be. There are also some offices, and the solitary confinement cell.

The side containing the bunks—there are no individual cells—is essentially a long rectangular cage of bars, set back from the windows about four feet and divided lengthwise by another wall of bars to create the two parallel tanks. There's no electricity in the building and no good source of light, just a few kerosene lanterns. Don't even ask about the bedbugs. As your prison buddy Ralph Fults says, "They all married and have families where I was. . . . When them lights went out they attacked you. Didn't nothing you could do about it but fight 'em."

It doesn't take long to learn that the farther into the recesses of the tanks you travel, the farther away from the central picket, the more you are in the realm of the building tender. One night in the dark tanks of Eastham, says Beecher Deason, he watched tenders kill two fellow inmates with a homemade dirk knife and beat a third nearly to death.

"Then the boy they had beaten was made to go down there where the boys had bled and wash up the blood," Deason says. "While he did that the building tender—the one who had done the stabbing—walked up and down the aisle, raving like a maniac. He licked the blood off his knife and asked us if any of the rest of us wanted to."

Eastham is a hellhole all right, but once in a while the tenders take it too far. Or they pick one fight too many with the wrong fellow. They misjudge somebody's courage, or their anger, or their desperation and find themselves one sloppy moment away from the protective guns of their friends the guards. They find themselves surrounded and outnumbered, outfuried. The homemade knives are coming toward them this time, into their guts and chests. The spilled blood in the back of the tank is theirs.

That's what happened to a tender the day you arrived, or the night before, to earn those boys their lashings with the reg strap. Everyone who comes to Eastham hates the tenders eventually.

It will happen again.

❋

Huntsville is a lot farther from Dallas than Waco is, and Bonnie doesn't visit Clyde quite as often as she thought she would. It's just much harder to get down there, almost impossible really, if she's going to keep her new job as a waitress in a year when it seems everybody's losing theirs. And Eastham Prison Farm is even harder to get to than Huntsville. The truth is, she doesn't hardly make it there to see him at all. And while it might be too much to say "out of sight, out of mind," her world does go on.

"She was a thoroughly normal girl," says her mother, "and in a few months began to take a new lease on life, and a new interest in the people about her."

Then she stops sending him letters, too.

"I don't know just when she stopped writing to Clyde," says Emma, "but I imagine it was along in the summer of 1930."

❀

> At that time they were real rough on you and you didn't know whether you went out this morning whether you was going to come in that night or not.
>
> —Floyd Hamilton

Why doesn't she write?

Every morning but Sunday now is the same.

"Twenty-two, Boss," the tender yells out, or whatever the day's size is for your squad, and out the door you go at five-thirty A.M.

"One, two, three, four, five, six . . ." you count off until you're all out there in the dawn light. Then the guard in charge of your squad hollers out, "Twenty-two," to let them know inside the building that they have the same number outside, as if someone could get lost in the doorway.

Then it's run to the work site. Not jog, but run full tilt, with the damn guards riding all around and behind you on their horses, wagging their pieces, as if they're just looking for a reason to haul a man out and give him some kind of hell.

The bastards.

"The men had lined up in front of the building preparatory to going to the fields," says inmate Gilkerson, who is at Eastham briefly during the time you are there. "At a given command the men started off towards the fields on A DEAD RUN! The guards at the sides and in the rear of the white-clad column kept their horses at a gallop, their shotguns wavering towards the line of convicts in a careless manner."

Gilkerson's lucky. He's visiting Eastham only as the trusty assistant to the chaplain of Huntsville, so he asks another prisoner why everyone is in such a hurry.

"Hell, man," comes the reply. "You haven't seen anything yet—just wait until they come in tonight." Sure enough, that night Gilkerson sees the men, after a long day hoeing in the sun, coming back in a cloud of dust. "They stumbled up to the halting line and many of them dropped to the ground, exhausted," he says.

Between the runs out to and in from the fields, it's nothing but work. By the time you arrive in May, the plowing and planting is done for the year; it's hoe time. Sure, it's hard, and they don't give you much water to drink—"We worked in the cotton fields all day, with only two cups of water for each man," says a fellow prisoner. And to call yourself out of shape is putting it mild, seeing as you have been sitting around in jail cells the past few months and weren't exactly doing hard physical labor in West Dallas before that.

You're luckier than some: it's not like you never hoed a row of cotton in your life. You grew up on farms, and your cousin Darrell Barrow says his parents always talked pretty highly of the times you worked out at their place. "A good boy," he says they called you. "They said he was smart and worked like the dickens in the field."

You must be working like the dickens in the field now because you're not getting punished for laziness or mouthing off, at least not officially. Plenty of your fellow inmates are not so lucky. Lacy Brown, a forger from San Antonio with a big scar on his upper lip, gets made to stand for six hours on the barrel for impudence not long after you arrive. So does his pal R. C. Rumsey, a little burglar from Oklahoma. Rumsey apparently doesn't learn his lesson, though, because in July someone has to sit on his head while the guards give him twenty lashes for refusing to work.

That first summer you're at Eastham, a thief named Albert Nichols gets eighteen lashes with the strap for not working. A cattle rustler named C. L. Ibeck gets beaten for fighting in the building. S. J. Covington gets it for attacking another inmate with a hoe. Roy Hammons also gets fifteen lashes with the strap for fighting, while your sometime friend Joe Palmer gets twenty-four hours in solitary confinement for gambling.

"Solitary" is just the new name for the old "dark cell" that Commissioner Simmons says is long gone from the system, and there's nothing solitary about it unless an inmate happens to be the only one subjected to it at a given time. Otherwise, as many men as will fit are shoved into the single narrow room—a dead-end hallway almost. There's a small barred window, ten feet up, that's more for air than light, though it lets in little of either. Inmates call the place the "piss hole," thanks to the smell, or just the "hole."

Most of the official punishing, though, isn't whipping or solitary; it's standing on top of that barrel until a man's knees buckle or his feet go dead and he falls off and has to get back up. Rollie Rector spends six hours on the barrel for laziness, as does T. H. Burke. Brownie King, a burglar who arrived the same day you did, stands six hours for jumping over to a different squad than he's assigned to, as does Eugene Fuller. Lee Mullinsaux gets stuck up there for destroying his shoes, something no one else sees fit to do. Usually the term is three or six hours, but on August 21, 1930, Fred Thomas, a holdup man with tattoos of wings and roses on his arms, stands for fully twenty-four hours on top of that barrel for refusing to work. There's a heat wave in late summer, a stretch of sun that can kill a man without any help from the guards; on another prison farm Jimmie Arnold, the real killer in that murder you were charged with, dies of heat prostration on August 20.

By September, with the sun burning down to make your ears ring, and the ground so hot it's just about throwing as much fire up from below, and the work getting on toward cotton picking, the squads start to get real tired of it all. It seems in September like every other day there's someone standing on the barrel, sometimes more than one, and sometimes more than one man per barrel. On Thursday night, September 8, while you and the other inmates rest at last from the long day's work and the hard run in from the fields, seven men stand for six hours into the night as punishment for "laziness." A few days later, it's two men, and then four men, and then six men. Cotton picking is going full and heavy now, and on September 22 six men are put on the barrel for nine hours after a full day's work for not picking fast enough.

But not you. According to the books, you never stand on the barrel. You are never beaten with the bat or sent to solitary. For the whole time you're at Eastham, in fact, there's no mention of you getting any officially sanctioned punishment. By the books you are, they'd say, a model prisoner.

Not that anyone believes that all of the punishments meted out at Eastham, or even most of the punishments, get written up with triple carbon copies on the "Daily Punishment Reports." "Dear Sir: I respectfully ask for an order from you to punish, by whipping, the following named convicts," reads the standard form. No. Most—and especially the most brutal or even deadly—actions by the guards go by unseen and without a whisper of complaint. They go by in the fields, and you're no exception.

"Once I visited him and found him with both eyes blackened," says Nell. She can't ask you about it at the time, since there's a guard present, but later you tell her they beat you up for complaining about the pace the hoe squad was setting. "He also told us that often the guards would ride them down if they lagged in their work," she says.

Charging a horse right up on an inmate is one of the guards' favorite tricks. "A horse stepped on me," says an inmate when Gilkerson asks him how his arm got torn up. Pressed for more information, the wounded man says he was unable to keep the work pace, so a guard ran his horse over him. The skin and some of the muscle from his bicep are torn and pulled back, and there is a clear print of a horseshoe in his flesh, but there's nothing in this world that's going to make that guy go to the rudimentary hospital up on the second floor of the building, near the guards' quarters.

"If I should tell the doctor how this 'accident' occurred I wouldn't live for twenty-four hours," he says to Gilkerson. "I would be taken out on a detail and I would be shot. The guard would say I attempted to escape and I would be where I couldn't do much talking. And no witnesses."

If anybody does ask questions, the guards always have a ready answer. "Shot while trying to escape" is all they need to say, and if the dead convict's family doesn't come and get it, his body ends up in an unmarked grave on what they call Peckerwood Hill.

"If you escaped, or wouldn't work, you's nearly dead," says Ralph Fults. "That's two things that you didn't hardly do—that's attempt to escape and not working. They'd kill you. They had guards that couldn't read 'n' write, they'd get thirty dollars a month, and what their theory was is you weren't sent there to be rehabilitated, you was sent there to punish. And they wanted to see how many notches get on the gun."

"They say, 'Come here, march him,'" he explains. "A guard come out and get 'em, and carry 'em right over the hill. You hear the shots; you cain't see it, and they come back here and say, 'They tried to get away.'"

It's not just your pal Fults who says that, either; everyone who's done time at the burnin' hell says pretty much the same thing.

"While I was on the Eastham Farm," says the dopehead Jimmie Mullins, who is there with you, "I saw five prisoners killed and the guards were exonerated."

So the bureaucratic fact that your official record doesn't show you on the barrel or under the bat doesn't mean you never run into trouble with the bosses and guards. Not by a long shot.

"He gave us enough trouble while he was here," the Big Captain of Eastham Farm, B. B. Monzingo, says of you.

And the lack of an official punishment record sure doesn't mean you don't hate every last one of those guards.

❅

Ralph Fults is one of the few men ever to successfully escape from the solitary unit at Eastham Prison Farm. The procedure with inmates committed to the cell at Eastham is to strip them, shave their heads, give them a couple of lashes with the reg strap, push them through the door, and toss in a

nightshirt after them. Despite all this, Fults gets himself put in there on purpose because he and a couple of others have a plan. Only nineteen years
old, Fults has already been an escape artist for six years.

As a child he was obsessed with Slim Jim, a comic-strip character who
always slipped away from the police. "So I got that on my mind about it's
just a game then," he says. "I was working in a locksmith and a gunsmith
shop—well, that's fascinating. I could pick handcuffs. I learned to pick handcuffs, locks, and things. I could open safes. So when I was thirteen, and got
in jail the first time, I picked the locks and handcuffs and got out of jail and
turned everybody else loose too."

It's a good stunt for a laugh—the kid who turns the jail loose—but he
gets recaptured pretty quick and it's been in and out of reform schools and
youth prisons for Ralph Fults ever since. Now here he is, nineteen, in the
state prison system at Eastham Farm.

"In other words," he says, "I graduated."

The plan for getting out of the piss hole doesn't involve picking any
locks. With hacksaw blades sneaked in with the evening's food by accomplices in the kitchen, Fults and four other men take turns standing on each
other's shoulders to saw on the window bars. When daylight comes they
cover their work with soap and grease, and on the fifth night, April 8, 1930,
they're out. They're out across the roof and down to the fields. Crawling
and scurrying across the land in slippers made from torn-up blankets, they
get past the dogs, who put up a howl but are temporarily ignored by the
guards.

"It was pretty hairy; we had to crawl right between two guards," he says.
"I tell you, old Geronimo never hugged the ground closer than I did that
night."

Three miles they slink, to the railroad tracks, where they've noticed in
recent weeks that a work crew has been using a motorized handcar. That
cart is their only real hope, because as soon as anyone finds they're gone,
the dogs will be loosed.

"I seen 'em put the motor handcar there and I thought if I ever get this
far I make it," says Fults. Make it, because the dogs won't be able to track
metal wheels rolling. "You got to beat the bloodhounds," says Fults. "You
got to get off the ground, you can't stay on the ground or they get you."

The hounds are always the main challenge for anyone attempting to get
away from the farms. "Every now and then, one of the convicts would try
and run for it," says an Eastham guard. "Well, everybody that was working
would have to go in for a lockdown. Just as quick as they'd find he's gone,
we would let the dogs loose and try to pick up the trail. Wherever they run

off from, that's where you want to go start dragging your dogs and pick his track up, following by horse. I've gone a many a mile through those woods on horseback trying to stay up with them dogs. You gotta stay up with 'em. Don't you lose 'em."

The guard stays close, says the Eastham dog sergeant from those days, "not only to prevent their killing the convicts, but also to prevent an armed convict, whether he has a gun, a club, or a knife, from killing the dogs."

It can get to be life or death for man or beast in pretty short order if a pack of six or eight dogs catches a runner out in the open without the dog sergeant nearby to call them off. They're liable to tear a runner pretty well to pieces unless he has a way to defend himself. So if he doesn't get to the river and lose them, or into an automobile, and he hears that barking getting loud on his heels, he's looking for a tree he can climb quick. Once that happens, it's just a matter of waiting for the guards to show up. But it's not necessarily over.

"They let the packs go after a runaway near dark," says another guard from those days, telling the story of one such "race" he was in on. They can hear from the sound of the baying that the pack has a man treed up, but when the guards arrive the boss doesn't call the animals off. Instead, he tells the bird to jump down from the tree into the mess of snarls, and when the treed man refuses to jump the boss pulls out his pistol and puts a bullet into the trunk of the tree. Guy still won't jump into the dogs, so the boss puts a bullet a little farther up, and again, until he's pointing the barrel right at the man in the tree.

"Boy, do we have a dead runaway or are you going to jump out of that damn tree?" he says.

Now the poor slob jumps, and starts screaming holy murder while those dogs go into him. Only for a few seconds, though; then the boss finally calls them off and marches the guy back to camp and tosses him in solitary to think about his bite wounds for a few days. He's lucky to live, actually: the same thing happens to another prisoner around then, a kid named Clarence Williams, only this time the guard doesn't get the dogs off in time.

"The hounds dragged him on the ground for nearly a hundred yards while the helpless boy was screaming to God above him," says a fellow prisoner. "The boy was covered with a mass of bites and his clothing was nearly stripped from his body. He was forced to march ahead of the horses back to the camp. When he staggered into the building even the old-time convicts shuddered at the sight." They leave him lying there in the tank, but when he starts to turn black, they take him to the hospital at Huntsville. He dies there, yelling, "Keep them off me, keep them off me."

So when Fults escapes, it's not getting out of solitary that's the crucial part, or even creeping like Geronimo past the various pickets. It's getting to the railroad tracks while that work crew's handcar is still in the area.

"I got out at two o'clock in the morning," he says, "crawled between two guards and got that motor handcar. And got away."

Away! Fults hides in a church loft for a few days, and steals some clothes. "They shave your head, they take all your clothes—I had a duck gown on, that's all," he says. He gets all the way to St. Louis. And Los Angeles. Then back to St. Louis, where in September he gets caught trying to pick a hardware store safe. They send him back to Texas. Back to the back of Uncle Bud's truck, where, for the last leg of the journey, he's chained next to a kid named Clyde Barrow. Barrow's on his way back to Eastham too, from a two-week bench-warrant trip up to Hill County.

In a stroke of what passes for good luck in a prison farm, Barrow's been sent up to Hill County for two weeks, right in the middle of the September picking season, to plead guilty to another handful of minor burglary and theft charges. Hill County is just south of Dallas, so he's seen his mama, his sisters, and maybe even his old man, though that's less likely. Maybe he's even seen Bonnie. It's like a vacation, but it's all over before it even seems to begin. Blink: here he is back on his way to the burnin' hell with seven more years on his sentence (but running concurrently with his fourteen years, so no big deal). Blink: back to Eastham, where, in the days he's been gone, there's been an average of three men standing on barrels every night for not picking fast enough.

This Barrow kid is all right, thinks Fults. He looks about sixteen or less. "He was just what you call a schoolboy when I seen him," says Fults, though Clyde's actually the older of the two by two years. In the back of the transfer truck they get to trading stories just to pass the time. You got a big family? Yeah, you got a big family? Yeah. Escapes, recaptures, girls. That kind of thing. They get to being friends.

Ralph's even got a dagger-and-heart tattoo on his forearm, too, though unlike Clyde's the accompanying initials are his own. They have a lot of things in common, but height's not one of them: Ralph's over five-ten, giving him nearly half a foot on Clyde. One big thing they have in common in the immediate run is neither one of them is much looking forward to getting back to Eastham. This is especially true for Ralph, who can pretty much count on getting the crap beaten out of him out in the fields somewhere.

"That was the rule," he says. "I'd escaped, and they'd pistol whip me. And they whipped guys with trace chains."

It doesn't come immediately. Fults and Barrow are assigned to East-ham's Camp Number Two, a sort of more primitive, wooden version of the big concrete building, which is Camp One. If anything, conditions there are even more squalid. "At Camp Two, located on flat land with no drainage, the sewerage stood in the open flat," says Commissioner Simmons.

The guards let Fults live nervous for a few weeks, knowing the inevitable retribution will come but worrying and wondering when. That's part of the punishment itself. Sure enough, early one day around about the middle of October, Fults finds himself nearly alone.

"While Clyde and I were working on the woodpile, three guards closed in, pinned me down, and beat me with a revolver," he says. Several other guards watched from their horses not far away.

Thud! To the jaw. *Smash!* To the side of his head.

What do you have to say now, boy?

Crash! Across the face. You gonna run again? *Crack!*

Huh? Pretty slick, aren't you, trash? A boot to the ribs, the butt of a pistol again.

Whack!

Then it stops. Fults, on his back, opens his swollen eyes as best he can to see what might be next.

"Suddenly, the blows ceased," he says. "I could barely see little Clyde—squared off, fists clenched."

It's an insane thing to do, bordering on suicidal. Clyde just stands there, furious, ready to take what comes his way and give back whatever he can. He's not out of control or crazy—more like in some kind of adrenaline-induced trance. It's a quality of coolness under fire that others will notice later in his life as well. At Eastham, though, unarmed and surrounded in the woodlot far from the main building, a prisoner might as well just ask the guards to shoot them both right then and there.

They don't shoot, though. The guards just stand there, looking at Fults, all puffy and bloody on the ground and not nearly so cocky as he usually is. They look at the Barrow kid, standing with clenched fists like some kind of joke. No one's afraid of the punk. No one cares one way or the other what happens to him. But for whatever reason, they let it pass. Their rage has subsided; they've spent their wad, so to speak. The kid's too pathetic to warrant action. Or maybe the guards just don't want to deal with the mess that two bodies would make on this fine fall morning.

They let it pass. For now, anyway.

"In retrospect," says Fults, "I'm reasonably sure his actions saved my life."

❀

You've had about enough.

"He was an awful sensitive guy and he couldn't stand to see those guys getting beat up all the time," Fults says about you. "Couldn't stand to see people beat up all around him, and they run a horse over him one time for nothing."

That particular run-in comes a few days after the pistol-whipping business: one of the guards finds you in a field, working like you're supposed to, and nearly runs right over you on his horse. Retribution, most likely. It wasn't an accident, that's for damn sure.

This time, though, the horse coming on you doesn't phase you much, according to Fults. He says you just stand there, grab the bridle, and stop the damn animal up short. Guess those days back in Telico with Buck, trying to ride various unbroke farm animals, finally paid off. The horse stops, you stare down that gun, just daring that high rider—Crowson, maybe—to put a bullet in you in front of the whole squad. He doesn't.

Shit, man, for a little guy, you're pretty tough. Or you've just had about enough.

"Yeah, I wasn't as bitter as Clyde. I been through that back down the line, way ahead of him, in Gatesville [a boys' reformatory] comin' on up, so I got out of a lot of that you know," Fults says. "Clyde, though, got bitter, he seen 'em—he saw 'em whip two guys with a short trace chain so they couldn't raise their arms one time, for they wouldn't work. And he saw 'em pistol whip me. And things like that. And begins to get bitter."

"He got real bitter."

Bitter, sure you are, but right around this time you start to get an idea in your head, too. An idea that slowly becomes more like a plan. You and Fults, and maybe some others, well, you aren't going to forget about all this. No way. You'll be back.

When you first bring the idea of a raid on Eastham up to Fults, though, he thinks you're just full of talk.

"I didn't pay any attention to him when he came to me, said, Let's get out of here and turn everybody loose," says Fults.

You're serious, you tell him. You keep talking about it: What you're going to need in the way of cars and guns. How many people you'll want. Who would be good, who can you trust, how it might be done. You talk day after day, on into the shortening days of winter, until eventually Fults figures you must be serious.

"He kept coming to me with it and finally I said okay, I'll go along," says

Fults. "I tole him, 'Okay, fireman, we'll get out first, and then come back and turn 'em loose.'"

❋

It always comes back to that, doesn't it? Got to get out of this living hellhole before anything else can happen. In the meantime, though, you can lay the groundwork and plan.

"Clyde and myself started the Barrow Gang in prison," says Fults.

Thinking and planning gives you something to do, something positive to occupy your mind about as the days and weeks creep by. But Fults is right: you can't do much of anything until you get out. Once in a while you might sneak word out to Harry McCormick, the writer for the *Houston Press,* about how bad things are in the burnin' hell.

"We had a way to get word to a newspaperman in Houston," says Fults. "We'd write in lemon juice and urine and you got to iron it out to make it noticeable. I don't know if it still works now, but anyhow we get that word to a newspaperman there's a guy on the spot and they is going to kill him tomorrow. He printed it in headlines in the *Houston Press,* they're going to kill this fellow, but you know they went ahead and killed him on schedule anyhow the next day."

Lot of good that did. Fults also says he and you tried to drop a tree on one of the guards' rat finks, but he ended up living. In terms of really doing something, of making them guards and commissioners sit up and say, "Whoa, what was that," in terms of your plan, you got to get out first. And you've only done what? Six months out of your fourteen years.

Fourteen years . . .

Your only hope is that your mother can get you a pardon, or parole. She's been talking to Judge Monroe, down in Waco, to see if he can help. And she's been trying to figure out how to get to the governor, too. But nothing yet. It might happen, it'll never happen; every day you think something different. You never know. But you do know you won't last fourteen years.

Escape? Guys are always trying to outrun the dogs and getting caught; you're not that stupid. Or, like your pal Frank Hardy, they try when they're off of the farm premises on a work detail: he got caught the same day he left. But if a car should make itself available, well then, all bets are off. Or even a gun . . .

No, realistically, your ma and the governor are your only chance. She comes down to visit in the middle of December 1930, bringing a few small gifts but mostly just the sight of her face and sound of her voice. And some hope.

"Sugar, mother just about got my time cut to two years, and I've been down here eight months already," you write in a letter to Bonnie a few days before your first Christmas in prison. "If she does get it cut, it won't take long for me to shake it off. So you just make it the best you can 'till I do, and then let me do the rest.

"Well, old dear, I don't know any news as usual, so be a sweet little girl and write your daddy real often, because I really enjoy your sweet little letters. Tell every one hello for me, and I wish you a merry, merry Christmas. Answer real soon. I send all my love to you. Your loving husband, Clyde Barrow."

(You have to say that husband business, not that you mind it one bit, but you have to say it because you're only allowed to write letters to relatives.) And you add something: "P.S. please send me one of your pictures."

It's true, Bonnie started writing to you again sometime in the beginning of December. You don't know why, and you don't care: the day that first letter arrives is one of the best in a long year of bad days.

"Why, honey, I couldn't hardly believe my eyes when I glanced at your handwriting on the envelope," you tell her. "So I took it and looked it over carefully and finally decided it was from you."

It's not easy to defend yourself when you're locked up and far away and people start talking about you. So you defend yourself in letters, and then worry that maybe it seems like too much. "Listen, Bonnie, who the hell told you all those lies on me?" you write.

And: "Sugar, what gave you the idea I wouldn't answer your letters? Sugar, you know I didn't say anything like that about my little blue eyed girl." And: "Listen Sugar, mother is not mad at you. She was down here last week and she asked me about you. She said she would like to see you. I told her she didn't want to see you half as much as I did, which is really true for I am just crazy to see my little blue-eyed girl."

And most of all: "Honey, I love you more than I love my own self and just because I have 14 years is no sign that I will be here always."

You won't be here always, but it sure feels like it sometimes. Only on rainy days and Sundays do you get a little blessed relief from the relentless and monotonous work in the fields and the woodlots. Not that there's any peace or quiet, really, stacked into the tanks with the rest of the men. But in those hours you sometimes work on little gifts to send home, painstaking projects that pass the time and make you feel, perhaps, still a part of the family.

"He loved his mother and he loved all of us, we were all a real close family," says your little sister Marie. "When he was in prison, well, he made this little necklace for me and sent it to me when I was a girl."

For Buck's wife, Blanche, you construct a little wooden box with a delicately carved lid; it's got her name on it. Blanche comes to see you probably more than anyone else. Almost unbelievably, two times when she comes to Eastham to visit, Buck comes along with her, and he's still on the lam no less!

Call it what you like—crazy, brave, dumb as a post. But that's Buck, as your daddy would say, going to a prison to visit his little brother while he's still an escaped con himself. That's Buck, your big brother who is smaller than you. You sure like seeing him and Blanche, and you make the box for her to show her so.

❀

Blanche isn't so sure about Buck's little brother Clyde, and the lengths to which her husband will apparently go for him. It's one thing for Buck to send her off visiting Clyde at that awful prison farm—she's perfectly willing to go down there several times without him, and does, taking presents and a little money for Clyde. But why does Buck have to be so stubborn and go along once in a while? Surely Clyde will understand why his brother can't come visiting.

"I was very worried on both of those trips," she says, which is putting it pretty mildly if a person stops to think about it. "Buck had escaped from another prison farm just across the river from Eastham. I was afraid someone would recognize and arrest him."

It's getting on toward the fall of 1931, and Buck and Blanche have been on the run for months. They got married on the run, up in Oklahoma. Went to Florida and had their honeymoon on the run at Amelia Island. They're in love on the lam. But it's wearing out—not the love but the will to keep it up, to always "run from place to place," as she says, "hiding from the law." It's worse than a prison sentence, she figures, because it's forever. It's as if they have no future.

There's a lot of talking between them in the car, on the road, and at night. "I loved this man who was hunted by officers of the law," she says. "He said he loved me, as I did him. He said he wasn't a criminal at heart. He told me he was tired of that kind of life."

Talk. Talk. Talk. Blanche knows what has to happen: "I told him that before we could become happy he must go back to prison and finish his sentence." She knows it will be hard, and not just for him but for her, too. But most of all, she knows it's their only hope.

"I begged him to give himself up and go back to prison. I was sure he wouldn't have to stay long," she says.

Buck's not quite there in his courage, though. He knows she's right, knows it in his head. Knows he needs her more than anything, and that he wants it to be over, too. Everybody's working on him; the Barrow brothers are like a family project to their women these days.

"Buck, we felt, was finally on the right path," says Nell. "Blanche prevailed on him to come home and talk things over with his folks."

Cumie agrees with Blanche and Nell about going back. And Henry, too, must think it's the right way to go though, as usual, he doesn't say much of anything that anyone remembers.

"He depended on Mama to spank us," says Marie. "He'd say, 'Cumie, make that kid do this,' 'Cumie, make that kid do that.' I don't remember my daddy ever hitting me in my life. He was easy-going. Just a real good old man. He said, 'If you can't say something nice about somebody, don't say nothing at all. Just keep your mouth shut.'"

Buck is way past spanking, of course, and Henry sits there listening to the women talking to the boy. Maybe they're right, Buck is thinking. Maybe after Christmas he'll go back. But not just yet.

Funny enough, what Buck is doing while out on the run is scraping together money—which is to say, committing small-time robberies, sometimes with Blanche along—so that Cumie can use it to try to get Clyde's sentence reduced. There's reason to be optimistic: money and lawyers are a good combination in Austin. But as far as Blanche can tell, the little brother is still going in the opposite direction.

"We were sure Clyde would be given a parole when he had been in prison two years, but Clyde couldn't believe it," she says. "Clyde said if he could get out he would go straight, but he couldn't take fourteen years at Eastham. He said if he didn't make a parole soon he was going to get out of there any way he could."

Blanche has almost, but not quite, gotten Buck to see the obvious. There's no way to get around prison or over it or under it; the only way is through it. Buck's almost there, but Clyde's talking nonsense.

"He begged me to bring a gun to him but I refused," she says.

Blanche is sympathetic enough: "He was doing really hard time."

But she's also firm: "I wouldn't help him escape."

CHAPTER 12

THE TANK

Ed Crowder likes to get that schoolboy Barrow kid in the back of the tanks, near what passes for bathroom facilities, and force him to take it hard up the ass. That's the word from Fults, anyway, who must have heard about it later, since he and Clyde are no longer together at Camp Two by the summer of 1931. What with Fults already being an escape artist and Barrow being full of attitude, it seems best to keep them apart, so Clyde is sent back to the big white building known as Camp One, where Ed Crowder is a building tender who apparently gets some kind of pleasure out of raping other men.

Crowder has been in jail now for four years, ever since he was twenty-four years old and was rounded up on a bank-robbing charge in Houston. Four of his brothers—he's got thirteen siblings—were initially hauled in for questioning, but Big Ed took the fall for the job. It was a brazen thing he did, walking right into the Citizens State Bank on Washington Avenue in broad daylight with two guns drawn.

"We looked at him and thought he had come in to try to sell some guns or something," says the vice president of the bank. "We had no idea he would attempt a holdup."

Everybody's standing there for a second or two before Ed clears things up. "You fellers had better get back there quick before somebody gets killed," he says. The vice president and the tellers figure it out then, and Ed goes over and grabs about $2,900 and heads out the door.

"Sure, I robbed the bank," he says to the police when they round him up less than an hour later. "Did it alone, but you can't find the money, I need it." They browbeat him, haul his siblings in and out, dig a bunch of holes in a field on a tip-off, but never do locate the cash.

When he gets to court a few weeks later, Crowder tells the judge the truth as he sees it: "I had to break laws in order to live." The judge doesn't buy it, though, and sends him away for forty years. The first two of these he's mostly at the Ferguson work farm, a place that, when it comes to roughness, gives Eastham a run for its money. The second two years he's mostly back at Huntsville, where he spends more than half of 1929 in solitary confinement for fighting.

By the time he gets to Eastham—he arrives a week after Clyde first does, in May of 1930—Crowder knows the system pretty well. In February of 1931 he takes twenty lashes on his back for not coming out of the building to work with a field squad, but by the time Clyde gets back to Camp One that summer, Crowder has risen to the position of building tender for one of the tanks. Now he stays inside, does a little cleaning, makes sure the water barrels are filled, and enforces order as he sees fit. He's friendly with the guards, who give him a free hand, and like all tenders he's de facto allowed to carry a dirk knife and a billy club, which no doubt come in handy when he gets the urge to beat the crap out of some kid and then rape him.

Big Ed Crowder's not really all that big: five foot eight and a half, and 151 pounds on his entry papers. But it's not necessarily the case that he physically has to overpower Clyde or his other victims: the threat of what he can do any dark night and pretty much count on getting away with goes without saying.

Nell says Clyde told her "he saw a 'lifer' knife a young boy to death before his eyes one night," though she doesn't say who the lifer was. "The man knew he was immune from a death sentence and he had nothing to lose."

However it is that Ed Crowder has his way with Clyde Barrow in the back end of the tanks, he may think he's got nothing to lose. Crowder may think that, but he's about to find out that he's literally fucking with the wrong guy.

❀

Okay, bastard, come and get it. You're walking down the tank, heading for the pissers at the back. You know he's going to follow you. Come and get it. C'mon, bastard. You want it? Come on.

You've got a pipe wrench in your hand, but no one can see it because you've got it inside your pants leg. It's riding there cool against your thigh, held there through a hole in your pocket. Snuck that heavy wrench in from outside, and not telling how.

C'mon, bastard, come and try it. You walk right past Crowder, daring him, and head for the latrines.

Ready, now, ready. Look like you're pissing while really you're gripping that pipe and listening. Listening. Sure enough, you hear him. He's taken the bait. He's coming. Ready. Ready. Not yet. Ready.

FUCK YOU, MOTHERFUCKING GODDAMN FAGGOT ASSHOLE! FUCK YOURSELF! You wheel around with that pipe coming out of your pocket already in full swing before the bastard even knows what's coming.

CRACK!

Splits his head just about open wide. Where's your hard-on now, see? Asshole.

Crowder falls to the floor, pretty much dead, and you're already on your way back to your bunk. Passing you is Aubrey Scalley, one of the other building tenders. He's got a dirk knife in his hand, gives himself a few superficial wounds with it and then stabs Crowder a mess of times. This isn't just to make sure he's dead. Scalley has agreed to take whatever heat may come from the killing. He's a friend of yours, and a tender with a half-century sentence: nothing much will come of it for him.

That's the story according to Fults, who says your deal with Scalley is to let him in on the big Eastham break you got planned. Henry Schuessler, a fellow convict who calls you a "pink-faced kid," says he saw it happen pretty much that way, too. Your friend Floyd Hamilton, on the other hand, who wasn't there at the time, tells a slightly different version.

"It was a stool pidgin and this group that [Clyde] was associated with, well, they all drawed straws to see who'd kill him. And they all ganged around him and do certain things, and of course when they all scattered there the guy is on the floor dead. Well, nobody knows."

He goes on: "The officials couldn't prove who done it, they just know that there's a bunch there and when they all scattered, well, there the man was on the floor and they couldn't say who done it. But I think Clyde Barrow killed his first man there according to what I hear. That is, it's rumored down in state prison where I was. And it's on the same farm where I was."

Either way, Crowder is most definitely dead, and the official story on the outside is that he was killed in a fight with Aubrey Scalley.

"One of the men—I don't know which—got out of his bunk and walked over to the other's," says the Big Captain of Eastham, B. B. Monzingo. "Then the fight began."

Monzingo is not the type to lose much sleep over convicts killing each other. He was fired from the prison system during the reforms of 1925 for excessive brutality toward his inmates, but he was rehired by Lee Simmons and put back in charge of Eastham. Still, even Monzingo, who doesn't really give a damn either way about the death of Crowder, thinks there's something a bit fishy about it all.

"Any of the fifteen wounds Crowder got would have caused his death," he says. "I don't see how he could have continued his fight with Scalley."

The story on the inside, meanwhile, is that you did it.

"It was he who slugged Ed Crowder on the head with an iron bar before another convict stabbed Crowder to death," says Harry McCormick, the *Houston Press* muckraker who has more contacts on the inside than anyone else.

❋

Buck can't rightly believe it's about to happen, but there's no turning back now. They're all sitting there packed into the car in front of the Walls at Huntsville—himself, Blanche, Cumie, Nell, Marie, and Nell's new husband, Luther Cohan. They've asked to speak to the warden, W. W. Waid, and are waiting for him to come out. It's two days after Christmas 1931.

Minutes pass and the doors open. Waid emerges from the building and walks down to the car. Can he help them? Now is the moment, and Buck finds his voice. He speaks up in front of his family and says that he's come to turn himself back in. He wants to do his time. He wants to be free.

"We gave the Huntsville officials the shock of a lifetime," says Nell.

The warden is surprised, but friendly and respectful. Looking at this poor family in this car come to turn in one of their men, he's even sympathetic. He tells Buck he's doing right thing, that it will be better in the long run.

"Warden Waid was very kind to both of us," says Blanche.

Buck sure hopes the warden is right—hopes, as Blanche puts it, that "the happiness we dreamed of would be worth waiting for." He says good-bye to his mama and sisters, then good-bye to Blanche. He gets ready to go with the warden back toward the big doors of the prison.

Blanche begins to cry. He kisses her and turns toward the waiting Walls, trying not to hear it too much, trying to stay strong. She's weeping and he just keeps walking, in his best-looking suit, toward those doors.

"It was like cutting my heart out with a knife to know I would be separated from him," says Blanche. "I had sent the man I loved back to prison, which to me was almost as bad as sending him to his grave."

Nell and Marie figure, Well, since we're here, we might as well take the visitors' tour of the prison. Nell's husband thinks it could be interesting too. But Cumie and Blanche don't have any desire to see any deeper inside the Walls than the waiting room, where, they've been told, they can pick up Buck's suit and other possessions as soon as he's changed out of them. There are other women there, waiting to see their men, talking quietly, or just trying to remember all the good news they can muster. It's not a happy room.

Then the guards bring Buck through—not to visit but just on his way through processing. It's too much for Blanche, the sight of him in those awful prison whites and a guard right behind him. She starts to howl, not just weep.

"I began screaming and crying," she says.

Buck, what can he do? He turns, gives her the best smile he can muster. Keeps going on out of the room. But it does no good; Blanche is inconsolable, crazy with grief. The other women in the room look at her and look away. It's hard enough being here for their own men without this. They turn their gazes on the wiry little woman with the tired face who must be somebody's mother.

"Someone asked what was wrong with me," says Blanche. "Mrs. Barrow told them the man who had walked through with a guard was my husband. Then they seemed to understand."

Buck's in.

❋

Buck's in! Can you believe it? Of course, he's not looking at fourteen years, like you are. He's only got whatever remains of his four-year sentence, minus whatever they take off on account of his turning himself in. You've got to wonder, What was he thinking? All you can figure is Ferguson Farm, where he run off from originally, must not have been as bad as burnin' Eastham, because no way in creation would you be turning yourself in if you got free. No way—every day that passes you're trying like hell to figure out how to get out.

Still, that warden's eyes must have near popped out of his head when Buck walked up. That sure would have been a sight to see. That's Buck for you. You never know what he'll do next.

Things aren't getting any better down here in the burnin' hell. Except for old Crowder being dead, that is. That's big. But it's hard not to notice another summer come and gone and still no word of paroles or pardons. Just promises. Just wait and see, be patient. That's easy for all them to say. The truth is, you just don't know if you can make it. The work is too hard, the place too mean; something even worse than killing old Crowder is bound to happen.

But maybe if you were even just up at Huntsville and off of this work farm, up at Huntsville with Buck . . . you could keep each other strong, look out for each other. The only way to get there, though, is to figure out how to get yourself admitted into the hospital. Maybe cut yourself somehow, get yourself sick or wounded.

You're not alone thinking this way. There's guys do insane things to get off these farms, and you're not just talking about trying to beat the dogs in a race for the river. Inmates have been known to shoot kerosene into their veins, pour stuff into their eyes, whatever they can think of.

"They would stick their foot in the commode and break their foot so they could go to the Walls and get drugs there," says Hazel Boettcher, whose father is the warden out at Eastham in the thirties. "It was a bloody, bloody time."

Mostly, though, inmates had "accidents" with the axes. "Fourteen men cut their hands and feet off in one week," says Ralph Fults. "That's just one week. That's how much punishment they was getting—they couldn't take it and they cut their hands and feet off."

"Yeah, I helped," he says. "I cut a guy's hand off, fingers, and one guy's foot. Course I got to tell you all of it to make you think that I'm not a sadistic or nothing person."

The foot belonged to a kid from New Jersey who never farmed a day until he ended up at Eastham, and he just couldn't keep up with the hoe squad.

"Well, they'd beat him up," says Fults. "This guard had a big old glove they called a tough nut. It had ridges on it, they catch him by the side of the head and beat him in the head."

So when the kid finally has enough of it he comes up to Fults and says, "I'm gonna run out."

"Well, that's committin' suicide," Fults says to him. "They got a shotgun guy and they got a rifle guy—you can't get away from both of them. . . . That's what they want you to do."

"You cut my toes off," the kid from New Jersey insists. "If you don't, I'm gonna run out and make them kill you too."

"Well, I was on the spot," says Fults. "I was afraid he was going to talk with them and the men'd kill me. I'm 'mutilating state property' if I cut his foot off. That's what they call that. But finally I did. I seen that he meant business and I told him to put his foot—we's cutting wood, tree sawing— I told him to put it up there on them log. We had double-bit six-pound axes. He stood and . . . I cut off about this much of his shoe off, all through the sole."

The guy who wants Fults to chop his hand off is different only in the details. He'd escaped once already, and the guards had let him know his days were numbered.

"He had got the word. And they was pretty strong. I was pretty scared. I didn't want to cut his hand off. I said, You'll be sorry if you ever live."

But the guy replies, "No, there's no way."

"And I said, Well, put it up there, and I did chop the fingers off," Fults says. "And I met him in Dallas a couple of years ago and he still says I saved his life."

There are dozens of stories like that, and toes and fingers are the least of them. An Eastham guard from those years remembers coming across two inmates in a woodlot who had cut each other's legs off below the knee, only the second guy hadn't done a clean job of it owing to nearly being in shock from the sight of his own severed limb there on the dirt and the tourniquet on his leg not doing such a bang-up job of stanching the blood. Another time at Eastham an inmate says he isn't feeling too well and asks permission to lie in the tank for the day. When he's told to shut up, go back, get his hat, and come out and get to work, he goes back as directed but comes out and throws his bleeding and severed foot through the bars.

"Now can I lay in?" he asks.

Once in a while the story of prison mutilations gets out through the grapevine to Harry McCormick or some other prison muckraker. Harry hears about it when guys are drawing lots and cutting themselves as part of an organized protest enforced by the heavies in the farm. No fewer than twenty-nine convicts cut their "heel-strings" while sitting at the breakfast table at Eastham. They tie their shoelaces around their legs and hack through their Achilles tendons, without the guards noticing anything until they see blood streaming out from under the table. That got out to McCormick.

"Dr. Veazey was the doctor," says Boettcher, "and Daddy told him, 'Bring lots of morphine with you. If they've got the guts to cut it I've got the guts to put it back together.' And they would take a hook and pull that [tendon] but they were always crippled after that."

Yet even when mutilations become an epidemic, there's not much sympathy from higher up in the system. "Between letting a few convicts bang themselves up and letting hundreds of them escape to bang up the public, I say let the convicts chop themselves," says Commissioner Simmons. "As long as they want to do that, I say give them more axes if they need them."

Nice guy. But that mass cutting and that little comment both come a few years after you're gone. That's right, gone and free. Sometime mid-January of 1932, out in the timber clearing trees with some other men, you put your left foot on a stump and get your buddy to do it. You look away. He says, You sure, Clyde? You say, Go.

Thwack. Couple of toes cut clean off, big one and some of the next one. Blood everywhere. Guard! Guard! We need some help, got a wounded man here!

Hey, guard.

That's gotta hurt like hell, but it works like a charm. You don't even get a chance to collect your stuff; Aubrey Scalley mails some of your personal photos home to Cumie for you, including, interestingly enough, one of you and your old girlfriend Grace. On January 16, you're back at Huntsville in the hospital. Maybe they let Buck come and visit you. He's sort of getting soft treatment for turning himself in; they don't even make him wear the stripes he's supposed to as a runaway.

Nell says you did it to escape the field work. Floyd Hamilton says the same thing: "He did this to get out of work or to get in the hospital so he could get some rest." And W. D. Jones, that neighbor kid from West Dallas, says you done it because you "couldn't keep up with the pace the farm boss set."

Blanche, on the other hand, who comes to see you and Buck that February and makes a point of mentioning that Bonnie never quite makes it to see you, says, "He did it so he would be sent to the Walls where Buck was."

What everyone agrees on is that it's a darned shame you weren't just a little more patient. Two weeks later, on February 2, 1932, Cumie's work finally pays off and your parole from Governor Ross Sterling—one of sixty-six paroles he grants that month—comes through.

You're out! On crutches, but out.

CHAPTER 13

BACK IN BUSINESS

She's been seeing somebody else for a while now, and why not? So maybe the feelings aren't as electric as they were with Clyde, but really, she's got her own life to live. Doesn't she? Clyde says he'll be out in two years, that Cumie's got a parole in the works, but what if there's not a parole? Or what if after two years it's, Hey, sugar, I'll be out after three years. . . .

Is she supposed to wait fourteen years?

Plus this new guy is a nice enough fellow, with no criminal record. (At least not that anyone knows about.) He's friendly to her, a good guy. Someone she can maybe see a life with. One who'll be there, at least, which is saying plenty. Twice now she's been crazy in love and twice now the laws have locked up her lover, so if it's not red-hot fire, so what? It's warm enough, and it's not behind cold bars.

It's no surprise that her mother is happy with the development. Emma's been taking a vacation from worrying about Bonnie. She's got plenty to think about with her younger daughter, Billie Jean, whose baby is now three months old, and whose husband, Fred Mace, got himself arrested for burglary and bank robbery just a few hours before that child was born.

"I was more relieved than I would have admitted to anyone," says Emma about her older girl, "and thought that Tom was the answer to Bonnie's problem, after all."

So yeah, Bonnie's seeing someone else.

❋

What does your sister really know about anything, let alone what kind of shirt a man needs in the world?

"I had a good girl before I went away," Clyde says to his sister. "I'm going to doll up now and go over there and see if Bonnie will still speak to me." *(Missouri State Highway Patrol file photograph. Used with permission.)*

"Listen, honey," says Nell, "nobody but bootleggers and gangsters wear silk shirts."

You're downtown in Dallas, standing in a store on your first day back. Your two sisters are taking you around to shops to get some new clothes for your new start in your new life. A new suit, and shoes, and a belt. It's real nice of Nell and Artie, especially with money being so tight and all.

But, darn it, they're not going to tell you what kind of shirt you're going to wear. You've been being told what to wear long enough.

"Nice people just don't go in for them, that's all," Nell insists. "You don't want an old silk shirt."

But you do want a silk shirt, a nice new one, and you get it, along with a pair of smooth kid gloves that Nell also has nothing nice to say about. She doesn't understand that after where you've been you need to look *good* just to feel human. Oh, yes, and dark glasses. You must have those too. You need to look *fine* if you're going to get Bonnie back.

Nell talks as if Bonnie's long gone, a hopeless cause. She says stuff like, You ought to get out and look for a job, and look for a girlfriend. Why look for a new girl, though, when you know right where the one you love is?

"I had a good girl before I went away," you tell your sister. "I'm going to doll up now and go over there and see if Bonnie will still speak to me."

❀

All of a sudden there he is in a beautiful new suit and tie, standing in the living room door of her mother's house. She's sitting there with, of all people, Tom, the other guy.

Tom who? she might as well ask. As soon as she sees Clyde standing there, with his crutches under his arms and his one-dimple smile waiting to light up like a beacon, she's off that couch and in his arms. And Tom, well, he's no dummy. Looks at Bonnie and Clyde and sees he's the fool. Heads for the door.

See you later, Tom.

"Shucks," says Clyde a few minutes later, putting his lips on her flushed cheek while she sits on his lap in a chair in her mom's little kitchen, "no decent girl would go with me, would they, honey?"

She laughs and kisses him back. He loves to hear her giggle. He loves his silk shirt.

❀

Massachusetts? Where the heck even is Massachusetts? You're barely back home from prison, only a couple of weeks, hardly off your crutches, and here everyone is telling you to go to Massachusetts?

It's mostly Nell, as usual. She's got some friend who has a line on a construction job up there. Says you should go there because it's so far away— the cops won't be bothering you and you can really make a clean start. Darn right it's far away.

You're not denying that the local laws don't seem much interested in letting you get your feet on any kind of firm ground. Not denying it and not surprised either: Why should they change?

"When he got out of prison, he tried to go to work," your pal Floyd Hamilton says about you. "He did get jobs at a couple of places, but two police officers found out where he was working, and they went out and told his employers that he was an ex-convict. And that he would probably steal from them, so they fired him. They just kept arresting him and putting him in jail."

Same old crap. Speaking of Floyd, the good news is that his little brother, Ray, who's your real pal from growing up, is out of jail too. That's thanks to Ralph Fults, who got out of Eastham a half year before you on a pardon. One day in January, just before you get out yourself, Ralph's walking down the street in his hometown of McKinney, Texas, and he hears someone yelling down from the jailhouse window. They yell to him that they got a friend of Butch's up here, or something like that, meaning a friend of yours. Turns out to be Raymond, who is in there for grand theft auto. Ralph's heard all about Raymond—how you grew up together and all. What's more, he knows Raymond's supposed to be part of the plan to bust open Eastham.

"Clyde had this buddy named Raymond Hamilton in the Collin County jail," Fults explains. "So I slipped Raymond some hacksaws, and we was the first three members of the Barrow Gang."

Good old Ralph. Slipped those blades into the bindings of some detective magazines and found a pretty girl in town to take them up to Raymond. Just a little reading material for poor little Ray, Officer . . . Ha, that's pretty good, huh? A hacksaw in detective magazines! But that business about forming the gang is just Ralph getting a little ahead of himself: you're still locked in at Huntsville yourself when Raymond—talking and singing all the time in his cell to cover the sound of his work—saws through those bars and slips away from that old county jail.

And now that you are out there's still no gang, really, because everyone is after you to go to Massachusetts and take this job. It's not just Nell, now—even Bonnie's ma is taking up the chorus.

"Maybe you'd get to like it up there," she says.

Maybe.

"If you and Bonnie love each other, I'm not going to stand in your way at all," she also says, which is nice of her, considering the circumstances. Unless, that is, Bonnie's ma is just trying to get rid of you by encouraging you to go north.

"My mother . . . my mother, um, um, she . . . ," says Bonnie's little sister, Billie Jean, trying to figure out the right way to put it. "At that time, Bonnie had a mind of her own. Mother didn't like, uh, her going with Clyde after Clyde had been in the penitentiary. But as I say, Bonnie was in love with Clyde. They were in love with each other."

Bonnie, too, thinks you should give it a try.

You do want to get a new start. You do want to do the right thing. Even Ray Hamilton is supposedly giving it a try: he's gone all the way up to Bay City, Michigan, and got himself a job where his father-in-law works. So, okay, you finally say; you'll go. And you do: all the way up there to New England at the end of February or the beginning of March. All alone, you might point out, since Bonnie can't afford to or won't come along.

"I am lonesome already," you write home to your ma only a few days after getting to Worcester and making contact with Nell's friend Jim. "Have you seen Buck yet? Tell him hello for me. I am going to send him a box, soon as I work awhile."

Buck doesn't get any box from you; you don't work long enough to send any presents. Less than three weeks after leaving for Massachusetts, you're back in Dallas. Even though you were seventeen hundred miles away from anyone who knows you and were going under the name of Jack Stuart, you still couldn't shake that feeling that the law was after you. It didn't matter that they weren't after you; you just couldn't handle not knowing a soul and being so far away from everyone after waiting so long to get out of Eastham and go home.

"Sis, I nearly died of lonesomeness up there," you say to Nell. "I've been away from you all two years. I've got to stay close to home."

✳

Neither Cumie nor anyone in the family is really outright pleased to see Clyde, except maybe Bonnie. That's not quite fair—a mother is happy enough to lay eyes on her son any day—but the fact that he's given up so quickly on what seemed like such an opportunity is depressing. Not to mention that the whole affair is a bit embarrassing for Nell, who went out of her way to get Clyde the job. Her friend up north could tell it wasn't going to work even before Clyde left; he sent a letter saying so.

More than the specific falling apart of the Massachusetts plan, though, there's a sort of general fatalism creeping into Clyde that is getting worrisome. It's like that bitterness that Fults is talking about. He's changed, they think.

"He just seemed like he got meaner like, or something or other," says the little one, Marie, about her brother after he gets out of Eastham.

"When he went to jail," echoes Nell, "he was still the sweet and likable brother I had grown up with. But prison life did things to him which changed that."

"I don't know," says Marie, "I don't know. He just seemed like he didn't care much anymore about anything."

"Clyde was restless," says Nell, "unhappy."

"He changed," says Fults, "from what you call a schoolboy into a rattlesnake."

❋

Snake or no, Ralph Fults is glad you're back. Since getting out of Eastham himself in August of 1931, he's been half-assed sitting around McKinney waiting for you to get out of jail too. He's been playing a little cards for spending cash and watching the newspapers for an announcement of your parole. That and, of course, his little adventure with the hacksaw blades for Ray Hamilton. He's not really making plans for the future; after all, you kind of have a plan together.

So it comes as a bit of a surprise to him when you up and go off to Massachusetts almost as soon as you're back from the burnin' hell. It's a decision that leaves him wondering if you're gone for good. Not that he wishes you bad or anything, or hopes you don't make it in the honest world. Not at all: Ralph's probably wishing you good luck up there in the cold. He just wasn't expecting it when he heard you were gone.

Chances are good Ralph isn't that surprised when he hears you're back. As soon as he does get wind that you're in town, he makes his way down to West Dallas on the interurban trolleys, and over to Cumie and Henry's filling station there on the Eagle Ford Road. You're not home when he arrives, though, so he sits and passes the time with Cumie in the little kitchen, or gives Henry a hand with pumping gas. Nell's probably around somewhere, and possibly Blanche, who is living there off and on while Buck's back in prison.

Living there not all that happily, you might add.

"I loved his people because he loved them and I knew it would make him unhappy if he thought I did not love them," says Blanche. "I loved his people, knowing they were jealous of me and of his love for me. Although they were not always unkind to me, they often showed me I was imposing on them by living with them and not working in town to pay my rent. And they all knew this was one thing Buck would not have wanted me to do."

Of Fults, Blanche says only: "He was this tall, good-looking twenty-something-year-old fellow."

Anyway, when Fults arrives at the filling station you're off at work, making yet another effort at your old job at the glass company. Once again, though, the cops show up and pull you out of the shop and start asking questions about who knows what. And who cares what? It's not you they're looking for, but it doesn't matter to the boss. He's had enough, and tells you it's just not working out. It turns out you've had enough, too. You head home, mad as hell, and find Ralph Fults there with Cumie.

"You showed up just in time," you say, looking at Fults. Then you go on to tell your mama that you lost another job and you've done trying to make a go of it.

"I'm never gonna work again," you tell her.

If Cumie tries talking some sense into you, you're not having it anymore. It's like something inside—your will, maybe—just finally broke clean through like a dry stick, and you can see there is only one road ahead that the laws are going to let you take.

"I heard him tell his mother in West Dallas 'I'm never going back.' He got a job and they kept grabbing him and got him fired," says Fults. "And he told her 'I'll never go back to prison, neither, I'll never stand arrest for nothing,' and he did. He told her that one day in West Dallas."

"I'll never go back to that hellhole," you say. "They're gonna have to kill me. I swear it. They're gonna have to kill me."

You grab a few things, and you and Fults are out the door, leaving your mama alone with her motherly thoughts. She won't understand, no doubt, but what are you supposed to do? You'll figure out how to tell Bonnie; maybe she won't care.

❋

"So we formed the gang," says Fults.

He's not as gung ho as Clyde is about reviving their old plan to go raise hell at Eastham. No, he might rather stay as far away from there as possible. But once again, his little pal won't shut up about it.

"He kept coming to me with it and finally I said, Okay, I'll go along."

Part of what changes Fults's mind is the thought that Aubrey Scalley and several other mutual friends of theirs are still inside, suffering and waiting for them. Scalley, in particular, Fults says, agreed to take the heat for Clyde's killing of Crowder in exchange for being allowed in on the big break.

"They was in what we called a living hell, you know," says Fults. "We called it a living hell down there, and we got close to 'em, you know. And they needed somebody, you know."

What Fults and Clyde need, on the other hand, are cars, money, comrades, and guns. "We was going to get two cars to go to the prison," says Fults. "Our whole idea was only to turn the people loose. We didn't plan to kill all the guards, but we planned to go down there any way we had to, and turn them loose."

The cars are going to be easy to get: Fults and Clyde are pros, as is Ray

Hamilton, who's back in town after his own attempt at clean living up north in Michigan ended pretty much the way your stint in Massachusetts did.

"If you lock a car we can get in, any locked car, and wire it up in one minute," says Fults. "If your doors were locked, whatever. 'Cause that was the things we was learning then."

Guns, at least the beginnings of an arsenal, come pretty quick too. Clyde starts by taking one of Buck's weapons from his parents' place on the Eagle Ford Road. "You better not lose that gun," yells Blanche. "Buck'll skin you alive." Then he and Fults buy a few more handguns and a couple of shotguns that they can cut down and customize.

"He had that sawed-off 16-gauge automatic shotgun along with him all the time," says W. D. Jones, the neighbor kid from Dallas who's not traveling with Clyde yet but knows what he's talking about. "It had a one-inch rubber band he'd cut out of a car-tire inner tube attached to the cutoff stock. He'd slip his arm through the band and when he put his coat on, you'd never know the gun was there. The rubber band would give when he snatched it up to fire. He kept his coat pocket cut out so he could hold the gun barrel next to his hip. It looked like he just had his hand in his pocket."

Coming by money takes a bit more effort. At around two A.M. on Friday, March 25, Fults, Hamilton, and Clyde cut their way through a fence that surrounds the Simms Oil Refinery. The refinery is only about half a mile down the Eagle Ford Road from where the Barrows and the Hamiltons live, making the risk of being recognized a bit higher than they might like. But the payoff is going to be high, too: a friend who works at the place says the payroll cash comes in every Thursday and is kept there overnight until payday, Friday.

There's no trouble getting through the fence, thanks to a pair of bolt cutters that they borrowed from Ray's older brother, Floyd. And no trouble either with the refinery's night foreman, Ray McClothlin, or the night fireman, J. L. Foster, who are working in the boiler room on the graveyard shift when they look up to see guns pointed at them. A quick search shows that they've got no money in their pockets, which is only mildly annoying, since pocket change is not what the three have come for.

"Well," says one of the bandits (no one remembers which), "we're going to crack open that safe."

The two night employees just shake their heads, maybe smile a bit, though that's not easy when someone's pointing a gun at you.

"Crack ahead," says Foster. "You'll just be wasting your time because there's no money in it."

No doubt he's lying, trying to protect the boss for some reason. A few seconds later the knob is knocked off, the tumblers are chiseled, and the safe is cracked. But damned if that night fireman wasn't telling it straight after all. When the door swings open there's not a penny of payroll inside. There's no money in the whole stinking office, as far as the three of them can find. It's not a nice moment: three guys with guns, two scared employees, and no money anywhere.

There's nothing to do, though, but tie up Foster and McClothlin and head back out the way they came. Back through the hole in the fence and across the railroad tracks to where their stolen car waits. Then out of West Dallas as fast as they can go without drawing undue attention.

What a waste of risk, not to mention time. Other small jobs start going better, though, including one where they manage to hit most of the businesses in a single town on the same night. "The corrupt police force actually posted lookouts on the streets while Clyde and I broke into every safe on the square," says Fults.

These little jobs still aren't getting them where they want to be, however, and at some point either Fults or Clyde comes up with the idea that maybe they're not thinking large enough—that maybe they ought to rob a bank. This is a big jump up for all of them, and Raymond, in particular, is wary of taking the step. He was just a car thief before he went to jail the first time, and basically he's pretty happy with the quick-and-easy-and-you're-out-of-there life. Fults and Clyde had to put a little pressure on him just to get him to go knob knocking. But to rob a bank! That means going in and pulling guns. He doesn't want to go, preferring to steal cars and sell them.

Fults, on the other hand, will steal only cash, on account of the first time he got thrown in jail was after getting caught trying to fence a load of stolen cigarettes. "We was stealing them out of railroad cars—the whole carload—and wholesaling them," he says, "and I got caught. After that I said I wouldn't steal nothing else I had to sell and I never did."

Clyde sides with Fults. Or, more likely, given his personality, he just announces what they're going to do.

"He was the complete boss, not Bonnie, like some have said," says W. D. Jones. "Clyde dominated all them around him, even his older brother Buck. Clyde planned and made all the decisions about what to heist and when to pull out and leave a job alone."

Clyde and Fults are ready to try a bank job, never mind what Ray Hamilton says. And never mind either that in 1932, banks are mostly in the news for not having any money in them: five thousand have closed their doors in the past two years. Banks are also in the papers every week for getting robbed. In fact, right there on page 1 of the Dallas papers on March 30, five days after the gang opens the empty safe at the oil refinery, is a story of some guys getting out of a bank in Minneapolis with $200,000 in broad daylight without even firing a shot.

Imagine! How much you think $200,000 weighs? Just the thought of those bags full of money is enough to make a man smile. Enough to make Ray Hamilton, who still doesn't like the idea of robbing banks but likes the idea of bags of cash, come around. Minnesota doesn't sound so bad.

In early April the three of them steal a car and head north, looking for a bank to rob. They find it, too, in the little town of Okabena, Minnesota. It seems ripe for the picking, not too big, not too small, not too far from the state line, where the laws will likely turn around. And, most importantly, in business.

They don't just walk in and say, "Stick 'em up," however. Even though this is the first bank any of them have attempted to rob, they know the fundamentals, both from talking to more experienced operators in prison and from experience on smaller adventures.

"You know robbin' a bank, a small bank anyway like that, there isn't too much danger in robbin' a bank. It didn't seem to take too much guts to do that" is how Raymond's brother, Floyd, explains the way they all looked at it. (Floyd is not yet a bank robber himself in 1932, but give him time.) "The danger is in getting away, and stayin' away."

Or as Ralph Fults puts the same sentiment: "Ninety percent of any bank robbery is runnin' your roads. Ten percent's all it takes to get the money, you know, but ninety percent is your getaway."

Clyde, of course, learned this lesson the hard way back in Middletown, Ohio, when he ended in the burnin' hell for two years on account of taking a wrong turn. That particular mistake is one he's not ever intending to repeat, and Fults is right with him on it.

There's plenty of good roads out of Okabena, going every direction and linked nicely, but winter won't surrender this year and there's still snow and ice on the ground. It's not so much slipping and sliding on the road itself that's worrisome, though it is a factor to be considered by a threesome of Texas boys without a lot of winter experience. It's all the snow and ice off the road that gives Clyde pause. The cars of the day are built for the roads of the day, meaning high clearance and decent traction for dirt and gravel roads, and one of Clyde's favorite tricks is cutting overland across fields and pastures and doubling back on a parallel road. The snow and ice, and the mud underneath it, are potentially enough to kill the plan.

"Clyde always believed in being prepared," says W. D. Jones. "One time, up in Tennessee, we were on the way to hit a cotton mill. We figured there was a big payroll there. But Clyde called it off, because there was water in the ditches alongside the road we'd have used and we wouldn't have been able to cut cross-country to make time on the getaway."

Clyde, Ray, and Fults run the roads, talking it through, scoping it out. Then they run the roads again. Pass the bank again. This is their job, after all; they're professionals now. Run the roads, watch the bank. But in the end, the snow and the ice are too spooky for Clyde and his pals and they decide to call it off and look farther south.

Farther south, they find what they're looking for in a plump little bank in Kansas whose president walks to work and opens the doors at precisely eight forty-five every morning. After the usual reconnaissance of the roads out of town, Clyde meets the banker at the door of his institution one morning and tells him calmly that there's a Colt .45 pointing right at him and if he just opens that bank door and goes on in as if nothing is out of the ordinary, no one will get hurt. Fults does the same with a couple of employees who unexpectedly show up early for work. Raymond is in the car waiting.

It goes off without a hitch, thanks, Fults thinks, to psychology in the form of a sawed-off shotgun.

"When we used the sawed-off shotgun strapped over a shoulder," he says, "there's a lot of psychology. You go in a bank and pull it up out of your overcoat, people never did try to grab it. Now I might have had a .22 or something, they might have tried to grab it. But there was a lot of psychology to that [sawed-off shotgun]."

They never even have to fire a shot, and in barely any time at all the bank president and his employees are locked away inside their big safe and Clyde and Fults are running out the front door with two bags stuffed full of cash. In the car, Raymond hits the gas and away they go. Across one state line, and across another state line, and finally to East St. Louis, in Illinois. There the three of them check into a hotel and count their take.

Thirty-three thousand dollars! It's just too easy. None of them have laid eyes on anywhere near that kind of loot before. Ray Hamilton in particular suddenly sees the light. He wants to be a bank robber from here out. Looking at his eleven-thousand-dollar share of the take, he also decides he doesn't really care to put his life on the line to cut loose a bunch of guys he doesn't even know down at the Eastham Prison Farm.

He's out, he announces, and that's that. Takes his share of the money and says, See you around fellas, and he's gone out the door. Up to Michigan, or some other fool place. Fults and Clyde, well, they look at each other. What are they going to do? It's his choice.

CHAPTER 14

FUN WHILE IT LASTED

I'm a pistol packin' papa
And when I walk down the street
You can hear those mamas shouting
Don't turn your gun on me

Now girls I'm just a good guy
And I'm going to have my fun
And if you don't want to smell my smoke
Don't monkey with my gun

—JIMMIE RODGERS

Hamilton! Can you believe it? He just ups and heads out on his own with his share of the take. He didn't even want to come along on the bank job in the first place and was just the driver and all, and . . . Oh hell, just let it go.

Fults, who doesn't think too highly of Hamilton's brains anyway, says the kid's never been in the burnin' hell, so how's he supposed to know or care about the guys there. Just let it go, there are other fellas who know what it's about. Guys we can trust. Guys who remember the bat and barrel and all. And you know Ralph's right. Who needs Ray?

"We recruited ex-cons as the other members of the gang," Fults says. There's Johnny and Al, who Ralph knows from reform school and coming up through the jails. There's also Ted, Jack, and Red, who are friends of yours, presumably from around Dallas and Denton. There's Ralph Alsup, Jack Hammett, Herman Hunter, and Gene "Fuzzy" Fezzel.

"We had about twelve guys that was workin' in fours," says Fults.

Plans for the raid on Eastham are going along fine, in fact, with a couple of boys working on different angles of the problem. Gear, cash, and guns are piling up at the hideout in the woods near Lake Dallas. Everything is falling into place for the raid. It's really going to happen. You know it is.

Not that there aren't a few close scrapes here and there, such as when you and the gang are all set to knock over both banks in the town of Denton, Texas, at the very same time. That's a great idea, by the way, two banks robbed simultaneously, cars screaming out of town in every direction, police not knowing who to go after, or maybe even what bank's been robbed. People saying, "Hey, they went that way" and pointing to all corners of the square. Damn! That's a plan to make you smile.

It's all set to go on the morning of April 11, 1932, but during the last running of the roads, the final circling of the courthouse square, Fults sees something he doesn't like. There's a car parked facing out instead of in. That's not such a big deal in itself; some folks like to do that, park out, not in. But sitting in the front seat of this car are a couple of Texas Rangers. Not quite Frank Hamer, but one of them is just as bad, maybe worse, and Fults recognizes him. It's "Lone Wolf" Gonzaullas. That guy doesn't miss once he pulls his weapon is what they say about him.

Old Lone Wolf sitting in the town square is enough to make any job go from "go" to "no-go" in about as long as it takes Fults to break an egg into a frying pan. You're not robbing any two banks this morning. It's a tense moment all around, and you and Fults both have to be thinking, as you look around the gang, that it's a mighty odd coincidence that two Texas Rangers would be sitting there on the very morning in the very square where you have been planning a big hit.

There's no time to worry about rats. At least Fults saw them in time, which is the kind of thing that makes a twenty-three-year-old like you feel more lucky than afraid. Ha! Nice try, Rangers, better luck next time. The good news is, you don't really need those bank hits: you got enough money left out of the big job in Kansas, though it's going fast with your buying the lot next to the gas station for your dad and giving chunks away to various other relatives. Not to mention plenty of big nights out with Bonnie. Just a few small jobs, some supply runs, and you'll be ready.

On one of these, you and Fults and Red are just northwest of Wichita Falls in Electra, Texas, when your car breaks down. There's nothing to do but get out and walk till you find another car to take. You don't get far, though, before up rolls the local chief of police. He's a big old boy named James T. Taylor, and he's riding with somebody who looks to be his deputy but is actually just a town water commissioner giving him a lift. Chief Taylor, who's sitting on the passenger side, rolls down the window and asks what's up.

"Could happen to anybody. He stopped me and Clyde in broad daylight," says Fults. "I told him we were going to get it fixed. He's there sittin' in the car, him and his deputy, but I'm standing up here, and I got a .45 automatic under my shirt. This button's unbuttoned."

Chief Taylor doesn't like the look of these boys in their fancy clothes, out here in the middle of nowhere. Or maybe he's already checked up on the broken-down car and figures it's stolen.

"I gotta take you down," he says, meaning down to the station for questioning.

"I looked at Clyde," says Fults, "and he walked around the other side."

Now the two of you have the car surrounded, and as the chief starts to get his handcuffs from out of his belt, Fults pulls his handgun. Over on the driver's side, you got your guns pointed right at the other fellow. It all happens real quick.

"Well," says Fults, "he didn't go up right then, you know. It hurt his pride, he's a big man . . . this big chief of police." But after a moment's thought, the big man slowly raises his hands up. The guy is huge, big around as a barrel.

"I don't want to hurt you, you know," says Fults, opening the door to let the chief out of the car. He relieves the big man of his service revolver, while you keep your guns trained on the driver. Right about now Red, for some reason only Red and God know, figures it's his chance to get away. He takes off across the fields, leaving you and Fults looking after him incredulously—at least Hamilton had the guts to say "See you later." But Red just leaves you and Fults there figuring out what to do with your two hostages.

Make that three hostages. What's this guy pulling up in a green Chevrolet and getting out of his car think he's doing? Turns out to be A. F. McCormick, the guy who called Chief Taylor in the first place. He's come to see if maybe Pretty Boy Floyd's been caught right here in Electra, and maybe, since he made the call, if there's a big reward coming his way. He figures out his mistake about the time Fults points a handgun at his heart and you yell at everyone to pile into his nice new car.

Next thing McCormick knows, he's in his own back seat going for a joyride with the chief of police, the head of the city water department, and two half-crazed armed bandits. One of them, Fults, is sitting next to him, pointing guns and saying we don't want anybody hurt. The other, you, is behind the wheel, driving slowly through town as if nothing is amiss.

You look around at all of them and apologize for the inconvenience.

Eight miles out of town, pretty much in the middle of nowhere, you stop the car and tell the three hostages to get out. See, no one needs to get hurt, but sorry, Officer, you can't have your gun back.

✳

W. N. Owens is just a rural mail carrier doing his job, taking catalogs along his usual RFD route like he does every day except Sundays and holidays. Neither snow nor rain nor heat, et cetera, et cetera. It's the same route every day, driving letters and catalogs and newspapers to the folks along the roads outside Fowlkes, Texas. Sure, it might be nice to have a more comfortable vehicle than this old jalopy of his, but truth be told, Owens knows he's got nothing to complain about: the U.S. Postal service is one of the best jobs going in times like these.

But what's this up ahead? A car stopped and a couple of young gentlemen standing near it, one on each side of the road. Must be broke down, Owens figures, and he slows a bit, thinking he'll stop to see if he can help. Maybe they just need a ride for some gas. We'll see.

Before he even gets to a stop, though, the two of them have jumped up on his running boards and, my goodness, they're sticking guns in his face. Pull it over, buddy, one yells, which naturally he does. Only a fool would try to do otherwise, after all. These boys look desperate and dangerous, though he can't see the eyes of the little one owing to the dark glasses he's wearing.

Now the boys are wiping down the Chevy, which is out of gas, as it turns out. Wiping it for fingerprints and then piling into his old mail car and taking over the steering wheel. Got any money? they want to know. Eight cents, he says, and gives it to them. He's got twelve dollars hidden away somewhere, which is either the bravest or the stupidest thing Owens has done in a long time. He'll find out which eventually.

They don't press it. They just take his eight cents, and he breathes easier. This is certainly not the usual day's work on the rural mail route, but that doesn't make it fun; they blindfold him, though why he can't say. He can tell they're going up and down and around on back roads. They go for hours that way, with the short one behind the wheel driving like a madman and chatting to him in a friendly way. Or at least as friendly a way as a man can who has recently stuck a gun in his face, commandeered his car, and blindfolded and kidnapped him.

They haven't eaten in three days, Clyde tells Owens. This is the fourth car they've stolen, he says. Fults just sits silently in the back, which is scary, but Clyde says, "Aw, don't worry about him, he's harmless."

They mention no names.

You might as well take that blindfold off, they tell him at last, and he does, in time to watch Clyde accelerate his poor old machine right through a chain that's stretched across the entrance to the toll bridge across the Red River. He sees the two men in the Randlett toll booth come running out, pulling guns, and fire uselessly at the back of the car as they speed across the river into Oklahoma.

Cool as cucumbers these two operators are. They stop at a lunch place along the road somewhere after crossing the state line. They don't have anything but the eight cents they got off him, so they give a big sob story to the owner about how hungry they are and all. The owner, a nice enough fellow, gives them a little food, which they share with Owens, who's no doubt thinking about that money hidden deep in his pants. Down the road a piece, at a filling station, the bandits use his stamps to buy a dollar's worth of gas.

They don't want his mail, however. When, about a dozen miles outside of the town of Fletcher, Oklahoma, Clyde finally stops the car and tells Owens he better get out here, they hand him his bags. Maybe they don't want to keep the mail because they don't want to cause Owens and his postal customers any more trouble than they already have. Or maybe Clyde's thinking about how his pal Turner went to the federal jail at Leavenworth just for stealing a couple of dollars from a U.S. post office. But then again, maybe not. Clyde in particular doesn't seem to be thinking about legal implications.

"In a few days," he tells Owens, "you're likely to hear that we're dead."

That's not the kind of thing a person hears all that often, even in the middle of this Depression out here on the edge of the dust bowl. It's like he's got a death wish or something. Still, the boy in sunglasses is cheerful enough when they're about to drive off and leave Owens there in the middle of nowhere, so Owens decides to ask Clyde a favor.

What are you going to do with my car? he wants to know. Nice and friendly, they tell him not to worry a bit—they'll leave it somewhere right out in the open where the police are sure to find it and return it to him.

But Owens has had some time to think during this mad drive. He's been thinking ever since he realized he probably wasn't about to get murdered, and it's occurred to him that maybe he can get a little more out of the afternoon's adventure than just the fright of his life and a good story to tell his friends and neighbors.

"Will you all do me a favor," he asks.

"Yeah, well, if we can," they say.

"Burn up this car when you get through with it," says Owens, "and I can get a new one."

✸

You and Fults look at each other and you just gotta laugh. Who doesn't like setting a car on fire? Especially when it's a good deed. Har har har. Didn't anybody ever tell that mailman that crime doesn't pay? Har, har, har.

"Yeah, he sure told us, be sure," says Fults. "You sure be doing a big favor, and I'll get a new car."

Of course, first you have to get good and far away from Fletcher, Oklahoma. As soon as you're out of sight of where you drop him off, you turn off the road you're on at the first chance and loop back in some new direction. Can't have that old thieving mailman telling folks which way to look. Then, somewhere along the way, you have to find another set of wheels for yourselves. That's easily done and in the plan anyway; his old rig is too slow for your taste.

Back across the Red River, though obviously not at the same bridge. Into Texas somewhere, you find a likely spot. Down out of the way, near a barn—there's no one around. Here we go, pouring gasoline on the machine and laughing, trying not to get it on your nice suits. Careful, man, don't be smoking right here right now.

Now you both stand back and flick that butt into the mess. Whoa. *Kaboom*. Can you believe it? Har har har. Almost burn your eyebrows off, that will.

"So we burned it," says Fults. "Took it down to a barn and gasolined it. Usually we just left 'em. We didn't go to all that trouble burning up a car."

Good for a laugh, it is, but too bad you can't stick around and watch it go when whatever's left in the tank ignites. No way, not with black smoke starting to pile up like some kind of Indian smoke sign telling everybody in the world to come on down and check out who is in this field. So it's just one last look, couple of laughs, and then it's "You're welcome, mailman, we got to be getting on the road."

"Well, we burned it up," Fults says again, thinking about it. "Took a lot of trouble, gasoline. Burned it over in Texas."

It was a fun trip. You didn't get rich and almost got yourselves caught. That big fat cop putting his hands slowly up and that car burning up, you'll remember those sights. And Fults is a good pal. But now you want to get home and see Bonnie.

Still, burning that car up was sure fun while it lasted.

✸

Clyde needs her help again. He and Ralph are finally back from wherever they were off at, some adventure or another, and now here he is smiling and kissing her on her neck and saying he needs her. And he does need her, in every way. She knows that better than anyone, just like she knows she probably shouldn't do a little favor for him.

But he's saying it'll be fun, honey, nothing dangerous, not nearly like bringing that gun into that old jail in Waco, and nothing happened then, did it? Naaaw, nothing will happen. She has to admit that it was actually kind of fun after it was done with, and the hiding out in her cousin's house was over; it made her smile just hearing about him trying to get out again. Now here he is saying just come along with Ralph and me. And there's nothing wrong with Ralph; a woman could do a lot worse for company than these two. She's got the time, unfortunately: the job at the place everyone called the Courthouse Café went the way of all jobs, and she's back to looking for work, along with just about everybody else.

What about Mama?

"Bonnie told me a few days after Clyde returned that she had a job with a cosmetic company demonstrating their face creams and lotions, and was going to Houston," says Emma Parker. "She did have the job. I made sure of that, and let her go, never suspicioning a thing."

No, Mama doesn't suspect a thing, or says as much anyway. And maybe Bonnie does have that job waiting; no one is saying she doesn't. But that's not where she's going, at least not first off. No, she's going to Weldon, Texas, to the Eastham Prison Farm.

We need to go on down to Weldon, Clyde explains, and get a message in to some friends who are still inside. They've written letters to Scalley keeping him up to date, using invisible ink made of alum, but now they need to confirm everything in person. Of course Ralph and him can't really go up to the front gate and just ask to visit, Clyde tells her—that won't go over. That will make them real suspicious. But, Bonnie, you're so small and pretty and smiling and all. And you talk so good, well, you can just go on up there on the regular Sunday visiting day and say you're Aubrey Scalley's wife or sister or something. Then when the guards aren't looking you can whisper or pass him a little note or something, and then we'll be out of there and can go have some fun.

Shoot, we'll have some fun times along the way before we even get there, and maybe after we'll go on down to Houston or down to the beach at Galveston. That's what we'll do. Come on, sugar.

"Course the original gang was Clyde and myself," says Fults. "And Bonnie Parker got in by accident."

The truth, more likely, is that she wouldn't miss it. Not if it means watching Clyde go off again without her, and she knows better than anyone that's what he'll do as long as he's got to do this thing back there at Eastham to get his head clear. Besides, what's she going to do? Stay in Dallas with Mama, crying and listening to Jimmie Rodgers sing "Pistol Packing Papa" while her own gun-toting man is off running around?

Oh it's true, Bonnie loves that Jimmie Rodgers.

"She had every record that he ever made," says her sister, Billie Jean. Bonnie loves him more than just about any other singer, except maybe Clyde. But Clyde mostly plays his saxophone, not so much sings.

"The singing brakeman?" someone asks Billie Jean, just to be sure they're talking about the same singer.

"Uh-huh," says Billie Jean.

Bonnie loves him.

> Yodelehee
> Oh de le hee hee
> Yodeloh hoo

❊

Bonnie won't sit home spinning her records if Clyde wants her along. What's she going to do? Go back to writing in her diary how nothing ever happens?

And just as Clyde promises, everything goes smoothly at Eastham. It's as easy as pecan pie compared to the adventure at Waco. Clyde and Fults get out about a mile from the building and go hide in the woods while she drives on in and bats her big blues at the guards and says that she's Aubrey Scalley's cousin. She could be in a school play. A little sweet talk—what else has Scalley got to do but talk to a pretty girl? She should have come and visited Clyde when he was here, but that's the past.

The moment comes. The guard's not looking. A lean in, a few whispers, and it's finished. Scalley's got the word that the big break is on, and he'll tell the others. Bonnie's done it. She's coursing with adrenaline now, buzzing like she's almost had a wreck, and driving kind of jazzed and jittery back out the dirt road, away from the horrible white building in the middle of those fields of sprouting cotton.

It's done, she tells Clyde when she picks them up in the woods. She smiles. He smiles. God, she loves his smile. He kisses her. Fults smiles. See, honey, it was easy.

My sweetheart understands me,
Says I'm her big shot.
I'm her pistol packing daddy
And I know I've got the drop.

You can give my new sport roadster
You can take my hard boil hat
But you can never take from me
My silver mounted gat

I'm a pistol packin' papa
I'm going to have my fun
Just follow me and you will hear
The barking of my gun

That was so easy. And now that it's over, it's hard to say it wasn't actually kind of fun fooling those gullible old guards, bless their hearts. Fun while it lasted.

❊

Everything is pretty much set to go now, except for a few loose ends. You need more guns for one, not because you're planning a war scene down there, but just so Scalley and the other Eastham boys have something to give themselves a fighting chance with after they're out.

The foursome of Fezzel, Alsup, Hammett, and Hunter agree to raid a hardware store in the town of Celina to get the needed guns and ammunition. They've seen a good supply there, they say. If they come across any opportunities for cash at the same time, that's fine too, but mostly they'll be going after hardware. They need a bit of hardware themselves and take with them some of the guns already collected at the Lake Dallas shed, including the nice service pistol Fults just lifted from that fat police chief up in Electra.

The other missing element to the plan are a couple of big, fast cars for the attack itself. This isn't an oversight; there's just no reason to have the cars until right before you're ready to go. You don't want them getting too hot, after all, and you don't mean engine heat.

The cars are your and Fults's responsibility, and you figure around the same night the other four hit Celina you'll go out toward Tyler, Texas, and find a couple of suitable machines.

"Think we'll have any trouble?" you ask Fults as you're getting ready to go.

"Naw," he says.

"Well, how 'bout takin' Bonnie?" you say.

Fults hasn't got any problem with that. "So Bonnie goes along for the ride," he says.

The ride's nice enough on the way to Tyler. You stop in the little town of Mabank along the way. It's not much of a place, a couple of blocks of single-story brick storefronts. You stay just long enough for Ralph to go into the H. Bock store there and buy a couple of boxes of ammunition.

"I saw some good guns in there," he says when he gets back out to the car. He's got an idea that you might want to have a backup if the boys going down to Celina strike out on their mission to get weapons.

"Coming back," he says, "let's just get some guns here in case they miss."

The ride is even nicer on the way back. You and Bonnie are now driving a fancy new Chrysler and Fults is right behind you in an equally swank Buick. The only problem with the new cars is they're fancy enough to grab the eye of David Drennan, the Mabank chief of police, who goes around to the back of the hardware store just as Fults is working his usual magic on the padlock while you stand watch. Drennan comes around the corner with a gun drawn, no less.

Pow! You take a shot at him and miss.

"The night watchman," says Fults. "We had a little shootin' scrape with him. He hid out on us."

Bang! Pow! Drennan fires back. He's ducked down right behind the Chrysler, where Bonnie's lying on the floorboards thinking this ride isn't as fun as it was a few minutes ago.

POW! Then he's gone, and a moment later the town bells are ringing and Fults is yelling, *Let's get the heck out of here!* and you're in the cars roaring out of town. But not far: it seems that Mabank, maybe due to all the bank robberies going on in Texas, has some kind of civic plan in place, because hardly are you out of the center of town than the road is blocked.

"They begin to blockade us on the road," Fults says. "Road graders, cars."

You slam the brakes, jam the wheel, and skid a fine U-turn, while behind you in the Buick, Fults does the same. He's not as good at it as you, but then again, not many people are. You practice Flying U-turns and reverse slides, and all manner of moves.

"Clyde was about the best driver in the world," W. D. Jones says a couple of Dallas cops told him. Like W.D. needs to be told. "Hell, I knowed that," he says. "I rode with him."

Fults manages to make the U-turn okay and you and he rip through

Mabank and start out in the other direction, only to find they got the road blocked at that end too. Where are they getting all these graders? Plus it's pouring rain now, getting muddy and all, so you can't risk going overland. Back through town a third time and finally, heading west, you seem to have found a route the townsfolk haven't blocked. You're flying along on a dirt road that's rapidly becoming a mud road. It's low clayey territory in the best of times and then, in a positive spring deluge near the swollen Cedar Creek bottom, it's all of a sudden no road.

Fults gets stuck first. You loop back, pick him up, but don't get very much more than a few miles farther before you, too, are up to the axles in the slurp. There's a house nearby, but it has no car—just a pair of mules, one of which is "known for its pitching."

Mules. You better be apologizing to Bonnie about the way things are turning out on this fun little trip when Fults lifts her to sit behind you on a smelly old mule for a cold night ride through an April rainstorm. Jesse James's fine horse this animal ain't. This is mules in the mud. C'mon, sugar, it'll be fun. You better hope she's laughing and cheerful about it.

Five miles riding on those damn animals gets you to another car, which ought to be the end of your troubles but only buys you another couple of miles before running out of gas.

Now you're wishing you had mules, trudging through the mesquite in the dawn. Bonnie's shoes are useless at first, then lost entirely. You pick her up and carry her. You are sorry you asked her to come along. Sorry for her and sorry for yourself. Trudging on into the daylight, knowing the whole territory is about to be after you. None of it's any good. Not the being sorry, not the trudging.

"Finally, a posse of about thirty-seven men had all three of us in a net and we begin to shoot," says Fults. "We didn't intend to give up right then."

Maybe it is and maybe it isn't thirty-seven men, but it is as many towns-folk as Chief Drennan of Mabank can round up. And they've got the three of you pretty well bottled up. You're lying together along the banks of a ditch or creek, near a country store where you tried to sneak over and get another vehicle but were spotted.

"Well, I got shot twice right quick, through the ditch, through this arm and got shot in the leg," Fults says.

It's looking like it's over, and by all rights it is.

But then suddenly you say, "I'm going to try to make it," and you jump up, leaving Bonnie and Ralph behind. You make a crazy mad dash right be-tween two armed men and off into the mesquite and creek bottom. And damned if you don't make it.

"He jump up and run right through 'em," Fults says. "But both of 'em was loading, they was behind trees, you know. Both of 'em told me they was loading the gun when he went through."

You're gone. You sure hope Bonnie understands.

❋

I believe to my soul
Somebody been riding my mule
Cause every time I want to ride
She acts such a doggone fool

You may call yourself the meanest gal in town
You may call yourself the meanest gal in town
Let me tell you baby
I'm going to turn your damper down.

—JIMMIE RODGERS

Did he really just run off and leave her in a ditch, surrounded by armed men? Did he say something like "I'm going for a car, I'll bust back down here and get us all out of this mess"? Did he really make it through there alive? Does she care?

Her clothes are torn. Her shoes are gone. Her body is scratched from the mesquite and bruised from that muleback trotting—and don't even mention that wet-mule smell. Next to her in the ditch Ralph is bleeding from his shoulder and his leg. He's in rough shape, poor thing, and wants her to help him load his gun, since one of his arms is no good. Tells her how to do it.

It doesn't come easy. Her hands are shaking from cold and hunger. That, plus the fact that she never trusted guns. Her cousin Bess says that their grandfather used to keep a big old revolver under his pillow and that when the two of them used to make the beds at their grandparents' house Bonnie would never willingly move the gun.

"Once or twice Bonnie touched it without knowing it was there, and such screaming I never heard," Bess says. "I used to remember those days after Bonnie went away with Clyde, and wonder how she ever learned to handle guns, load for him, even fire them herself, for I never saw anyone a bigger coward about them than she was when we were kids."

She may be scared, but she's nothing if not a quick learner, and Fults talks her through it. Put the bullets into the clip, the clip into the gun. That's right. He takes the pistol in his good hand and turns to her.

"If you don't give up, they gonna kill you," he says. "Just tell 'em you don't know where I went, you see."

She agrees. It's the only way.

"I'll hold my fire and you give up," says Fults. She goes.

The laws are all around Bonnie immediately, surprised to find that one of the desperadoes is a woman. A tiny young thing, a girl really, soaked and miserable looking. She's not carrying any weapon, but they arrest her and she gives the story just like Fults suggested. She doesn't know where he is, she didn't know what kind of boys they were when she got in the car, she's scared, she's sorry, she just wants to go home. The third one? She doesn't know who he was or where he is.

Fults, who had moved off a little bit before she went up over the ditch, can hear her getting questioned. "She tol' them that," he says. But he's listening a little too carefully to Bonnie and not paying enough attention to slipping away from the posse. Or his leg is so bad off he can't get far anyway.

"I let a guy slip up on me while I was listening to the conversation," he says.

"I think I got him," someone in the posse yells.

It's no use: Fults is surrounded. "I let another dude slip up behind me with a sawed-off shotgun," he says. "So they got me out and took me to jail."

So much for Clyde riding back to the rescue.

The little calaboose at Kemp is just a cube of bricks behind the block or so of commercial buildings that make up the downtown. It's a single room, about twelve by twelve feet, and open to the air through two small barred windows and a metal gate. There's nothing comfortable about it, but by the time Bonnie and Fults find themselves locked in for the night, in all likelihood she's just glad to be anywhere other than in that ditch with bullets flying.

The two of them are in there wondering what's next. Fults isn't going to die from his wounds at least, though they haven't patched him up a bit. She and Fults are wondering, too, about whether Clyde made it away. There's not much chance he'll be coming by to bust them out; that much is clear from the armed guard keeping watch outside. Them and the gawkers who start showing up as soon as it's light enough to see in.

"I remember my momma going down there to look," says a townswoman named Abbie Lou Williams. "Bonnie got so mad she spit in my mother's eye. That really tickled my father as no one ever had the nerve to stand up to my mother before."

Yeah, she's glum and angry and full of vinegar. Not to mention embarrassed and anxious, not the least about what her own mother will say.

Fults tells her not to worry. The laws haven't anything on her, and he'll back her up on the story that she had no idea what she was getting into. Hell, it's almost true, isn't it? He gives her a piece of advice, too, in case she should ever be tempted to try her luck again on the road with the likes of him and Clyde.

"I told Bonnie you better stay out of that car," he says. "Told her don't get in that car with nobody as hot as we are."

❊

It's a bad week that's looking worse all the time. First Fults gets himself shot, and he and Bonnie get arrested, and you barely escape with your life. That's Tuesday night, April 19. A couple of stolen cars later, and you're out of Kemp and on to the hideout at Lake Dallas. There you hook up with the members of the gang who were supposed to have already raided the town of Celina for guns, only to find they haven't gotten around to it yet.

So you get in on the job, which goes only marginally better than the fiasco in Mabank. Around midnight on Wednesday, you and a couple of pals pistol-whip the Celina night watchman from behind, *wham,* giving him a nasty wound to the temple. But what do you care? You take his two dollars and his two pistols and drag him over to the train tracks and lock him in a boxcar. Next it's the mayor of Celina's turn: he gets a pistol stuck in his ribs as he's coming out of town hall after a late night at work. He, too, gets relieved of his cash—fourteen dollars—and goes in the boxcar. Two more citizens are locked in there, too, before you and the boys get down to the real business of the evening: breaking in through the back door of the hardware store.

Which turns out to be a drugstore because somebody miscounted the number of storefronts when you all went around back. A total waste of time, not mention risk. Bandages? What do we want with stinkin' bandages? You don't even touch anything in the store. The next door down proves to be the one you're looking for, and you manage to get a number of decent shot-guns and some shells. Before you can really clean the place out, however, *CLANG CLANG CLANG,* the damn town fire alarm starts going off just like in Mabank. Someone saw you.

The only thing that really goes right about the raid in Celina is you're able to make a clean getaway. Not that the laws don't see you and jump into their own car to give chase. They do. But unfortunately for them, you boys thought to reach in and take the sheriff's keys out of his ignition.

Ha! That's good for a laugh, at least. Back to the shack with the guns you go, laughing together at the thought of those cops' faces when they realized they weren't going anywhere in their police car tonight. Sitting in their car with no keys, watching your coupe disappear down the road. Dumb old cops should learn how to hot-wire.

Maybe it's all going to work out after all, even without Fults or Hamilton, and, hell, you'll bust Fults out that old county jail one of these days anyway.

Not as soon as you think, though, because the next day, when you're out at the hideout testing out the new guns, who should roll up but the stinking laws. What's with your luck these days, anyway? Your own at least holds enough that, as usual, you manage to slip into the thicket and away without getting arrested. The cops get Jack Hammett and Fuzzy Fezzel, though, and within days they also have Alsup and Hunter locked up.

As for the guns and whatever is left of your money from the big bank job with Hamilton and Fults, which isn't much at this point, that's all gone.

One week. Only last Sunday you were sending Bonnie into Eastham to tell Scalley that the big plan is set to go, and now here you have pretty much the whole gang in jail, and Bonnie, too. You got no money, no guns, no cars, no girl. Things have to get better. Right?

❈

Fults can't believe what he sees. After one night in the little calaboose at Kemp, he and Bonnie were transferred to the county jail at Kaufman and put in separate cells. Now he's been transferred again, this time to the Collin County jail, in McKinney, where a couple of the boys from the gang are being held after the raid on the hideout on suspicion of being involved in the Celina burglaries. That's disconcerting enough, but what really surprises him is seeing the mailman from Electra there to identify him as his kidnapper. It's Owens, the man whose car he burned up!

"Yeah, that's the guy," Owens says when they bring him in to look at Fults. The defrauding mailman doesn't crack a smile or anything, even though his local paper has stated that "no trace of the Owens car has been reported to officers here."

"Well, I didn't tell them about burning up the car," says Fults. "But he's the first one that identified me. Down there that time when they bring the chief of police down."

That's right, he's there too, big Chief James T. Taylor. After no one in Celina could identify the shiny lawman's pistol that turned up with the suspects, a sharp detective remembered reading about Taylor's little adventure the week before and called him up to see if he might want to come down and identify his gun. So here he is, pointing the finger at Fults.

There's no sense fighting it, and when the time comes Fults tells the district attorney he's ready to make a deal.

"Will you take fifteen years?" the prosecutor wants to know.

"I said, 'Yeah, if you'll turn Bonnie loose, sir,'" says Fults. "I did. I took fifteen years for Bonnie. I said Bonnie didn't know what we was gonna do, she was virtually kidnapped. But I did take fifteen years to make that deal with the district attorney to get her turned loose."

"I was too big to be an outlaw," he says another time, referring to how Clyde always slipped away and he always seemed to get caught.

"I should have stayed at home."

❀

"Only a mother can appreciate my feelings when I walked into that Kaufman jail and saw Bonnie behind the bars," says Emma Parker. "Death would have been much easier."

She doesn't bail her daughter out. She just doesn't have the money, though she could probably scrape it together by borrowing all over, and maybe selling some things. Also, the nice woman who runs the jail, Mrs. Adams, calls her over and gives her a little advice.

"Don't do it, Mrs. Parker," she says. "When the grand jury meets in June they'll give her a no-bill. Let her alone. She's not suffering, and time to think matters over may mean all the difference in the world."

❀

The jail is not so bad, really, except for the crazy woman in the cell next door. The keepers—a husband and wife—treat Bonnie nice, let her sit outside once in a while. She gets visitors now and then. Her mama comes, of course, though that was hard at first. She can't help but cry to see her mama so sad; makes her so ashamed. Makes them both ashamed; makes them both cry. But it gets easier.

Buck's wife, Blanche, comes down, too, along with Clyde's little brother, L.C. They are nice to do that, and they give her the news that Clyde's okay. She's glad of that, even if she's not quite sure how she feels about him taking off and leaving her and Ralph to their fate. Maybe he was really planning on coming back and rescuing them, but there's no arguing that in the end he didn't. Still, she can't deny that her heart is sure glad he's not killed somewhere. Or even caught.

Blanche and L.C. tell her not to worry, that the laws have nothing on her. It's not even worth trying to bust her out, which Clyde would do if she wants. Better to get out clean since they have no case. Everyone says that: they got nothing on her. Wouldn't it be nice, then, if they would let her out. They won't tell her how long she'll be in for, and though the police are always friendly and polite, they just won't take "I don't know" for an answer. It's always the same with the damn *they*!

"Bonnie was in there for a month or two before they turned her loose," says Floyd Hamilton. "They was trying to make her tell who the other people were and she wouldn't do it."

Darn right she won't do it. So days go by, and weeks go by. It's no fun, but it's not so bad either. So much time on her hands, maybe she'll finally write something! This is not how she expected to get to being a writer, she has to say, but she'll take it. She even has an idea.

It's the story of a country girl who moves to the city and falls in love with a bandit, a gangster really. She learns the talk and the walk, and they get into a scrape, you see, in a robbery that goes bad, and she ends up taking the fall for him. And now she's in prison, telling her sorry tale in gangster slang to a fellow inmate. Only it's not going to be a story, Bonnie thinks, but a poem. Or a ballad, like Jimmie Rodgers might sing. She calls it "The Story of Suicide Sal," and it ends with a murder:

> I took the rap like good people,
> And never one squawk did I make.
> Jack dropped himself on the promise
> That we make a sensational break.
>
> Well to shorten a sad lengthy story,
> Five years had gone over my head
> Without even so much as a letter—
> At first I thought he was dead.
>
> But not long ago I discovered
> From a gal in the joint named Lyle,
> That Jack and his moll had got over
> And were living in true gangsters style.
>
> If he had returned to me some time,
> Though he hadn't a cent to give,
> I'd forget all this hell that he's caused me,
> And love him as long as I live.
>
> But there's no chance of his ever coming,
> For he and his moll have no fears

But that I will die in this prison,
Or flatten this fifty years.

Tomorrow I'll be out on the outside
And I'll drop myself on it today:
I'll bump 'em if they give me the hot squat
On this island out here in the bay . . .

The iron doors swung wide next morning
For a gruesome woman of waste
Who at last had a chance to fix it.
Murder showed in her cynical face.

Not long ago I read in the paper
That a gal on the East Side got hot,
And when the smoke finally retreated,
Two of gangdom were found on the spot.

It related the colorful story
Of a jilted gangster gal.
Two days later, a sub-gun ended
The story of "Suicide Sal."

Sal gets her revenge. But it's just a story, a work of fiction. Bonnie, the real Bonnie Parker, sitting in her cell listening to the lunatic lady in the next cage over, wonders what she'll do when she gets out if Clyde comes around. What will she do if he comes by, flashes that dimple and those teeth, and asks her to get "in that car," as Fults put it.

Or maybe Bonnie does know exactly what she'll do if Clyde opens that car door.

CHAPTER 15

THE BEGINNING
OF THE ROAD

Guitar strings? What in the world? It's the middle of the night.

Tell them to go on their way, for goodness sake, Madora Bucher is thinking. Her husband, John, is too friendly. What's that you say you want? he's calling down from the living quarters above their store. You want guitar strings?

The two boys below in the street shout up, Yes, that's right, and call him by name. They've got a Ford parked in front of the store. They seem to know Bucher, though of course the sign in front of the combination garage, gas station, and jewelry store says his name.

Yes, Mr. Bucher, sorry to bother you and all, we're the boys who were in earlier looking at knives with you, remember? There's a dance down in town and the guitar player has busted a string, you see, and so we're hoping you can just open up long enough so we can get a replacement. For the guitar player, you know—otherwise the party will have to stop, and we're real sorry to bother you so late.

It's the middle of the night, right around midnight. It's well past time for a sixty-two-year-old man and his fifty-one-year-old wife to be asleep. John and Madora Bucher have been in business for thirty years or more, but they just recently moved their shop from downtown out here to the edge of Hillsboro so that they can fix cars and sell gas in addition to Bucher's regular career as a jeweler and an optician. Cars, they think, are the business of the future, and the move was a success. There were costs involved in relocating the shop out to where the cars go by, however, and he and Mrs. Bucher aren't surviving these recent hard times by turning away sales.

Their five children are almost grown, but four of them still live at home. Guitar strings at midnight? A sale is a sale.

So Bucher says all right, wait a minute. But just to be safe, he tucks his old Colt .45 pistol into his belt. Madora hears him heading down the stairs to turn on the lights and open the store.

Moments pass. Maybe she hears their muffled talking through the floorboards, him going to the back of the store, getting the guitar string. Hears them clumping back to the cash register. Now she clearly hears her husband calling up to her to come on downstairs. We need you down here, he says. Madora, come and open up the safe. These boys only have a ten-dollar bill.

Oh, for goodness sake, a ten-dollar bill for a twenty-cent purchase. But she gets out of bed and heads down to the shop and opens the safe. She's the one who can remember the combination. She's making the change, turning around—

BLAM!

She sees her husband stagger. Just a single shot that rips through the old man's heart and out his back. Blood pouring out of her sweet old man. He's on the floor, and beside him his old gun, fallen either from his hand or from his belt before he even got a chance to lift it.

These horrible boys! In a fury she reaches for the gun herself now, but one of them gets to her, holds her, tells her to put the gun on the counter, which she does. And there's her darling John, with his mustache and his droopy ears, and his kind eyes, lying there on the shop floor, not moving, his life draining away.

Why?

The horrible boy steps over him to the safe, scoops out the money—they could have had the money—and the diamonds—they could have had the diamonds! And then steps over poor John again and they let go of her and run out the door to the car idling there in the street.

He's dead already. Madora knows it. Her John is gone.

❀

From where you sit behind the wheel of an idling Ford V-8 you hear it: BLAM. It's not a sound you were hoping to hear, because absolutely no good can come of it.

From the front of the store come running what remains of your big Eastham raid gang, Ted Rogers and a kid named Johnny. They've got a pocket full of diamond rings and about fifty bucks, which is good, but they're agitated as hell.

The old man pulled a gun, they tell you as soon as they jump in the car. I had to shoot him, I had to, says Ted. They're pretty near certain he's dead. And the old lady saw us too, they say. They're shook up all right, and you're thinking to yourself, Well, that's it, then, and you floor it out of town.

At least, that's one version of the story of how John Bucher died. You tell your sister Nell that you didn't stick around once you heard the gun. She finds you hiding behind the Barrow gas station on the Eagle Ford Road the day after the killing and grills you about whether you were involved.

"No, Sis, good God, no! I told those dumb eggs not to use any gunplay—and I beat it the minute I heard the bullets popping."

It's not exactly the statement of complete innocence she's looking for.

"Listen, Sis, don't start bawling me out," you say. You try to explain that you didn't even go into the store because the Buchers would know you. You used to pal around with one of their kids. So you were just waiting in the car, and you warned the other two not to shoot the place up: "I told them two or three times to be careful about any gunplay." Nell's still not impressed.

"I don't know how the shooting started," you say at last. "I just heard somebody scream, and guns popping, and I stepped on the gas and beat it. I don't know how they got away and I don't care."

Driving off in the getaway car is hardly heroic, but it's what you tell your sister the day after the crime. What you tell Floyd Hamilton somewhat later is that the shooting was started by someone inside the store.

"Clyde told me when he went in there and robbed the people—he and these other two fellows—that the man was standing in front of his safe and there was a trap door open to the upstairs. The man actually lived upstairs with his family and they could look down, right down on the safe and the cash register," says Hamilton. "And he said when they was robbing them, a shot rang out. And when this shooting started they run and shot back. And he told me he didn't think he shot the man. He thinks somebody else did."

You tell Floyd the whole thing might have been a trap laid by the Bucher boy you used to run around with. "Clyde tol' me that it was a possibility that this boy set his daddy up in order to kill him and throw the blame on somebody else," he says.

"I got an idea that he figured that if something happened to his daddy that he was the only one that had any brains and he would be the one that inherited everything or take charge of it," you tell Floyd. "I don't think we hit him, we just shot back to stop the shooting and run."

A bit far-fetched, sure, especially since all the newspaper reports only talk of one bullet fired and found. Still, the possibility of some inside involvement might help explain why, of all the businesses in Texas, you chose to rob one where the people know you. For his part, Floyd's inclined to believe you, but for other reasons.

"See Clyde, during all his career and places where they had robbed people, he always admitted he did the killing, or if it was a killing that happened or anything like that, he would tell details." Floyd doesn't always paint things in the best light for you, seeing as he's usually looking out for the reputation of his little brother, Raymond. But he does say your versions of events usually match up pretty well with what he knows for himself, or hears from others in the small, rough world you both belong to.

"So I'm quite sure he would have admitted that down there as quick as he admitted anything else," he says. "I kind of think he was right."

Nell believes the version you told her for pretty much the same reasons. "I'm not excusing Clyde. I'm just telling," she says. "We believed Clyde when he said he didn't do a certain robbery or murder, because he admitted so many crimes to us, often crimes that the law knew nothing about. Why should he lie to us? What was one robbery more or less during a spring and summer that was filled, not only with robberies, but murders?"

The funny part about Floyd's opinion on all this is that when Mrs. Bucher goes with the police to look at pictures of likely suspects, she doesn't pick you or either of the guys who were with you. (That sure suggests you didn't go in the building.) Who she picks is Floyd's little brother, Raymond, and he wasn't even in the state of Texas that night! Some say Raymond Hamilton looks a bit like Ted Rogers—the actual killer that night—and maybe he does. It shows what good eyewitnesses are: Ray is in Michigan, hauling water at the construction site where his dad works.

Better Ray than you, you guess, but there's no denying that the police are on to your crowd. On May 7, a week after the killing, the police ask Mrs. Bucher to come down to Dallas to look at another suspect. They caught him the night before, shot and wounded him, in fact, in a scrape up in the Oak Cliff neighborhood of Dallas. It's Billie Jean's husband, Fred Mace, Bonnie's brother-in-law. Police have been after old Fred a long time for a string of things, but this time Mrs. Bucher gets it right and tells the laws that Fred is too tall to be one of the killers.

It's just a matter of time before your name gets attached to it. Sure enough, the sheriff of Hill County puts out a poster offering a $250 reward with your picture on it. And there's good old Frenchy Clause listed right next to you. Poor old Frenchy, rather, since he had about as much to do with this murder as the last one they tried to charge the two of you with. Seems your pictures have been picked out of the police files by the victims of a couple of small-time robberies and the laws are figuring, Well, it almost worked last time, so let's try to get those two for murder again.

They don't have a case against Frenchy. Too bad you can't say the same thing for yourself. You know as well as anyone that it doesn't much matter whether you did or didn't pull any triggers, did or didn't get out of the car. You were at the scene of the crime this time. They're getting closer. There's no turning in now, or turning back either.

Not that you were ever thinking of doing that anyway. These days you don't go anywhere without a gun.

❈

Ray Hamilton doesn't think it's all that funny that the police are looking to question him about the murder of some old man in Hillsboro. He shows up in Dallas just a few days after the murder, hoping that in the months he's been gone the cops might have forgotten about those couple of burglaries and what all they had him down as a suspect for. The money from the big bank job with Clyde and Ralph is long gone. Working construction in Bay City with his old man is old news. He figures he can slip back into the Big D and carry on having fun with his old pals.

Lucky for him, Clyde's already warned Ray's big brother about the situation.

"Clyde just come to the door after he got wanted by the police," says Floyd. "Well, he come up, knock on the back door, and he's carrying his sawed-off shotgun—he usually carried this 16-gauge Browning automatic shotgun with a sawed-off barrel and stock. And he come ask me about Raymond. That's when I first heard about him being wanted by the police and that is for murder. And Raymond being wanted for murder."

There's nothing the younger Hamilton can really do about it, except avoid being caught.

"Raymond had been associating with Clyde, and the police knew he had been round with him," Floyd explains. "And Raymond come back down here visiting and we told him he was wanted for murder and so he didn't go back to work."

Seeing as Clyde's in the same situation, and seeing as it's not really anybody's fault that the old lady picked the wrong picture out of the lineup, Hamilton figures he and his old neighbor might as well lie low together. After all, he and Clyde have had some good and profitable adventures over the years.

"He went and looked Clyde up," says Floyd, "and they went pallin' together."

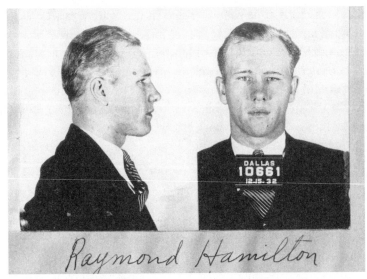

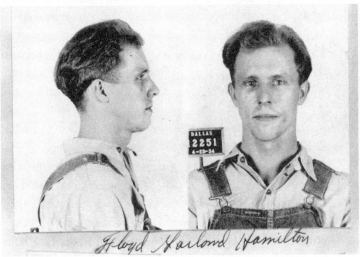

Clyde's pal and fellow bank robber Raymond Hamilton, top,
and his older brother, Floyd Hamilton, bottom. (*From the collections of the Texas/Dallas History and Archives Division, Dallas
Public Library.*)

For a while the two wanted men camp out in the open lands to the
south of the city. Both are kind of dandies, however, and they like their fancy
clothes more than life on the range. As soon as they can scrape together a
little cash, by the usual methods, they get themselves set up in a cottage in
Wichita Falls. Their plan is to use it as a base.

❋

"I'm through with him" is what Bonnie tells her mother as soon as she gets out of jail on June 17, 1932.

Just as everyone predicted, the grand jury no-billed her for lack of evidence (and thanks to Fults's plea deal) and let her go free. Emma's overjoyed to get her daughter back, naturally, and pretty much the first words out of her mouth are warnings about the danger of hooking up with that Clyde Barrow again.

Bonnie tells her not to worry. "I'm never going to have anything more to do with him," she says, and Emma believes her. Heck, maybe Bonnie even believes it herself.

Emma believes Bonnie again a few weeks later when she announces that she's at last found a job. It's another waitressing position. The only problem is, it's up in Wichita Falls, so she'll have to move there. The job must have opened up pretty quick, since Bonnie doesn't even have time to personally say good-bye to Emma, who only hears the news from her own mother when she gets home from work one afternoon. It's odd, certainly, but jobs are scarce and maybe there's a good explanation.

"You see, I wanted to believe her more than anything in the world," says Emma. "I discovered later that she was lying to me about everything."

❁

For a few weeks in Wichita Falls, it's like the life Bonnie always thought she'd have.

"Well, they wanted what anyone else—any other two people that were in love—wanted," says her little sister, Billie Jean. "They wanted to live right. They wanted to be married. Live right."

It's fun, living right for a while in the little cottage with Clyde and Ray. He and Clyde are like peas in a pod, about the same height, same weight, same taste for fancy clothes. Only Ray's blond hair isn't nearly as thick as the nice wavy black crop that grows on top of Clyde's cute little old head. No, Ray's hair is downright thin; he's going to be bald someday not too far off, bless his heart. Makes him look older than Clyde even though he's not.

Raymond's chatty and fun, always got a wisecrack and a good line. She likes him; he keeps them both laughing. But don't get any ideas about funny business, no matter what people may say now or write in the newspapers down the road—like "they are known to be rivals for the favors of Bonnie Parker, twenty-one-year-old bandit girl." Ray's always got his own girlfriends and wouldn't dare trying anything with her even if he didn't. Just ask him.

"Bonnie and Clyde are in love," he says. "She is jealous of him and he is jealous of her. Clyde doesn't 'gal around' any at all. Bonnie is the only girl he ever thinks about."

Raymond's correct about that: she's the only one for Clyde and aims to stay that way. (Though that awful old girlfriend Grace is in Wichita Falls, which Bonnie can't be too happy about.) Only a thoroughbred fool would risk getting Clyde mad, and though Raymond may not be as smart as he thinks he is, just like Fults says, he's not crazy.

Saying the little cottage in Wichita Falls is the life she imagined might be taking it a little far, given the nature of Clyde's and Ray's line of work and all. It's nervous, nervous all the time, of course, though the boys are pretty good about keeping their adventures out of town, so at least around Wichita Falls they figure they're not going to get recognized. Still, Bonnie is not inviting the neighbors over for iced tea or anything. Not inviting the other girls from the waitressing job she told her mother about, either. That is, of course, if she really has that job.

Once in a while Bonnie might tag along with Clyde and Ray, staying in the car while they stick up some out-of-the-way gas station. As Nell says, there are lots of crimes all over the place that summer, crimes which at the time they take place no one connects with Clyde or Ray, or Bonnie. But after the fact—after they are famous—everybody's certain every little job on the highway must have been theirs. The police think a couple of gas station jobs in Lufkin have the look of Clyde. Some say Clyde and Ray are the ones who on July 16 stick a gun in Roy Evans's face at the Palestine Ice Company and get away with almost a thousand bucks. A bank down near Houston says it was robbed by Ray and Clyde. The post office at Port Sullivan, Texas, thinks it must be Clyde and Ray who break in on the night of June 24 and steal four hundred blank money orders.

On the evening of July 29, Clyde and Ray definitely walk into the interurban station in Grand Prairie—the electric streetcar line runs right through that town on its way from Dallas to Fort Worth. Earlier in the day they hid their car in the town cemetery and changed over to a nice new Chevy they found parked outside a school. The station is empty when they enter, just the way they want it. The ticket agent puts up no resistance when he looks up from his post to see a gun barrel pointing straight at him, just like they hope he will. It all goes off without a hitch, in fact, except for the fact that there's only $12.75 in the till.

Mostly Bonnie stays behind, having had enough excitement in Kaufman. Or, if the plans are for a job near Dallas, Clyde might drop her at the filling station to visit with Cumie, Blanche, and Marie. That's where she is a few afternoons after the interurban robbery, on August 1, when Clyde, Ray, and a kid going by the name Everett Milligan* knock over the Neuhoff Brothers Packing Company to the tune of about $440. The drill is pretty much the same as ever: they steal a car to use for the job and plant their getaway car in an innocuous spot. Then they drive to the plant and the kid keeps the car idling while Clyde and Ray, "roughly dressed," barge into the company office.

"I was at the front of the office and Mr. Henry and Mr. Joe were at the back," says Elsie Wullschleger. She's Henry and Joe Neuhoff's office assistant. "Two men came in and I asked them what they wanted. They didn't pay any attention to me, but kept on going, and then I saw guns in their hands. I called Mr. Henry and he and Mr. Joe turned around and saw the bandits."

"Where's the money," Clyde says as if he knows for certain that Monday is payday at the company. He rips the telephone out of the wall.

"There it is," says Henry Neuhoff, pointing back to Elsie Wullschleger's desk. She's been carefully counting out the week's payroll and putting it into envelopes for the employees.

"The bandits stood there and we asked if they wanted us to hold up our hands," says Joe Neuhoff, "and they said no but for us not to move. Hamilton then put the gun in his shirt and went in to Miss Elsie's desk and got the money, putting it in a paper bag he had with him."

Then Raymond goes and drops the bag and the coins start rolling around on the floor. He bends over to start picking it up and Clyde yells at him to forget the coins, just leave the stinking change behind and let's get going.

"Where's the other phone?" they demand, and one of the Neuhoffs points. That they seem to know about the number of phones, witnesses will tell police, indicates that there may have been some inside information on the job, maybe from an employee. Like the first phone, this one is ripped from the wall.

Clyde and Ray now put their backs together, and with one of them keeping his pistol pointed at the three in the office and the other keeping an eye out on the lot outside, they turtle back through the office door, turning at the last second to leap from the loading dock down to the waiting car.

"I went outside as they were leaving and got their license number," says Joe Neuhoff, "but I got back inside when one of them looked back and I saw his pistol."

Back at the Barrow gas station, Bonnie's listening to the radio. Henry's always got that radio tuned in for news flashes, so it's no imposition.

"Listen over the radio, honey, and see if we make our getaway," Clyde had told her when they dropped her off.

---

* An alias: his real name was Ross Dyer.

"Don't say things like that," she'd yelled back. "It's a jinx."

Only this time it isn't a jinx, and sure enough she hears a police bulletin announcing that the Neuhoff plant has been robbed. Not long after that she hears what she's really listening for: a car pulling up fast from the Eagle Ford Road. His voice—C'mon, Bonnie, let's be going. Now!—and she piles in. It wasn't such a clean getaway from Neuhoff to the filling station, he tells her. They were chased for a couple of blocks by a pair of cops who thought they were just chasing a pair of speeders. With Clyde at the wheel, naturally, the boys got away.

Still, it's best they all lie real low for a while. Clyde and Ray have pulled too many jobs in a row; they're getting too hot. One good thing about these hard times is there are abandoned farmhouses pretty much everywhere you want to look, and there's one out by Grand Prairie that will be good for a couple of days. A couple of days go by, though, and it's not exactly feeling cooled off all that much in Texas. Not enough anyway that Clyde and Ray want to go back to the cottage in Wichita Falls, and they sure can't go back to Dallas. They had best be going on up to Oklahoma, where neither of them is wanted for anything. He'll be gone just for a while, Clyde tells Bonnie, until things cool down a bit more.

She can go along, sure, but won't she be happier at her mom's? She can visit some, and see Billie's baby. Get some rest. Get cleaned up. It's better. He drops her off near where her mama works, and then heads north in a car stolen that morning in Corsicana. Emma Parker can't get out of work early, however, so Bonnie waits for her at her house.

"I didn't mention Clyde to her until late that night when we were sitting on the porch alone," says Emma. "I asked her then if she'd seen him."

"You know I wouldn't have anything to do with him, Mama," Bonnie says. Says it flat out, just like that, without a hint of anything unusual. "Not after the trouble I got into down in Kaufman. No, I haven't seen him and I don't want to see him."

Emma believes her daughter again. Or doesn't push it. Mother and daughter sit there on the porch in the dark, listening to the sounds of the city, and the insects, and thinking their own thoughts between making small talk. Up in Atoka County, Oklahoma, meanwhile, Clyde and Raymond and Everett Milligan are stopping in at a little outdoor country dance in the rock-crushing and lumber crossroads called Stringtown.

❊

"We were just big old boys . . . schoolboys," says Duke Ellis. Ellis and a couple of his friends from high school have a four-piece string band that plays out around Atoka County whenever their parents will let them, which is more and more now that they're actually getting paid a little bit for their time.

"A dollar was as big as a wagon wheel," Duke says.

Tonight is actually the band's second appearance at the open-air dance pavilion in Stringtown, and the crowd is bigger than last week's, thanks to some advertising and all the fun folks had last Saturday. "Pavilion" might be putting a bit of a bigger hat on the outfit than it really deserves. "They had an outside dance platform about thirty to forty feet square with a banister around it and a small gate at one end for the dancers to enter," Duke says. "There was a canopy or pavilion-type cover on the back side for the band to sit."

So it's not exactly a grand ballroom, but no one really cares. It's a perfect summer evening, a cooling-off Friday night with lightning bugs flickering and just the tiniest crescent of the month's moon beginning to show. Hardworking folks from the rock-crushing plant and the lumber mill are stopping by to enjoy life a bit. Maybe some farmers come in from their fields, bringing their daughters even. For reasons no one can remember, only two members of Duke's band can make it; Duke himself on guitar and his buddy Ed Mills on the fiddle are the evening's entertainment. No matter: they're keeping the crowd happy, which is keeping the organizer happy.

"It was a typical dance of the time," says Duke. "We would play awhile and the man in charge would say, 'All right boys, up to the bar' and everyone who wanted to dance would go up to the bar and pay a dime for the privilege."

On the stage, Duke and Ed are having a good old time, playing their songs and watching the pretty girls dancing down below with their fellas. Folks being folks. "One man had a brand-new white hat of which he was very proud," says Duke. "After he paid, each time he would put the hat near us where it would not get soiled or dirty."

"It was great fun and it was especially nice to get paid for doing something you really enjoyed doing," he says. "We had a big bunch there. We were having a good time."

❉

You pull up at around nine-thirty and park behind where the band is playing. Milligan says he wants to stop and go have a dance or two. After some talk, you and Raymond don't see why not. The three of you have been on the road pretty much all day now, up from Corsicana, where you stole the car, and Dallas, where you dropped off Bonnie. You're tired, and maybe a dance will do you good. What's more, Milligan and Raymond have been sipping a little from a jar. Or if they haven't got a jar yet, they plan to find one there in the parking lot, which should be easy enough, never mind prohibition. It's Oklahoma, after all.

"Akota County was full of honky-tonks and there was plenty of wildcat whiskey and Choctaw beer during those days," says Ted Maxwell, whose father is the sheriff. "Of course they were drinking," says Duke Ellis, who sees you pull up and park back there. "It seems everyone had a drink at that time . . . moonshine."

You might even have a sip yourself, though that's not normally like you. In fact, Ray, who's there with you, says, "I never saw him take a drink of whiskey in my life. He's got his mind on his business. You know what that is." But Ray might just be exaggerating; you're known to have an occasional sip when you're feeling safe—just not much and not often.

"Clyde was pretty smart," says Bonnie's sister, Billie Jean. "He figured if he drank he wouldn't stay alive."

At any rate, it feels real good to be across the line, out of Texas and into Oklahoma. It's pleasant enough to just be sitting in the car hearing the music; too bad you don't have your saxophone. Ha! You could join in like you used to at your uncle's down in Corsicana, though of course this country string band stuff isn't really your kind of music. You're a horn player, after all, a city man who could show these hicks a thing or two. "Melancholy Baby" is your favorite song.

> Come sweetheart mine
> Don't sit and pine
> Tell me of the cares that make you feel so blue
> What have I done
> Answer me, hon . . .

There's nothing wrong with fiddles and guitars, mind you. The two kids aren't bad at all, and as long as only one of you goes out to dance at a time, what can go wrong? That's the plan: two of you stay in the car and make sure it doesn't get parked in by other cars, while the third goes and puts a dime down and has a dance with some local honey. It's sure nice to have dimes. You all take a turn.

"Clyde Barrow and Ray Hamilton danced a little," says Duke, who notices from his perch up on the bandstand that the strangers are only coming out one at a time. "I don't recall any misconduct by either. It was my impression both had been drinking, but not much, and I did not see them get out of line."

Milligan stays out on the dance floor most of the time, which is no surprise, really, since he's the one of the three of you not wanted for murder. You don't care. You and Ray are happy enough to stand around by the car and listen to others having fun. The only problem is, you have to keep moving that car around as the crowd grows, and this eventually catches the eye of Sheriff Maxwell.

He's sitting across the way with his thirty-year-old undersheriff, Gene Moore. They are in Moore's brand-new Chevrolet, and according to another deputy, Oscar Folsom, they aren't expecting any trouble. They partly came up from the county seat at Atoka to check in on the dance at Stringtown just to get a ride in Moore's new machine.

"Gene will go with me," the sheriff says by way of telling Folsom to stay behind and mind things down in Atoka. "I want to ride in his new car, and haven't got to, so far."

It's a line that sticks in Folsom's head because it's one of those little decisions that changes everything. "If Gene Moore had not bought a new Chevrolet," he'll say later, "I might have been the one that was killed."

POW!

Sheriff Maxwell has barely gotten the words out of his mouth. He's walked up toward your car, seen you getting back in, seen a jar of whiskey, some say. He says, "Consider yourselves under arrest." Or he says, "Drop it," depending on who is telling the story. In either case, the words are lost in the roar.

POWPOWPOWPOW! POW! BLAM!

You're not listening and neither is Ray, though he'll always say for the rest of his life that he never shot anyone. Ray can say what he wants because Sheriff Maxwell is lying in the dirt with at least half a dozen bullet holes in him. What you say about it is "I don't know."

"You mean—you mean—you killed those men," Nell's going to ask you later, and you'll shake your head and say, "It's an even break whether I did it or Raymond. We were both shooting all the time."

"I didn't see the shooting start, but rushed to the side of the platform to see what was happening when it started," says Duke Ellis. "Maxwell was standing by the side of the car, and someone was shooting him with a pistol. They kept shooting until he fell, and it took him a long time to fall. I think he was shot seven times."

Get in the car! You're yelling and firing. Start the goddam car! Let's get out of here!

Almost unbelievably, Sheriff Maxwell, with seven bullets in him, isn't dead. He's bleeding bad there, crumpled up on the ground, but he gets his own gun out and starts firing at your car as it screeches out onto the highway.

He even hits a tire, or else you just lose control, because you're barely out of the parking area before one wheel is in the ditch and the car rolls.

Now here comes another cop. The young undersheriff, Gene Moore, has been sitting there in his brand-new car, bought to please and transport his wife and three young children. He didn't get out with Sheriff Maxwell to check out the strangers because the two lawmen had earlier apprehended a woman who they are pretty sure is an escaped convict. He's guarding her in the car, but when he hears the gunplay, he's out in a second and over to help his boss. He pulls his own weapon out, takes cover behind an old beat-down Model T Ford. He can see everything, sees you getting out of your overturned car, raises his gun. Takes aim.

Only you see him first, or Ray does.

BLAM! The sawed-off shotgun.

"He had his gun out and raised it when he was hit," says Duke. "I saw him fall, and was sure he was killed instantly."

Duke is right about that. Moore is dead pretty much when he hits the dirt. One blast, one spray of pellets, and Gene Moore is gone, though no one in his family knows it yet. Only he and the kid guitar player know it.

"I guess I was the last one to see Gene Moore alive," says Ellis.

❋

"They gunned my father down with a shotgun," says Russell Moore. He's one of three kids under the age of nine left behind. His grandpa had been rich, but lost it all in the stock market crash.

"My father had us to feed, so he became a deputy sheriff and was glad to have the job. I'm told he was easygoing and people liked him, and that's why they picked him."

It's too late for him now, boy, and you're real sorry about that. That lawman is dead in the dirt, all right, and you're trying to get that car out onto the road.

"My mother was still young and pretty when it happened, but she never married again," says the dead man's son. "She hasn't had a date. Oh, we used to tell her that maybe she . . . well, let's not talk about that now."

Damn right let's not talk about it—we're trying to get the hell out of here.

"The roughest thing for me was growing up without a father. My grandfather was helpful and understanding. But it isn't the same."

You're sorry, you really are. This isn't how you planned things. You weren't bothering no one, just having a sip and a dance like everybody else until that cop came up on you.

"The only material possessions I had of his were a hat, his gun belt, and a gold railroad watch," says Moore. "And a picture. He was a very tall man. They tell me I look a lot like him."

Look at it this way: What were you supposed to do? Stand there and get arrested and sent to the electric chair? It was him get killed or you, and this time it was him. Sorry it had to be some kid's pa and all, but that's how it is. Sorry, kid.

❋

It's like a nightmare up on the bandstand. Mayhem. People running, diving, getting under tables. Bullets are flying everywhere.

"For about five minutes there was a heavy gun battle between the law and desperadoes," says Duke. "People were running in every direction."

With the sheriff down and Gene Moore dead, just who these other laws are is anybody's guess. Duke says he saw the town marshal there and enough other lawmen that he wonders if they somehow knew Clyde and Ray were around. With Clyde firing off his automatic weapons—*rata rata rata rata*— while Ray collects up what he can from the upturned car, it just sounds like a war zone.

"They scrambled out and began to shoot out all the lights," says Duke. "They may not have been trying to kill anyone, but may have been shooting high to keep us all scared, and believe me, we were."

Right about now, with the lightbulbs exploding and fire spitting out of the barrels of guns, Duke and his fellow musician Ed Mills figure out that high on the bandstand isn't where they want to be. Like everyone else, they take off running.

"Ed was in front of me and was holding his fiddle up high to protect it from damage by the weeds or brush. Every time we went out to play his dad would tell him to be sure and not let anything happen to that fiddle, and he wasn't if he could possibly help it."

They see one guy who tried to jump a barbed-wire fence and ended up astraddle it. They pass a ditch where the man with the new hat is lying low, regretting that he put his prized headgear on the stage after all.

"Oh, Lord," he says, "if I only had my hat I'd go home."

Duke says, "As much shooting as there was, I don't know how someone else escaped being shot. Everyone ran. I remember hearing people calling in the dark, trying to find someone, but afraid to come out in the open. It sounded like a herd of sheep that had been scattered were trying to get back together."

As quick as it starts, it's over. The shooting stops. People crawl out from wherever they are. Raymond and Clyde, having scooped up all the weapons and ammunition they can carry, have found a culvert running under the railroad tracks and have run through it into Stringtown proper, where they quickly find a car to steal and are gone. Milligan, the third in their party, who was on the dance floor when the shooting started, slips away in the fracas and catches a bus back to Texas.

In the sudden quiet, the dancers pull themselves off the barbed wire and out of the ditches and take stock of things.

"After the two men got away, we went to take care of the men who were shot," says Duke. "Charley Maxwell had been shot so many times, I didn't see how he could possibly live, but we put him on a bed and someone called an ambulance from McAlester. Before it arrived, his blood had soaked through the mattress, was dripping on the floor.

"After we had taken care of the sheriff, I told them I saw the other man fall and was pretty sure he was dead. We went out to where he was, and he was dead. We carried his body into the house."

❀

Dear Friends of Eugene's and ours: It is impossible for us to express in words our thanks for all of the kindness and sympathy that was bestowed upon us at the death of our father and husband. But by the help of our Lord and Savior in days to come we will have the opportunity to show our appreciation for all of your love.

May the Lord bless you all.

Mrs. E. C. Moore and children.

—*Indian Citizen-Democrat*

❀

Oh for God's sake the wheel is off and you're what, less than fifteen miles from Stringtown. What kind of car owner doesn't grease his bearings and check his lug nuts, for crying out loud. It's about as funny as a rubber crutch. Damn thing's so broken down you and Ray can't even get it off somewhere in a hollow to hide it. Now the first person who comes by will find the thing sitting here with three wheels and no doubt they'll know about the disaster that just was back there at the dance. Shit!

At least there's a house not far away, up there at the crossroads. A house nearby is not a given out here in wherever the hell, Oklahoma. Even better, they have a car, also not a given out here in wherever the hell, Oklahoma. It's a powder blue Model A, and your first choice is to steal it. Except the lights in the house are on, or they hear you and Ray coming up the drive, or the dog barks, or whatever . . . there's talking to be done.

You and Ray have worked out what you're going to say, which doesn't mean you don't have a weapon under your coat in case you need it. You just hope you won't need it. It's been enough already tonight. A woman and a man and their twenty-one-year-old son, whose name is Haskell, come to the door.

We've had an accident just down there, see, and my wife down there is hurt real bad, you say. She needs a doctor. Can we get a ride or borrow your car and take her to get some help? She's hurting.

"It was about twelve o'clock when they came to our house," says Mamie Redden. "No one drove the car but Haskell and myself. Mr. Redden did not drive and the Clyde outlaw put up such a pitiful story. We, of course, offered to help. Mr. Redden let the boy go with them."

Oh, God bless you, thank you, thank you, all that nonsense. You're a good liar when you need to be, even if you never were in the school plays. Full of charm, all right, but you're not even backed fully out of the driveway yet when one of you has a pistol at Haskell's ribs and is telling him to keep his mouth shut if he knows what's healthy for him. At the bottom of the driveway, you tell him to turn not as if the car will be pointing toward your wreck, but the other way. Mamie Redden sees it.

First she calls out to her son, but with that gun in his ribs he doesn't answer his ma.

"I thought you were going to get the woman that was hurt," she calls out to you now, with a hint of fear creeping into her voice.

"Oh," you say without missing a beat, as if you knew what she was going to ask. "We just decided to go get the doctor and take him over where she is."

She turns to her husband as their car—now your car, thank you—disappears down the road.

"Now they got my boy and the car," she says to him. "There is something has to be done."

The man is not as alarmed as his wife might hope. He thinks she's making a mountain out of it. As she says herself, she's "always quick to take a thought." Or maybe Mr. Redden just feels impotent, given that there isn't anything, really, he can do in the situation.

"You beat all I ever saw, you have always got something with everything," he says to her, thinking it might calm her down a bit. It doesn't.

"That caused me so much worry I could just feel every hair on my head standing straight up on my head," she says.

On down the road, the kid's pretty good to have driving. Turns out he's a mail carrier and knows every little back way and shortcut there is in the territory. Little bugger takes off on you, though, when his car runs out of gas near Sardis, Oklahoma. You and Ray are just in the process of flagging down and commandeering the vehicle of some traveling salesman when Haskell sees his chance and takes off into the thicket. He goes fast, considering he's got a pretty bad limp from a broken leg that wasn't set right when he was a kid. He's got a worse limp even than you with your chopped-off toe. You yell, Come on back, we won't hurt you or nothing. Ray yells too, but the kid stays out there.

Can you blame him, really? You let him be, and head south in the third car. He'll be okay, and he is, though the woman he later marries says that all his remaining days, until he dies at the age of ninety-one, "he never answered the door at night." Yeah, you guess not. But it's not like you hurt him or anything—just borrowed his car.

The laws are swarming all over the hills of Pushmataha County, with bloodhounds now, thinking they got you bottled up somewhere near where you left the first car. But all they're getting for their trouble is some exercise: you and Ray finally have a car that will go a few miles and you're driving it like hell all night long back to Texas. Back to Dallas, in fact, to get Bonnie.

❊

She's been glued to the radio since the first announcements of the killings up in Oklahoma. A suspect named Everett Milligan is under arrest up in McKinney, taken off a bus. The police think the other two are going to be caught any minute up in the Kiamichi Mountains. A deputy in Atoka thinks he wounded at least one of the bandits.

The endless afternoon becomes evening, and she announces to her mother that she has to get back to Wichita Falls. Has to work the next day, or something like that. Can she borrow the fare for the early bus?

Of course, of course. Emma doesn't make much at the factory all week, but of course. She digs in her purse and finds the change, gives it to Bonnie. It's about eight o'clock in the evening now.

"We were again sitting on the porch, saying very little," Emma says. "A car drove up in front of the house with a boy in it whom I had never seen before. Bonnie ran out and talked with him a few minutes. She came back and said she had a ride to Wichita and wouldn't wait till daylight. She gave me her bus fare, took her handbag, kissed me good-bye, and left."

So much for lying low in Oklahoma and letting Texas cool off. Before the week is out the police have you and Hamilton figured as the Stringtown dance hall killers. The trail of cars, and maybe some fingerprints, helped them a little. But the real break is that Everett Milligan spills the beans to a couple of detectives from Dallas who interrogate him on Sunday night in

Atoka. He's back there, having been arrested off the bus in McKinney, Texas, and taken directly back to Oklahoma for questioning. He's back there saying whatever he needs to, to make it clear that he was just dancing when all the hell broke loose. He's naming names.

"They gained definite information from the man held as to the identity of the two men in the shooting" is how the *Dallas Morning News* reports it on Tuesday. Yeah, you read that paper, or one of the other Dallas rags saying pretty much the same thing. It also says, "The two desperadoes have been sought by Dallas police for several months in connection with hijackings here and a filling station murder in Hillsboro several months ago." Those clues are not lost on you.

The Oklahoma papers don't mince words. "Positive identification of the two who escaped was furnished Sunday by Constable H. Hunt of Grandview, Texas," says the *Indian Citizen-Democrat*. "One of them is Clyde Barrow, wanted for murder of J. Bucher, a merchant of Hill County, Texas, and [the other is] Raymond Hamilton, pal of Barrow and wanted for highjacking and other crimes."

Milligan says something else interesting as well. He tells the Dallas lawmen that the reason he isn't afraid to identify who he was traveling with is that they can't harm him as long as he is "cooped up" in jail. That may be true, or it may be wishful thinking, but Milligan also says he's darned sure the police can chase you and Ray Hamilton all they want to but they will "never capture them alive."

He's got that right, and you say pretty much the same thing to Nell when she comes up to your car window at a secret roadside meeting outside of West Dallas a few days later. She doesn't recognize you at first with your bright red hair, which is thanks to Bonnie.

"I guess I used a little too much ammonia," Bonnie says from the passenger seat. "But he wanted it red, Nell, and he's got it red."

Nell's thinking Bonnie looks more tired and worn out than she's ever seen her. What starts your sister crying, though, is when you tell her that yes, you and Ray were the shooters up in Atoka. She's not laughing at your jokes about getting blond wigs and passing yourself off as Bonnie's sister anymore, or any of that. She's crying and telling you that it might still be possible for you to turn yourself in, cut some kind of deal.

You cut her off, tell her it's beyond that now.

"It's set now, sis, and you might as well stop making a row every time you see me. We'll have a little longer together—Bonnie and me," you say. Maybe you'll get a few years if you're lucky, or just a few months. Nell looks over at Bonnie, who nods and snuggles up when you say this.

Then when your luck runs out, suddenly it will all be over. "Out," you say, giving Nell your best devil-may-care smile. "Out—like Lottie's eye."

First, though, they gotta catch you. So much for Texas cooling off. So much for Oklahoma being cool. Or, maybe, for anywhere ever being cool again. But you have to go somewhere, because you can't stay here and you can't turn yourself in.

❀

She knows it as well as he does.

"Bonnie realized that Clyde faced the chair already," says Emma, "and she didn't believe he had a chance in the world to clear himself of it."

Still, she doesn't have to go with him, does she? Could say to him, You know, Clyde, loving a burglar and a bank robber is one thing, but a murderer . . . see, sugar . . . that's something else. But she doesn't say anything like that. Bonnie goes with Clyde, and no one who knows her says there is any hemming or hawing about it at all.

"After they killed this officer up in Oklahoma," says Ray's brother, Floyd, "they picked Bonnie up and she took them out to her aunt in New Mexico—the state of New Mexico."

We can all lie low at Aunt Millie's for a time, she says. It will be like those weeks in Wichita Falls. No one will know us, none of us are wanted there. Having her along will make the traveling a little easier, and not just because Clyde loves her company. Two men and a woman aren't what the laws all over Texas and Oklahoma are looking for, at least not yet.

Of course she goes.

"They wanted to be married," says Billie. "Live right. But, um . . ." Her voice trails off while she looks for words, looks for thoughts. "Seem like this happen—you know, everything happened just all at once. And they went—so far that—they were afraid that they couldn't—you know, give up . . ."

W. D. Jones, who's been hanging around more and more with Clyde's little brother, L.C., says it slightly differently. "Clyde just wanted to stay alive and free," he says, "and Bonnie just wanted to be with Clyde."

❀

Millie Stamp isn't all too pleased to see her niece Bonnie Parker appear out of nowhere in a fancy new car with her husband, James White, and his friend Jack Smith. Well, that's probably not entirely fair: she's happy enough to see the girl at first; it's been years since she's seen any of Emma's children, and Bonnie's all grown up and polite enough and all. Tiny thing, isn't she, though. Her husband is plenty friendly too.

It's just there's something off about them. Some sort of nervous energy that's just not really right. And the guns and all, lots of guns. It's a bit puzzling.

"I was irrigating my patch when I first saw them," says Bill Cobb, a melon farmer who is renting five acres from the Stamps. "At first I thought they were just schoolkids visiting, but they were out by my cantaloupes practicing shooting. I was upset when they started shooting at them and was headed down there to jump them out when the motor died on my irrigation pump. By the time I got it fixed they had stopped shooting."

Shooting off guns isn't in itself anything all that unusual in West Texas or southeast New Mexico, though there aren't a whole lot of people just wasting shells these days like they got money to burn. No, what really gets Aunt Millie to wondering, and worrying, are the bloody clothes Bonnie asks her to wash. Those and the stacks of cash she finds stuffed under the mattress. Blood and cash—along with the guns—are enough to get her, in a sly moment, to call Bill Cobb in for a look.

"There were solid packs of money," he says, "the most money I ever seen." He agrees with Aunt Millie that they better figure out a way to get word to the sheriff, and they make a plan for Millie to come on out to the melon patch Sunday morning and pretend to be helping him water the crop. From there, she can sneak away to the neighbor's and make a phone call.

The crazy thing is, just as she's heading out to the melon patch, Aunt Millie falls over and doesn't move. She's worked herself into such a nervous state thinking about the cash and the guns and the blood, and what she's got to do without the people sleeping in her house figuring it out, that she faints. From where he's standing down among the cantaloupes, it looks to Bill Cobb like maybe she's been shot or killed or something. It's not good, and he runs up to the door of the house only to discover she's just wilted.

"I threw some water on her face I got from the ditch," he says, and she revived. She's okay, she says. She still wants to do it, she says. Okay then, says Cobb, and they head down to the patch.

It all goes off without a hitch. Aunt Millie makes the call and gets back home without Bonnie, Clyde, or Raymond ever suspecting a thing. Heck, they're not even out of their pajamas.

The hitch comes after Deputy Sheriff Joe Johns arrives.

❋

He gets out of his car. Starts walking around the fancy new Ford V-8 coupe in the yard. Looking in the windows and such. Trunk is locked. He comes to the door and knocks. Knocks again. He knows they're in there, because

Millie Stamp told him to come on over while they're still in bed. Knocks
again, and finally a girl comes to the door. Must be the niece, he figures, a
little thing not five foot tall with blond hair.

He asks about the car, and she says it belongs to "a couple of boys up here."

"Well, tell 'em I'd like to check this car," he says.

"All right, I'll tell 'em," she says and goes back in. It'll take them a
minute to get dressed, she tells him.

He wanders back down toward the machine. Girl seems nice enough. He
turns his back to the house in order to look at the car, which is a mistake.

Next thing he hears is "Stick 'em up." Instead he moves his hand toward
his holster.

BLAM! Clyde squeezes the trigger. Dirt flies.

"I started to reach for my gun but a warning shot from a shotgun fired
into the ground made me change my mind and I put my hands up," says
Deputy Johns. It's a smart move.

❋

You keep a gun on the deputy sheriff while Raymond gets to work tearing
out the ignition wires on his car and on another vehicle nearby. Bonnie appears, and they start loading the cash and other belongings back into the
trunk of the coupe.

"We're ready to drive," you say when the trunk closes with a thud.
"Jump in."

The Ford coupe with the big V-8 is your favorite car, the one you always
try to steal if you can. It's got enough speed to outrun just about anything
else on the road and big steel doors that will stop most bullets. But it only
has a front seat, so you order Deputy Johns to get in the middle. Bonnie
will have to sit on Ray's lap. It's okay—she's light and Ray don't mind.

Now all of a sudden here's Aunt Millie come from somewhere begging
you and Ray not to hurt the damn deputy. No doubt she's the one who ratted on you.

"Shut up," you say, not losing your cool. You're not any happier about
the situation than the old lady is, and you're not in any mood to make nice
to her anymore, either. Damn if she doesn't keep it up, though. She's down
on her knees of all things, in the driveway dirt, begging you not to kill the
deputy.

"They told her shut up," says Deputy Johns, "but they did say they
wouldn't hurt me."

Johns is not all that sure he believes that promise, though, particularly
since you're barely out of Carlsbad before you and Raymond are so worked

up and angry at Aunt Millie for turning you in that one or the other of you suggests turning right around and going back and killing her dead.

"Oh, don't do that, fellows," Johns says, and of course you don't. Bonnie would never have it, for one, and neither you nor Ray are really that type. But you tell that deputy that you might just have to kill him if he doesn't behave. Tell him that more than once, too.

"I told him I guess it was his business," says Johns. That's a pretty cool-cucumber answer, you guess. Kind of pushing it under the circumstances, seeing as Raymond's got a gun sticking in his ribs and such. But you let it pass. You don't have any intention of killing him unless you have to; you just want to see if he'll scare. Just see how it feels to be on the other end of power for a change. He doesn't scare, though, and that's all right too.

Deputy Johns isn't the type to beg. "That feeling of thinking that you are near death is hard to describe," he says. "I wasn't nervous but kind of half resigned to it, but with the determination that I would take every chance offered to battle them should the time actually come for the end."

When you're not far out of Carlsbad, you plant the accelerator pedal on the floor and point the car for Texas. You're figuring, correctly, that the laws will be looking for you and Ray to head toward the Mexican border—or anywhere else other than Texas. So much for New Mexico being cool. Well, at least you love driving and you got a V-8 under the hood.

"We weaved in and out among traffic and along slippery, muddy roads at sixty and more miles per hour," says Johns, who has come to sound more scared of your driving than your gun. "After hitting a mud hole at one place which so covered the windshield with mud that the driver couldn't see through, he leaned out the door and drove at seventy to eighty miles an hour. How he drove like he did without wrecking the car I can't imagine."

Once or twice, in fact, you do come a bit too close to another car and rip the bumper off it, or dent a fender. Drivers are pulling over, getting run off the road, shouting and cursing. Folks are honking and yelling, but what do you care? Once you're past Odessa, Texas, and figure there's no way the laws are expecting you, you're just flying along in that V-8 toward San Antonio with Bonnie and Ray and the good deputy along for the ride.

At times you talk to Deputy Johns. You tell him you can't go back. "If we ever get caught, it's the electric chair for us," you say. Or Ray says. Somebody says it; Deputy Johns isn't sure who. And it doesn't matter since it's true for both of you. You even explain to him that you tried to go straight, but the laws in Dallas wouldn't let you. You were even trying to be good in New Mexico until the nosy deputy himself came along. Right, Bonnie? Ain't that right, Ray? Why'd he have to do that?

Mostly you just ignore the hostage. "I didn't question them much but did a lot of listening," Johns says. "Once they talked in a slang or language that wasn't familiar to me. Another time, sometime late at night, they drove up before an old abandoned place and slowed up. 'Here's the place,' Barrow said. What he meant I never did know and they drove off."

❀

In the middle of the night, in the middle of nowhere, somewhere past the Pecos River, out on the Edwards Plateau, Clyde finally pulls over and off and out of sight of the road. He's been driving hard for what, three or four hundred miles since Carlsbad now. He says he needs some sleep or he *will* crack the car up. He and Ray lie down and close their eyes, while Bonnie, no doubt with a handgun, keeps an eye on the tied-up deputy.

No one's had any food. Everyone is covered with dust. Legs are cramped, but sleep comes fast out on the flat highlands under the Texas stars.

In the quiet after the boys are asleep, Bonnie asks the deputy how he's liking his new life as a thief.

"I never had had much experience," he replies to the girl, whose name he thinks is Honey because that's all they call her. "This was the first experience I ever had."

"You've just had twenty-four hours of it now," she says back to him. "And we get three hundred and sixty-five days of it every year."

❀

Five-thirty in the morning. Fifteen miles outside of San Antonio. You pull over and tell Johns it's time to get out of the car. Good a spot as any, with no houses in sight.

You ask him if he has enough money to get back to New Mexico on, and he says yes. You ask if he's sure, because you can get him some if he needs it, but he says no, he's got money. You make as if to return his gun to him, but then pull it back as if having a second thought.

"No, Sheriff," you say, "this is a pretty good gun, I guess I'll have to keep it." Instead you give him your hand to shake.

"You sure have caused us a lot of trouble, Sheriff," you say. You tell him he better not leave this spot for at least an hour.

He shakes your hand and says that you "caused me just a little trouble, too, and not a little worry."

He's not all that bad for a sheriff. You get in the car with Bonnie and Ray, adjust your dark glasses, and give him a wave.

"You haven't been bothered much," you say to him, and drive off.

CHAPTER 16

MERRY CHRISTMAS AND A HAPPY NEW YEAR

I know Clyde Barrow and Bonnie Parker. Have known Clyde Barrow about eleven years, and met Bonnie Parker two or three times prior to the occasion a day or so before Christmas Day, 1932, when I went with the two of them from Dallas, Texas, to Temple, Texas, on which occasion Clyde Barrow tried to hold up a grocery store. . . .

—W. D. JONES

Ray Hamilton wants out.

Exactly why he wants out depends on whose family you ask. "Course Ray never did get along too good with Clyde because he always considered Clyde a little bit too trigger happy," says his older brother, Floyd. "You know, he shoot too quick."

Clyde's sister Nell, on the other hand, says, "Right after the escape at the bridge, Raymond Hamilton decided he wanted to go home to Michigan and visit his father. Clyde and Bonnie took him."

It's no doubt some of both: a little bit personal and a little bit personal protection. In any given situation, Ray's more likely to reach for the sky, while everyone knows that Clyde's going to reach for his gun. Either way, the escape at the bridge that Nell's talking about seems to help Raymond clear up his mind a bit about the future. Bullets smashing through your car window can have a way of doing that.

The bridge is the one across the Colorado River in Wharton, Texas, which is on the way from San Antonio to Houston. They reach it not long after dark at the end of the day they dropped off Deputy Johns. The only thing that's changed since leaving him to find his way home, which he does after a visit with the San Antonio police department, is that Clyde and Bonnie and Ray are about 175 miles east and are traveling in two cars. They picked up a sedan in the town of Victoria along the way, because it was there and because it's always better to have a second car. The sedan's a Ford V-8 naturally, this year's model. Ray's driving that behind Clyde and Bonnie in the coupe.

Clyde hates long bridges. Or, rather, doesn't trust them, and not because he's scared of heights or thinks they're going to break down or anything fool crazy like that. He hates them because he figures if he were a cop trying to catch a guy in a car, he'd be thinking a long bridge is about as good a place as any. And the bridge over the Colorado is long and narrow.

It would be one thing to head across that bridge if they thought no one had any idea where in the Southwest they were, but somebody saw them steal the sedan in Victoria and even gave chase for a few blocks. The guy chased them right about to where they turned toward Houston, which means toward this bridge.

In front of him, Raymond sees Clyde pull over onto a side road before the span, and he pulls the sedan in behind. Clyde just wants to see what they can see, and talk a bit about their plans once they get into the city of Wharton, on the other side of the river. He wants to clear up where to meet if they get split, that kind of thing. Plans made, and nothing looking amiss, they pull back out on the road and head for the bridge. Not too fast or anything, just a normal speed that won't attract attention.

The next thing Ray knows, Clyde's slamming on the brakes up in front of him, just before he gets onto the bridge. He's reversing that coupe at top speed, slamming the brakes again to spin the car around in a skid, and then sliding it directly into second gear so he can speed right back up without ever coming to a stop. It's a move Clyde practices out on back roads and now Hamilton wishes he could do it too because here's Clyde driving straight toward him, meaning he's seen something wrong. Hamilton turns the sedan around to follow.

Blam!

Inside the coupe Bonnie's got to be screaming. Clyde just fired his sawed-off shotgun straight through the windshield of the car at Deputy Seibricht of the Wharton Police Department. Seibricht has just stood up in a ditch next to the road and is aiming to shoot into the car as they pass. It was his flashlight signal to his men on the other side of the bridge that made Clyde turn around, most likely.

Blam! Another shotgun blast from the coupe.

Now it's Ray's turn. Clyde didn't hit the deputy with anything more than windshield glass, and Seibricht's standing there waiting for Hamilton in the sedan to pass him. Ray's hoping those steel doors Clyde talks about are as good as he says they are and pushes the gas down and ducks below the dashboard, flying past that cop as fast as those eight cylinders will push that car, hoping it doesn't go off the road before he's past the firing range.

Pow pow . . . pow.

Seibricht squeezes off a couple of good shots into the door of the sedan and thinks he may have injured the driver. But if any bullets make it through the panels, they don't make it far enough into Ray to wound him that anyone knows about. No one's hurt on either side of the law in the big shootout at the bridge, and down the road a few miles Clyde and Bonnie hop into the sedan and they leave the coupe behind full of fingerprints for the cops to find.

Those bullets got close enough to make Raymond think, though. Two firefights, one kidnapping, and a shitload of driving—hundreds of miles of it with someone sitting on his lap—in the course of little more than a week.

Ray wants out, at least for now, and maybe for good. It doesn't have to be immediate, but he lets Clyde and Bonnie know that he'd like to get back up to Michigan for a time.

❋

That's okay with you, and no big surprise either. He ran out on you and Fults once before, didn't he? And that was after Fults busted him out of jail, no less. No doubt he'll get himself caught and hope you'll bust him out again.

You and Bonnie will miss him, but Ray's not always as good at following orders as you might like. And ever since the big score up in Kansas, all he ever wants to do is rob banks, though how he's going to do that on his own is anybody's guess. Hard enough to pull off decent jobs with only the two of you. Plus, Raymond is always complaining about being on the road. Even Bonnie doesn't complain like Ray does about wanting to sleep in a house. Like he's too good for tourist camps.

Still, there's no hard feelings, and splitting up for a time is probably just as well now that the papers are full of stories about two short guys and a small woman with blond hair. The Dallas papers don't always put your names in their stories yet. They just say sly things like "the description of the girl fitted that of a Dallas girl who detectives said has been identified as a frequent companion of the two West Dallas men."

Poor little honey, she can't go home anymore either. And to make matters worse, she just about shot her little toe off trying to learn how to use a pistol. Actually, it's the toe next to her little one, whatever you call that one. For a couple of days in early September you're all hiding out at the Muckleroys', your aunt and uncle's place in Martinsville, Texas. Cumie's come down, along with L.C., for a visit. It's a happy few days, but then—who knows how it happens—*pop*, and the bullet grazes the tip of Bonnie's sweet little toe. Shot herself in the foot, just like the old joke! Now she's just like you, missing some toe.

You wish you could stay in Martinsville longer than just four days, but with the kidnapping in New Mexico and the big escape at the bridge, people are starting to think they see you every time a crime happens in Texas or thereabouts. It's getting too hot again. A trip up north to take Raymond home might not be such a bad thing.

"After staying in Michigan for about a week or so, Bonnie and Clyde started out 'just driving' again and left Raymond up there," says Nell. "The two kids drifted down into Kansas City and played around awhile, going to shows, eating at the best restaurants, having their nails done, buying some clothes. Bonnie got a permanent, too. They stayed in Michigan, Kansas, and Missouri till the last of October."

Doesn't that sound nice? Nell heard it somewhere—no doubt from you and Bonnie—and it might be half true. But somebody kills that old grocer in Sherman, Texas, on October 11. Somebody comes into the store right around closing time and asks for ten cents' worth of bologna and some eggs, hands the kid at the counter a dollar, and as soon as the register is open pulls a gun and grabs about sixty dollars from the till. The old man who's just got done slicing the meat sees what's going on, comes out from behind the meat counter, and gets real foolhardy.

"Young man, you can't do that," he says, and gets between the gunman and the door. He won't shut up or get out of the way. Gets hit in the head by this mystery gunman, sending his glasses flying. Gets shot. *Bang.* And shot again. *Bang.* And again after he's already on the ground in the doorway of his store. *Bang.*

One more shot, this time at the counter kid, produces only a click, as the gun jams. They're all three all the way out on the street now, the dying grocer, the short bandit, and the counter kid, Homer Glaze. Glaze watches you— or whoever it is—run down the street. "The bandit doing the shooting was described to police by Glaze as being about 20 to 25 years of age, small and of a light complexion," says the local paper the next morning. "This description was phoned to every police department and was also broadcast over radio stations in Dallas."

Sixty miles to the south, in the Dallas sheriff's office, that description sounds a little too much like somebody they know. Deputy Denver Seale sends a picture of you up to Sherman, and the local sheriff, Frank Reece, shows it to Glaze. He looks at it closely. Nods his head. Looks like the guy, he says. "The bandit whose photo has been positively identified by Homer Glaze," says the *Sherman Daily Democrat,* "is wanted in half a dozen cities in Texas and Oklahoma for robbery or murder."

No way was it you, you say to Nell; you and Bonnie were up in Kansas. And it's true that the witnesses who saw the killer jump into a car and drive off say there were two other men in it but no women. But Floyd Hamilton says you told him a completely different story.

"He told me that he was in there robbing the man that owned the place at the cashier cage and he said—I believe he said—he looked like a big Swede or something and was a butcher."

"Directly I look up and here he come running up behind me," Floyd remembers you telling him. "He was between me and the door going out. . . . I couldn't get out. I backed all the way up in the corner and I kept telling him to get on away with that meat cleaver, and he just kept backing me on up in the corner and I finally shot him. Said I didn't want to, but I did, and I got away."

It doesn't matter much to Howard Hall or his wife, Emma, whether it's you or anybody else that left him with three holes in his chest. He's dead within the hour.

For that matter, it doesn't seem to matter much to you whether they charge you with it or not.

"They just hung it on us for luck," you say to Nell. "But what's the difference, now?"

❀

Someone else besides Glaze sees you in Sherman that day.

"I knew it was him the instant I laid eyes on him," says Walter Enloe. He's working in the Grayson County jail in downtown Sherman, bringing food to the prisoners. It's lunchtime, about five or six hours before Howard Hall will get shot across town, and who should come walking in the front of the jailhouse but Clyde Barrow, probably the most wanted man in three or four states.

"Mr. Graham knew it too," says Enloe, referring to the jailer who's also there when the desperado comes in and announces that there's a prisoner in the jail that he'd like to visit. They know who he's looking for: his little brother, L.C., in there waiting to be tried on a charge of stealing automobiles. It's not visiting hours, however.

"Clyde said he wanted to visit, but we told him that nobody could visit while we were feeding the prisoners," says Enloe. "When he left, he didn't just turn around and walk out—he backed out with his hands in both pockets of his overcoat."

❀

Two days after the killing of Howard Hall, Sheriff Reece puts out a wanted poster with your picture on it, offering two hundred dollars as a reward for your capture. "He is a thoroughly dangerous man and will not hesitate to kill," the poster says, which you have to admit is not untrue. "He is said to stay at tourist camps." That's also pretty accurate. You particularly like the kind of roadside place that has a carport or even a garage attached to each of the cabins. That way you can unload your guns and such straight into the little cabin without anybody getting too nosy. If there's a door to close, so much the better, to keep the snoops away from your nice new cars.

The poster also says, "He may be accompanied by Frank Albert Clause." Well, maybe when that poster is put out you are, but not any longer. Poor old Frenchy. He's always getting his picture stuck next to yours on posters, it seems.

By the end of November, you and Bonnie are lying pretty low in Missouri and running pretty low on cash. Frank Hardy and another guy, Hollis Hale, are running with you now that Hamilton's gone, and the bank in Oronogo, Missouri, looks like an easy mark. Oronogo is a small town, but busy enough that there might actually be money in the vault. Bonnie goes in and looks the place over a couple days before, to get an idea of the layout and the number of employees, and comes back with a good report. It doesn't seem excessively guarded or anything.

Best of all, from your point of view, the town is an easy run from Joplin, which is kind of like a little Kansas City in the way it opens its doors and doesn't ask too many questions of strangers with money. "In those days, Joplin was known as 'the first night out,'" says George Kahler, a Missouri State Highway Patrol man from that time, "meaning it was about one day's drive from Chicago when things got too hot up there." Joplin's also, you can't help but notice, down in that southwest corner of the state where it's an easy jump across the line into Arkansas, Oklahoma, or Kansas. State lines are good things because most cops can't cross them. State lines are real good things, you should say.

Oronogo Bank, on the other hand, is a disaster from the get-go. You and

Frank go in with guns drawn, and everything's as Bonnie said it would be. Not too many people, not too many employees, but the teller is some kind of lunatic. Doesn't put his hands up when he's told, but ducks down and—

Pow pow pow.

Goddamn if he doesn't start shooting a gun out of some hole in the counter. "They started popping at us the minute we got inside the door," you tell Nell later. "We'd have beat it right then if we hadn't needed money so bad."

Bang pitchee.

Shit. Stay calm. Do your job. Thing is, the teller can't hit anybody from down there because he can't see out.

BLAM!

You fire the sawed-off shotgun into the counter about where you think he is, but it doesn't do any good because with banks getting robbed all over these past couple years, the owners of the Oronogo one have put a wall of steel under the counter. You're not shooting a machine gun, no matter what the newspapers say the next day, and no shotgun is going through that.

Pow pow pow.

BLAM!

Now Frank's shooting too. It sounds like a damn war until finally the teller's gun jams and the only customer in the place—some poor train dispatcher from Joplin—begs the teller to just stand up and put his hands up, which he wisely does.

You or Hardy smash the glass in the door between the lobby and the back of the bank and reach in and open the door, not even feeling the cut in your hand. Just start dripping blood on the bank floor.

"Leave him alone! Get the money and let's get out of here," someone yells, either you or Frank, no one remembers. One of you is sticking the gun in the teller's ribs, telling him what a fool thing it was to start on shooting like that.

Of course all the noise has raised a little attention out in the street. Maybe more than a little.

Bleeeep bleeeeeep bleeeeeeeeep bleeeeeeeep.

There's the car horn now, from out on the street. That's the kid, Hollis, behind the wheel of the getaway car, telling you and Frank to hurry it up inside as he sees the whole damn town starting to gather out there.

"They're robbing the bank, they're robbing the bank!" a guy working a drilling rig across the street is yelling.

"Leave him alone! Get the money. . . ."

No time for the big haul that might be in the bank safe. Frank scoops up whatever cash he can while you keep the teller and customer covered with the sawed-off shotgun. Out the door, into the car, and down the street.

CRACK! CRACK! A couple of guys with rifles fire at the car as it passes a garage a block down from the bank.

Rata rata rata you fire back through the window, hitting no one but sending glass flying and putting a couple of holes in a truck at that garage.

"We had a shooting scrape," you say about it later. "Shot up an oil truck."

No one from Oronogo follows, and when the police come to ask questions all the witnesses can say is that you were "well dressed" and not Pretty Boy Floyd. By then you're long gone. After the usual quick switch from a car you stole locally to your getaway Ford, you head back to a tourist camp in Carthage, where Bonnie's waiting. Along the way Frank counts out the take. Just eighty dollars, he says, and divides it three ways. It's pathetic, a joke, but you'll take it. Only the next day, after Frank and Hollis go off, supposedly for supplies, and never come back do you read in the paper that the take was more like "less than 500."

"The thief," says Nell, "had stolen from the thief."

❋

Hamilton's gone. And Frank and Hollis are gone. It's just her and Clyde again, and that's okay with Bonnie, though the money's thin. It means, too, that she has to drive getaway now instead of waiting outside town somewhere while the boys go in and do business. She parks outside a bank they've been looking at for days, watching it, planning. Just keep the car running, he says, and he'll be right back. This is scarier than sitting, but it's also better. At least she doesn't have to wonder as long about what's happening.

They pull up. Clyde goes in. She slides over, under the steering wheel. She loves him so much. It's so unfair, what they made him into. Hope he doesn't get hurt. Hope he doesn't have to shoot anyone. Hope he gets enough money so they can live forever. Hope and worry. Worry and hope. He goes in and draws his guns.

C'mon c'mon c'mon c'mon . . . what's taking him.

Good good good here he comes. She slides over, to let Clyde into the driver's seat. No shots fired means no trouble. That's good.

No money either, though. Clyde says, Sugar, there was only one old man in the bank. Says he looked up at the weapon and said, "I wisht you'd put that gun up and stop trying to be so gol-darned funny. This bank's been closed down four days. There ain't no money in it. That's what's the matter with it."

Sure it's funny later. Not even that much later, maybe. Sure, go on and laugh. And Bonnie sure does. No one shot, no one hurt. Laughs are scarce enough in this world. Even Clyde, once he cools off a bit, comes to think it's a good laugh.

"Clyde was telling me about it later on, laughing about it," says Floyd Hamilton. "It was kind of funny after." (Floyd actually thinks it happened while Clyde and Ray were together and that it was Ray who ran into the bank, but that's just Floyd always giving credit to Ray, isn't that right. Floyd's all right, though, bless his heart.)

"We thought we'd run into a bank with a lot of business," Clyde tells Floyd. "But somebody else done stole it all and changed the books and he was in there trying to figure out how much he'd stole."

Ha ha ha ha ha ha. They still need money, though. And Bonnie thinks wouldn't it be nice to get home and see their people at Christmas. Can we, Daddy? C'mon, sugar.

"I want to see my mama, honey," she says.

Dallas is about as dangerous a place as the two of them can go, but as always, sweet little old Clyde heads the car in that direction. Bonnie has been that way her whole life, crazy about her mom, and crying inconsolably when she gets to missing her. Even her little sister teases her about it now and then. Clyde doesn't seem to mind too much when she asks him to take her home and she tries not to do it all that often, just when things get real desperate in her heart. It's the one seminormal thing Clyde can still give her, after all. Plus, she knows deep down, he needs to see his people as much as she does.

Of course, it's not as simple and normal anymore as just dropping her off at her mama's and saying I'll see you later and heading over to the gas station. She's only been running with him full-time for a few months now, but those days seem long gone . . . "we get three hundred and sixty-five days of it every year." It's one of the saddest things, come to think of it, not being able to go home, but there it is.

"How we got and they got in touch with us," says Billie Jean, "is Clyde's daddy had a filling station and, uh, they would come by and have a note and throw it. And put it in a Coke bottle or something, and throw it out at the filling station.

"And Clyde's father would pick it up and they would tell us where to meet 'em." Usually the meeting place is on some country road out of town, a place chosen by Clyde because he likes the way he can see cars coming or going and, whenever possible, because there are a couple of roads going different ways nearby.

"L.C., usually—my youngest brother—was the one that would take us out to see where he was at, you know," says Marie Barrow about the days they found a Coke bottle with a message in the dirt by the station. "And my mama would cook beans, you know, or corn bread, or something to take to them to eat." Red beans, Bonnie's favorite food, becomes sort of a code between the families.

"I've got a big pot full of beans and some corn bread," Cumie might say over the phone to Emma or to Nell, and they would know there was some news or a meeting afoot.

"But it wasn't no big reunions," says Marie about the meetings, "it was just seeing 'em."

Seeing them. Seeing her mama and her little sister, and her sister's babies—to hold those babies—that's what she needs. Those precious hours out in some lonely piece of road with her people and his people all sitting around having a picnic . . . those make the long hours and days on the road disappear. Almost disappear.

It's the same for Clyde. "He come around there all the time," says Marie. "Mom used to mark on the wall how many times. He couldn't stay away, poor thing."

They get back within drive-through distance of Dallas around the beginning of December 1932, staying here and there. No one's saying exactly where, of course, but often they're out at the hideout in Grand Prairie or some other abandoned farmstead. She's as happy as current conditions allow, seeing folks reasonably regularly; though in hindsight, December 25 of 1932 is about the worst Christmas Day in her twenty-two years on this dried-up and mean old world.

❀

W. D. Jones is a footloose kid having a good old time on Christmas Eve. He and his best pal, L. C. Barrow, are cruising around West Dallas in Henry Barrow's Model A. The two have been friends since way back in the days when both of their families had just come to the city from farm country and were living in the squatters' camp under the viaduct. W.D. had it even harder than the Barrow boys: a year after his family moved into a real house not far from the Barrow gas station, his dad, sister, and oldest brother all took sick and died of the flu. His ma almost died too. He can't read or write, and he has already been convicted once, along with L.C., for stealing cars.

Tonight, though, sixteen-year-old W.D. isn't thinking about the past. "We had a half gallon of whiskey with us and were drinking this freely," he says. Even better, he and L.C. also have Maudine Brennan and another girl in the car with them, and they have just been at a Christmas dance. W.D.

"All the girls thought he was good-lookin'," says Marie
Barrow about W. D. Jones, shown here (on left) with
Clyde. *(Missouri State Highway Patrol file photograph.
Used with permission.)*

never has trouble getting girls to go around with him, what with his smoky
good looks, gray eyes, and jaunty style.

"All the girls thought he was good-lookin'," says Marie Barrow. "He had
several good-lookin' brothers too."

Be that as it may, Maudine and her friend are well-behaved young ladies
who can't stay out too late, and nothing the boys can say will change that.
L.C. and W.D. aren't exactly good boys, having been in trouble with the law
once or twice for acting as mules for moonshiners or for other petty crimes.
But they drop the girls off at home close enough to on time. With nothing
better to do, they head on down the Eagle Ford Road to a hangout by a
small concession stand. It's past the Barrow garage, out near the gravel pit.

There's a couple of fellas there, and L.C. gets out to talk, but Jones stays put, trying to keep the world from spinning. "I was pretty drunk by this time," he says.

(A word or two are in order here about W. D. Jones and the words he says. Not that he's a liar, necessarily, but everyone knows he has what might be called a tendency in his tellings of things to pretty much always be either drunk or asleep whenever anything goes wrong or a dumb decision gets made. The habit doesn't make Clyde or Bonnie angry with him. Clyde figures a guy's got to say what a guy's got to say, especially if he's talking to the law, which W.D. finds himself doing eventually. "He told quite a few tales after, you know, he got caught," says Marie Barrow, "but we all knew that, you know, that he did it on purpose to keep from, you know, getting in too much trouble himself, so you can't blame him for that. 'Cause Clyde, you know, had told him to tell anything he wanted to.")

So, anyway: "I was pretty drunk by this time," W.D. says about Christmas Eve of 1932, and "Clyde Barrow and Bonnie Parker passed by where we were. They were driving a Ford V-8 coupe, with two wheels on the running board, khaki top. L.C. saw them and suggested that we follow them, which we did. They drove on down a side road to a gravel pit and we drove up behind them and parked there."

L.C. gets out of the car and goes up to the coupe to see what his big brother is up to. They talk a moment and then L.C. yells over to W.D. to come on over to the car, that Clyde wants to speak to him.

"Clyde was wanted then for murder and kidnapping," says W.D., "but I had knowed him all my life. So I got out and went to his car."

"We're here to see Mama and Marie," Clyde says to him. "You stay here with us while L.C. gets them."

Doesn't take much convincing, especially since W.D. and L.C. are out of drink and Clyde and Bonnie have a jar of moonshine in their car. He's got nothing better to do than sit and have a sip with them, and anyway the Barrows are just about family. Plus there's no denying there's something a bit exciting about being around L.C.'s famous older brother. Marie says W.D. is always looking for a chance to tag along with Clyde.

"He hung around up and down the roads, Eagle Ford Road, lookin' for Clyde to come by," she says. "W.D. just wanted to go along with him."

Soon enough on comes L.C. with Mrs. Barrow and Marie, who's getting pretty and pouty at the same time. Maybe there's other Barrows and Parkers come along, too, to wish each other a Merry Christmas all around.

It's a nice visit. There are the small pleasantries. The hugs. Some food. Some of the talk is about their neighbor Ray Hamilton, who has naturally got himself caught again. He did all right for a while, robbed the same little bank south of Dallas in Cedar Hill twice in a row, which is kind of good for a laugh. But even funnier, though not for Ray, is how he got himself rounded up a week or two back up in Bay City, Michigan, along with another West Dallas neighbor, Gene O'Dare.

The way Floyd Hamilton tells the story, "some girl that Raymond was familiar with, you know, trying to go with, took him to a skating rink. She supposed to have put him on the spot." Either she or some boy Ray worked with told the laws they might find a couple of bank robbers at the rink. The way Special Agent F. A. Blake of the United States Bureau of Investigation (soon to be renamed the FBI*) tells it, a kid named Frank Walsh, who they think is really a bank robber named Jack Rayburn, promised not only Hamilton but "Clyde Barrow and Pretty Boy Floyd, who were supposed to be there at that time for the purpose of robbing a bank."

Poor Ray: West Dallas boys don't grow up to be very good skaters. (No one will ever see Clyde Barrow on skates.) Even if Ray gets to the edge of the rink, those skates make for pretty tough running. No, he and Gene don't get to the edge of the ice before those northern lawmen catch them. They hit Gene over the head with a billy stick when he tries to pull something out of his pocket, and Ray's pistol doesn't do him any good either. Within days both are on their way back down to Dallas in the company of deputy sheriffs Denver Seale and Ed Caster. In fact, Ray's over there in the county jail, right across the viaduct, this very night. Merry Christmas, Ray! Welcome home!

It's no real laughing matter, though. Not if you're Clyde Barrow and those deputies are looking for you even more than Ray. In fact, the first telegram sent down from Michigan to Leonard Pack, the Dallas detective who once dragged Clyde out of his mother's kitchen, reads, "RAYMOND HAMILTON ARRESTED BAY CITY MICHIGAN WITH J C CLARK ALIAS DUNN WHO MAY BE CLYDE BARROW." They should be so lucky.

With Ray, the laws are pretty certain that they have got the killer of old man Bucher. Clyde knows better, and though he's got no real love lost with Ray, he does have this idea that a man who was involved in a crime doesn't let another take the fall for a crime he didn't commit—especially if it might mean the electric chair. He'll bust Ray out one way or another. He'll bust him out regardless of that Bucher business.

Ray knows it too. "I'll wait my chance and be out before you know it," he says to anyone listening at the Dallas County jail. "And when I do I'll team up with Clyde again and all hell will never catch us."

---

* To avoid confusion, from now on the Bureau, by any other name, will be called the FBI.

On a similar note, Clyde's been trying to figure out how to bust old Ralph Fults out of the Collin County jail, in McKinney, for months now. Can't let him sit there taking the long rap while him and Bonnie are still out free. Last week, in fact, Bonnie walked right into the jail to visit Ralph, gave him some cigarettes, and told him to be ready. As luck would have it, though, they moved Ralph off to Huntsville at the last minute.

There's lots of news. They could talk all night with their families if it wasn't so cold and they weren't so tired. Wouldn't it be nice to be sitting around a Christmas tree or cozied up under a blanket instead of sitting around in cars at a gravel pit sipping moonshine? Around midnight Clyde decides it's time to move on. He calls W.D. over.

"Clyde suggested to me that I go with them 'down the road,' as he put it, but did not say where," W.D. says. What Clyde wants is someone who can keep watch while he and Bonnie get some sleep. "I went. I know now it was a fool thing to do, but then it seemed sort of big to be out with two famous outlaws. I reckoned Clyde took me along because he had knowed me before and figured he could count on me."

At about two in the morning on Christmas Day, they pull into a tourist camp in Temple, Texas, about a hundred and thirty miles to the south.

"They slept on the bed," says W.D. "I had a pallet on the floor."

❉

It's a chilly Christmas morning and Doyle Johnson's family is letting him sleep in at his mom and dad's house on Thirteenth Street in Temple, Texas. His wife and his new baby are awake, though, visiting with his mom and some of his in-laws, the Krausers. They're sitting there enjoying the morning when Doyle's wife looks out the front window and notices two men getting into her and Doyle's brand-new car, releasing the brake, and pushing it down the street. What are they doing? she wonders for a second before realizing that of course they must be trying to steal the sporty little Ford roadster. She calls her father, Henry, and her brother, Clarence, and they head out into the street, yelling at the men to stop. Her mother-in-law, meanwhile, goes to wake twenty-seven-year-old Doyle.

In the street, Clyde is yelling at W.D. They just robbed a small grocery store, and on their way back to the car where Bonnie's waiting they passed the roadster with the keys in it and Clyde told W.D. to climb on in and start it up. Only due to the cold or something, W.D. can't get the thing going. Now all of a sudden here come three people out of the house running toward them.

"That's my boy's car! Get out!" yells the older man.

Clyde can't believe that W.D. can't get the damn car started, and yells for him to just slide over in the seat and he'll do it himself. Right then, though, Clarence Krauser catches up to the car, and Clyde jumps right back out and pulls his pistol. Tells them all to get back to the house and no one will be hurt, and they retreat, all three of them.

Before Clyde can get the roadster going and get them around the corner to where Bonnie is, however, Doyle Johnson comes running out of his house. Either he didn't see the gun that scared off his wife and his in-laws, or he doesn't care, or he's still asleep, or he's just plain not thinking. Or he's stupid.

"Get back, man, or I'll kill you," Clyde yells, but Doyle doesn't listen. He jumps up on the running board, grabs Clyde by the collar, and starts trying to choke him.

"Stop, man, or I'll kill you," Clyde yells again, putting his pistol up to Doyle Johnson's chest.

Pow!

Clyde fires his .38, but either he's just squeezing off a warning shot or Johnson's got his hands on the pistol, because the bullet goes into the ground.

Bang! A bullet from W.D.'s .41- or .45-caliber "thumb buster" pistol slams into the left side of Johnson's neck about halfway between his head and shoulders and travels downward from right to left through Doyle's spinal cord and stops about a half inch under his skin. Doyle Johnson falls off the running board, bleeding and paralyzed, and within a day of being dead.

Johnson's wife is screaming now, running back toward her dying husband. Someone else is hollering for somebody to call the police. There's noise all over the street as Doyle lies there dying. Clyde finally gets the car running, and he and W.D. screech around the corner, taking a hard left onto Avenue F, where Bonnie's waiting. The plan, if there was one, would have been to change cars and go off in the newly stolen roadster, but that's out of the question, so they abandon it two blocks from the dead man's house.

"We piled into her car and lit a shuck out of town," W.D. says. A mile or two down the road, Clyde pulls over.

"Boy," he says, using his regular nickname for W.D. "Boy, shinny up that pole and cut them phone wires. We don't want no calls ahead." W.D. does it, no problem, and from then on cutting wires becomes his specialty, and it's real effective, as the police are only starting to get radios in the biggest cities.

Farther down the road Clyde speaks up again.

"Boy, you can't go home," he says. "You got murder on you, just like me."

Then he tells W.D. to get in the turtleback of the car and pushes that pop-up seat right down on him and latches it so it looks like it's only him and Bonnie in the car. It's hell of uncomfortable down there, but there's nothing to be done about it under the circumstances of half the state looking for two men and a girl in a car like theirs.

"Didn't let me out of there until we got into the tourist camp," says W.D. "And when we left the next morning he did the same thing."

Of the killing, W.D. says, "Clyde gave him fair warning."

❋

It's Saturday night, New Year's Eve, about to be 1933. In Washington, Governor Roosevelt from New York is toasting his victory at the polls the previous November and getting ready to take over the reins of government in a country that's a mess. There are twelve million unemployed, thousands of banks have already shut their doors, and most of the others are just barely hanging on. Not that anybody outside of the big cities much likes the banks, since mostly what they've been doing seems to be taking away people's farms. It's the height of hard times, but none of that is stopping folks in Dallas from firing off guns and sipping homebrew. Those factories still in business are getting ready to blow their whistles to mark the arrival of a new year. A new year, a new president—it can't get any worse. Can it?

Up in the Dallas County Criminal Courts building, which overlooks the construction site that will come to be called Dealey Plaza, as midnight approaches there is a literal changing of the guard under way. Smoot Schmid, the giant redheaded former bicycle salesman who has finally won his first two-year term as Dallas County sheriff in a runoff election, is going cell to cell, counting prisoners. The last thing he wants is to find out after he is sworn in at the stroke of midnight that there are fewer prisoners actually in the jail than on the books. That's happened before in Dallas, and it got to be an argument about when so-and-so went missing.

This could have waited until Monday morning, but the old sheriff is just as anxious to be done with responsibility for the three hundred–odd prisoners in the lockup as Smoot Schmid is to pin that badge on his own chest. Smoot, who has had that nickname since high school (and is also sometimes called Bigfoot on account of his size 14 boots), doesn't pretend to be some "two-gun" cowboy sheriff. Sure, he'll pose for the paper with a pistol and a huge smile, but he ran more on dollars and cents than bullets and big hats. He promised to bring a businessman's attitude to the job, and he spent more time talking about cutting costs than he did spouting tough law-and-order lines. In fact, his only previous public service consisted of sitting on a grand jury. He won because he's a born politician and because, among other things, it seems like he knows everybody in town.

That latter statement includes more than a few of the West Dallas boys who've gone wayward in the years since they hung around his cycle shop.

"Say, don't I know you?" the story goes he says when he gets to Raymond Hamilton's cell.

"You ought to, you big-footed son-of-a-bitch," says Hamilton. "You used to buy hot bicycles from all us boys from West Dallas."

It's a good story that might even be true. Ray always talks big and tough to his keepers after he's been locked up. Smoot can talk big, too. "Don't worry about that job security," he tells another former kid from the neighborhood, Ted Hinton, who he's just convinced to quit his job at the post office and become a deputy sheriff. "I'll be sheriff forever."

As for Smoot Schmid's plans for focusing on the nuts and bolts of running the county jail and not riding tall all over the county in search of bad hombres, well, that starts to change less than a week after he takes the oath of office when somebody with a sawed-off shotgun blows away a deputy sheriff just across the river, in Raymond Hamilton's sister's front yard.

❈

I always felt—sick inside—sick and cold and weak—and a sort of dull wishing that I'd never been born. You see, sis, it's hard to make you understand, because you've never faced it. But it comes so quickly and it happens in an instant—you're there and they're there—they've got guns and you've got guns—you know it's going to be you or them and there's no time to think about anything else. You grit your teeth and come down to it—they do the same, unless you beat them to it. In that case, they're telling the story and not you, next day. Then it's over and done and no going back—you've killed a man—you see him lying there, if it's daylight and you've time to wait and look. Life's gone—you took it—will never live and breathe and laugh again. But if he'd beat you to it, you'd be lying there like that. It gets mixed up—it seems senseless—the whole business—them killing you—you killing them—you wonder why you were born—why anyone was ever born—why God should bother with the whole mess. And you feel so helpless, so unable to do anything about it—and then you run away and get sick, and that's all.

—Clyde Barrow

It just doesn't end. How are you supposed to know that there are four laws hiding out in Lilly McBride's house on the night of January 6? They aren't even waiting there for you, but for Odell Chambliss,* a pal of Raymond's and yours who sure as heck isn't going to show. He dressed himself up as a woman and snuck out of town weeks ago, shortly after robbing a bank in Grapevine. Actually, there is a way you're supposed to know that the cops are at Ray's sister's house: she's supposed to put a red light in the window if trouble is brewing. That was how you left it earlier in the day when she said the cops had been nosing around looking for Chambliss.

You aren't even looking for trouble by dropping by. You're not out to rob someplace. You are just hoping to find out the news about Ray if there is any. You're working on your plans to help him escape, get some saw blades to him, along with a radio to cover the noise of sawing. Okay, so you're looking to help bust him out of jail, but that's it. It's nothing to get to gunplay about. But that just seems to be your luck these days.

You and Bonnie and W.D. are out driving in circles like you usually do whenever you're in Dallas. Takes some of the fun out of being home that you can't stop anywhere for too long. A few minutes at Bonnie's mother's house on South Lamar Street, just long enough for W.D. to run to the door and fetch Billie Jean back to the car for a ride out to some country road where you can talk a stretch in peace.

"I was about half drunk and didn't pay any attention," says W.D., as usual. "We drove out on some country road, and stopped and all got out of the car, and Clyde Barrow, Bonnie, and Billie Parker all had quite a conversation, which I did not listen to."

Bonnie has been drinking a bit too, something she's starting to do a little more often. "I let her have at it about once a week," you explained to Nell later, "because the poor kid's nerves can't stand the strain. She's not built for this sort of thing, and it gets her."

Then out to Lilly McBride's house, where there's no red light, so Billie Jean hops out and knocks on the door but gets no answer. Then back to Mrs. Parker's house to drop Billie off at home again, and back around to the Eagle Ford Road to stop in and say hello to Mrs. Barrow—barely staying there long enough to get out of the car. Then around the corner to Floyd Hamilton's house, passing Lilly McBride's another time or two and seeing there is a red light on. At Floyd's, you leave Bonnie and W.D. in the car and go around back to have a talk, no doubt about the plans to get Ray

---

* He is sometimes referred to as Chandler or Chandless.

out. After a few minutes it's back to the car and around the corner again to Lilly McBride's house, where the red light is now off.

What you unfortunately don't know is that the red light is off because the two deputies, one constable, one attorney from the prosecutor's office, and one Texas Ranger who are inside waiting for Odell Chambliss have finally figured out what is going on and told Maggie Farris, another of Ray's sisters, to put it out. They notice your coupe passing the house over and over again and not stopping, and they're not buying Maggie's line that the light has to stay on for her little babies to sleep.

Your car is loaded with weapons, as usual. You got your 16-gauge shotgun, the one you sawed down the stock of and keep under your overcoat pretty much at all times, held there with its inner-tube strap around your shoulder. In the car is another sawed-off shotgun, a rifle, and assorted handguns. Once again, Bonnie and W.D. stay in the car; you'll only be a minute. You get out with one of the handguns, and of course the sawed-off is swinging under your overcoat. You tell W.D. to be ready to drive.

"I crawled over Bonnie and got under the wheel," he says. Like most of the houses in the blocks along the Eagle Ford Road, the McBride place isn't much more than four small rooms and a roof. It's wider than some of the shotgun houses, with all their rooms in a row like a railroad car, and has a narrow covered porch across the front. It just about backs up onto the edge of your ma and pa's filling station.

From the car it looks as if either no one is home or everyone's asleep, and you get all the way to the porch before you figure out that it isn't so. Maybe you see someone moving in the room to the right of the door. Maybe you even hear Special Ranger J. F. Van Noy telling the others to get out their guns. That's what he does when he looks out and sees you coming and sees that you're carrying your sawed-off.

Or maybe you just don't like the look on Maggie Farris's face when she opens the front door.

BLAM!

You fire that shotgun through the window to the right of the door, into the room where Deputy Sheriff Fred Bradberry and Ranger Van Noy have been waiting. They dive for cover and start firing back.

POW POW! BANG!

In the back room of Lilly McBride's house, Deputy Sheriff Malcolm Davis of Fort Worth and an investigator from the Tarrant County district attorney's office hear all hell suddenly breaking loose on the other side of the thin walls. It makes no sense to open the door between the back and the front of the house, however, as there is no way of knowing who is doing the firing and in what direction. Instead Davis, who at fifty-one is a five-year veteran of the department, runs out through the back porch and around the house.

Sitting in the car outside the house, Bonnie and W.D. also hear the shots and start firing from the car. W.D. naturally says it's Bonnie doing the shooting, with a handgun, just as her people say it was him, a version that fits a little better with the police accounts of rifle fire from the driver's seat.* Either way, neither Bonnie nor W.D. hit anybody. But you do.

"Just about the time the shot was fired I saw two men come around the corner of Lilly McBride's house, on the side of the house nearest the Eagle Ford Road," says W.D.

"Hold on there," Davis yells when he sees you on the porch. There's no time. You turn to him.

BLAM!

"Then the shot rang out and Bonnie Parker told me to start the motor," says W.D. "I saw one of those two men fall, and I began starting the motor."

Fire spits from the barrel of your sawed-off and six shotgun pellets, shot from pretty much point-blank range, rip Deputy Sheriff Davis's heart to pieces. You're running between the houses, jumping on the running board of the Ford now, screeching around the corner, maybe firing off a last round. You're gone off into the rain that's starting to fall, tearing along out of Dallas with a siren you stole off an ambulance in Waco howling to make people think you're supposed to be driving that fast. Off into the rain, into the mud, into a ditch even, so you have to pay a couple of farmers a couple of bucks to hitch their mules to your bumper and pull you out. A good day's wage for them, it turns out.

Behind you in Lilly McBride's front yard the officers are gently lifting Davis into the back seat of one of their own cars and heading for the hospital. But there's no point in the exercise.

"He was known to friends and fellow officers as a quiet-mannered, curly-headed bachelor who liked to catch big catfish at Lake Worth and to invite his friends to help him eat them," says the local paper about Malcolm Davis. "The Davis fish dinners were famous in Fort Worth."

He's dead on arrival.

---

* Many years later, when there's no chance of legal consequences, W.D. changes his story. "As far as I know, Bonnie never packed a gun. Maybe she'd help carry what we had in the car into a tourist-court room. But during the five big gun battles I was with them, she never fired a gun. But I'll say she was a hell of a loader."

CHAPTER 17

JOPLIN, MISSOURI

*Clyde Barrow, will o' the wisp gunman, and a woman com-
panion attended a party in South Dallas that lasted into
the small hours of Monday morning, police were reliably informed a few minutes before they surrounded the house to
find their quarry gone. . . .*

*Barrow, wanted in at least three murders and a long list of
holdups, was the guest of honor at the party, according to
secret information received by the police.*

—Dallas Evening Journal

So it's back on the road. Bonnie knows it was inevitable, but that doesn't
mean it wouldn't have been nice to stay around Dallas a little longer.
Just long enough for a few more meetings with her mom and sister, a
few more hugs, a few more plates of red beans and corn bread. But that
killing of the deputy there in Lilly McBride's front yard . . . that changes
everything. The papers are talking about the "West Dallas Mob," run by
the young and ruthless Clyde Barrow and Ray Hamilton. Dallas is hotter
than ever, in the middle of winter. Even her name is now turning up in
print.

It's kind of funny, actually. As soon as Odell Chambliss turns up back
in Dallas with proof that he actually spent the day Malcolm Davis was
killed in some jail cell in California, a sheriff over in Fort Worth starts saying

he's sure that Clyde's companion was either the world-famous Pretty Boy Floyd or Bonnie Parker. That's something, isn't it? Pretty Boy Floyd or her little old self. She's famous now. Wonderful. Famous means she never gets to go home.

Once the heat gets on their trail, Clyde will drive for days straight. "He believed in a nonstop jump in territory," W.D. says, "sometimes as much as a thousand miles—whenever it got hot behind." And it's definitely hot in Texas, so she, W.D., and Clyde are on the road.

Sometimes she doesn't mind the road so much—the hours in the passenger seat watching the scenery fly by at seventy, eighty miles an hour, maybe more if Clyde can make the car go faster. It's good scenery sometimes, open fields, empty prairies, grass forever like the ocean down in Galveston. Stars like you wouldn't believe when they pull over so she can relieve herself. A person can see anything coming, good or bad, from miles away out there, which is good, though of course seeing can also mean being seen. No sound but the whine of the motor and the rush of the wind coming through the window.

"There was never a whole lot of talk among us when we was on the road," says W.D. Hours pass with no one speaking. Then, out of the blue, Clyde speaks up.

"Honey," he says, "as soon as I find a place, I'm gonna stop. I'm tired and want to get some rest." But then hours more can go by before he finds a place he likes.

"He always called her 'Honey' or 'Baby,'" says W.D., "and she called him 'Daddy' or 'Honey.' W.D. calls her "Sis" and calls Clyde "Bud."

Hours and days go by on the road with no real destination but lots of places to avoid. It's not always prairies. When they get into Louisiana there are those thick woods, piney smelling and safe. Or up in the Ozarks there's the springs you can take a swim in, in warmer seasons. In North Carolina, Clyde announces they're going to go to Durham to see the Camel cigarette factory. He buys her a Brownie camera there in Durham, and some film, which is sweet of him. Taking pictures will be fun.

Sure she gets tired of eating sandwiches off her lap, not being able to sit down anywhere for very long and have a nice supper. It would be fun to go shopping together with Clyde sometime, like a normal couple, instead of always sneaking in one at a time while the other two park off somewhere. It'd be nice to just do her laundry when she wants to instead of leaving it at a washing place one week and circling back around a week later to pick it up. Or not circling back to pick it up—often as not Clyde just has everyone

"Bonnie was always neat, even on the road," says W. D.
Jones. *(From the collections of the Texas/Dallas History
and Archives Division, Dallas Public Library.)*

buy new clothes. Or, in some cases, he and W.D. steal new clothes. In Fort
Smith, Arkansas, they stick a gun in a tailor's face and take eight nice suits,
six of which they throw out.

Everything that should be little work is more of a production, but she
does it somehow.

"She kept her hair, you know, fixed nice all the time, even under those
conditions," says her sister, Billie.

"Bonnie was always neat, even on the road," says W.D. "She kept on
makeup and had her hair combed all the time. She wore long dresses and
high heels and them little tams on her head. She was a tiny little thing. I
reckon she never weighed more than a hundred pounds, even after a big

meal. But them big meals was usually bologna and cheese sandwiches and buttermilk on the side of the road."

There's a lot of things that would be nice if they were just a little bit different in this old world. But she doesn't mind the road sometimes, especially if she has a supply of her cigarettes, Camels. She sits, has a smoke, and thinks. Creates.

"She would think up rhymes in her head and put them down on paper when we stopped," says W.D. "Some of them she kept, but she threw a lot of them away."

He's right about that: most of them get tossed or forgotten along the way. But she's got the beginnings of an idea for a poem—or a ballad, really—that she knows she wants to finish. Knows she will finish if they can just get a place to settle down a bit so she can put it on paper.

It starts out like this:

> You've read the story of Jesse James—
> Of how he lived and died;
> If you're still in need
> Of something to read
> Here's the story of Bonnie and Clyde.

No one calls them "Bonnie and Clyde" back home. It's always "Clyde and Bonnie." Clyde and Bonnie this, Clyde and Bonnie that. Even in the papers, Clyde and Bonnie. But "Clyde and Bonnie" has no proper rhythm. And beside, nothing rhymes with "Bonnie" but everything rhymes with "Clyde."

Clyde won't care one bit, especially since there he is in the same line as Jesse James. He's going to love that. She loves Clyde. If only they can settle for a bit, she'll get it done.

"Run, run, run," W.D. says. "At times, that seemed all we did."

❈

Dallas police waited expectantly Monday night for another tip-off on the whereabouts of Clyde Barrow after three squads of heavily armed officers awakened sleepers at two houses on Harding Street in South Dallas early in the morning on information that the West Dallas desperado and a companion were at one of the houses.

Captain Norman D. Bailey led 10 officers in a futile search of the houses. Both places were surrounded by police armed with machine guns, riot shotguns and teargas bombs.

Presence of the long hunted West Dallas gunman was reported
by a man by telephone.

—*Dallas Morning News*

It's hot in Texas all right, cops running around with machine guns and
tear gas every time someone feels like phoning in and saying Clyde and Bonnie are at a party. Smoot Schmid and his deputies at the county sheriff's office
and Captain Bailey and his boys at the city police department aren't the only
lawmen sniffing around, either. Almost by total coincidence, across town at
the FBI, a request has come in from Michigan to look into a strange clue. The
FBI, still an obscure but growing branch of the Department of Justice,
doesn't have a lot of jurisdiction. Its agents can't go after murderers and bank
robbers, for instance. They can only chase people who steal a car and take it
across state lines. Or who kidnap someone, a crime that recently became a
federal offense in the aftermath of the stealing of the Lindbergh baby.

What the FBI has is an empty prescription bottle with a number and a
sticker that says "Nacogdoches, Texas." It turns up in a car stolen at Effing-
ham, Illinois, and then found abandoned a few weeks later in Pawhuska,
Oklahoma. The National Motor Vehicle Theft Act, which makes it illegal to
take a stolen car across state lines, is the FBI's ticket into any case that
might be interesting, and finding a bottle from Texas in a stolen car that
apparently went from Illinois to Oklahoma qualifies as interesting. Some
articles of women's clothing found in the car distract the agents for a while,
but eventually the paperwork filters down to Texas so that local agents can
look into this bottle from Nacogdoches. At the beginning of March, a couple of days after the police raid on the party in West Dallas, agent Charles
Winstead writes up his report to send to Washington and elsewhere.

The local police down in Nacogdoches are a little ahead of the "government men," as the agents are known, having already been asked by
their counterparts up in Illinois to look into the prescription. They haven't
gotten very far, though. The prescription belongs to a Mrs. Jim Muckleroy, a nice old lady who lives in Martinsville, Texas, and tells the officers
she has no idea how her bottle got into the stolen car. "She stated she had
no relatives in Illinois; that there are several families in that vicinity who
visit her home, but none of whom were missing from that community."

That's good enough for the local police. "She did not know how the
bottle got out of her possession and into the stolen car found abandoned
near Pawhuska," they conclude, and they don't even bother sending a letter
with their findings up to Pawhuska. But Winstead won't let the bottle drop,

and eventually Mr. Muckleroy, who is "an elderly man and bears an excellent reputation in the community where he has lived all his life," tells the G-man he wants to talk somewhere where Mrs. Muckleroy won't find out what he's saying.

"After thinking over the matter of the disappearance of the medicine bottle," Winstead writes in his report, Mr. Muckleroy's wife "finally recalled" that a few months back her sister Cumie Barrow had come to visit, along with Clyde, Bonnie, L.C., and Marie. L.C., old man Muckleroy explains, was "afflicted with venereal disease, and asked for a bottle."

Once old man Muckleroy gets talking, it's like a load off his chest and he doesn't stop. He tells Winstead "that he does not know where Clyde and his wife live, but they just go all over the country; that Clyde has served time in the Texas State Penitentiary, and was released sometime shortly after Christmas, 1931 . . . that he does not know the maiden name of Clyde's wife, but thinks they married in Dallas." Muckleroy has had about enough of his outlaw in-laws, as it turns out. A few weeks later he and Mrs. Muckleroy tell the agents that though Clyde and Buck haven't been around in a while, "should they put in their appearance in that vicinity they would risk the consequences and immediately notify the local authorities."

Winstead and his colleagues live in Dallas; they know all about Clyde and Bonnie and Ray Hamilton and the "West Dallas Mob." Heck, it's in the dailies every day. For the benefit of his superiors back at national headquarters, though, and because there's a strict form to these documents, Winstead goes on in his report to include physical descriptions of Clyde and Bonnie. He gives directions to the filling station on the Eagle Ford Road, though he doesn't seem to be completely familiar with the street names across the river. He lists Clyde's career highlights.

"Clyde Barrow is wanted for the following crimes:

April 30, 1932—murder, Hillsboro, Texas
May 12, 1932—robbery, Lufkin, Texas
Aug. 1, 1932—robbery, Dallas, Texas
    " 4, 1932—murder of sheriff, Atoka, Okla.
    " 14, 1932—kidnapping Deputy Sheriff, Carlsbad, NM
    " 15, 1932—Released Carlsbad Officer in San Antonio, Texas
    " 15, 1932—Theft of car Victoria, Texas.
    " 15, 1932—Shot at Deputy Sheriffs, Wharton, Texas.
Oct. 8, 1932—Robbery, Abilene, Texas
    " 11, 1932—Murder & Robbery Sherman, Texas
Jan. 6, 1933—Murder, Tarrant County Deputy sheriff at Dallas, Tex.

"The local state and county authorities, including State Rangers, are watching for Barrow to show up in Dallas as he has announced that he intends to visit his mother whenever he desires if he has to shoot his way in and out of Dallas," says Winstead in conclusion. "He is a killer and without warning has killed and shot at several officers, who merely approached him."

It's the kind of report—and the kind of semiscientific sleuthing—that is pretty much guaranteed to whet the appetite of certain persons higher up in the Bureau. And does.

"The Federal Bureau of Investigation," says the recently renamed Bureau's young and ambitious director, J. Edgar Hoover, "became interested in Barrow and his paramour . . . through a singular bit of evidence . . . a prescription bottle, which led Special Agents to a drug store in Nacogdoches."

❊

"The room was still dark and someone was holding me, kissing my lips and eyes." Blanche doesn't know if she's asleep or awake. "Something was going on."

"Baby, wake up," a voice says. *His* voice says. She's waking up.

"Daddy, is it really you, or am I still dreaming?" Blanche asks.

She's not dreaming. It's really true. Buck is out. Her man, Buck, is home. He's in her room here in Denison, Texas, seventy-five miles north of Dallas, where she's been working at Buck's sister Artie's beauty parlor. Working and waiting, waiting, waiting. Writing letters to the governor, to the prison, to whomever. Waiting. He's here in her room a little earlier than expected, but who cares? He's kissing her lips, kissing her eyes, kissing her. She's awake now, all right. She's definitely, deliriously awake now.

"Daddy, is it really you . . ."

"Baby . . ."

Buck's out. Buck's home. Blanche can't remember being happier.

"I was too happy," she says. They drive down to Dallas, and even the indignity of being pulled over on suspicion of being Clyde and Bonnie doesn't dispel the mood.

❊

Down in Dallas, at the filling station on the Eagle Ford Road, Cumie and Henry are in a good mood, too. Their boy is out of prison, ten days after his thirtieth birthday. Not just out on parole, like Clyde, either. Buck got a full pardon on March 23 from Governor Ma Ferguson. That pardon is thanks partly to the efforts of Mrs. Barrow, but even more thanks to the efforts of Blanche.

"I personally was instrumental in securing his pardon," she says.

Cumie doesn't care one whit about how Buck got his pardon or who did what. She's got more than enough on her mind. Buck's home, and that's one less child to worry about. Don't forget L.C., poor little guy, still waiting trial. And Clyde. Clyde, Clyde, Clyde . . .

Who knows, Cumie thinks. Maybe, just maybe, Buck coming home is the start of a turn around a corner that's been a long, long time coming. She's got to hope that, anyway, because Buck seems pretty stuck on thinking that he can somehow turn Clyde and Bonnie around. Thinks it's his duty as a brother.

"I used to dream at night that Clyde had been caught and brought to the death house," he tells Nell. Buck's job at Huntsville included sweeping out the room where they keep Old Sparky, the oak chair with straps and electrodes and a persistent smell of death. "I'd wake up in a cold sweat. I couldn't have stood it if that had happened while I was there. Something has got to be done to make Clyde straight with the law again, Sis."

No one in the family really believes it's possible. Haven't they all tried a dozen times or more to get Clyde to turn himself in, tried to get him to make some kind of deal for his life? And doesn't Clyde always say it's no use anymore, that he's sure to get the chair? "Blanche, you know I can't stop now," Clyde says. "You know I've gone too far already to stop."

"You fool around with Clyde," Nell tells Buck, "and you'll land back in the pen with a life sentence."

Clyde's not exactly making it easier on Buck by telling him to stay away or anything like that. He has no intention of coming in from the cold. But as soon as he gets wind of the news that Buck's out, he wants to see his big brother.

"Buck got out of the penitentiary," says Cumie, and "stayed around the house about a week and then he and Blanche went down to her mother's farm near Seagoville. A night or two later Clyde and Bonnie drove in, stayed only a short time, and they left to go down to the farm to see Buck."

Blanche's parents are the ones who answer the front door at around midnight to see Clyde, W.D., and Bonnie. They've never met any of them before. "We had not been in bed long and had just dozed off to sleep," says Blanche, "so when they ask for Buck their voices wake Buck and I, who were sleeping in a bedroom on the second floor. . . . We knew their voices when we first heard them."

Buck jumps out of bed and hurries downstairs. The last time he saw his little brother was just over a year ago in Huntsville, where he had just turned himself in and Clyde had just been transferred to recover from chopping his toe off. It's an emotional reunion for both brothers. There's more than water under the bridge; there's been a flood go by that carried the very real chance that they'd never lay eyes on each other again.

Buck tells his in-laws not to be alarmed, that everything is all right. Don't worry that these two boys coming into your house in the middle of the night are carrying sawed-off shotguns and this girl has had one or two sips. They're family. Don't worry, they're family. Okay, maybe the girl has had three sips.

"Bonnie was so drunk she could hardly walk," says Blanche.

They head up to the bedroom, so Blanche's parents downstairs can try to get some sleep. "All of them come over to the bed, where I was, and sit down," says Blanche. All of them except W.D., that would be. He sits by the window to keep watch in case they were followed out to the lonely farm.

"After greeting me, Bonnie sat on the side of the bed. She seemed glad to see me, and I was glad to see her. I had always felt sorry for her, having to live the life she was living, never a minute's peace, and she had often told me she was happier when she had something to drink, so I did not blame her for staying drunk most of the time if it made her feel better."

Bonnie looks worn out to Blanche, "as if she had not slept in a week." Buck and Clyde are talking in one corner. W.D. is keeping an eye out the window. Blanche hasn't even begun to suspect that Clyde might ask Buck to go off with him. She thinks that even if Clyde did ask such an outrageous thing, her Buck would say no. Not worried at all about the brothers' conversation, she tells Bonnie to come on and get in bed.

"Try to get a little sleep," she tells her, but Bonnie wants to talk. "She said it was so good to have some woman she knew to talk to, that it sometimes was so lonesome for her just driving in the company of men all the time."

Blanche says she understands, having done it herself for the few months she lived on the lam with Buck before he turned himself in. Now and then during the evening Blanche hears bits of what Clyde is saying in the background—"Blanche knows where the place is and knows the country well," he says at one point. At another point he says something about busting Ray Hamilton out of jail. But Blanche isn't really paying attention. She and Buck aren't going anywhere with Clyde and Bonnie; Buck's promised her that.

The problem is, Blanche finds out around four in the morning that Buck's also promised Clyde the opposite. It's not pretty, but Blanche puts her foot down. They're not going. It's the darkest hour, just before the dawn, and Bonnie and Clyde need to be on the road. They all plead with her. Clyde says nothing will happen. Buck says nothing will happen. Bonnie says she'd love the company.

But Blanche is adamant, and Clyde, Bonnie, and W.D. eventually leave without her and Buck. Blanche won't even go down to the car to see them off, but Buck does, and promises Clyde he'll talk to her some more. She's crying when he gets back upstairs, not hysterically or anything, just weeping at the fight she knows is coming and maybe at the outcome she fears is inevitable.

"I know nothing will happen to us," he says, even though she tells him over and over again that the police have come right out and informed her that they're going to be watching like hawks to see if Buck gets back with Clyde. He won't listen to reason or tears, and finally Blanche tells her husband how she sees it, how she hopes the best for his little brother but doesn't think Clyde would do as much for them.

"He will shoot to kill if the officers should run in on him," she says. "And if we were with him, he would not think of you. He would only think of getting away and saving his own life. Hasn't he run away and left you before, lying in the street shot down by officers, not knowing or stopping to see if you were still alive?"

Blanche isn't sad now. She's mad as hell at Clyde for even putting his brother in such an unholy bind. Didn't Clyde promise her that he would go straight if he ever got out? He promised her this when she was just about the only one in the family, including Bonnie, who was going to visit him at Eastham. She doesn't trust Clyde; she hardly even likes him.

"Didn't he run away and leave Ralph Fults and Bonnie near Kaufman?" she goes on to Buck. "Ralph was shot in the arm. He and Bonnie were taken to jail. He didn't even try to get Ralph a lawyer, or do anything for him. Do you think he would stop to think of what a tight place he may have you in? Especially if the officers should corner him and we were with him? Considering the many murders he is wanted for now? No, he wouldn't!"

"I know nothing will happen to us," Buck keeps saying, as if repeating it will make it certain. He, too, is crying now. Can't she see that he won't be able to live with himself if his little brother were to get killed without his even trying to turn him around? "I may never see him alive again if we don't go," he tells her.

Buck's mad too. If she won't go with him, he says, he'll have to go alone.

She's lost the battle and knows it. Letting him go alone is even worse than going with him, and not only because she'll miss him. Alone with Clyde, Buck's sure to do something stupid. Worse, Clyde will never let him go once he has him. "I thought if Buck were alone with Clyde," she says, "Clyde would try to kill his love for me."

She'll go to Joplin, she tells her husband. He promises it will only be for a few days.

❀

"The morning they left," says Cumie, "Buck sent me word he was going off for a while with Clyde and try to straighten him out. He sent me word he was leaving his pistol at home and was not going to get in any more trouble."

Somewhere, it doesn't matter where, you stop the car. Come on, you tell Bonnie and W.D., get out of the car, let's make some pictures. You bought Bonnie that Kodak Brownie camera and film and haven't used it yet. Come on. It's a camera with film, and here the three of you are—you, Bonnie, and W.D.—on the road on the run and free. At least for the moment.

C'mon, sugar, let's make pictures. Everyone does as you say. They always do, and besides, it's fun. One of you, sitting at the wheel of the car.

Click.

One of Bonnie looking sweet out of the car window, peering like a little child with her hands on the door and her head barely coming up to the opening. Isn't she sweet. That's great, honey.

Click.

And of course a couple of W.D. He's leaning back on the car looking much bigger and badder than his seventeen years.

Click.

Wait wait wait, get one of us kissing. W.D. takes the camera and you take Bonnie in your arms and put your left hand—the one holding your cigar—up by her neck. Your right hand slides down around the small of her back, pulls her sideways a bit. She leans into you, and up on her tiptoes. You're just on the side of the road there, with a dirt cutaway for your background, but you kiss her movie-style. W.D. clicks.

"They do a lot of lovemaking," W.D. says later to no one in particular. "She makes over him a good deal but he does a lot of it himself."

And take one of me picking her up, holding Bonnie up. She puts her hand at your neck and her chin on your forehead. Is the car in the background? Get the car in the background.

Click. Click. Click.

Did you get it? Did you? Good. Now one of us, you and me, W.D., looking good. And you do look good in your suits.

It's fun now. Give me that cigar, Clyde, she says. Or take this cigar,

Bonnie, he says. Doesn't matter. She doesn't smoke big fat cigars, but it's going to be a funny picture. Like a school play. She takes the cigar in her mouth, the pistol in her hand. Hikes her leg up on the fender.

Click. That's going to be famous, that picture.

She's looking so good in her little beret and that hugging dress. Somebody suggests one of Bonnie sticking Clyde up. Ha! She takes the shotgun, points it at your belt. Takes her fingers—long fingers for such a little thing—and puts the tip of one of them right on your chest. Smiles. You got to say you don't entirely like someone pointing a gun at your belly. Not even if it's Bonnie. You smile a bit, but mostly just look her in the eye.

Click.

Fact is, she pointed a shotgun at you for real once. Or as for real as it ever gets between you and Bonnie.

"One time she did pick up Clyde's shotgun and threaten him with it," says W.D. "He'd said something to me because the jack I was using to change a flat tire kept slipping. Clyde thought it was taking too long. Bonnie come to my side and held Clyde at gunpoint. He turned around and walked off."

W.D. figures it was just the law on their tail that was making Clyde jumpy. "The heat back of us was getting close enough to put Clyde on edge at anything. I finished changing the flat and took the shotgun from Bonnie so Clyde could come back to the car," he says. "We'd been drinking white lightning, and you know how that is."

Sure you and Bonnie fight—what man and woman don't? It's always over the stupidest things, too, isn't it. You go at it once like cats and dogs over whether or not you need a can opener to open sardines, have a big old fight over how to get the darned fish out of the can.

"Why don't you go on home to mama, baby?" you say when she really gets under your skin and starts itching like a chigger. "You probably wouldn't get more than ninety-nine years. Texas hasn't sent a woman to the chair yet, and I'd send in my recommendation for leniency."

"She'd laugh at him then," says W.D., "and everything would be smooth again."

One smooth time in those weeks, you're driving along as always and there's a road sign that's just crying out to be shot at.

Rata rata rata.

Ha!

"Clyde liked to stay sharp and would sometimes hit the car brakes all of a sudden, bounce out to the roadside and open up with that automatic rifle on a tree or a sign for practice," says W.D.

Clyde with a road sign he's recently used for target practice. *(Missouri State Highway Patrol file photograph. Used with permission.)*

Damn right! Look at that hole in the sign! Get that camera, Bud. Take a picture. You get out of the car, put your arm through the hole you blasted in the sign with the Browning. You hang your hat on the top of the sign and tell Bonnie or W.D. to take the picture.

Click.

And let's get all these guns out and stick 'em all over the front of the car and get some funny ones. Come on. Yeah, that's good. The car is decorated all up like a Christmas tree with pistols and sawed-offs and Brownings. And that deputy's fancy pistol right up where the hood ornament goes. That's too good. That's rich.

Click. Click.

Can't wait to see those. C'mon, let's go find Buck and Blanche.

✳

Things haven't been this nice since those times last summer, after Bonnie first got out of jail and she and Clyde and Raymond had their little place in Wichita Falls. Those were good days. It's hard to believe now that that was only half a year ago, since it seems more like forever ago. Or it seems like just yesterday that they were in Wichita Falls. Yesterday or forever, depending on her mood.

Bonnie's in a good mood now, which means not looking back and not thinking ahead. For a while, it looks like maybe Blanche has won the argument with Buck and they aren't going to show. Clyde doesn't believe it for a second, but Bonnie wonders. She can't blame Blanche for trying; it's what she would do in the same situation. She told Blanche as much.

"If I felt I would lose Buck again after all those long weary months of waiting for him to be free, she did not want me to go against my better judgment," Blanche says Bonnie told her before she and Clyde left her mother's house. "She told me everything that had happened to them in the past six months and how she wished she and Clyde were as free as Buck and I were. She said she hoped we could stay that way."

For their sake, that *is* what Bonnie hopes. For her own sake, though, she sure hopes they show up in Checotah, Oklahoma, as planned.

And . . . they do. Poor Blanche, but even she's decided to make the best of it now that they're all together. Bonnie, Clyde, W.D., Buck, Blanche, and Snowball. Blanche tried to leave the dog behind, under the care of her mother until she and Buck got back from what was supposed to be a short trip, but Buck refused. He'd been long enough without his wife and his dog, he told her. Snowball comes with us.

It is fun, as even Blanche has to admit, especially once they get out of the tourist camp and set themselves up in the little apartment at the edge of Joplin on April 1. Buck handles the renting, saying to a neighbor, "You don't need to be afraid of me. I'm a civil engineer and I live near here."

The ground floor is entirely a garage, big enough for four cars, though the neighbor uses half of it. Upstairs is a handsome two-bedroom apartment, cozy and with lots of windows across the front and slight arches over the interior passageways. It's a little square, with a kitchen and a bedroom at the back, a living room and another bedroom at the front. And, of course, a bathroom. Nothing big or fancy: sitting on the john, a person's knees pretty much touch the edge of the bathtub. But a bathtub means regular baths. Bonnie's not complaining.

Buck and Blanche take the bedroom at the front, looking out on the street, and Bonnie and Clyde take the slightly smaller room at the back. W.D. sleeps on a cot in the living room, which is a change, since usually he just squeezes right into bed with Bonnie and Clyde rather than sleep on the floor. "We used to laugh at him and tell him he was afraid to sleep alone," says Blanche, "but he would take the teasing good naturedly."*

It's tight in the apartment with five people and a dog, and they're not all used to living with one another. Blanche likes everything nice and neat, keeps her and Buck's room all tidy, with the bed made and such. Clyde and Bonnie's room, on the other hand, is a wreck, with the bedsheets all over the place and clothes in heaps. And, always, guns scattered around.

"He was never more than an arm's reach from a gun," says W.D. about Clyde. W.D. says Clyde even prayed with a gun. "Even in bed, or out of bed on the floor in the night, when he thought we was all asleep and couldn't see him kneeling there. I seen it more than once. He prayed. I reckon he was praying for his soul. Maybe it was for more life. He knowed it would end soon, but he didn't intend for it to be in jail."

Blanche likes the shades and curtains open to let the air in and so she can see out. Clyde, on the other hand, will never open the curtains, in case someone's peering in from somewhere. He's obsessive that way: won't let any delivery boys carry groceries or laundry up, even when Blanche tells him it seems stranger for a woman to carry them up and he can just hide back in his room.

"Those people are always bothered with nose trouble," he says. End of discussion: Blanche meets the deliveries at the door. So it's cozy at times in the apartment in Joplin, all right, particularly for Blanche, who doesn't want to be there.

Compared to a car seat or the tourist camps that Bonnie's gotten used to, on the other hand, the place is a castle. It's even built out of stone, like a fortress. The apartment feels designed for them; there's even a big hideaway closet over where the stairs come up from the garage that's just right for storing the guns. There are lots of guns, especially after Clyde and Buck

---

* Rumors about Clyde's sexuality and the possibility that W.D. and other gang members may have participated in various kinky arrangements all seem to have originated long after the death of Clyde and Bonnie. Without exception, the witnesses and family members who actually knew Clyde and Bonnie deny any such possibility. "I've heard stories since [their death] that Clyde was homosexual or, as they say in the pen, a 'punk,'" says W.D. He thinks the rumors may have started because Clyde was small, quiet, and polite. Or because he sometimes dressed in women's clothing to escape detection when visiting Dallas, or because of his slight limp from having chopped off his toe. "I knew a lot of convicts the years I was in prison—some of them years on Eastham Farm, where Clyde had served his time—and none of them had a story on him being a punk. Matter of fact, nobody, not the police who questioned me for hours and hours or the reporters who got in to see me, ever mentioned it. . . . It's just recently, more than thirty years since Clyde was killed, that I've heard the story. I was with him and Bonnie. I know. It just ain't true."

knock off a nearby National Guard armory. The closet is stacked with them, and there are more in the cars.

Clyde and Blanche aren't always disagreeing with each other. Clyde, who likes to cook, is pretty much the only one who helps his sister-in-law prepare meals. And neither of them can fathom what it is that Buck and Bonnie like so much about eating pickled pigs' feet. Clyde leans more toward french fries and creamed peas, which seem much more sensible to Blanche. (W.D. will eat anything.)

For a couple days Clyde and Blanche go mad for jigsaw puzzles. But most nights, Bonnie and the boys sit around drinking beer—it's legal again!—smoking, playing poker, and cleaning guns until all hours of the morning. Blanche, who prefers whiskey to beer and doesn't play poker, is nonetheless a good sport about it. She either plays solitaire or sits on Buck's lap and tries to learn how the different hands work. But some people just aren't meant for poker, and usually she falls asleep in her chair. Everyone sleeps in.

"Clyde could hardly get Bonnie or W.D. awake the next day. He worked with them for hours, or until he got mad because they would not get up," Blanche says. "Bonnie seldom got up before twelve noon or one o'clock. Of course, none of us were early birds because we stayed up so late."

They're having fun, sliding into a routine that feels suspiciously like a real life, except that, of course, no one is exactly working for the money. (Once in a while, Clyde and W.D. go off for a night or a couple days at a time and come back with a new infusion of cash.) While they're gone, Bonnie and Blanche go shopping some days, or take in a movie.

"Every time we went to town we came back with our arms loaded with ashtrays, glassware, small picture frames, and anything else that was pretty or that we wanted or needed, plus a lot of things we didn't need," says Blanche.

On one of these excursions Bonnie buys herself some black construction paper and white ink. She loves the cozy little kitchen at the back of the apartment, with its built-in furnishings and sweet suburban views of trees and respectable houses. She sits there afternoons, while Blanche gets to work on dinner or neatens up around the apartment. She sits and works on her writing. Other times she sits in the middle of the rug in the living room. White ink on black paper will be perfect, Bonnie thinks, for a dramatic finished copy of "Suicide Sal."

"All of us had a lot of fun together," says Blanche about those spring weeks in southwest Missouri. "But to me there always seemed to be a shadow hanging over us, like a dark cloud."

Blanche says that as if Bonnie doesn't know that cloud. That old cloud? It's always there.

❀

"It was April 13, 1933, that I experienced my baptism of fire, so to speak," says George Kahler. Like a lot of states in the early 1930s, Missouri has a brand-new state highway patrol force, and Kahler is a member of the inaugural class of 1931. He's had a few adventures in his brief tenure as a lawman, mostly having to do with learning how to ride his Harley. Now, though, a lead has come in that a string of robberies in the area might be connected with the people living in an apartment on Thirty-fourth Street, just across the Joplin town line. Specifically, during the robbery of the Neosho Milling Company, a man and his wife were held hostage while the safe was cracked, and their descriptions of the bandits' car in particular "seemed to fit the folks in the house."

This isn't the first time Kahler's been by the apartment. The odd behavior of the tenants there has not gone unnoticed over the past two weeks. "Neighbors said the residents of the house had several cars, all with license plates from different states," Kahler says. Cars that they parked facing out rather than in, like everyone else. "They rarely left in the daytime, but were seen coming and going at all hours in the night. Apparently none of them worked."

It's the little things that make people nervous. As one neighbor says, "They lived there with their curtains down all the time." The guy who delivers the laundry tells Kahler there's one guy living there who won't let anyone see him. People can't be arrested for being shy and keeping their curtains closed, however, and a check on the registration of the one car parked outside didn't turn anything up.

Kahler drops it until the Neosho burglary convinces him and a colleague named Walt Grammer to get a search warrant and take a closer look. A constable named Wes Harryman, who has the credentials to serve the warrant, comes along with them. They also invite a couple of Joplin city policemen—Harry McGinnis and Tom DeGraff—along for support, even though the apartment is technically just outside the city line.

"We decided that Grammer and I would go in one car—it was Captain Elsick's Model A sedan—and Harryman and two Joplin detectives, Harry McGinnis and Tom DeGraff, would follow in the other," says Kahler. It's about four o'clock in the afternoon when they set off.

Kahler and his fellow officers don't know it, but the people inside the apartment have been getting suspicious of their neighbors as well. Blanche, in particular, is certain that the neighborhood private watchman—whom they also pay to keep an eye on their car—is sniffing around too much. And the fellow who has the use of the other half of the garage is a worry. Just the night before Kahler gets his search warrant, in fact, Clyde and Bonnie have a huge argument over the decision to bring another stolen Ford V-8 back to the apartment to put in the garage. She knows it will make the place hot, and Clyde's just as certain it will be fine overnight until he and W.D. use it on another job and ditch it.

"They kept arguing until they both were mad enough to fight, which is what they did," says Blanche. "And Clyde wasn't very easy with her. He knocked her across the bedroom a couple of times but she got up and went back for more. Bonnie had tried as best she could to keep the place from getting hot. She did not want Buck and I to get into trouble and have to live the life she and Clyde were living."

W.D. has seen it before. "I never knew him to jump on anybody with his fists except Bonnie," he says. "He whipped her occasionally." It always passes. "He slaps her across the face when she crosses him, but they kiss and make up."

Not this time, though. Bonnie goes to bed mad and Clyde takes W.D. and leaves to pull a job somewhere. The two of them will be back tomorrow night, he says, and then we'll all leave. Okay?

Blanche goes to bed angry too. She's had her own smaller version of the fight with Clyde's brother, telling Buck that if he won't leave the apartment with her she's going home alone. They've given Clyde his chance to reform, and enough's enough. Buck agrees to leave the next day, or the day after that at the latest.

"All of us had the jitters," says Blanche, "and felt as if a bomb was about to explode." All of them, including Clyde, have plans to be out of the apartment within the next forty-eight hours.

Before any of them get a chance to pack up and leave, however, Kahler and his colleagues set off from the Joplin Police Department with a somewhat flimsy search warrant for whiskey that's really just a cover for their desire to take a closer look at the cars.

"While the others served the warrant, Grammer and I were to check identification numbers on the car parked between the houses," Kahler says. "We didn't realize who we were dealing with. If we had, we'd have lined up a lot more help."

❊

"Oh Lordy," you yell. "Let's get started."

You've just driven back into the garage with W.D. scrunched down low under the dashboard. You always tell him to do that when you get into town or near where you are going, so he's used to it; it keeps all those big noses on the corner guessing about how many people are in the car. Sometimes you even put poor W.D. in the trunk, but not this time.

Buck is in front of the garage when you pull up, having just finished doing something to his car, which is kept around behind the apartment. There are two pairs of swinging doors, and he opens the set on the left to let you back the car in, which you do and then get out and start talking. Just as he's getting ready to close the doors again, damn if he doesn't see two cars pulling around the corner. It's the law, he tells you.

Inside the lead car, Patrolman Grammer, who's in the passenger seat, sees Buck closing the doors of the garage.

"Step on it," he says to Kahler. "We'll get up there before they get inside."

"So I stepped on it, but of course those Model A's didn't have much scat," says Kahler. "They looked up, saw us coming, and casually moved inside the garage, pulling the door shut behind them."

Kahler pulls up just as Buck is getting the big swinging garage doors almost shut behind him, and Grammer jumps out before the machine has even come to a full stop.

"Hey, fellows," he calls out. "Just a minute, we want to talk to you."

BANG! You don't want to talk to him. *Rata rata rata.*

"Their reply was a burst of gunfire from a pistol or rifle," Kahler says. He and Grammer are damn lucky to be alive. "The first shot barely missed both of us, passing through the car."

"Cover the back!" Kahler shouts to Grammer, who doesn't need any more encouragement to run around behind the house. Kahler himself manages to scramble out of the car to relative safety around the corner of the house next door.

Now the second police car rolls up and all hell starts breaking loose.

"DeGraff, who was following us, headed his car against the garage doors, trying to catch them with the bumper of his car," says Kahler. "At the same time, Harryman jumped out and ran inside the garage, a distance of about three steps, firing one shot from his gun as he entered.

Bang.

BLAM!

You or Buck answers with the sawed-off shotgun right into his chest. He's dead.

Pow. Pow. Pow. Harry McGinnis has gotten out of the back seat of the second police car, made his way over to the set of doors on the right side of the garage, and is trying to shoot his pistol through the window.

BLAM!

Another shotgun blast goes into him, severing his right arm below the elbow and hitting him in the face and chest as well. He falls. Behind him, DeGraff retreats around the corner. You switch to a Browning and stick the muzzle out the crack and point it in DeGraff's general direction.

Rata rata rata. You love these guns! You hate these goddamn cops. DeGraff can't believe how bad the day is turning out to be.

"It was just one of those places you get into and you can't get out of," he says. "You get into one of those hot spots and there you are."

Kahler, from the opposite corner, takes advantage of the attention you are paying to McGinnis to get off some shots, aiming through the garage door at where he thinks whoever is holding the rifle he sees sticking out of the crack is standing.

Pow. Pow. Pow.

"I aimed about where I judged his body to be and put two or three bullets through the door. He dropped the weapon and ran inside," says Kahler.

"Oh Lordy," you yell loud enough at some point that Blanche and Bonnie can hear you upstairs in the apartment. "Let's get started."

Bonnie is writing and Blanche is finishing up a game of solitaire when they hear the shooting start. They think for a second that there's nothing more going on than you getting one of your guns jammed and misfiring. That's happened before, but when Buck comes tearing up the stairs and starts yelling at them to get ready to leave because the cops are surrounding the place, they start to move around, collecting their stuff. Bonnie grabs a gun, goes to the window, and fires it.

"But I know I didn't hit him," she says later. "He ran off down the street. Then before I could fire again a slug came through the top of the window and glass shattered all around me."

Buck almost tackles her, yelling, "Get back, for God's sake!"

Downstairs, W.D. sticks the business end of one of the stolen Browning automatics out the garage doors and lets loose in the general direction of Kahler.

Rata rata rata. Fire spews out of the muzzle. *Rata rata!*

"I felt sharp pains in my face and neck," says Kahler. "I thought, My God, half my head is gone." He's been hit only by fragments of stone chipped loose by the bullets, though, and decides his little .38 handgun is like a joke compared to the Brownings and whatnot. He runs for better cover around the house. W.D. keeps up the barrage.

Rata rata rata.

"How he missed, I'll never know," Kahler says. It must be Kahler's lucky day, because W.D. actually thinks he hasn't missed when Kahler trips on some chicken wire as he's running and falls to the ground. W.D. thinks Kahler's dead or at least out of commission and turns his back on him to look around for DeGraff.

"Where did the other son-of-a-bitch go?" Kahler hears him say. He's got one more bullet in his pistol.

"From about twenty-five feet away, I took careful aim and fired," says Kahler. "The slug hit him just beneath the right shoulder blade. He fell back inside the garage."

When W.D. staggers upstairs with a hole in his chest and blood coming out everywhere, Bonnie and Blanche really get moving.

"Blanche, they shot me! I'm dying," he says to Blanche, who up to this point has been trying to control Snowball. "Please do something for me."

He says this over and over again. He also says, "Leave everything . . . y'all get down in the car."

He falls against Blanche, who is on her way into the bedroom to grab her purse. He wraps his arms around her neck and tells her he's dying. It's all Blanche can do to keep from falling over herself. Buck's back downstairs with you, loading guns into the car and getting Harryman's corpse out of the way so you can get the car out of the garage when the time comes. In the brief lull in the shooting you run out the front of the garage to release the brake on the police car that's blocking your exit.

"Get in the car," you yell to no one and everyone. W.D. is somehow back down the stairs and getting pushed into the back seat. Here's Bonnie, too.

"Take the guns with you, Bonnie—never mind anything else," you yell to her. "For God's sake, honey, run!"

And here's Blanche, who helps you push the cop car out into the street, until she gets herself all worked up over the sight of a dead man. What does she expect to see in a gunfight?

"I started to push it and saw another man just outside the door," she says, "lying there with what looked like his brains blown out and running down his shoulders and onto the ground. It looked as if one arm had been torn off by the bullets."

Blanche almost forgets to let go of the police car as it starts to coast down the hill. She's out in the middle of the driveway when the shooting suddenly starts up again. It's either DeGraff or Kahler.

Pow pow. You're hit, but not down yet, bastards. Not when you're holding a Browning automatic rifle in your hands.

Rata rata rata.

"I saw Clyde stagger," says Blanche. "He had a rifle and was almost bent over double, shooting as fast as he could. I could feel bullets whiz by my head."

Rata rata rata.

Hit but not down yet, bastards.

Blanche screams and takes off down the street, Snowball right behind her. Buck calls her back, and she turns and looks at him. She comes back, mostly because she wants to get Buck's pardon papers and their marriage license out of the house. Snowball, though, has had enough and keeps going.

"That was the last time I saw our little white dog," says Blanche.

Now, according to Bonnie, you're the one that won't get in the car. Buck hasn't let Blanche go back upstairs and they're all in the car and you're still out there firing away on the BAR at God knows who.

Rata rata.

"For God's sake," Bonnie says to you, "come and get in the car."

"Not till I get the dirty rat that shot me," you say, and give one more blast—*rata rata*—after which you come and jump behind the wheel and say a prayer to the God of V-8 engines and plant that pedal on the floor.

"We seemed to almost jump out of the garage to the street," says Blanche. You're gone.

"DeGraff and I fired several rounds at their fleeing car but to no avail," says patrolman Kahler. "We would estimate about two or three minutes' time elapsed from the time we arrived in front of the garage apartment until they were gone."

It starts to rain. Then pour. It rains so much, in fact, that over in Texas the Trinity River overruns its banks and floods West Dallas, nearly washing away the old squatters' camp under the viaduct.

❋

Missouri State Highway Patrol
Joplin, Missouri,
April 14, 1933

Subject: Report of raid at Thirty-fourth and Oakridge drive . . .

While waiting for the ambulance which arrived about five minutes after called, we searched the garage, finding one sawed off shotgun with fresh blood stains, one 30-06 rifle wrapped in a quilt in the back of a V8 Ford Roadster. The Roadster proved to be stolen from Miami, Oklahoma on the night of April 11th.

The ambulance arrived, we loaded McGinnis and Harryman in it and then proceeded to search the apartment above.

In a closet of the apartment, we found one Browning Machine Rifle and three 30-06 rifles. In one of the overstuffed chairs we found one 41 Colt pistol, frontier model. Among the effects we found a bunch of Kodak pictures and negatives of Clyde Barrow, Bonnie Parker and another man and woman as yet not positively identified. A marriage license of Ivy (Buck) Barrow to Blanch Caldwell, and Texas ownership papers to the Marmon Sedan, in M. B. (Buck) Barrow's name. Also Buck Barrow's pardon papers from the Huntsville, Texas Penitentiary signed by Governor Miriam Ferguson, dated March 23, 1933. . . .

Signed
Walt Grammer
Geo. B. Kahler

Later, George Kahler remembers one other thing that he and Grammer found in the apartment that they forgot to put in their report.

"On a table lay several sheets of black paper on which Bonnie Parker had been composing a poem," he says, "in white ink. She had evidently been writing when the shooting started, because the ink was still wet."

❋

"He was on the porch with the paper in his hand when they shot him to pieces," says Wes Harryman's oldest son, Claude. This is years later, when everyone, including George Kahler, has forgotten about Harryman shooting his pistol. The accepted truth by that time has become that Harryman was politely pulling out the search warrant when he was gunned down, as if that little fiction will somehow make the murder worse and the loss easier for Claude and his mother and siblings to bear. They can no longer afford the farm that was their father's main occupation.

"We sold the farm. I worked in the packing house butchering animals for $1.50 a day. My mother sewed for the WPA," says Claude. "It was a long haul. It wasn't until my brothers and sisters grew up that I could make plans, get married, settled out on my own place."

❀

July 10, 1933

Special Agent in Charge
U.S. Bureau of Investigation
Kansas City, Missouri

Dear Sir:

A young man giving the name of TOMMY HARRYMAN . . .
has appeared in Dallas and says he is a brother of J. W. Harryman, Constable, who was killed by the Barrow brothers at
Joplin, Missouri.

He states that it is his intention to ascertain the hideout of
the Barrow brothers and either kill them himself or assist others
in so doing.

He has not yet contacted this office, but it is expected he will
do so in the near future; and in order that I may know how to
deal with him will you verify . . . that J. W. Harryman has a
brother Tommy. . . .

Very Truly Yours,
F. J. Blake
Special Agent in Charge
[Dallas Office of FBI]

❀

"When I came to next, we were in that Ford V-8 sedan on a country road,"
says W.D. "Clyde was driving at the time, he was driving very fast. We headed
for the Texas Panhandle and drove as fast as we could away from Joplin."

There's blood everywhere in the car, mostly from W.D. but some of it
from Clyde, who has a bullet in his chest but won't let anyone else drive. Buck
was hit by a ricochet, but the bullet didn't break his skin, just gave him a
nasty bruise. Bonnie's freezing cold in nothing but the negligee she was wearing when the shooting started. Blanche is pretty much in a state of shock, still
clutching the deck of cards she had been playing solitaire with, thinking
about how the future has all come crashing down just as she knew it would.

"I think I must have gone insane for a few minutes," she says. She is crying, yanking at her own hair. "W.D. was trying to pet me and begging me
not to cry. He was suffering himself, but was begging me not to take it so hard.
Buck was trying to tell me it hurt him just as bad as it did me, but I couldn't
see how it could."

Poor, sweet old W.D. He's just a big, dumb kid and he's hurt the worst by far. They all think he might die, in fact, though they're not telling him. He thinks so too. There's a hole in the front of him, and another in his back, but he just can't believe the slug went all the way through him. Thinks he must have been shot twice.

"My belly ached so bad I thought the bullet had stopped there," he says.

Finally, near a country store, Clyde stops the car for gas and oil and aspirin and rubbing alcohol. They head down the road another short piece and pull over. Hold still now, they tell W.D. Hold still now.

"Clyde wrapped an elm branch with gauze," says W.D., "and pushed it through the hole in my side and out my back. The bullet had gone clean through me, so we knew it would heal."

They pour a little rubbing alcohol into both sides of the wounds for good measure, which hurts almost more than the stick. Clyde's bullet isn't deep, and Bonnie works it out with a hairpin. A little alcohol in that hole, too, and then back on the road. All night long.

It's a godforsaken mess, and even Clyde seems to know it for once.

"Bonnie and Clyde said they were very sorry they had gotten us into trouble," says Blanche. "But saying they were sorry didn't do any good."

CHAPTER 18

THE MIDDLE OF THE ROAD

"We didn't go back to Joplin anymore after this gun battle," says W.D., "but rambled around for several months through a good many states, Texas, Oklahoma, Kansas, Indiana, and Louisiana."

That's pretty much all there is now, rambling around, working the state lines. Never stop, never stop, never stop. Once in a while, they might stay at a tourist camp, where they can clean up a bit, but never more than a night or two at the most. Most nights they sleep in the cars or camp out on the ground, with one always keeping watch while the others sleep.

"I lost all track of time we drove so much and so fast, most of the day and night," says Blanche, who adds a few states to W.D.'s list: New Mexico, Nebraska, Iowa, Illinois, Missouri, and Arkansas. "I do not know what filling stations or stores were robbed during this period of time, but I do know that our money was obtained through hold-ups or robberies."

They change cars whenever the opportunity presents itself, and pull off small-time burglaries and robberies when the cash runs short. W.D.'s not much use at first, given the hole in his chest, but Buck's not even pretending not to take part anymore. Why should he? It's all over the newspapers that his pardon and marriage license were in the apartment at Joplin.

"I'd get the chair," he says when anyone tries to tell him he can still turn himself in, say he was just visiting his brother and that he didn't fire a shot. "It's no use," he says to Clyde. "I've got to stick with you now."

They aren't making any major heists. Just hit-and-runs at gas stations and small stores. "We never had a great deal of money," Blanche says, "yet we always had sufficient for our needs."

And, of course, pretty much the first order of business on Clyde's list after the rubbing alcohol is guns. Less than a week after the shoot-out in Joplin, a Ford sedan with Missouri plates and carrying three men and two women turns up in Plattville, Illinois.

"One woman was a blonde, the other a brunette, and both looked like hard characters," a witness says.

One of the men, a small guy with a southern accent who "had a rather thin face and sickly looking" comes into the grocery there. He buys a little something and asks casually at the checkout counter if there's an armory in town. Next morning, when the supply sergeant shows up at the armory he discovers that the front door is wide open and all the locks in the place are busted. Three Browning automatic rifles are gone, along with ten pistols, assorted other rifles, and a whole carload of parts and accessories. Even the bayonets and scabbards are gone.

After that Clyde, for one, breathes a little easier.

❀

Smoot Schmid is not having the glorious inaugural year as Dallas County sheriff he imagined. Within a few weeks of the killing of Deputy Davis in Lilly McBride's front yard, two other local lawmen are gunned down. Not by Clyde Barrow and his gang, it turns out, but to the voters of the county it doesn't much matter. Nor does it matter to them that this lawlessness seems to be all over the Midwest, with Pretty Boy Floyd up in Oklahoma, John Dillinger, Baby Face Nelson, and Machine Gun Kelly up in wherever. Doesn't matter that people are robbing banks and shooting it up all over this Great Depression Dust Bowl Hard Times—whatever they decide to call it next.

What matters is that crime feels a little out of control and that West Dallas is Smoot Schmid's territory more than anyone else's, and he's not going to be sheriff forever, like he promised his protégé Ted Hinton, if it stays like this.

Even the newspapers are starting to poke fun at the fact that Schmid and his deputies don't even know who is in Barrow's gang and who is not. "Jesse James Next?" the *Dallas Morning News* quips in a headline about the changing list of names being bandied about. That's real cute. They should try to catch him.

In other words, says Hinton, "the clamor was growing to get the Barrows."

When word gets to Schmid by telegraph on the day of the gunfight at Joplin that Buck's pardon papers and some other evidence implicating the Barrows have been found, Schmid immediately wants to send a deputy up to have a look at the evidence. His first choice for the job is Bob Alcorn, an experienced lawman who has served as a deputy under previous sheriffs. When word comes that there's a roll of film with pictures of the gang goofing around, Alcorn tells Smoot he wants Ted Hinton to come along with him. Up to this point in his brief career as a lawman Hinton has mostly been serving subpoenas and carrying out other relatively low-profile jobs, but both Schmid and Alcorn know his real value to the department is his knowledge of West Dallas, from his years hanging around the bike shop and working as a Western Union messenger. He knows Clyde and Buck and all of them from growing up, and pretty much had a crush on Bonnie when she was a waitress.

"In all modesty, I probably knew more people—particularly the hoodlums who were up to no good—than any other deputy on the force," says Hinton. "Bob Alcorn and I drove through all of the night that remained and reached Joplin from Dallas the following morning."

Hinton knows as soon as the film is developed and he gets a look at the pictures, for instance, that the movie-star-handsome relaxed-looking mystery man wearing a pin-striped suit and leaning against a stolen Ford is not Pretty Boy Floyd, as some have suggested. That's just old W. D. Jones, another kid from West Dallas. And he knows without a doubt that that's definitely Bonnie Parker—"a woman who would be noticed in any crowd," he says—leaning up against Clyde with her hand on his chest and her cheek on his shoulder.

Alcorn wants to stay in Joplin for a few days, sniffing around, but Smoot Schmid knows the trail is more likely to come through Dallas again than Joplin. Clyde and Bonnie are long gone from Missouri, on the road to who knows where. He calls Alcorn and Hinton home.

Sheriff Schmid can take some professional comfort in knowing that the other local lawmen, the Dallas city police, aren't doing any better than he is at this point, even though they, too, have officers who've known the Barrows for years.

"In my opinion he is the most desperate character with which police of the Southwest and Middle West have to contend," says Doug Walsh of the police department's identification bureau. He's been picking Clyde up on suspicion for years and knows the family. "He would often send word to me through his mother. He told her if he ever wanted to talk he would get in touch with me, but that if I should ever meet him by chance, not to walk toward him or he would shoot."

The police can say pretty much the same thing back to Clyde at this point. According to the papers there are some seventy officers "well armed" with guns, descriptions, photographs, and "shoot-to-kill" orders. Like Schmid, Walsh knows that Clyde and Bonnie come back to town regularly: "His mother and father admit his visits, but so far our department has not been successful in catching him in the act."

As for the G-men from Washington, Frank Blake, the "special agent in charge" of Dallas, has a tracer on all mail going to Henry and Cumie, Emma Parker and Billie Jean Mace, and Blanche's family. That's about all he has, though. The New Orleans agent gets wind of the gang traveling near Logansport, Louisiana, in the weeks after the Joplin shoot-out. But, he reports to headquarters, the trail "all at once dropped off the earth."

All the laws are in the same situation as Smoot Schmid, with their ears to the ground and their guns loaded, waiting for the gang to turn up somewhere.

❋

You've got guns, but money is short, food is short, tempers are short. The good news is, guns can get you money and money will fix the other two. The other good news is that it looks like W.D. is going to live, though he'll always have a "hole large enough to put your thumb into" on his chest. All you need is a bank to rob, and there's one in Ruston, Louisiana, that looks ripe.

The plan is the same as always: steal a reasonably local car to use for the getaway from the actual job scene, and then ditch it when you make the switch back to your current machine. You find a nice-looking Chevy parked just up the street from the bank, let W.D. out, and, good morning, the keys are in it. Maybe your luck is about to turn, but goddamn if some local hero doesn't come charging out of a house and try to jump on the running board just as the car takes off. Lucky for him, he doesn't quite get there and grab something to hold on to or he'd be dead right now. Come to think of it, he's pretty lucky he's not dead either way, because instead of giving up like a sensible person he calls for his neighbor to come out.

"I had my car parked in front of a boardinghouse across from the high school, says Sophie Stone. "Soon after lunch I saw Mr. Darby come running out of the boardinghouse shouting that someone had stolen his car. We got in my car and took off after his car, which was still in sight."

There's nothing to do but pull out behind them and chase along, getting madder by the minute because it's obvious you're not going to be robbing the Ruston State Bank this afternoon. Eighteen miles out of Ruston, near the village of Hico, Stone and Darby finally give up trying to catch W.D. and turn around. Mad enough to blow a gasket, you stop and flag them over. Darby gets out of the car thinking you're a friend of theirs, looking to help.

Not exactly.

"Clyde jumped out of his car cursing and saying we'd spoiled his bank robbery," says Stone.

When Darby tells you that it's his car up there ahead that's been stolen, you let him have it. "He hit Mr. Darby over the head with a pistol," Stone says.

Whack!

"The man said something smart, which made Clyde even madder," explains Blanche, who is watching the scene from the back seat of the gang's car.

Meanwhile, Bonnie is giving Sophie Stone pretty much the same treatment, pulling her out of the driver's seat by her hair, cussing her out, and finally popping her on the back of the head with the butt of a pistol. Stone says her long braid kept her from being hurt too badly, but the whack is enough to make her compliant.

"Mr. Darby was still dazed and wasn't able to say anything. I kept begging them to let us go, but they told me that I'd better shut up, so I did," she says.

Still furious, you throw their keys in the woods and order them to get in the front seat of your car, between you and Bonnie, because there's no room in the back.

"The back seat was a regular arsenal of weapons and ammunition and a dirty man was in the back seat. I think he was Clyde's brother Buck," says Stone. She's right about that. "He was drinking and he needed a shave," she says.

Blanche is also back there, but Sophie Stone doesn't mention her. It could be she's just too afraid to look behind, as Buck keeps piping up drunkenly about killing them both.

"They told me that when they got ready they were going to tie us up to a tree and blow our brains out," she says. "Well, naturally, I was terrified. I didn't know what to do."

Where the hell is W.D. anyway? You're basically just driving around now at top speed, going past a few places where you think maybe he's pulled over and hid. You've got your police siren, and you get it going at likely spots, trying to rustle W.D. up.

"If W.D. had left the car someplace and was waiting in the woods he would know we were looking for him by the way Clyde blew the siren," says Blanche.

Where is that boy? Nowhere, it seems. You drive on, faster and madder, while this woman who screwed everything up blabbers on nervously about absolutely nothing. When some ammunition you're storing in the glove compartment keeps falling out you practically bite her head off, telling her to either hold the glove box shut or hold the ammunition, one or the other. You're snapping at everyone now, even Bonnie.

"Once Bonnie whined that she was thirsty when we stopped in a filling station, with hidden guns being held on us," says Stone. Bonnie wants to go in and get a cold drink, even though just about the whole countryside around here is probably looking for you by now. What is she thinking? "Clyde spoke roughly to her and handed her the filling station water hose," Stone says.

Sophie Stone notices that Bonnie is wearing a red dress and red shoes to match, but if there's anything glamorous about being a bank robber she's not seeing it.

"She was dirty, they all were," she says. And hungry. Once Bonnie finds out that Stone works as a home demonstration agent, all she wants to talk about is food. "She said she was terribly hungry and asked if I'd been preparing any foods that day," says Stone. "She asked me to describe the foods."

How talking about food can make a person anything other than more hungry is a mystery that might just make you madder if you let it bother you, let it sit there like some underhanded comment about how you're not providing enough food. Goddamn! Woman can drive you crazy sometimes, and you don't even want to get to thinking about Buck back there, too drunk to be of any help if trouble starts.

Only after dark, after you give up on finding W.D. anywhere short of Dallas, do you start to relax. Start to let it drift out the window with the night breeze going by at ninety miles hour. Across the Louisiana line into Arkansas, and past midnight into tomorrow, you even start to enjoy the prattle of this goofball woman who took off trying to chase down the bloody Barrow Gang. Of course you're not telling the two of them that that's who you are. And if this Dillard Darby fellow—what kind of name is that, Dillard Darby?—keeps thinking you're Pretty Boy Floyd, which he does, it's all right by you.

You tell Stone and Darby that you've "got to liking them," and even apologize to Darby for smashing his head so hard. You hope it didn't hurt too much, you say. What do you do for a living, you ask, just making conversation.

An undertaker? An undertaker? He's not kidding, either. Darby answers that he's an undertaker, which is a conversation stopper in just about any situation but sets Bonnie to cackling with laughter.

"I know we're going to get it sooner or later. I know you would really enjoy embalming us. Promise us you will," she says between guffaws.

Blanche says Darby answers that he hopes you all live a real long time, which is funnier in a way than whatever Bonnie is finding so amusing. It's obvious that Dillard Darby, undertaker, wishes you were dead at this very moment and is just too chickenshit to say so. You drive past a guy fixing a flat tire on the side of the road, hurtle past him so fast and so close you knock the jack out from under the car and send him diving for cover.

"Clyde didn't see the humor," says Stone.

She's right about that, too. A mile and a half later you slam on the brakes and ask Dillard Darby if he's got any money. He answers twenty-five cents. Get out of the car, right here, you tell them. You get out behind them.

"I thought that they were going to shoot us just like they said," says Stone. She and Darby are just about petrified with fear.

"But Clyde gave us a five-dollar bill so we could get back home," she says. "Then they roared off and just left us there."

❀

The bandit car ran into a herd of about twenty pigs and two sows on the flight northwest of Lucerne and killed two of the pigs. The bandit driver was an expert at the wheel or he would have been wrecked.

—*Pharos-Tribune*

"When we drove through Palestine, Texas, we bought a newspaper," says Blanche. "Our names were in big headlines."

With W.D. gone, it's just the four of you now, Bonnie, Blanche, Buck, and you. Driving, driving, hiding, robbing, driving, and then reading about yourselves in newspapers bought here and there or, more often, stolen from mailboxes along the way.

"I would say that we were in Oklahoma and Texas just traveling from one place to another, never staying but two or three days at one place, for about six or eight weeks," says Blanche.

There are some laughs along the way, the usual after-the-fact-guffaws over robberies or burglaries that nearly go bad. You all laugh to let the nerves go, the way a normal person standing under a woodshed roof might laugh after nearly getting caught in a hailstorm.

"We had to laugh to keep from crying," Blanche says.

Running over the pigs on your way out of Lucerne, Indiana, qualifies for some chuckles. That whole job is a bit of a botch, starting with Buck making too much noise on top of the safe where you and he have been hiding all night, waiting for the employees to arrive for work. Just before you're about to jump down and make your move, a teller named Lawson Selders hears something and looks up at Buck.

"Put 'em up," he has to yell from up there, instead of from the ground. Buck points his pistols, but instead of putting his hands up, Selders dives for the open door of the safe. The other teller, Everett Gregg, is already in there.

Pow.

Buck fires off a shot, missing Selders by a couple of inches. Then *rata rata* you fire a spray through the front windows of the bank at some nosy passerby who is gawking in. Glass goes everywhere, but the guy on the sidewalk manages to dive out of the way without taking a bullet.

Down from your hiding place, you boys now figure it's too risky to follow the employees into the vault to get the money, what with Selders and Gregg firing their own guns out the safe door in your general direction. The bank apparently stores a couple of weapons in the vault for precisely these situations.

Damn!

So it's out the back door without the big haul, turning around only long enough to fire a mess of bullets into the back windows of the bank. Bonnie and Blanche have brought the car around as planned and are waiting in the back seat for you and Buck to jump in the front.

Away you go, with the usual roar and squeal of tires. But damn if just about the whole town hasn't come out to see what all the shooting is about. Here comes some old man tottering down to the side of the road carrying a big old log, and damn if he doesn't throw it out in front of the car, hoping to cause a wreck. You swerve off the road.

According to Blanche, you start yelling at Buck to shoot the guy, but Buck won't do it. According to your sister Nell—she says she got it from you yourself—it's Bonnie you yell to about shooting the guy, and she won't do it.

"Why, honey, I wasn't going to kill that nice old man," Bonnie says when you yell at her. "He was white-headed."

Maybe that's the way it happens, maybe it's not. The townspeople of Lucerne are of the opinion that Bonnie and Blanche weren't shy about spraying bullets out of the car windows as you drove past a crowd of gawkers gathering near the town church, wounding two.

"Those who saw the bandits leave town were alike in their stories that the women did a large part of the shooting and probably all of it dur-ing the parting fusillade," says a reporter for the local paper who talks to them that afternoon.

Blanche says it was only Bonnie who did the shooting.

They say just about the same thing up in Okabena, Minnesota, a week later, on May 19, when you and the gang shoot up the town on your way out. Again you and Buck hide out overnight in the bank, only this time when Blanche and Bonnie pull up to the back door you come running out with almost fifteen hundred dollars, which is more like it. This time the reporter says, "As the woman driver started a fast getaway, one of the men poked his machine gun through the rear car window, while the second woman han-dled one out of the side window, and riddled the back of the store."

Rata rata rata rata you pretty much shoot up the whole town. When you're gone, they pick bullets out of the farm implement store, the hard-ware store, several upstairs rooms of the hotel, the barbershop, the black-smith shop, the gas station, a car or two, the grain elevators, and, of course, the bank.

"Just across the tracks the raiders let loose at a hitch-hiker who flagged them for a ride," says the *Okabena Press,* "while a little farther they scared the horses of Morrison's incoming school bus."

No one in town is even hit, though, so they can't call it murder, can they? Ha!

All you can do is laugh. Or what about the time that maniac comes run-ning out of a hardware store with a shotgun after you and Buck and starts firing and you have to just jump on the hood of the car and hang on while Bonnie hauls on out of town? Ha! That was hilarious. You on the hood there hanging on for dear life and Buck on the back bumper firing his pis-tol and the guy running down the sidewalk blasting away.

"Bonnie said she could hardly see the road because of him climbing around on the car like a monkey," says Blanche. "Bonnie kept laughing at Clyde because he looked so funny on the hood."

That one would have been even funnier if you and Buck didn't both end up with buckshot in your ass. Blanche cuts Buck's out, except for a few deep ones in his leg. You leave all yours in. What can you do but laugh. Laugh and start looking for another bank or gas station to rob, you guess.

It's not all laughs. Not by a long shot. Sometimes it seems like if you're not fighting with Buck about whether it's safe to rob a bank—he wants to make a big score, you want to pull off a couple of small jobs—you're fighting with Bonnie about whether it's safe to go back to Dallas. She even pulls a pistol on you over that one time and Buck has to take it away from her.

"She was going to shoot him," says Blanche. "But Buck grabbed the gun out of her hand, threw it back in the car, and told her she was crazy. He always tried to separate them when they fought, expecially if one of them got too rough with the other."

And if you're not fighting with Bonnie you're trying not to slug Blanche for some damn thing or another, trying not to slug her because that will start another fight with Buck. Or trying to make peace between Buck and Blanche when it's their turn to fight.

Don't believe it? Try driving around with your in-laws for the rest of your life. In two cars when you have them—even splitting up for a day or two at a time—or crammed into one car when you must, you drive all over the country it seems. Around Mother's Day you send Blanche into Dallas on a bus to arrange a family meeting out on a lonely road near Commerce, Texas. You give her a couple hundred dollars to distribute to various Barrows and Parkers.

It's a bittersweet reunion all around, with Cumie trying to convince Buck to turn himself in and him saying he can't. And Emma Parker trying to get Bonnie to come in and her saying she won't.

"Let's don't be sad," she tells her mama. "He'll be killed sooner or later, because he's never going to give up. I love him and I'm going to be with him till the end."

Another time, when Emma keeps pushing her, she says, "Mama, we've gone too far. They'd put me in the electric chair."

The only thing to do when things get glum is keep changing the subject, keep telling stories. Emma tries her best to put up the appearance of understanding. Cumie does the same. It isn't easy on either of them, though.

"They talked about everything that had happened since they had last seen each other," says Blanche, "but it was hard to keep the mothers from crying."

A few hours of trying not to be sad and then it's over. Time to get back in the cars. Back on the road to wherever. Back to Oklahoma, Missouri, Louisiana, all the way to Florida even. Not Alabama, though. Buck and you are both real careful about Alabama. "They were afraid if they got caught they would embarrass Uncle Billy," says Clyde's older sister Artie. "He was our mother's brother, and he was the head warden of the Alabama state prison."

It's a crazy pace. "We traveled so fast and through so many towns and states that I lost all track of time," says Blanche. "I often didn't even know what day it was. We lived in the car day and night with very little sleep, just driving like mad, going no place."

❋

In the dark, Clyde doesn't see the sign showing the road to the new bridge. He and Bonnie have just picked W.D. up on a short trip into Dallas and are returning to meet up again with Buck and Blanche, who went to visit Blanche's dad. W.D. is dozing, as is Bonnie, while Clyde, as usual, is driving as fast as he can make the machine go.

So fast, in fact, that he doesn't see that sign and doesn't see that the old bridge is gone until it's way too late. Oh Lordy. Hold on.

The car is in midair now, turning sideways, slamming onto the dry bed of the Salt Fork River near Wellington, Texas. It's tumbling, rolling over on itself, spilling gasoline and battery acid. His head smashes against the windshield, or maybe through the windshield, breaking his nose and cutting his face in a dozen places. Maybe he has a concussion. W.D., who is not quite two months into his recovery from being shot through the chest, isn't much better off. He's all busted up in the face like Clyde and at least momentarily knocked out. But at least Clyde and W.D. are able to get free of the car. Bonnie is trapped.

"The car caught fire while Bonnie was still hung inside," W.D says. Bonnie screams.

This isn't how she has been imagining it will end, screaming in pain and fear, wide awake in a cloud of black smoke with burning gasoline seeping over her leg and hip. Or is it battery acid from the battery compartment under the floor? Or both? It doesn't matter. She's pinned there while her leg is on fire. This is worse than the bullets she's been imagining. She's seen bullets. This is worse. Slower, scarier, and it surely hurts more.

She screams out to Clyde to help her, help her. She's burning to death. Help! If he can't help her then shoot her, she cries. Where is he? But Clyde is barely becoming conscious himself. She burns, screams, and then, finally, passes out.

When she comes to she's being carried up from the riverbank. A couple of farmers, Jack Pritchard and his brother-in-law Alonzo Cartwright, saw the wreck happen from the porch of Pritchard's parents' house up the way. They've run down to see if anyone survived, and with their help Clyde and W.D. manage to get her out of the wreck, but she's in a bad way.

"The hide on her right leg was gone from her hip down to her ankle," says W.D. "I could see the bone at places. She'd been burned so bad none of us thought she was gonna live."

They're taking her back up to the house, where Mrs. Pritchard takes one look at her leg and says only a doctor can treat such a bad wound.

"Can't afford it," insists Clyde emphatically. He tells the women to just do what they can, and Bonnie, hearing the talk of doctors and ambulances, rouses herself enough to agree that she absolutely cannot go to a doctor. She's drifting in and out while the Pritchard women work on her as best they can with what they have.

"She had dirt and sand on her face and in her hair and her leg was blistered pretty bad around the knee," says Gladys Cartwright, who helped her mother bathe Bonnie. "All we had to treat her was some salve."

This business of absolutely no doctors is making Jack and Alonzo nervous, and they were nervous already from having seen the guns down in the car. Not as nervous as Clyde, though, who has suddenly realized that in all the confusion and fear about Bonnie he didn't bring adequate firepower with him up to the house. Hard to believe he doesn't have at least a handgun in his pocket, but now he wants some proper weapons and probably wants to hide the ones that are in the wreck, get them ready for a quick pickup when the time comes. He's noticed that there's no decent set of wheels here at the farm—these Pritchards must be pretty hard up with just a funky old Model T. They'll take that if they have to, but if it doesn't start or someone gets nosy, he and W.D. might just need those Brownings before they get out of here.

Clyde tells W.D. to keep an eye on Bonnie and heads back down to the river. As soon as he's out of earshot, Alonzo Cartwright picks a moment when W.D. is with Bonnie and slips out the kitchen door and into that Model T. He releases the brake and starts it rolling in neutral down the drive. When he hears someone yelling behind him, he pops the clutch and putt-putts away.

❊

"What can we do for you?" Paul Hardy asks. He's the marshal of Wellington, Texas, and he and Sheriff George Corry have just locked up a couple of drunks and are figuring the night's work is pretty much over when Alonzo Cartwright comes careening around the corner and jumps out.

"There are two boys and a girl at our house," Cartwright whispers, as if it's a secret that might get out. "They ran their car off the dump of the new road and into the river. They are bad hurt. They had some guns in their car."

So much for the night being over. Sheriff Corry starts to say something about how if these strangers have guns he better go by his office at the courthouse and pick up some heavier weaponry and ammunition, but Cartwright is insistent about getting going right away.

"They are all hurt pretty bad, especially the woman," he says. "You better hurry." The officers relent.

"Let's go," says Corry. They pile into the sheriff's relatively new Chevy and stop at the drugstore just long enough to call an ambulance before heading out toward the Pritchard place.

"Wonder how those birds ever managed to miss the detour sign?" says Corry at one point.

"It beats me," says Hardy. "Must have been drunk."

Then they are at the house, which is strangely dark, almost deserted looking. It's deserted looking because Clyde and W.D., having figured out that Alonzo has gone for the law and that there is no other car on the premises, have the entire family herded together on the floor in the room with Bonnie. They've warned everyone about making any false moves. There's a single kerosene lantern, burning just enough to cast long shadows.

Hardy and Corry come in through the back door of the house and see the family in the next room. "They sat on the floor of that dim room," says Hardy, "huddled together, motionless." Not for the last time is Sheriff Corry regretting that he didn't pick up those heavier guns back at the courthouse.

"Where are the two boys," Hardy asks.

"On the front porch," answers Pritchard without looking up, which Hardy thinks is strange and worrisome. Nonetheless, he heads for the porch while Sheriff Corry goes over to where Bonnie is lying.

"How are you feeling, young lady?" Corry asks. "Are you badly hurt?"

She just mumbles something incoherently while he takes her pulse. Hardy, not finding Clyde and W.D. on the porch, sticks his head back in to say, "There isn't anyone out here." Corry gets the lantern and comes out to have a look.

It's the moment Clyde and W.D. have been waiting for: both lawmen well lit and alone. Out of seemingly nowhere they appear, Clyde with his Browning, W.D. with a shotgun.

"Get 'em up, and get 'em up high," Clyde barks, and up go Corry's and Hardy's hands. He's a sight to see, standing there looking down the barrel of a BAR, with blood all over his white shirt from his broken nose and other cuts. He's wearing only one shoe. W.D. steps in closer and levels his shotgun at Hardy's head. He's a mess, too, but has what Hardy thinks of as a "cheap Panama hat" pulled down low over his face.

"Keep 'em up," Clyde repeats. "And no tricks."

Almost unbelievably, like Lazarus, suddenly Bonnie comes through the front door. Leg bleeding and oozing, no doubt half delirious, she's a shocker in her bare feet and print dress. "Her blazing eyes and quick movements presented a striking contrast with the bleeding pitiful weakling we had seen on the bed two minutes before," says Hardy.

"Take their guns," says Clyde, and while he and W.D. keep the weapons

THE MIDDLE OF THE ROAD

trained on the officers, Bonnie goes into the pocket of Hardy's pants for one pistol and takes the sheriff's from his holster.

"You boys are just in time," says W.D. He's taking the sheriff's handcuffs and cuffing the two lawmen together and shoving them into the back seat of the car they came in. "We want to borrow your car."

Clyde slips into the driver's seat, keeping a gun on the cops in the back, and tells W.D. to go and get Bonnie, who must have collapsed again after her heroics.

Blam!

"I jumped with such nervousness that Clyde jammed his gun into my ribs," says Hardy. Hardy is about as scared as he's been all night because he thinks Alonzo has managed to make it back from town and has snuck up with some other lawmen and all hell is about to break loose, during which Clyde Barrow will no doubt get rid of his hostages. Hardy and Corry later tell the FBI that Clyde and W.D. were both exceedingly nervous, jumpy, constantly cursing.

"I knew Clyde would not leave us alive," he says. "I knew he would not let a posse overpower his brother"—he thinks W.D. is Buck—"without going to his assistance."

Clyde jumps back out of the car to try to see what's happened.

"What's going on?" he says when W.D. appears out of gloom.

"Aw, that dame reached for a gun and I gave her a shot in the hand," he says. Turns out Gladys Cartwright, the one who helped her mom clean up Bonnie's wounds, had figured since the bandits were out of the house, why not lock it. W.D., seeing her reaching for something over the door, thought she was going for a gun and let loose with the shotgun through a window. Put six buckshot pellets in her hand, but missed the baby she was holding in her arms.

"Let's get out of here," W.D. says. With Bonnie moaning in the front seat between Clyde and W.D., and the cops in the back, they head down the driveway. W.D. points Hardy's own pistol at the laws, in case they do something stupid. "Step on 'er," he says to Clyde once the doors are all closed.

At the bottom of the driveway they see headlights coming.

"I wonder if that is the fool who went to town?" Clyde asks of no one, turning out his headlights. "If it is, I'll kill him."

"He made the statement calmly," says Hardy. "I believed every word he said."

But the car goes on by, over the new bridge that Clyde missed, and is gone. Clyde turns and follows, passing it not far from the bridge but paying it no attention. They're late for the meet up with Buck and Blanche at the bridge in

Sayre, Oklahoma. A couple miles farther on he pulls over and moves Bonnie to the back seat, with the officers, to try to make her more comfortable.

"He set them in the back seat with Bonnie across their laps, and we drove on to meet Buck and his wife," says W.D.

For a brief moment, Clyde wants to turn around and go back to the wreck site to pick up a stack of license plates they forgot in the car—"a dumb trick," forgetting them, he says—but Bonnie is alert enough to tell what a ridiculous idea that is, and he has to agree. Once they're on the road again Clyde relaxes a bit, except when other cars approach. Invariably, he tells Bonnie and W.D. to be ready, and they put hands on their guns. Then he hogs the middle of the road, practically running the oncoming car off into the ditch, so that there's no way the other driver can take his eyes off the road long enough to look in Clyde's car windows. There's not much traffic after midnight in the Texas panhandle and western Oklahoma, though, and after a bit Clyde gets downright chatty, says Corry later.

"Did you coppers ever hear much about the two Barrow brothers?" he asks over his shoulder.

"No, I can't say that I have," Hardy says, lying through his teeth.

Clyde, Bonnie, and W.D. all bust out laughing when they hear that. Still laughing, Clyde tells them in all seriousness that if he knew they were hunting the Barrows he'd kill them both. Corry chimes in that he's got no record of them at the sheriff's office either, which is also a lie. More laughs.

"Don't you mugs ever read the paper?" Bonnie asks. She might laugh more if it didn't hurt so much.

❋

You get to the bridge where you're supposed to meet Blanche and Buck and they are nowhere to be seen. They probably gave up on you, or got skittish sitting there too long and went off. They're supposed to have left a note at the far end if they did take off, but seeing as no one's around out here in the middle of nowhere you might as well give the horn and flash the lights some, just in case they're nearby in the woods.

Beep beep beep.

Three short blasts, that's the signal. "We set there a few minutes and we heard another horn at the far end of the bridge," says W.D.

Sure enough, your honking wakes Blanche and Buck where they fell asleep waiting and Buck flashes his headlights and *beep beep beep*s back at you to let you know he's here. Thank God, he's here, you're thinking. Good old Buck. You turn on your headlights and start walking across the bridge to talk to him before he shows his face too much to the laws.

"Then we saw Clyde on the bridge," says Blanche. "He looked like he had been in water. He was carrying his shotgun. He told us they had been in a wreck and that he thought Bonnie was dying. He also said he had two officers he had to get rid of. That really woke me up good."

Blanche gets some decent clothes together for you and W.D. and makes a place in the back of their car for Bonnie to lie. Make it as comfortable as possible, you tell her, but don't come over to the bridge. You don't want the two laws to see either her or the car. Buck, on the other hand, you tell to come and help you deal with the two cops.

"What we gonna do with these coppers?" asks W.D. You think for a moment and then answer, "Let's march 'em down the river a piece and tie them up."

"I think this was one of the happiest moments of my life," says Hardy. "I had the slight assurance that I was not going to die."

Slight assurance it turns out to be, and passing. "Buck was all for killing the two lawmen," says W.D.* "But Clyde, thinking how gentle they had been with Bonnie, said no."

You and Buck follow the two handcuffed men down along the riverbank away from the bridge, pointing guns at their backs. After about two hundred yards you tell them to stop.

"What would you do if we turned you loose?" you ask them. When Hardy answers that they'd just try to get home, you correct him.

"Yeah, I know," you say. "You'd run your legs off getting to a phone."

"What you gonna do with them?" Buck asks, even though you've already said you plan to tie them up. "Want 'em tended to?" He raises his handgun and points it at Hardy.

Hardy is a brave man, but he's scared now.

"Standing with your back against a tree, facing two desperate men with drawn guns is a feeling you cannot put into words," he says. "I braced myself for the impact of a pistol bullet—and waited, the longest second of my life."

You say to Buck, "Yeah, they've been pretty decent cops," as if the two aren't even there listening to the conversation. "But I've said I'd never take a cop for a ride and let him live to squeal his head off."

You say that, but you don't let Buck shoot them. As always, your word goes. The two of you tie them up with barbed wire taken from a nearby fence. It's not polite, but it's all you got. You tie them pretty good, but not so tight that they won't be able to get loose with some effort.

---

* In her later statement to the FBI, Blanche insists it was Buck who wanted to spare the officers.

Walking away, Buck turns around one last time and levels his gun at the two tied men. But you call him off.

"Come on," you say to your older brother. "Let's get going."

"I will never forget that moment as long as I live," says Hardy. "I believe he saved our lives."

That's right, copper. Don't you forget it.

※

Blanche doesn't think Bonnie will make it. Truth be told, Blanche isn't too sure about W.D. or Clyde either, but Bonnie's by far the worst off.

"Bonnie was a mass of burns and cuts on her face, right arm, and leg," she says. "Her chin was cut to the bone. Her chest was caved in, although no ribs were broken. She was screaming and moaning like she was dying and appeared to be unconscious. All of us thought she would die before daybreak."

Bonnie doesn't die, though. All three of them, Bonnie, Clyde, and W.D., should be going to see a doctor, but of course that's out of the question. So they drive on away from the tied-up cops, Buck behind the wheel, Bonnie with her head in Clyde's lap in the back seat, W.D. with his head on Blanche's lap in the rumble seat. Across to Oklahoma they go, and then Kansas. Blanche goes into drugstores along the way for bandages and Unguentine, aspirin and whiskey. They find a tourist camp to hide out in for a few days, and then another.

"When she was so bad at first, we had to carry her to the toilet and take her off when she finished and put her back in bed," says W.D.

W.D. begins to heal first and is able to help Buck with the necessary trips out at night for funds—"it took $9 a day worth of Unguentine to put on her leg"—and after a few days, Clyde, too, feels better. He's strong enough to go out and find a doctor willing to see Bonnie and keep quiet about it. Bonnie tells the doctor it's just a bad stove accident, which he doesn't believe but doesn't say anything about.

Clyde also finds a supply of Amytal. "Dope," Blanche calls it. That helps the pain, but it makes Bonnie mean when it's wearing down. She comes limping out of her bed one day, tearing open the scabs and getting her leg bleeding again, ranting and raving about having it out with Blanche once and for all—calling for a fight, calling Blanche "excess baggage," and accusing her of being "afraid to shoot coppers."

"Just lay down and shut up," says Buck, and when W.D. appears she eventually does. Clyde's not around, having snuck down into Dallas to see if he can bring Bonnie's mother or sister back with him. Blanche is about fed up with nursing, and Bonnie's desperate to see her mother. Clyde gets to Dallas and decides it would attract too much attention to bring Emma. He comes back with Billie Jean instead, which is almost as good.

"I went to Bonnie because Mother wanted me to go and because I wanted to see my sister," she says. "I always thought each time would be the last time."

Billie's come out on the road with them once in a while in the past for short trips, when Bonnie's gotten particularly lonesome or sick. Or just to hang around with W.D., who she has a small crush on. Plus, her husband is a convicted thief. So she knows the drill, knows the outlaw life, and is more than willing to come with Clyde if Bonnie needs her. Leaving Dallas, she and Clyde even get chased for a few blocks by Ted Hinton, but he recognizes Clyde just a second too late to put up a decent chase.

"I was confused because I did not recognize the young woman beside him as Bonnie," Hinton says. "I saw that he recognized me, saw his car dig in and speed faster. My heart pounded; I spun my roadster into a U-turn and held the pedal on the floorboard. In a moment, or perhaps even less, I had lost sight of him."

The incident made Hinton want to get a faster car, he says. It also made him determined to get Smoot Schmid to put him full-time on chasing Clyde Barrow.

※

Billie Jean Parker Mace is no wide-eyed lily-livered wallflower. Still, she's horrified at the condition of her big sister when Clyde finally gets her back to Arkansas.

"Bonnie's leg, all the muscle—she was burned to the bone on her calf of her leg, and the tendons back here cut," she says. "I mean burned!"

It's bad, but at least they've found a good place to lie low for a while— a tourist camp near Fort Smith, Arkansas. They check in on June 15, 1933.

"They were real nice," says Billie Jean. "Course they didn't know who we were or anything. And they'd bring Bonnie's lunch over and you know. And their daughter was a nurse and she doctored her quite a few times, you know, doctored her leg."

The nurse's name is Hazel Dennis, and at her insistence Clyde twice manages to get doctors from nearby Fort Smith to come out to the tourist camp to treat Bonnie. When the second of them, Dr. Walter Eberle, asks how she got the injury, Bonnie tells him a camp stove exploded about six weeks before. Eberle knows this is a lie, as the burns are only two weeks old at the most, and asks her for her name, but when Bonnie starts to speak a little too freely, perhaps because of the morphine, Billie clamps her hand over her sister's mouth. Eberle just keeps working on the burns, but thinks to himself that he might mention this whole strange situation to the sheriff. Perhaps considering his own health, after Clyde has paid him handsomely he forgets all about making that call.

Bonnie's going to make it after all. The rest is doing her good, but suddenly they're back on the road again. On June 23, while Clyde's taking care of Bonnie, Buck and W.D. get themselves into a scrape with some laws over near Fayetteville, Arkansas, after robbing a grocery store. There's a shootout in Alma that leaves a town marshal named Henry Humphrey dead, with two bullets in his gut and another one in his chest, followed by a car wreck that leaves Buck bloody. In other words, the gang is hot as all hell again and have to move out to the woods before anyone at the tourist camp figures out who it is that's been renting those two cabins for the past week.

"Don't get excited now," Clyde says to Blanche. "Buck's all right. He's in our cabin." She's been pacing the floor, wondering why Buck and W.D. haven't returned. Clyde tells her they've been in a wreck but they're okay.

The important thing now, he tells her, is to look calm and work quickly. "Put your bags in the car before you come to our cabin," he says. "Don't act as though you are in a hurry when you are walking to our cabin."

Blanche does as she's told, walking as calmly as she can muster. But Buck sure doesn't look okay when she gets over to the other cabin. He's a bloody mess.

"One's ankle was almost broken," says Billie Jean, "and they had knocks and all, all over their heads and, oh, they looked terrible."

"Oh, Daddy, are you hurt badly?" Blanche runs to Buck and asks.

"Oh, honey," he says. "I believe I killed a man."

❊

"We had to leave," says Billie Jean. "And we only had one car and it was a roadster so, uh, we had to have blankets. It was cool at night, you know, and we knew that we'd have to go out in the woods. It was—we had to have blankets and clean sheets for Bonnie. So, um, Clyde took the blankets and the clean sheets and he left ten dollars on the chest of drawers for, you know, to pay for the sheets and the blankets.

"So we went out in the woods and stayed for a couple of days."

❊

You have to take Billie Jean back to Dallas. It's not fair to put her in such danger when things are so hot with the cops after the murder in Alma and you've moved out of the tourist camp at Fort Smith and are living in the woods and all. Plus, it looks now like Bonnie's going to pull through, though she'll never walk right again.

"Bonnie never got over that burn," says W.D. "Even after it healed over, her leg was drawn under her. She had to just hop or hobble along."

Thing is, Billie doesn't want to go, and not just because she's worried about her sister.

"She and W.D. had become sweethearts not long after Clyde brought her to Fort Smith," says Blanche.

You don't have a problem with her and W.D. loving it up, particularly. Her husband is in jail and she's almost as pretty as Bonnie, in a darker-eyed way, so you can understand why W.D. might take a liking. And she's got spunk, too, like the time you all had to squeeze into one hotel room. You don't have but a couple of dollars left in the kitty, so she and Blanche and Bonnie rent the room and you boys sneak in the back window.

"So the lady had been back once with the towels and the water and we thought that was over, you know, so we let 'em in the window," says Billie Jean. "And, uh, and it wasn't long till she was knockin' on the door. Well, we had to hide them. And there was a, um . . . oh, not a good room, you know. Not for two dollars. And, um, so we hid them behind this curtain, which is like about two feet or a foot coming on down to the floor and here she came back for something and, uh, we were scared to death she's gonna look over there and see the three men's feet."

It's almost too much to keep in without cracking up. Three hardened killers, wanted bank robbers and all, hiding out behind the curtain from some little old lady with a washbasin.

"Well," says Billie Jean, "you know it was just one of those things that, uh, we thought was real cute after it was over."

She's a real good egg, Billie Jean, knows a good laugh when she sees one. Like the time you and Buck and W.D. come back from an armory raid all dressed up in uniforms and scare the living daylights out of the girls. Ha!

"Like to scared us to death," says Billie Jean. "We started climbing out the windows to run, and it was them."

Your favorite joke, though, was on Buck, after you stole that doctor's bag out of a car to find medicine for Bonnie. Billie Jean saw it all, and kept a straight face the whole time. You're out at this lake in the woods, a big beautiful lake, pretty enough to make you just as happy not to be in a dirty old tourist camp. And Buck keeps going through the doctor's bag, playing with the stuff. He's listening to everyone's heart and all.

"Clyde," he says over and over again, "let me give you a shot, let me give you a shot."

Naturally you're not interested in Buck's doctoring.

"Oh, Buck, get away from me," you say. "I'm not going to let you use that old needle on me." But he won't let up. So finally you give Bonnie and her little sister a wink and say, "Okay, I'll let you shoot me."

He's real happy now. Gets that needle out of the bag real careful and all, getting some medicine in it. Says it won't hurt and all, and sticks it in your arm. You give it a few seconds to take effect and then . . .

"Clyde just keeled over," says Billie Jean. "It like scared Buck to death. We knew that Clyde was putting on, you know . . . you know he's scared to death that he has killed Clyde. I mean they just were, you know, were really cutups."

You love Billie Jean. She's a real good egg. But it doesn't mean you're going to let her stay around to get into the kind of trouble you and Bonnie are in. Most likely Bonnie too, much as she wants the company of her sister, is insisting that Billie leave for her own good. (Other times when she's been afraid Billie might get caught she's told her to go.) No. Billie's going home, and W.D. is staying with you.

Sometime before you drop her at a train station, though, you all drive into a gas station looking like a freak show from the circus. Bonnie's sick under a blanket. Buck and W.D. have bandages on their heads and black eyes and all. You're hiding under your hat as usual, with your busted nose still looking like a grapefruit. Blanche is wearing this horse riding outfit and dark glasses she picked up in Dallas last time she was down there. All of you are crammed into a little roadster.

The attendant keeps looking at Billie Jean, with her nice red hair and put-together outfit. She's the only one acting remotely normal. He looks at Billie Jean and then around at the rest of the passengers. Then back at Billie Jean.

"I bet that filling station man thought, 'That redheaded woman, she got mad and whipped 'em all,' " you say when you've safely pulled away.

You laugh. You all laugh. What else is there to do? You're all still alive, aren't you?

CHAPTER 19

PLATTE CITY

"They couldn't keep two cars," says Blanche. "Buck could not drive because of his hand and Clyde always wanted W.D. to be in the car with him."

They've been all over the place in the three weeks since sending Billie Jean home: Oklahoma, Texas, New Mexico, Colorado, Nebraska, South Dakota, Minnesota, Illinois, Indiana, Ohio, Kentucky, Tennessee, Alabama, Mississippi, Louisiana, Arkansas, Kansas, Iowa, and Missouri, according to Blanche. Mostly they're sleeping out on the ground if they stop at all, or in the car (or cars, as the case may be), leaning on one another. Once in a while Clyde lets them spend a night in a tourist camp, but not often. Buck can hardly drive with his hand all smashed up.

Along the way there's the usual string of cars stolen and eventually tracked down and written up in a growing stack of reports by the FBI's G-men. The reports are sent to Washington and to Dallas, where Hoover has consolidated the case, an endless stream of single-spaced, carbon-copied data that are disseminated around the country, always with a list of "undeveloped leads" for other offices to follow up on. "These three subjects," one typical report reads, "were positively identified as parties who abandoned the Ford coach motor . . . at Clayton, which car was stolen from the Durant Nursery Company, Durant, Okla., and . . . on July 3, a Ford V-8 Tudor sedan . . . was stolen at Clayton by the same parties who had previously abandoned the Ford coach in question."

There's also the usual string of gas stations stuck up for small amounts of cash. If there's talk of bank jobs, they don't materialize. But, of course, the need for guns and ammunition—a need that's turned into an obsession, really—must be slaked. On July 7, while W.D. stays behind to take care of Bonnie and keep guard in a tourist camp, Buck and Clyde raid the armory at Enid, Oklahoma.

W.D. says they "brought back so many guns it looked like a gun factory. There were some forty-six government automatics, forty-five pistols, several rifles, and two or three cases of ammunition."

It's kind of crazy, really, the number of guns they're hauling around. "More guns and ammunition than I had ever seen at one time in my whole life," says Blanche. "They also had several pairs of field glasses. They said we needed the glasses to scan roads to see if they are blocked so we don't drive into a trap."

Blanche usually sits up on the car hood and keeps watch with the field glasses while the others sleep. Bonnie almost never leaves the back seat of the car—she's still healing up—and the boys are dead tired from driving or late-night prowls.

There's no plan except to keep running. No strategy except to keep well armed and awake to whatever end comes along.

Sitting up on the hood of the car night after night with her military binoculars, Blanche thinks about the four wounded and weary people asleep behind her. She thinks about the hundred and whatever ridiculous number of handguns and rifles stuck into every loose space in the vehicle, the bullets in the glove compartment, and those wrapped in inner tubes in the trunk. She can't even put her feet down in the car without them resting on weapons. She thinks about how Clyde and Buck have taken to fighting all the time again, about this and that, stupid stuff that wouldn't matter except Clyde's so gun crazy he's always pulling and maybe one day he'll shoot his own brother. "Clyde wouldn't fight fair," she says.

And why can't Buck just leave him? And W.D. too? He clearly wants out, but here he is letting Clyde tie a string between the two of them so that if W.D. wakes up Clyde will wake up too. What is it?

"Clyde dominated all them around him, even his older brother Buck," says W.D. "I followed him, just like everybody who was ever with him did."

Blanche is following Buck, though, and Buck's promised her that as soon as they find another car the two of them will take it and leave his little brother. They'll leave him forever this time. They'll go to Canada, maybe. And never come back. One more night, he tells Blanche, one more night or two at the most.

❈

You got some money in your pockets from robbing three gas stations in a row in broad daylight up in Fort Dodge, Iowa, this morning. One, two, three—you and Buck and W.D. hit all the stations in town, carrying the attendants along with you in the car as hostages from station to station so they can't run to the police. Works like a charm and after the last job you let them go, put the pedal down, pick the girls up from the woods where they've been hiding, and . . . you're gone.

Now, though, everybody needs a rest. You got money, you're tired, you're hungry, you're thirsty, you're dirty. You've come three hundred miles south from Fort Dodge pretty much without stopping, and those little brick cabins attached together by a garage out here in the land of nowhere that you just drove past look perfect. Just across the way is the Red Crown Tavern, a gas station, and a café. You're a little close to Kansas City for Buck's liking— at a crossroads a few miles south of Platte City, Missouri. But Buck's not running the show, is he? Bonnie needs a rest. She's still in bandages and on crutches, for crying out loud. You all need a rest. You're going back there to see if the cabins are available. It's July 18.

It's late, after eleven o'clock, when you settle into the two brick cabins. (You pulled the usual stunt of hiding two people under blankets in the back seat so the management would think there were only three of you in the party.) The cabin you and Bonnie share with W.D. has direct access into the double-door garage that connects the two cabins, but the one Blanche and Buck have only has a door to the outside. Blanche goes across the street for a mess of food and beer. She complains about ordering so much food for what is supposed to be just three people, but she's always complaining about something these days. Like they're going to care or notice how much food you order. Everybody is on a short fuse. Buck's so mad about some damn thing or another that he's not even talking to you, staying over in his cabin as much as possible.

"Just get the food," you tell Blanche. "Bring back some chicken if they have any."

And, of course, you're right and Blanche is wrong. There's no trouble. The food and beer are a blessing and everyone, even little old worrywart Blanche, gets a little more cheerful and sleeps in all morning the next day.

As soon as she wakes up, though, Blanche starts in again talking about how you all ought to be moving on. Says she's the only one going out to get food and whatnot, and people are acting strange out there. Says the man she gave the money to for another night in the cabins seemed suspicious. Says everyone went all silent as soon as she came in for the dinner food and then started talking again as soon as she walked out.

"The girl who waited on me stood and stared at me for a few seconds, as if she had seen a ghost," Blanche says. That kind of thing all day long, even though you and Buck are watching out the window with binoculars every time she goes for food. Watching with rifles by your sides.

You tell her it will be fine for one more night, and she says, "If we all get killed here tonight, you can't say I didn't warn you."

You tell her to go to bed. You'll all leave in the morning. Earlier than you think, as it turns out.

❊

Sheriff Holt Coffey of Platte County isn't taking any chances. Not after what happened over in Joplin a couple of months ago with the Barrow Gang. And not after what happened only one short month ago just thirty miles down the road in Kansas City. The Kansas City Massacre it's being called: three machine gunners mowed down four lawmen and the prisoner they were escorting. Out of nowhere, they just cut the lawmen to pieces with bullets on a busy morning in the middle of Union Station and then disappeared. The current prime suspect in that crime is Pretty Boy Floyd, but no one really knows who did it, and no one has been caught.

Sheriff Coffey's got more reason to wonder if the strange and secretive collection of men and women in the Red Crown cabins are the Barrow brothers and their girls than he does to think it might be whoever did the Kansas City Massacre. The manager of the Red Crown tells him they've blocked up the windows with newspapers, are always peering out to see if anyone's coming, and won't let any employees into the cabins to clean up and whatnot. He says they rarely come out except for one woman who collects their food, though Coffey himself watched Blanche and Buck having lunch in the Red Crown. More interestingly, Coffey's also gotten word from a local druggist saying a stranger came in and bought tannic acid and bandages; pharmacists all over the Midwest have been told to be on the lookout for travelers buying odd supplies. The papers everywhere have reported that the lawmen from Wellington, Texas, who were kidnapped say Bonnie Parker is seriously burned, and tannic acid baths are considered beneficial to burn victims.

Whoever it is in the cabins, Sheriff Coffey knows from the license number they gave when they checked in that they are driving a car that was stolen from a doctor in Oklahoma. They're not on the up-and-up, and in this day and age he's not taking any chances. He's coordinating his efforts with Captain William Baxter of the local troop of the state highway patrol, some of whose men frequent the Red Crown and have also heard of odd behavior by the cabin renters.

"We had no two-way radios in our patrol cars then, so when the troop headquarters had a message for us, they'd phone restaurants where we made regular stops," says Tom Whitecotton. He's one of the state highway patrolmen, though he's wearing a seersucker suit and a Panama hat instead of his usual uniform, having come straight from a day of desk work. "The Red Crown Tavern near Platte City was one of the stopping places. They serve good food and a lot of the boys ate there."

Sheriff Coffey and the local prosecutor's office have also contacted Coffey's big-city counterpart down in Jackson County, which includes Kansas City. Sheriff Tom Bash is bringing up his armored car and some deputies with machine guns. Sheriff Bash will also bring some heavy steel shields, the kind meant to stop bullets. If the people in the cabins are who Coffey thinks they are, he doesn't intend to be outgunned like those poor fellows in Joplin.

Everyone is on the scene by around midnight, thirteen officers in all, but the lawmen decide to wait until the tavern has closed down for the night before taking any action. If it comes to bullets flying, there's no sense in having more of an audience than necessary. At one A.M., they get ready to go.

"We stationed two Platte County deputies on top of the Red Crown Tavern," says Whitecotton. "The armored car, with two Jackson County men inside, was parked in the driveway, blocking the only escape route. A deputy and I were set up at the end of the driveway as backup, and the rest of the officers were arranged strategically around the cabins."

With machine guns in one hand and armored shields in the other, Sheriff Coffey and Captain Baxter make their way up to the cabin where Buck is asleep and Blanche is trying to get there too.

❉

Blanche hears Coffey's knock and shakes Buck awake. "Then I jumped over the foot of the bed and began putting my clothes on," she says.

Buck whispers to her to ask who it is.

"The sheriff. Open up!" comes the answer.

"Tell them the men are in the other cabin," Buck whispers. "And shout it loud enough so Clyde can hear you."

"Well, come on out here yourself," comes the answer from outside the door.

"Wait until I get my clothes on and I will come out," Blanche yells. That's always been the signal to the others in the gang that there's trouble at the door—"wait until we get dressed."

"Well," says Sheriff Coffey after a minute goes by with no sign of activity inside the cabins, "let's give them some gas."

❋

"That's the law," you say to W.D. as soon as you hear Blanche yelling through the door in the other cabin. You grab your BAR from under the bed. It's a beast of a weapon, with its barrel and stock sawed down to make it easier to handle in a car and a special triple-long clip that you got someone to weld together for you. You call it your "scattergun," and you can rattle off sixty rounds without changing clips.

Oh Lordy, here we go. You look out the window and, sure enough, laws are everywhere and they've got a car parked blocking your way out of the driveway. You start giving orders. "He told me to get out there and start the car," says W.D. "He started shooting out of doors and windows."

Damn right.

Rata rata rata rata rata rata you're just unloading bullets in a torrent. So is everyone else in the vicinity. It's a war all of a sudden, with Buck and W.D. firing their weapons, and all the cops letting loose with their Thompson machine guns brought up from Kansas City.

"Bonnie had given me the key out of Clyde's pocket to the car, and I started the motor, and shooting was coming from all directions," W.D. says.

The two guys at Buck's door—Sheriff Coffey and Captain Baxter—are driven off immediately, their lives barely saved by their steel shields.

"I saw my father stumble back as the bullets struck the shield," says Clarence Coffey, the sheriff's nineteen-year-old son and deputy, who is watching from the kitchen doorway of the Red Crown. "Everybody else was down. My father was playing possum under the shield."

When young Clarence fires off a bit of defense for his father, you or Buck turn a BAR momentarily toward him.

"I guess they saw me there in the corner and decided they'd kill me," he says. "I couldn't get in the door and I couldn't run for it. They started shooting me with everything they had." He's hit in the foot and the arm before you eventually turn your attention back toward the closer threats.

"Baxter staggered backward, unhurt and still holding his gun and shield, but Holt Coffey ran for cover," says Whitecotton, who sees him go, but in the bad light thinks he's one of the Barrows making a break for it.

"There's one of 'em," Whitecotton yells to his partner, Ellis, who's a little closer than he is. "Get him."

Blam. Trooper Ellis fires his shotgun at the fleeing sheriff, putting some buckshot in his backside but not wounding him seriously.

"He believed till his dying day that Clyde Barrow shot him, but it was actually a state trooper," says Whitecotton.

The truth is, you're not even paying much attention to the two cops trying to get themselves away from outside Buck's door. He can handle those. "My husband used a Brownie Automatic and I believe that he had three clips," says Blanche later. "There were also two .45 Colt automatics and I think that there were about five or six clips—that is, full clips—for these two guns."

No, you're working on the number one problem, which is the cop car that's parked in the driveway, blocking your escape. The cops think it's bulletproof, but what do cops know? It's not BAR-proof. At this range your .30-06 bullets are going right through that thing's thick windows and not-thick-enough walls. Those four coppers inside are getting nervous, whether you have time to notice it or not.

"The armoured car from the Sheriff's Office, of Jackson County, containing four deputies, was pulled up in front of the garage door to the cabin to prevent the gang inside from escaping," the G-man from the Kansas City office is going to type up in his report to Washington in a few weeks' time. "This armoured car has bullet proof glass and has armour plate around the bottom. The bullet proof glass was riddled and there were 8 holes altogether in this 'armoured' car. It was shot up like a sieve."

Yeah, they're getting nervous all right, especially after one of your bullets sets their horn going.

Beeeeeeeeeeeeeeeeeeeeeeeeeeeeeeeeep.

Rata rata rata rata rata. Those coppers oughta be nervous. You'll tear that whole car to shreds with the scattergun if you have to.

Rata rata rata.

When one of your high-powered bullets goes through the plate and then through the steering column of the car and then through both knees of one of the deputies in the car, they've had enough.

"The car that seemed to be breaking down one of the garage doors started backing away with its horn screaming," says Blanche.

There's a lull in the shooting. The time is right now.

"Are you all right?" Buck yells across the thirty feet or so that separates his shot-out windows from your shot-out windows.

"Yes," you say. "Are you both still okay?"

"Yes."

"Let's get away from here," you say, and then bark an order to W.D., but W.D. is frozen.

"Clyde told me to open the garage door and I was afraid to do it," says W.D., "and he came and together we opened the door."

The car is running, filled with whatever guns and whatnot you've had a chance to load in. Bonnie, bless her heart, has managed to drag herself into the car without any help. W.D. is firing beside you. The law is finally backing away. You have to move now or never. Now, Buck. *Now.*

Since Buck and Blanche's cabin doesn't have a door directly into the garage, they have to make a break for it. "Maybe we can make it while they're reloading," says Buck, and they open the door and go for it.

"When they did," says Trooper Whitecotton, "Captain Baxter opened up with his machine gun."

RATA RATA RATA you return the favor. W.D. returns the favor, too. *Rata rata* Buck fires while running out the door behind Blanche.

"It seems to me that I was the first out the door," says Blanche. "My husband following after me. I got to the car and heard a shot fired and looked back and saw Buck fall."

She screams, "They've killed Buck," and goes back for him. Clyde comes running over too and wants to know where the shots came from. She points. He picks up Buck's BAR by the barrel, burning his hand, but gets it up and returns fire—*rata rata rata*—to give Blanche a little cover while she struggles to get Buck back on his feet. Buck's got a hole in his head.

"When we opened the [garage] door Buck and Blanche were right in front of the door," says W.D. "Blanche was holding Buck up, holding him under his arms. Clyde told me to go out there and get Buck. I refused to do it, and Clyde went out and got him just about to the door, and handed him to me, and I took hold of him then and while I was putting Buck in the car Clyde was shooting."

Rata rata rata rata—Fuck you, coppers—*RAT RATA RATA RAT RAT.*

"The hail of bullets from both sides was terrific," says Whitecotton. "I hit the dirt, seersucker suit and all."

You hit the gas, flying past the armored car in reverse, past the seersucker in the dirt, firing out the windows with help from W.D., slamming on the brakes, throwing the wheel over to spin the car around and the transmission into second gear, barely losing any momentum going from reverse to forward.

A bullet comes through a window, spraying glass into Blanche's eyes. Sixteen or seventeen slugs come into the car in other places but don't hit anyone.

You're gone.

❉

"They can't survive their own heat. They're too hot!"

Raymond Hamilton, 20, former bandit pal of Clyde Barrow, from his solitary confinement cell in the county jail here, Thursday expressed the belief that Clyde and his brother, Ivy (Buck) Barrow will be captured or killed within the next sixty days.

"Did they kill somebody else?" Hamilton inquired when told by a Times Herald reporter the Barrow brothers early Thursday figured in another gun battle at Platte City, Mo. He was told they made their getaway, with a woman, after wounding two officers.

"Luck must be with them," he said. "But it won't be long before they lose their rabbit's foot."

—*Dallas Daily Times Herald*

"May God spare my boys," says Cumie. She's standing in front of the filling station talking to Sheriff Smoot Schmid, but really, "May God spare my boys" is the kind of thing a person says to no one in particular. Or to God.

A reporter from the *Dallas Daily Times Herald* asked Schmid to take him over to see Mr. and Mrs. Barrow, and the sheriff apparently figures it can't hurt his image any to be seen on the job in the days after the news is all over every paper that the Barrow brothers had yet another big shoot-out with the police and disappeared. The reporter and a deputy stay in the car, listening, while Smoot uncurls his six-foot-ten self from the vehicle and stands towering over the poor old lady that Cumie has become in the past few years. Henry Barrow, wearing overalls and a weary look, is also there.

"I'm going to tell you the truth," she says to the sheriff. "The truth is I don't know where Clyde and Buck are right now."

The sheriff nods and pushes her for a few more details about the last time she saw Clyde. She did see him not that long ago, Cumie says, out at a secret place near Belton, Texas. But she's not telling where exactly, or even when the meeting took place. She'll only say, as if to taunt the friendly sheriff, that "we had a long talk and then they brought me back home."

Most of what she knows is the same as what everyone knows, she says, what they read in the papers or heard on the radio. She also knows that the laws aren't trying to capture her boys anymore. They're looking to kill them, she says, and Smoot can't look her in the eye and deny it, with the newspapers reporting "shoot to kill" orders and such.

"They're living on borrowed time," Cumie says to the sheriff. She's got tears in her eyes, and wipes them away. "I know that as well as you do."

There's a young boy at the filling station who looks to be about eleven hanging near to Henry and Cumie, listening and watching. When the reporter in the car gets wind of the fact that it's Buck Barrow's son from his first marriage, come for a visit with his grandparents, he can't resist leaning out the window and asking a question or two.

"What do you want to be when you grow up?" the man from the newspaper asks Marvin Barrow Jr.

"I want to be a cowboy and wear two pistols," the kid says.

Even Cumie has to smile at that, if only for the little boy's sake. Henry puts his arm around his wife, as if to protect her from something. They stand there together looking at the sheriff. But old Henry Barrow doesn't say a word for the reporter.

❊

It's all a blur, really.

Tires go flat and are changed. Or not changed, depending on if the boys have a spare somewhere. "We ran for a long while on the rim of one of them and ruined it," W.D. says. Bandages are changed or not changed, depending on if they can risk going to a drugstore or can "borrow" some old sheets from a farmhouse. It's not just Bonnie's kind of oozy scabby wounds, anymore, either. She didn't get any new injuries, and neither really did Clyde or W.D., to speak of, but the hole in Buck's head is bad and won't stop bleeding and Blanche's face and eyes are a mess. She's blinded, in fact.

"Most everything was wet with blood, as if dipped in water," Blanche says of those first hours after the escape from the Red Crown. "The floorboard of the car was so soaked we could hear the blood gush under our feet."

Worst of all, perhaps, is that Clyde for some reason can't seem to get out of the neighborhood. He can't find the bridge he's looking for and has to loop back over the same one a couple of times. It's not like Clyde; he must be shook up by what he saw of Buck's head. There's no way Buck can live with that, is there? They all know it, though no one's saying it.

Buck's going in and out of making sense. He doesn't remember that he's supposed to hide under the blanket when they're getting gas and pops up like a monster in a movie right when the gas station boy is pumping. Even Clyde says they're going to get caught this time, and that's just not like him.

Bonnie's in the front seat with Clyde, wondering what they always wonder, which is maybe this is the time they've been running from all these months. Buck and W.D. are in the back with Blanche, who is mostly holding Buck's head, trying to hold it together really, trying to keep more from coming out. She's telling him to rest. Telling him not to die.

Finally, in the morning, Clyde finds his way out of that corner of Missouri and heads north into Iowa, leaving behind a trail of bloody bandages that farmers will find and report to police. Near the town of Dexter, only a couple of hundred miles north of the Red Crown instead of the usual eight hundred or a thousand, he pulls into some woods. They can't go farther; if Buck's going to have any chance at all, he has to rest.

Clyde knows the place he wants, having been there a year before. It's on the outskirts of Dexfield Park, an abandoned amusement park of sorts, long since gone bust in the hard times. He pulls in under an oak tree, and he and W.D. drag the cushions out of the back seat of the car to try to make a comfortable place for Buck to rest. They make a place for Bonnie, too. Blanche is able to wash her eyes a bit; she can see a little out of one of them.

Clyde's getting ready to go into town for some food and bandages.

Bonnie's thinking some version of what they're all thinking at some level: so this is what it's come to after all. The burned, the bleeding, and the blind, sleeping under the stars, hoping that Clyde can get them some bandages and food. They are the hunted—"like a wounded, trapped animal," as Blanche says. At thirty, Buck's the old-timer in the crowd, and they all know he can't make it, no matter what Blanche says. He's got a fever now.

Thirty! That sounds so old. How does anyone live that long? She's just twenty-three and so tired, so ready for . . . no, not yet. Let's not talk about those things. . . .

Clyde's got W.D. at work spreading river mud all over the car. Spreading it real thick, as though it got sprayed up off the road, even though there hasn't been rain in a while.

Clyde can't exactly go into town to buy food and medicine with seventeen bullet holes in his car. He's thinking that he needs a new car.

❋

It's a terrible risk, what you're doing, and you know it. Going back to the same place day after day for five meals and a block of ice, and then going across the street and getting bandages, alcohol, and salves is sure to raise questions among the people of Dexter, Iowa. But what else can you do? Buck is in no condition to move yet and may not ever be, and you have to eat and dress your various wounds. So you take what comfort you can from the fact that while the folks at the two stores must be getting suspicious, they don't seem overly nosy, and on Friday, Saturday, and Sunday, you dutifully return the used plates and silverware and order a new round of food. Bonnie, as always, waits in the car, keeping it running.

By the third day in the woods near Dexter, the bullet hole over Buck's right eye is starting to smell a little rough, and his fever is starting to run a little high. You can see his brain through there when you change the bandages. Blanche will hardly leave his side.

"We put ice on his head," she says. "That seemed to give him more relief than anything else we did." He wants her to lie down beside him, which she does, though she's afraid to let herself fall asleep lest he die on her without saying good-bye.

"Buck wasn't out of his head," says W.D. "I talked with him a lot there."

He's not out of his head, but he's getting there, sometimes pulling the bandage off his head and digging at the wound with his fingernails. He's in no condition to move, as a sort of trial run on Sunday proves. You all load back into the car and head to Perry to look for another car, one in which you can move on. You find the car, another V-8 of course, that W.D. gets going with no trouble. The adventure nearly does Buck in, though. He can't sit up, and can't get his breath lying down. You decide to put off leaving Dexfield for one more night.

First thing in the morning, though, first thing, you're going to move out. Everyone agrees. W.D. gets to work transferring all the guns and gear from the old car to the new one. That night, a screech owl gets into the tree above the car and won't shut up with its insane *hoohoohoohoohoohoo* that sounds more like some kind of escaped lunatic laughing than a self-respecting owl.

"I could have screamed from hearing it," says Blanche. "But we were afraid to shoot it because someone might come to investigate. Clyde tried to frighten it away but it always came back."

Fucking bird. First thing in the morning you're out of here.

❋

It doesn't matter how the cops get there. Somebody finds a bloody shirt in the woods and reports it to the local laws. Somebody else finds some dirty bandages. Somebody mentions the five meals a day and the bandages and ice once too often, or takes note of the holes in the side of the muddy car with the yellow-haired girl sitting in it waiting for her man to come out of the drugstore. Somebody sees something, says something, calls someone. It was bound to happen eventually, and it does.

"Officers became suspicious and got in touch with state officers who thought the gang was the Barrow Gang that had shot their way out of a tourist camp near Platte City, Missouri, last Wednesday," says a reporter for the local paper. "The state men decided to try and capture the gang early Monday morning and reached the scene about midnight and made their plans."

All night long on Sunday they guard the roads and watch the river cross-ings. More members of the posse gather. "Police officers, state men and county deputies and vigilantes from Stuart and other towns appeared on the scene," says the paper. No one knows for sure how many lawmen and volunteers eventually get there, as more keep arriving. More than fifty men, say some re-ports. Two hundred, say other reports. The chief of the state bureau of inves-tigation will be in an airplane flying low and hopefully coordinating ground efforts. First thing Monday they make their move.

"I was roasting some wieners we had left from supper the night before," says W.D. "Clyde and Bonnie were sitting on the cushion when they saw the officers coming."

"Look out!" Clyde yells and jumps up and lets loose in the direction of a line of men coming out of the underbrush about fifty yards away.

Rata rata rata rata.

No one, not even Clyde, is in the mood to hear that sound this early. But the laws are asking for it, coming at them out of the woods, and W.D. goes for his gun as well. The posse lets loose with their own fusillade of every-thing from machine guns to rusty revolvers to farmers' shotguns. It's a war all right.

"Shooting was going on before I could get straightened up," says W.D. "One buckshot is still in my lip, one in my right little finger, one in my chest just above my right nipple. These buckshot I still have in me. I was shot through the calf of the left leg with a bullet, and a bullet from a machine gun struck me in the chest above the right nipple. I also was shot in the left wrist, but don't know what with, and my right thumb was also shot. I was knocked down by the machine gun bullet that struck me in the chest, but I got to my feet again and went back around the car, and I think it was there that I got the shot in my thumb."

He's standing there behind the car, bleeding out of a half dozen places. "I looked his way and saw blood streaming down his face," Blanche says.

"Clyde, I'm shot," W.D. yells. "I can't fight any longer."

"I'm shot too," Clyde yells back, "but we gotta keep fighting."

Rata rata rata rata rata bang pow rata blam. The overwhelming fire-power of the BARs temporarily flattens the relatively underarmed posse.

"I heard Clyde curse one of the officers and say, 'I'll get you for that,'" says Blanche.

"Clyde was yelling for me to start the car like he always did when trou-ble happened and I got in and tried to start it," says W.D. "Bonnie got in the car too. I don't know whether Bonnie did any shooting there or not. I was so scared I couldn't get it going, and Clyde was shooting all the time, and he came and stood by the door by my side and emptied his rifle standing there."

W.D. is so shot up and nervous that he can't get the engine to catch, so Clyde yanks him out of the seat and climbs in. The V-8 roars to life. After a short trip down the way they came it's obvious they aren't going to get out that way, and he puts it in reverse to turn around. Over the sound of the warfare comes a low grinding thump that's even worse in its way than the constant gunfire.

"When he tried to turn around again he backed the car up on a stump and it hung there and we couldn't get it off," says W.D. "He made me get out and try and pry it off with a rifle, and we couldn't do it."

They're stuck, and the other car has been shot to shreds by the posse. It's got four flat tires and a radiator full of holes.

"Let's run," says Bonnie. Clyde reminds her that she can't run on one leg but she insists she will, and the truth is there is no other choice. He tells W.D. to pick her up and he'll cover them with his BAR.

"Clyde decided to abandon the car, and told me to carry Bonnie, which I did, and we went off through the woods," says W.D. Behind them, Blanche tries to help Buck out of the car.

"Come on," Clyde yells to them from about ten feet away, and turns to lay down another barrage of bullets in the direction of the advancing posse, sending them diving back onto their bellies again.

"I got my arm around Buck's waist and tried to follow, but when we were about twenty feet up the hill Buck fainted," says Blanche. "Clyde, W.D., and Bonnie were still running and shooting. They saw Buck faint and pull me down. I called to Clyde, but they didn't stop."

Buck revives a bit.

"Baby," he says to Blanche. "Leave me. You can get away alone. I'm too tired to go on."

She refuses.

"Please go," he says again. "I love you too much to let you get killed because of me. And don't commit suicide."

"Daddy," she says to him, "I don't think you have to worry about me doing that. They will do it for me because I'm not leaving you."

They make it a little farther into the woods, and Blanche lights them a cigarette. She can hear Clyde in the distance, yelling, perhaps calling for them, but she knows they're not coming back for her and Buck.

"I didn't expect any help from him," she says. "I knew we were on our own."

After the cigarette Blanche and Buck are able to move again, but not far. They settle in behind a huge log and wait.

Up ahead, Clyde, W.D., and Bonnie are also catching their breath. Bonnie's bandages are long gone, and the wound on her leg has cracked open again and is bleeding. She's bleeding from a couple of buckshot wounds, and from countless scratches from the race through the underbrush. W.D. is full of holes, as is Clyde. But at least they seem to have temporarily lost the posse.

Their only hope, Clyde figures, is if he can get them a car. He tells W.D. to take care of Bonnie and they watch him limp off with his rifle in the direction of the road. The last time Bonnie was left with a wounded man waiting for Clyde to go get help, he never made it back and she ended up in jail. She's not thinking about that now, though. Too much has passed for Bonnie to worry about Clyde making a run for it on his own; if he were going to do that, he would have done it months ago when she was half dead from her burns. She's worried he'll be killed.

Rata rata rata.

Blam pow bangbangbang pow.

There it is. They hear Clyde's BAR going off and being answered by a barrage of returned fire. Then silence. Who knew that silence could be so horrid. She's more than worried about Clyde now. She's almost certain.

"They got him this trip, Bonnie," W.D. says when the silence grows too long.

"My heart turned to ice," she says. "They'd got Clyde."

There's nothing more to do. He's gone. It's over, except for the end.

"I wish I had his gun," she says, and W.D. tells her she wouldn't be able to hold them off for long even if she had a gun.

"I could kill myself," she tells W.D. "He's finished and I don't want to live."

That was always their deal, and now Clyde's gone and gotten himself killed without her. She's crying and begging W.D. to kill her, though how far this talk goes is not really clear.

W.D. never mentions it at all. Like everybody who knows them, he says how they "didn't intend to ever be taken alive. They was hell-bent on running till the end, and they knowed there was only one end for them." Or: "Bonnie was like Clyde. They had grit. They meant to stay free or go down together."

But W.D. saying Clyde and Bonnie had a death wish is not the same as saying he once seriously thought about putting a bullet through Bonnie

Parker's weeping head to help her keep up her end of a suicide pact. Billie Jean, on the other hand, says her sister later told her flat out that "W.D. already had the gun to my head—cocked and his finger on the trigger."

❋

"There they are!" Blanche hears someone in the posse yelling to the others. Buck hears it too and rolls over and tries to get his gun in a position to shoot.

Bang pow. He squeezes off a few shots, which are immediately answered with a barrage of bullets from, among others, a national guardsman with a machine gun.

"It seemed as if the log in front of us was being cut in half with a saw instead of bullets from machine guns, rifles, and shotguns," says Blanche. At last, one of the slugs finds its mark, and Buck's body jolts against hers.

"Baby," he says, "they got me this time."

He hugs her hard at first; then, in a moment she'll never forget, he goes limp. Now Blanche goes half crazy, thinking he's dead. The buzz saw of bullets keeps coming, though almost miraculously she's not hit.

"I just went mad, screaming and begging them to stop," she says. She's got her hands up over the edge of the log to show the crowd of gunners that she's unarmed. But Buck's not dead, and when he moves, she pulls them back down to hug him.

"Baby," he says, "don't get up, they will kill you."

The guns begin again.

"We lay there holding each other tight, murmuring to each other I love you no matter what happens I will always love you," says Blanche.

The bullets continue, and the thought comes into Blanche's head that her husband is dying no matter what. Maybe in a few minutes, maybe in a few hours. Whenever, but he's on his way and maybe there's no real glory in dying in the dirt behind a log with one or two more pieces of angry lead in what's left of him. Not when there's a chance of a bed in a hospital, or even a jail. A chance for a quiet end.

"Don't get up, baby," he says for the second time, "they will kill you." It's over, though, and Blanche isn't listening anymore.

"Daddy, whatever they do to me I'll always love you," she says and stands up.

"She got up from back of the log," says one of the posse. "She had on a pair of boot breeches, she had a pair of nice riding boots, she had on dark glasses. She didn't look too clean."

"My husband is lying on the ground, he can't move," she tells them.

"Well, we didn't really believe that," says the posse man, "so we de-

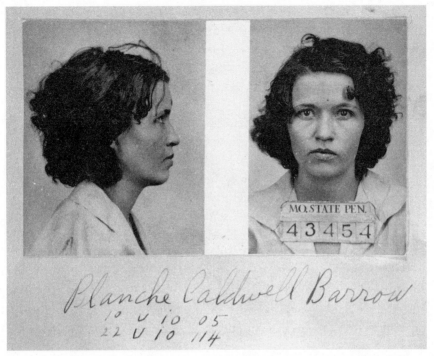

Mug shot of Blanche Caldwell Barrow taken after her capture at Dexfield Park, Iowa, on July 24, 1933. *(From the collections of the Texas/Dallas History and Archives Division, Dallas Public Library.)*

manded that he stand up. And is he armed? Well, she didn't answer that. She came out and stood at one end of the log or a little bit beyond. And we kept telling him to get up, come out. And she was, well, she was pretty hysterical."

It's really over, though, the shooting and everything. Buck's clearly not going to be a danger to anyone in his condition. "Buck had very bad pallor, ghastly looking pallor," says a posse man. "His brain was exposed; you could see this man was on his last legs and wasn't going to live too much longer, which he didn't."

The posse closes in. Two men take Blanche by the wrists; two take control of Buck.

"Buck would walk for a while and he would seem to pass out and they would have to drag him for a few feet and maybe stop and then he'd get his feet under him again and maybe walk a way," says the posse man. "We covered, I suppose, better than a quarter of a mile when we got to the area where everybody has seen the famous picture taken by the register photographer."

Click. Buck's there in the fetal position at the base of a car, barely visible in a crowd of men, including one in overalls and a sleeveless undershirt on his knees, leaning over Buck's head. Blanche is there in her dark glasses and riding clothes. As the posse man says, she doesn't look altogether clean or in control of her emotions, both of which are understandable given the circumstances.

"I never knew if Buck was mad because I gave myself up," she says. "I only did it so he could die in a comfortable clean bed and not be torn to shreds by more bullets."

At the hospital, after an examination and some work on her wounded eyes, the laws put her in handcuffs and take her away.

"Good-bye, daddy, good-bye," she screams over her shoulder, but it's not clear if Buck hears her last words to him or not. He's not dead, won't be for a few more days, but he and Blanche will never see each other again.

❋

"Are you all right, honey?" you ask Bonnie when you crawl back through the underbrush to where she has just been trying to convince W.D. to kill her. She nods.

"Are you all right?" she asks.

You've got four bullet wounds in you—one in your leg, one in your shoulder, one across your face, and one who cares where at this point—but you nod, too. You're alive, anyway. There's no way out near the bridge where you've just been, you tell her and W.D., but you think you found a place not too far away where you can ford the river, and then, maybe, you can get a car up on the road.

"Can you make the river, kid?" you ask W.D. He's going to have to carry Bonnie across, with your arm useless and your leg nearly so. He nods. He's bleeding out of his chest, but his legs and arms are still in working order.

Okay then, and you head off.

"I was carrying her on my back—half stumbling, half swimming," says W.D., but he manages to make it across the river. Bonnie's almost passed out now from lack of blood and sheer exhaustion. He's carrying her over his shoulder like a corpse, up the muddy bank and into a cornfield. You're out a little bit ahead, with nothing but a handgun. There's a farmhouse up ahead with three men in the yard who are looking out in the direction of the gunshots but who don't see the three of you in their cornfield. There are cars in the farmyard as well.

You tell W.D. to rest by the fence and you rush up on farmers, waving your pistol and demanding one of the cars.

"We had three cars, but since it was during the Depression, we could only afford tires and gasoline for one, a 1929 Plymouth," says Marvelle Feller. He's nineteen, and along with his dad, Valley, and a hired man named Walter Spillers he's been up since daybreak feeding cattle and gazing out across the river occasionally to where the noise of guns has broken up the usual bird-song. When they point to the Plymouth, you yell to "buddy" to come on out of the cornfield, and W.D. appears by the fence with Bonnie over his shoulder. You tell the kid standing there to go help him get her over the fence and not to put her on the ground as she's been shot in the leg and the stomach.

"Since Bonnie was hardly conscious and bleeding badly, Clyde ordered me to carry her to the car," Marvelle says. "He'd been shot through the cheek-bone and grazed. He'd been shot in the shoulder and, uh, when you're nineteen and you see a guy with blood running down the guy's face, been shot a couple times, you kind of do as he tells you to do."

Everybody does exactly what you tell them to do. When the mom and sister come out of the house saying they've heard on the radio that there are dangerous men in the neighborhood and old man Feller tries to yell at them to get back inside, they don't go back in because you tell them you'll shoot someone if they do. When you threaten to shoot the dog if it doesn't stop barking, they make it shut up. When you can't figure how to shift the crazy transmission on the Plymouth, they lean in the window to show you. What they don't know is that you ran out of bullets over on the other side of the river.

"We didn't have nothing to shoot with no more," says W.D.

It might be kind of funny if you weren't all half dead. And if Buck wasn't probably dead back there in the woods. It's better than funny, though. Maybe even better than bullets. You got wheels and you got gas. You're gone.

CHAPTER 20

SOWERS

"How can they avoid seeking medical attention if either is badly wounded?" a reporter asked Hamilton.

"Huh," Raymond laughed. "That's a cinch. Clyde knows how to get medical attention as easy as anyone. He'll just kidnap himself a doctor or a surgeon and take him along on a tour. . . .

"They're saying they'll catch them before the end of the week; I say they're dead wrong.

"They got away at Joplin, didn't they? And didn't they outsmart a small army of coppers at Platte City? Where are they now? Not in any jail yet—and if I know anything they won't be for a long time . . .

"I'm a lot safer here in jail than Clyde is at large, but I'm still predicting they won't get him for a long, long time."

—Dallas Daily Times Herald

"I just know that if I don't see Buck before he dies, I'll never get to see either of them alive again," says Cumie. "It's been so hard to stand! I don't care what people say, they're my boys and I love them."

Smoot Schmid is back at the Barrow garage again, with a reporter in tow, talking with Cumie and Henry. He gives the sad old couple what news he knows about the shootout up in Iowa, but mostly, of course, he's hoping to glean a little information from them, hoping they'll slip up and say something—anything—that might be useful. It seems he knows more than they do.

"Have they got Clyde?" they want to know. "Did he get away?"

Schmid nods. The Barrows are either just acting dumb or looking for confirmation of what they've doubtless already heard over the radio. Old Henry's always got that radio running. He's more talkative than normal, though, no doubt shaken up by the news that Buck's on his deathbed. He tells Schmid how Buck went to try to get Clyde to change his ways and just got caught up in the gunfights by accident, how Buck doesn't deserve what's happened to him. As for Clyde's possible whereabouts, however, Henry's got no news that he's willing to part with. He knows Clyde has been to Dallas but says he hasn't seen Clyde himself since last January.

"I know you think they are bad boys," he tells Schmid. "But they are our boys. I've never been in any trouble on my own account, but this has brought me lots of trouble and grief."

Cumie is planning on going immediately to see Buck. Schmid gives her a letter of introduction to the police up in Iowa, asking them to let the poor old lady visit her dying son. She's grateful for that, for his civility under the circumstances. Henry won't be making the trip, though Emma Parker, who is desperate for news about her wounded daughter, will go.

Cumie's grateful again, a week later, when Schmid and his deputies do the family the service of keeping uninvited gawkers away from the funeral. She's not naive enough to think that he and his men—and the Dallas city police and the federal men—are there just to protect the privacy of the Barrows of Eagle Ford Road in their moment of grief. The rumor all over Dallas is that Clyde is going to disguise himself in one of his wigs and dresses and attend the funeral, just like the rumors up in Iowa claimed that he and Bonnie were going to come in a blaze of guns and bust the dying Buck out of the hospital. Cumie knows the deputies and officers in the cars tagging along to the graveyard after the service are looking for Clyde under every woman's hat brim, but she is nonetheless grateful for the decorum they provide the fifty invited guests.

"The fact is every person at the funeral was identified or recognized," says Deputy Hinton. "I would have known him, despite a beard, despite a bonnet he might have worn, or under any other disguise. We were on the lookout, believe it or not, for just such a stunt."

Some of the guests are reporters with notepads from the local dailies.

They hear "Mother Barrow" say "it's so hard to give him up." And "Oh, why did he have to go this way." And "He always was so sweet to his mother. God take care of him. I'll be with him soon."

❀

August, 1933

Dallas TX R6 Box 112a
Mr Ed Prtly,
Kind Sir Chief of Detectives,
    Will you pleas write me just what charges thair is against Buck or Marvin's . . . car you all I understand have thair. I am the mother of Marvin Barrow and as Marvin is dead and was very inisent in the killing at Jopling I now want to bring his car home and also his clothes. . . .

Sincerely a friend
Mrs. C J Barrow
Dallas Tex R6 Box 112a
Marvins Mother

Dear Madam:
    In answer to your letter of August 3rd will state that all clothing taken from the house where Marvin and Clyde lived at the time of the killing of the officers here, is in the possession of the State Highway Patrol. . . .
    In relation to the Marmon car which was the property of Marvin, will state that the same was attached by the families of the murdered officers. . . .

Respectfully yours,
Ed Portly
Chief of Detectives

❀

Now that Buck is in the ground forever and Blanche is in jail for who knows how long, W.D. is thinking about conversations he had with the two of them in the days camped there at Dexfield Park. Clyde and Bonnie would go into town for supplies and he would get a chance to talk with good old Buck, who had known him all his life, after all. Buck's head was a mess on the outside, but he and Blanche were good to talk to about all the stuff W.D. didn't really feel like Clyde was going to want to hear him say.

"W.D. told us how tired he was of the outlaw life," says Blanche. "He said he wished he could leave and forget all about it. We told him he might have a chance to do that if he left right away and went to work someplace. No one knew he was with us or had his fingerprints. He was young."

That's how he was feeling, all right, and that was *before* the army of cops and farmers and patrolmen and who knows what all showed up and put a couple more bullets in him.

That first day after they get away from Dexfield is just plain crazy. They quickly steal a new car in Polk City, Iowa, but even getting gas is a risky operation.

"We was wearing some sheets that was left in the car," W.D. says. "We'd cut holes in them to stick our heads in. Bonnie was lying in the back seat all covered up. The gas-station man looked at us funny, but it was wear sheets or show how bloody and shot up and muddy we was."

They're in shock, really, feeling more full of holes than blood, like they been drug through a knothole backwards.

"We were all so sick that time went by without our knowing it," says Bonnie. "We lost track of days. Eventually our wounds began to heal."

Things settle down once the bleeding stops. Clyde almost immediately swings by the armory in Platteville, Illinois, the same one he and Buck had knocked over once before. He and W.D. break in exactly the way Clyde did before only to discover that the company is off on maneuvers and has all the equipment with it. Third time's a charm, however, and when they come through town again in a couple more weeks they get six pistols and five BARs. That has to relax Clyde a little bit; cleaning and cutting them down gives him something to do around the campsites. It's always campsites—they're not sleeping anywhere but the car, in a driveway of a house if they can't find a road off to nowhere. Cops won't stop to check out a car in a driveway like they will one that's off the side of a road. They're homeless, just like they were before Buck got killed.

W.D. can't get that out of his head: Buck got killed and here they are doing just what they were before.

"We traveled all around in this car," he says, "through Nebraska, Minnesota, and into Colorado. In Colorado we saw a newspaper that said they were looking for us there, and we thought they were getting pretty hot on our trail so Clyde turned back through Kansas and down into Missouri and back into Oklahoma and across into Mississippi."

Nothing's really going to change: buying bandages, stealing doctor's bags out of cars, stealing cars, stealing money to buy gas and sandwiches to get them through to the next state. And, of course, hoping to avoid the other thing—the bullets—but knowing that somehow the bullets will come again.

"The robbing and killing never stopped," W.D. says, "and neither did we."

Clyde's healing up nicely now. And Bonnie, Jesus, she looked like she was going to die for a while there, but she didn't die and she's slowly getting stronger too. She'll make it as long as they make it, and W.D. hopes they make it a long time. Without him. Toward the end of August 1933, Clyde puts him out of the car not far from Clarksdale, Mississippi, with orders to steal a new vehicle for them.

W.D. has done some scary stuff in the eight months he's been with Clyde and Bonnie—hard to believe it's only eight months; it feels like a lifetime—but not bringing that car back to Clyde and just taking off and leaving them to their own devices is up there on the list. It's not that he's some kind of slave: that business about being chained to trees at night and Clyde always watching him is just some hogwash he'll tell the police later, like happening to be passed out every time someone happens to get killed. That said, it just seems easier to slip away than to try to tell Clyde to his face that he's leaving. He steals the new car like he's told, but then pulls a sort of Clyde on Clyde himself.

"I drove on up the road and he was supposed to follow me, but I turned off on a little country road," he says. "This was at night when I got on that country road, I cut my lights off and he didn't find me."

W.D. adds, "I'd had enough blood and hell."

❀

Scars on body of W. D. Jones:

Round Bullet wound 6 inches below R. shoulder in side ranged toward back and came out 1 inch to right of backbone about center of small of back. Received at Joplin, Mo:

Dexter, Iowa:

Bullet wound scar about 3 inches above right nipple and 1½ inches to right of breast bone. Buckshot under skin about 1½ inches above and left of right nipple. Buckshot under skin in right little finger between first and second joints. Scar across second joint of right ring-finger. Scar near end of right middle-finger left side. Gash scar inside of right thumb from end downward. All of right hand wounds from being shot near Dexter, Iowa. 1 small round wound on left lower leg back above ankle. 1 small cut scar at heel of left palm outer. 1 buckshot under skin inside left lower lip. Small cut scar left cheek above corner of mouth. 1 small scar from shattered or spent bullet in left eyelid.

Burn scar on back of upper right leg center 6 inches long by 2 inches wide at widest part, received in auto wreck near Wellington, Texas.

—FBI document 26-4114-144

❀

It's just her and Clyde again for the first time in a long time. Bonnie can't really blame W.D. for slipping off, not after what they've all been through. He'd be a fool not to leave. Heck, she and Clyde would love to leave off running with themselves too if it were possible. Still, it would have been nice if W.D. said good-bye, but she can understand that too.

She and Clyde are living entirely out of the car now. Or, rather, living in the car now. They're lower on money, more often hungry, more often dirty.

"We lived in little ravines, secluded woods, down side roads for days that stretched into weeks," says Bonnie. It's nothing they haven't done before. The road is tiresome, but mostly it's a loyal friend. She has her poetry to read and write in her mind, or occasionally on scraps of paper. There's plenty of time for that. Somewhere along the way she gets a little book of poems, a ten-cent pamphlet really, entitled *The Most Wonderful Collection of Famous Recitations Ever Written.* Maybe Clyde picks it up at a drugstore as a little gift.

The print is tiny, making it hard to read on all but the smoothest roads. There are almost sixty poems, most of them tragic ballads, to read aloud to Clyde if he's interested or just quietly to herself if he's not. There's "Gunga Din" and "Guilty or Not Guilty," "The Boston Burglar" and "Life Is But a Game of Cards," with its memorable last lines:

> No matter how much a man may win, or how much a man may
> save,
> You'll find the spade turns up at last, and digs the player's grave.

One of Bonnie's favorites, a sad tale of an artist felled by love called "The Face upon the Bar-room Floor," is there and she copies the opening lines of that one down. It's the middle of the poem, though, that sounds more like her own hard-luck ballads, "Suicide Sal" and "The Story of Bonnie and Clyde":

> You've treated me pretty kindly and I'd like to tell you how
> I came to be the dirty sot you see before you now,

"We lived in little ravines, secluded woods, down side roads for days that stretched into weeks," says Bonnie. *(Photograph by Floyd Hamilton, collection of John Neal Phillips.)*

> As I told you, once I was a man of muscle, frame and health,
> And, but for a blunder, ought to have made considerable wealth.

Another of her favorites, "You Beautiful Girl of the Street," isn't there, but it doesn't really matter since, Billie Jean says, she can quote it at will.

> Within your barren heart there lies
> The cherished hope, that when
> The evil thing within you dies,
> Your love will live again.

Her own autobiographical poem "The Story of Bonnie and Clyde" is coming together a bit more:

> There's lots of untruths to these write-ups;
> They're not so ruthless as that
> Their nature is raw;

They hate all the law—
The Stool pigeons, spotters, and rats

They call them cold-blooded killers;
They say they are heartless and mean;
But I say this with pride,
That I once knew Clyde
When he was honest and upright and clean

But the laws fooled around,
Kept taking him down
And locking him up in a cell
Till he said to me,
"I'll never be free,
So I'll meet a few of them in hell."

The road gets dimmer and dimmer;
Sometimes you can hardly see;
But it's fight man to man,
And do all you can,
For you know they can never be free.

The road is not only getting dimmer, it's starting to feel a little pointless as well.

"We felt that the end of the trail was near," says Bonnie, "and we wanted to be close to home when death came out to meet us."

Clyde points the car toward Dallas.

❄

Hard as it is to believe, it almost seems easier to hide out in Dallas than on the road. All fall, you and Bonnie are in the area, not staying in town, of course, but coming through pretty regularly or getting word to everyone to meet you out of town somewhere. Bonnie's mother figures that during all of September and October, and halfway through November, you visited with family members just about every night. That's probably a bit of an exaggeration—a distant cousin in Alabama says you and Bonnie stopped by there in mid-October—but for the most part you're around Dallas.

It's heartbreaking at first, because it's so obvious you've barely survived the past few months. "Bonnie was still unable to walk without help," Emma says. "She was miserably thin and much older. Her leg was drawn up under her. Her body was covered with scars."

Not everybody in both families is interested in coming out to see you. Bonnie's brother, Buster, for one, doesn't want to have anything to do with you. You've known his wife, Edith, even longer than you've known Bonnie; Edith even thinks she introduced you to each other. But Buster is tired of getting interviewed by all manner of lawmen every time he shows his face in his own hometown, and more than that, he knows you're going to get his little sister killed. He thinks you're nothing but trouble.

You do feel like a damn failure. You got Buck killed and Bonnie all torn up. You don't even have any stacks of money these days to show for it. W.D.'s gone. Your own ma isn't taking the stress and loss of Buck all that well. She looks old now.

Still, it's a blessing to be back, even if it means putting on a wig and lipstick now and then to get through town.

"I remember that several times that Clyde had a red wig Bonnie had purchased for him," says Billie Jean. "And, uh, in the daytime she would put the wig on him and put lipstick on him, and fix his face up, you know. And, uh, one time, when he was fixed up like that coming in he ran into a deputy sheriff. And this deputy sheriff had put Clyde in jail so many times. It was out close to Irving, this little town, and uh, the deputy sheriff waved to Clyde. And Clyde waved to the deputy sheriff, who never did know who they were."

That was damn funny. Ha! It still feels good to laugh. Good to be home. Good to eat Ma's red beans and rice. Maybe the coppers just plain forgot about you. They've got a lot to worry about. Sure they did. Ha! It's grim to laugh, too.

❋

> The Irving News wants to compliment our big, 250-pound, double fisted, hard-working sheriff for the consciencious [*sic*] manner in which he has conducted the law enforcement of Dallas county. He has put a lot of wallop into it, but at the same time his big cheery smile has proven that he is the friend of all, whether in low or high position.
>
> —*Irving News*

The truth is, Smoot Schmid's first year in office as sheriff (hopefully for life) is not ending on all that much better a note than it started, and not getting Clyde Barrow and Bonnie Parker is only a part of it. On September 5, 1933, just about the time Clyde and Bonnie show up back in the neighborhood, Harvey Bailey single-handedly kidnaps his jailer and breaks out of Schmid's county jail. Bailey is probably the most important criminal awaiting trial in the country at that time. The feds think he was the trigger man at the Kansas City Massacre. His arrest, however, came at the hands of the Dallas FBI and the Fort Worth police—and not the Dallas sheriff's office—in connection with the equally sensational kidnapping of Oklahoma oilman Charles Urschel earlier in the summer.

Making things worse from a local publicity point of view, only a few days before Bailey's escape Schmid posed for the newspapers with a tommy gun in his hands to show how seriously he was taking the custody of the famous gangster. He tried to look tough as a boot in the picture, with a suitable scowl, but it's not clear the newspaper is going for the new tough-guy image.

"Sheriff Fondles Submachine Gun," reads the headline.

Bailey is caught only four hours later up in Oklahoma, but still, the whole episode is an embarrassment. Schmid tells the grand jury looking into the escape that it was all the jailer's fault, which it was, though passing the buck is generally unbecoming to a Dallas sheriff.

"The kidnapped jailer was a farmer at Rheinhardt when he was given a job as deputy jailer by Sheriff Smoot Schmid," says the *Dallas Evening Journal* with a sniff.

The department can't even seem to get proper credit when credit is due. When Ted Hinton, acting alone, manages to round up a pair of high-profile murderers, the city police department ends up taking all the credit. "Sheriff's Office 'Hot,'" says the *Dallas Dispatch* when it gets wind of the tiff between the two local law enforcement agencies. "After six months of surface cooperation the police department and the sheriff's office are again at cross purposes."

Now that the word on the street is that Clyde and Bonnie are back in the neighborhood, Schmid wants Ted Hinton to work pretty much full-time with Deputy Bob Alcorn on tracking them down. He doesn't say it for the record, of course, but the unspoken truth that everyone in the department knows is that if the sheriff's office can get Bonnie and Clyde, then the politics—well, the politics will take care of themselves.

"It would be completely accurate to say that Sheriff Schmid wanted nothing so much in the world as to capture Clyde Barrow and Bonnie Parker and to walk them down Main Street of Dallas and show the world what he'd done," says Hinton. "His reelection would be assured. Hell, he might have become governor if he could have made it happen that way, but the man was pipe dreaming."

Part of the problem is, despite Hinton's great contacts and best efforts, he's mostly coming up dry. Hinton thinks it's because Clyde has been spreading money around for so long that no one will give him up.

"There couldn't have been more than five hundred adult people living in all

of the region known as the 'Bog' at that time, and I probably could have recognized all of them and called them by name," he says. "Even my good sources
in West Dallas now were beginning to hold back on me—for it seemed half
the people out there were either related to Clyde and Bonnie or were old
school friends sympathetic to their predicament if not their choice of careers."

Bonnie, in her poem, says it's something even stronger than money.

> From Irving to West Dallas viaduct
> Is known as the Great Divide
> Where the women are kin,
> And the men are men,
> And they won't stool on Bonnie and Clyde.

One big break comes when they get word that W. D. Jones is in Houston
and Alcorn drives down and brings him back up to the Dallas County jail.
They keep his presence a secret from the press and other law enforcement
agencies, mostly because they don't want Clyde to know that they know
whatever W.D. might be telling them. He's telling them mostly that he was
a prisoner of Clyde's, and was asleep pretty much every time someone got
killed. Sheriff Schmid and his deputies don't buy that one bit, what with all
the witnesses saying W.D. was firing BARs and shotguns just as furiously as
Clyde, not to mention the pictures of him all smiles and fancy suits and
guns and such that were found at Joplin. W.D. does confirm a lot of information about the past and about Clyde and Bonnie's habits, but he's not
much use on their current whereabouts. After all, he was in Houston mostly
because he doesn't want to run into them again.

"God, I'm glad to be in this jail," W.D. says to Hinton during one interrogation. "Don't ever make me leave it while Clyde's alive."

Without reliable tips, the sheriff and his deputies mostly just keep an
eye on the family and hope to get lucky.

"We have trailed the women of both the Barrow and the Parker families numerous times and have seen them meet a car, but we never got close
enough to be sure Clyde was there," Schmid says. "We felt sure he was, but
could not start anything for fear of shooting some of the women."

Finally, in October, one of Bob Alcorn's contacts in West Dallas starts
dropping hints that he knows Clyde's movements. This is just what they've
all been waiting for, but Alcorn's nervous. He trusts his source well enough;
it's his boss he's worried about. As a career lawman who used to work with
the Dallas city police, Alcorn does not have all that much confidence in the

glad-handing former bicycle salesman turned sheriff. Ted Hinton, meanwhile, is hardworking and talented, but there's no getting around the fact that only one year before he was a mailman. In Joplin and Dexter, Alcorn saw the evidence of what kind of firepower anyone who tries to go up against Barrow is likely to face, and he's not so sure he cares enough about Smoot Schmid's reelection to run the risk of the sorts of heroics the sheriff is hoping for. But Schmid isn't listening to reason.

"Alcorn failed to convince Smoot that he couldn't say merely, 'Stop in the name of the law,' and slip handcuffs on Clyde Barrow,'" says Hinton.

On October 28, Schmid decides to use a tip from Alcorn's source to spy on a Barrow-Parker gathering out near Duncanville, Texas, rather than round up all the law enforcement people he can to try to put them on the spot as planned. He tells Alcorn it's because he wants to be sure the informant is reliable, which is another way of saying he's more worried about bad press the next morning than he is about catching Clyde. Alcorn doesn't want to lose his job at the sheriff's department in the middle of the depression, but he decides to put out some feelers behind his boss's back. He gets together with his old friend Doug Walsh at the Dallas Police Department and tells him the whole story, confiding that they have everything they need to get Clyde and have blown it once already.

Walsh says there's nothing he can do: Schmid won't listen to anyone from the police department. Walsh puts Alcorn in touch with E. J. Dowd, one of the special agents in the Dallas office of the FBI. "He stated he would like to work with the Dallas Division Office [FBI] and the police, and in this context suggested seeing Smooth Smith [sic]," wrote Dowd in a memo to his boss after the meeting.

Schmid can smell the prize, however, and isn't interested in sharing the glory. When Dowd comes to him saying the Bureau has got some good connections and has been tracking Clyde all over the Midwest and, without mentioning Alcorn's leaks, suggests combining forces, Schmid brushes him off.

"Sheriff Smith [sic] declined to do so, stating he was now close on Barrow's heels, and at the present did not think it would do any good to divulge his plans, etc., to the Dallas division office," complains an internal FBI memo dated November 6, 1933. "He stated that after following the same for about two weeks, he might ask the assistance of the Dallas division office, but at present preferred to work alone."

Schmid thinks it will all be over within two weeks, maybe even sooner. Two weeks after the FBI memo, Alcorn gets another tip.

✻

It's the day after your ma's birthday, on a road near Sowers, Texas.

"We had met Clyde at Sowers the day before and he told Mother to meet him back out there the next night, which was the first time he had ever had her or any of us meet him twice at the same place," says Marie Barrow. "So we met. And, uh, evidently somebody told 'em we was coming out there."*

In the car going out to meet you and Bonnie are your ma, Emma, Billie Jean, L.C., Marie, and Marie's relatively new husband, Joe Francis.

"We usually met them in a field where we could see for miles, you know, so we drove down and we had to signal. Just turn on the lights, off and on, so many times and they'd know it was us, and we'd know it was them," says Billie Jean. "Bonnie said, 'Clyde, let's don't go. I don't feel right.' And he said, 'They're already parked, so let's go.'"

Marie says the misgivings came not from Bonnie but from you, that your vaunted sixth sense gave you second thoughts. "We saw his lights coming so we thought. Here he comes, but when he got to right beside us he said he had a hunch, or he might have accidentally seen something over in the gully, and he didn't stop beside of us—he just kept going," she says. Whoever has the hunch, it's a little late.

Rata Rata Rata Rata.

This time the Browning automatic rifle is in the hands of Alcorn, and Ted Hinton and Smoot Schmid have a couple of tommy guns, and deputy Ed Caster has a repeating rifle. This time it's your car door that's no match for the steel-jacketed slugs.

"They got about a car's length in front of us and all these sounds like firecrackers—oh, just popping," says Billie Jean. "Then I realized that it was guns, and the boy that was driving the car had never turned his lights out. He had the lights trained right on the car, on Bonnie and Clyde. I reached over and turned off the lights and we backed out."

"It was just fire all across the sky," says Marie. "You know, shooting. And of course we left right quick and my mother got down and Mrs. Parker got down and I was too stupid to get down, I guess, 'cause I said, 'Mama, he's got away because he's still going.'"

Marie's right. You are still going, firing back at them as you tear away.

---

* "I don't really know who it was," says Marie Barrow about the informant. "I know that my brother L.C. tried to get Ted Hinton to tell him in the later years who it was, but Ted Hinton would never tell him. So it had to be Billie Jean or it had to be Joe Francis. It had to be one of the two."

Hinton, who after Alcorn died claimed the whole event was due entirely to a hunch of his own, may not have disclosed who the informant was because he may not have known. One thing is certain: nothing in her character or actions suggests it was Billie Jean, making Marie's motive the only interesting thing about the insinuation.

Rata rata rata.

"Bonnie was shooting, too, from the rear window," says Hinton, who also says the whole thing started with Sheriff Schmid standing tall and telling you to halt in the name of the law. "We had managed to load the car full of holes, to knock out its windows and flatten a tire, but it only zig-zagged crazily and disappeared."

That's right, Sheriff. You're all shot up again, with a bullet from the BAR that went through your car door then through both your knees and on into Bonnie's leg. There may be other bullet wounds too—who's counting?—and there's car glass everywhere. Yeah, old Smoot the bike salesman got a piece of you. And more than that, he got you real mad with all that shooting when there's a bunch of old ladies and innocent folks around. He could have killed your ma, and Bonnie's too, had things really got going.

But you're more than still going. As all the Dallas papers shout out the next day, the sheriff and his deputies didn't get you. The press is after Schmid, and to get the reporters off his back he announces with great fanfare that he's got a member of the Barrow gang locked up and they should come in and read the twenty-eight-page confession.

"Alcorn winked at me," says Hinton. "The wink meant that Smoot could handle the situation nicely."

Good work, Sheriff, but W. D. Jones is not Clyde Barrow by a long shot. You may be half dead, it's true. But half dead is half alive, and most of all you're gone.

"It won't be nice to run across Barrow now," says Schmid's deputy Ed Caster.* "He's hot and nothing will stop him."

❁

"Barrow has vanished in thin air" is all Ed Caster and Bob Alcorn can say in explanation to a reporter a few days later. "We haven't any idea where to look for him, although how he escaped without being shot is a miracle. We had expected that we would hear from him before now."

"He seems to bear a charmed life," says Caster, who thinks he might have been the first to arrest Clyde, back in 1923 for stealing a motorbike. "He has been shot many times, I believe, but he has always survived without the apparent aid of any doctor."

Bonnie's sister Billie Jean, who also saw the rain of bullets fired on the car, is equally mystified—though in a thankful way—by the escape.

"I don't know how they got through the field. But they did. The car was all

---

* This could have been Alcorn. Both were talking to the reporter, but the context suggests Caster.

shot up," she says Bonnie later told her. "Bonnie and Clyde were wounded real bad. So, um, they drove and drove and drove. They were both bleeding so bad.

"They made it to a well. Way out, maybe in West Texas somewhere, they made it to a well. Clyde got out of the car and he had to crawl to the well—crawl so far—and he passed completely out from loss of blood. Bonnie saw him crawling; she was trying to get out of the car.

"They don't know how long they laid there," Billie goes on, "but Bonnie woke up with Clyde bathing her wounds. He had finally made it to get the water and she woke up with him bathing her wounds. They were injured real bad. They left there and they went to Oklahoma."

Clyde is hurt worse than Bonnie this time, and while holed up in a deserted house in Vinita, Oklahoma, he gets treatment from a nurse named Hattie Crawford. She comes down on a bus from nearby Miami, Oklahoma, after being met outside her apartment by two unidentified men who offer to pay her well to make a house call. It's all pretty mysterious. Billie Jean says that "some of Pretty Boy Floyd's people" helped out, which may be: the FBI thinks that while Clyde and Floyd aren't particularly friendly and don't cooperate on jobs, the two gangs share a number of hideouts.* For her part, Nurse Crawford says that she knows Bonnie from back in 1925, when Emma Parker and her children briefly stayed in Miami "and she was well acquainted with them."

Crawford doesn't get a good look at any of the men, however, because they make her do her work by flashlight. They also make her so afraid that she doesn't tell anyone about the encounter for a week, by which time there's nothing left in the house in Vinita for the cops to find but some bloody bandages.

---

* Jimmie Mullins: "Clyde said that one time in Oklahoma he and Bonnie needed medical aid—I think right after their wreck at Wellington—he went to a cousin of Pretty Boy Floyd and he got him [Clyde] some medicine. Clyde said he never met Pretty Boy Floyd, and that cousin said he had not seen him in a year and a half."

CHAPTER 21

EASTHAM, AGAIN

Even the prison grapevine telegraph, usually good for 15 or 20 different versions of any prison affair, was silent.

"The 'finks' (prison term for informer) and the 'good people' (trustworthy accomplices) know nothing about this deal," a two-time loser on the Eastham farm told The Press. "Maybe it will leak out later but right now everybody is 'uptight' (in a bad way) and won't talk."

—The Houston Press

Floyd Hamilton is a great friend, always willing to take a message to someone in Dallas for you, or bring your mom out for a meeting. But whenever Floyd Hamilton says he wants to talk to you, you know what it's going to be about: getting his little brother Raymond out of jail. He's been at it ever since Raymond got himself caught on that skating rink up in Michigan last spring. Back then he was all hot about breaking Ray out of the Hillsboro jail, and then when that didn't happen he wanted to knock over a bank to hire a lawyer. But Floyd wouldn't agree to work with anyone else and you didn't think you could rob the bank with only two people, so that fell through too.

Now here you are in January, barely healed up from the ambush at Sowers, and here's Floyd with that ratty old drug addict named Mullins. You remember him vaguely; he turned up at Eastham just a few days before you chopped your toe off and got out of there. Maybe you remember him just because he's one ugly cuss: just about your size, but with that dope-addict sallowness and most of his teeth gone and what remains discolored. His arms are all tattooed up and down with daggers and scrolls and horse's heads and skulls and crossbones and a girl's head. He acts like he remembers you, anyway.

Mullins says he's a good pal of Raymond's, who by now has been transferred to Eastham himself (where he's announcing to everyone who will listen that his pal Clyde is going to come and bust him out one of these days). Floyd believes Mullins is on the up-and-up because he's got this special ring that Raymond told Floyd to look out for on somebody coming with a message. There's no surprise about the contents of good old Ray's message.

"I put it up to Clyde about rescuing Raymond from the Eastham Farm," says Mullins. "He and Bonnie agreed that they and I would pull the job."

The way Floyd tells it, you don't want to go at first because you don't want to get near the place, and Bonnie has to talk you into it because she thinks with Raymond out the two of you will get back to robbing banks and making big money. "She clapped her hands and said, Boy, that would be good, we'll get Raymond out, says we won't go hungry anymore, says he'll really make the money."

You like Floyd, but that's just like him to make Raymond sound like this big brave bank robber—who never kills anyone, of course—while you're somehow the chicken who can't feed your girl. This after you pretty much spent your last six months in Eastham and your first six months out of Eastham planning a raid on the place. The whole thing was your idea in the first place! Hell, you've written to Aubrey Scalley four times, telling him to give the word and you'll come and get him. Maybe if Raymond didn't get himself caught so much he wouldn't need busting out so often.

You can't leave him in the burnin' hell, though. As you tell your pa one day during a quick visit at the filling station, "The only thing to do is to go down there and get Raymond or die trying."

What you say to Floyd is that you do want to help his little brother. He's one of your oldest pals, after all, and 366 years is an awful long stay at the burnin' hell. Sure you'll help him out; it'll be fun to see Raymond again. You and Bonnie will be there with a car and some clothes and guns and all. But you're not smuggling those guns up under that bridge near the woodpile. You're not going that close to the camp, what with your wounded leg and all. You tell Floyd he and Mullins can plant the guns.

"I can't admit that I went down and put the guns," says Floyd. "But I'll say arrangement was made to plant the guns and put 'em in, and they was close enough to the building you could see three-tier bunks and you could recognize men walking back and forth there. Mullins recognized some of his friends 'cause he was just out a few days, and there was a guard about less than a hundred yards settin' in a tower reading a magazine and, uh, the bloodhound dog pen was just about thirty feet from us and they was just tearing the building up. And this guard never looked up."

It's a long night for Floyd. Clyde, Bonnie, and Mullins go down to the Trinity River bottoms and camp out. Floyd, on the other hand, goes back to Dallas, picks up his wife, Mildred, and drives back to Eastham Farm in time to make the Sunday afternoon visiting hours. Raymond is brought into the visiting room, and in a moment when the guard is out of earshot Floyd tells him what he wants to hear.

"I told him everything was set up and the guns was where he wanted 'em and that not me but Clyde and Bonnie would be waiting on him."

Yup. You and Bonnie and the dope fiend Mullins will be there. You'll be waiting with your BARs and sawed-off shotguns in the deep, cool fog that rolls off the Trinity River in the predawn and covers the land around Eastham that morning like Vaseline.

❋

"Come on, son," you say to Henry Methvin when all the gunfire and horn honking is over and you've made it clear to Mullins and Hamilton that you don't care what plans they made, anybody who is here at the car and wants a ride out of the burnin' hell with Clyde Barrow is going. Come to think of it, it's too bad old Aubrey Scalley didn't get the word or couldn't get here. Where is he?

Seven people in a Ford coupe is a full car, all right—you, Bonnie, Raymond, Mullins, and Joe Palmer, with Hilton Bybee and Henry Methvin jammed into the trunk. But it feels almost like having a gang again. More than that, it's like you are Moses parting the waters, taking those boys out of the burnin' hell. Fuck, they could get you at the next bridge but you're laughing now. You've been there, you know that guard Crowson they shot, you been buttfucked and beaten, you picked their cotton. Well, now you got a whole load of their boys in every spare space in your car, and your foot is to the floor on the gas, as usual. Ha!

"Clyde was driving," says Mullins, "and he really put a car over the road."

It starts right out on a good note when you pull in to get gas with five people crammed into the car seat and two in the trunk and the attendant looks at you and says, "Did you hear about the prison break? Clyde Barrow and Bonnie just liberated Raymond Hamilton."

"You don't say," you say.

"Yes, Bonnie and Clyde went right into the dining room while they was eating breakfast and took Raymond and shot two guards, said one of them wasn't expected to live," the kid says. No one even cracks a smile. You just pay the fellow and go on your way.

The first couple of nights you all hide out in the vicinity of Rhome, Texas. Floyd and your little brother, L.C., bring food and clothing and take Mullins away with them. After that, for a while it's fast cars and fast money again. One of the first stops after stealing a few more cars is a quick raid on an armory for weapons. Then Hamilton and Palmer rob a bank near Joplin on January 22 with you and Bybee driving getaway, and everyone in the group gets about four hundred dollars. When Mullins hooks back up with the gang on Friday, January 26, looking for the money that Raymond promised him in exchange for setting up the raid, he finds out you've been real busy.

"They all talked about having robbed some mercantile stores in Oklahoma and getting clothes and of having robbed a bank in Iowa and getting $6,000 or $7,000 out of it. They also talked of two or three other bank jobs they pulled on that trip—one in some little town in Kansas and one in Oklahoma, but I can't remember the names of the towns," Mullins says. "Billie Parker, Bonnie's sister, was with them on that trip to Iowa and stayed with them for a while after that meeting that night." Hamilton and the other escapees chip in to give Mullins a part of what they owe him.

"I was supposed to get $2,000 for putting those guns there on the farm," Mullins says, "and I got about $650."

For what it's worth, Mullins, a known liar who is cooperating with the police by the time he says all this, also says that "Billie Parker was Henry Methvin's woman friend, but she gave Palmer, Methvin, and Raymond the gonorrhea, and they all got to quarrelling and sent her home. Both Clyde and Bonnie are afflicted with gonorrhea. They quarrel a great deal."

Mullins presumably knows better than to say that kind of stuff to your face, because he's still alive. Even without knowing the garbage he's spreading, it's fine with you that you don't ever see him again, though Floyd and Ray do.

Next to go is Hilton Bybee, who announces on Monday, January 29, that he wants to keep on with the bank robbing and get some "sure enough money." He tells you where you can find him if you need him and sets off in the direction of Lubbock, taking his big plans with him.

"Clyde didn't care," he says. "Just wanted to ride around and get by."

Getting by may not be good enough for Bybee, but it should have been. His career as a big-time bank robber lasts all of one day and doesn't include any bank jobs. He's arrested trying to steal a car in Amarillo on Tuesday. Ha! That's the kind of thing that makes you glad you risked your life to get him out of the burnin' hell.

Just about the same time, Billie Jean goes back home and Joe Palmer decides to take a break from the gang. Poor old Joe, he was sick as a dog already when they broke him out of Eastham. Funny thing is, he didn't even know it was Clyde driving the getaway car from Eastham until they were twenty miles down the road, but he's loyal as a puppy to him now.

Mostly Palmer's loyal because he thinks Clyde saved his life. "I was in the back of the car asleep, with a fever of 105. Clyde and Bonnie were on the front seat and I was on the back with Raymond. I woke up to find Raymond with a gun in his hand, and Clyde trying to drive and hold his hands at the same time. I didn't find out till later when Clyde told me that Raymond wanted to shoot me in the back and throw me out on the side of the road."

Who knows if Hamilton really would have done it. Palmer's his friend, after all. Hamilton is mostly talk most of the time; Palmer even says the reason Hamilton was so mad at him in the first place was "because I had called him a punk blabbermouth braggart." Hamilton probably wouldn't have pulled the trigger on Palmer, but the fact that Clyde turns around and slaps Hamilton for even suggesting such a thing sure makes an impression on good old Joe.

"Clyde maybe was a murderer and killed folks, but he was sure good to me and the boys, and he toted fair," he says. "I was asleep in the bottom of the car when the bank was robbed, but he split the money six ways with us all." Between his poor health and the situation with Hamilton, Palmer decides to lie low with his piece of the take and checks into a hotel in Joplin. You promise to come back by for him in a month or so. In the meantime, that leaves you, Bonnie, Henry Methvin, and Raymond, and you're getting tired of Raymond faster than you thought you would.

❀

Former Texas Ranger Frank Hamer is glad to hear that his old friend the prison commissioner, Lee Simmons, has done his homework and gone to Governor Ferguson to make sure the politics are all cozy before coming to him with this proposition that he hunt down Clyde and Bonnie. He's got no interest in getting involved in a situation where either politics or legal niceties are apt to pull the rug out from under him before the job is done. After all, he's making more money right now as a private security man in the oil fields than he ever did in twenty-seven years as a Ranger. He's making more, in fact, than Simmons is offering him to go after Barrow. He doesn't need this job, though he has to admit it's his kind of assignment: he knows full well what Simmons means when he says "take Clyde and Bonnie off the road."

It would be wrong to suggest that Frank Hamer, Texas Ranger, enjoys killing. He doesn't, but he's got plenty of experience at it. More experience, even, than Clyde Barrow, which is saying something. By the end of his career—and he's near the end at the time of this conversation with Simmons—Hamer is said to have killed either some thirty-eight men or fifty-two men, depending on who is counting and whether they're counting Mexicans down along the border in his early days. Hamer doesn't confirm or deny the number, saying only that they all either refused to come in quietly or tried to escape. As a general policy, he prefers to keep his mouth shut and let his reputation speak. And it does; the "angel of death," they call him.

"How many men have you killed?" a reporter asks him.

"I won't talk about it," he replies.

"They say you have killed twenty-three men, not counting Mexicans," says the reporter.

"I won't discuss it," says Hamer. "All my killings were in the line of duty. It was an unpleasant duty." But later, in the same conversation, when the reporter asks coyly how many gunfights the Ranger has been in he says, "I don't mind telling you that I've been in fifty-two of them, counting the scrimmages we had with Mexicans and smugglers along the Rio Grande."

Once the shooting starts, Hamer, who claims to be able to see bullets as they fly through the air, and can shoot a hundred plates out of the air in a row without missing one, usually finds his mark.

"Does your conscience bother you?" asks the reporter.

"Not a bit," he says.

Hamer has a few questions for Simmons. He wants to know how long the prison commissioner thinks the job will take, not because he doesn't want to make a commitment but because he doesn't want to sign up if Simmons has unrealistic expectations.

"No matter how long it takes," Simmons assures him, "I'll back you to the limit." Simmons wants revenge for the killing of that guard at Eastham, and even though Clyde didn't do it, it's Clyde he wants most of all.

"No matter how long it takes" is the right answer as far as Hamer is concerned. They also review what tools Hamer might have at his disposal. Simmons tells him that he's discussed with Governor Ferguson the possibility that Hamer might need to be able to strike a deal with someone to put Clyde on the spot. She's agreed that once Clyde is captured or killed, she will grant clemency from the state of Texas to anyone who might have helped Hamer. There are various rewards on Clyde's head already from counties and states all over, but this particular carrot—the offer of clemency—is something that none of the others chasing Clyde and Bonnie have. It will be Hamer's biggest weapon in some ways. He agrees to take the assignment.

Hamer knows full well why Simmons has come to him for this assignment. Just in case he doesn't, however, after Hamer has accepted the job the prison commissioner gives him a little parting advice.

"Captain, it is foolish for me to try to tell you anything," Simmons says. "But in my judgment, the thing for you to do is put them on the spot, you know you are right—and then shoot everyone in sight."

Hamer looks at Simmons and doesn't respond.

❀

The Dallas underworld is in a speculative mood concerning the recent brazen outburst of Clyde Barrow and the more daring "burst out" of Raymond Hamilton. Many members of the grapevine circuit here believe Clyde and Bonnie are near the parting of the ways. They also think Bonnie, and not Barrow, was the originator of the plot which brought Hamilton his freedom and Bonnie another pawn.

It is no secret that Bonnie is the impelling force behind Barrow's recklessness and murderous escapades. She writes the orders and Clyde carries them out while Bonnie stands to the side and watches his victims squirm in fear or wriggle in the dust in pain.

Underworld characters think the prison break means one of two things—either Bonnie and Clyde are ready to call it quits or that she decided they had been quiet too long and it was time things started popping. Back of it remains the fact that she once was madly in love with Hamilton. Perhaps her mind recalled those days and nights spent with Ray, and she couldn't bear to think of him locked behind bars with nothing but four walls staring him in the face. Perhaps her vanity told her she could hold the love of both Ray and Clyde.

The most logical conclusion, according to a sneak thief here who knows both of the fugitives, is that they realize too many officers are after them, particularly Clyde, and capture is only a matter of time if they remain together. And Bonnie, after leading Clyde on a merry chase, is ready to take up where she left off. If so,

Raymond Hamilton may soon find himself in the big-time, that
category of fugitives who brave machine guns and rifle bullets
for the fun of "showing up" officers.

—*The Dallas Dispatch*

It's amazing what those newspapers will say, isn't it? Bonnie is used to
reading that she and Clyde have committed pretty much every crime reported in every state over the past couple of years. She even jokes bitterly
about it in her new poem:

> If a policeman is killed in Dallas
> And they have no clew or guide;
> If they can't find a fiend,
> They just wipe their slate clean
> And hang it on Bonnie and Clyde
>
> There's two crimes committed in America
> Not accredited to the Barrow mob;
> They had no hand
> In the kidnap demand,
> Nor the Kansas City Depot job.

Anything else—any bank job or gas station stickup—is likely to get
their names attached to it. She and Clyde have always read the papers reli-
giously. Part of it's just self-preservation; if the radio or newspaper says the
police think the gang is in Oklahoma, well, that's as good a reason as any to
head down to Louisiana. The news also relieves the boredom of life in the
car: she reads out loud the happenings in the big world as they fly along
through it. Finally, she'd be lying if she denied that she and Clyde are not
amused by how famous they've become. Who wouldn't be? In more than
one car that they leave behind along the way the cops find clippings of stories about them. Some say she and Clyde even send their own pictures and
poems into the paper for publication.

Take that business about her with a cigar, for instance. "Clyde's cigar-
smoking moll" is how it seems she's always described now. It's been cigar-
smoking, gun-totin', and bloodthirsty ever since those pictures from Joplin
got into the hands of the papers. What they don't know is she was just play-
acting in those, with the guns and cigar and all. She smokes Camels, not
cigars! That cigar-smoking stuff bothers her, and it bothers her mother
even worse.

Bonnie's least favorite picture of herself, which
earned her a reputation as "Clyde's cigar-smoking
moll." *(Missouri State Highway Patrol file photograph. Used with permission.)*

"I think it's just dreadful the way the newspapers talk about her," says
Emma. "Why, she doesn't smoke cigars at all."

As for Bonnie running the gang, that's almost worth sending a card to
the newspaper to say thanks for lightening up the day. If she's running the
gang, why is Clyde telling her to go home all the time? Ask Joe Palmer.

"Not many people know about Clyde Barrow," says Palmer. "He was a
friend to me, if to no one else. And he wasn't a coward. He tried a dozen times
in my presence to get Bonnie to consent to let him give up, in a trade for her
liberty. He wanted to give up and take the rap, the chair if necessary, to save
her. Every time, she'd say 'no,' and say: 'When you go down, I'll go with you.'"

Good old W. D. Jones has it right. He's in jail telling nutty stories about
being chained to trees by Clyde, bless his heart, but he says, "I always figured
some of them reporters was holed up somewhere with some booze during

the time they claimed they'd been off with the law in hot pursuit of the outrageous Barrow gang. They was just writing from their imagination."

Where else could this idea of her being in love with Ray come from?
(Okay, maybe from Floyd, who thinks everybody loves his brother as much
as he does.) Now, W.D. is at least good-looking. W.D. is cute! But Raymond? (As if she feels like getting frisky with anyone with a bullet in her
knee and a burn up her leg and who knows what else hurting.) If Raymond
really is Bonnie's love slave, her "pawn," why would the first thing he wants
to do when she and Clyde bust him out be to send Mullins and Floyd into
Wichita Falls to find Mary O'Dare? Mary is Odell Chambliss's little sister,
so they've all known her forever from around Wichita Falls and West Dallas. She used to be married to Raymond's other best pal, Gene O'Dare, but
promptly divorced him when he got locked up.

"I didn't love Gene, but I married him," she says. "It was just one of
those things." She immediately got remarried, to a poor slob bootlegger
named Barney Pitts, but knowing her, she'll leave him in a second for Raymond if he finds her. What Raymond sees in her—she's positively rat-faced,
and Clyde thinks she's a rat fink, too—is anybody's guess. But there it is:
Hamilton's not any more interested in Bonnie than she is in him.

Bonnie could have guessed that being back together with Raymond
wasn't going to be a round-the-clock picnic, and it isn't. Twice in the past
Clyde's helped get Ray out of jail and twice in the past Ray's up and quit on
him, after all. It's not that Clyde wants Ray to be thanking him all the time,
or anything like that, and they're good friends. Raymond's just not a fol-
lower and, of course, neither is Clyde, so while it's fun for a few weeks that
winter for old times' sake, tempers start to wear thin fast.

Once Raymond tracks down Mary O'Dare and she starts riding with the
gang, tempers wear even thinner even faster. Even the kid, Henry Methvin,
hates Mary. (Palmer says O'Dare is constantly trying to seduce Methvin
when Hamilton isn't around but he, sensibly, is more interested in Billie Jean.)
They call Mary the washerwoman and won't let her go anywhere alone.
She's a washerwoman with fancy aspirations, though: she and Raymond are
always wanting to live it up.

"Long as I had money," says Hamilton, "I slept in the best hotels. There
wasn't no use to stop in tourist camps, or sleep in cars when the hotels
needed a little money so bad." To Bonnie and Clyde, that sounds like a
comfortable way to get caught or, more likely in their case, killed.

The inevitable split with Raymond Hamilton, when it comes, is, not surprisingly, over a combination of money and Mary O'Dare. On February 27,
Ray, Clyde, and Henry Methvin rob the R. P. Henry Bank in Lancaster,

Texas. The job goes over without a hitch; Methvin drives getaway and Clyde, with a sawed-off shotgun, and Ray, with a pistol, work the bank like pros.

"I never saw two calmer men," says the cashier, L. L. Henry. "They quietly told us what to do. Apparently the robbery was carefully planned. When the money was gathered up, they made us go to where they could see us as they backed out the door."

On the way out, Clyde returns some cash to a customer named Worley, telling him, "We don't want your money. We just want the bank's." Worley's grateful to have his pay returned, but he's not starry-eyed.

"The shotgun that one was pointing at us never wavered," he says, "You could tell by looking at him that he would shoot in an instant if he thought it necessary."

When the bank robbing is over, though, the calm demeanor of Ray and Clyde slips away. They've switched cars, picked up Bonnie and Mary, and are on their way to Oklahoma. Clyde's driving, as usual, with Bonnie beside him, and Ray starts dividing up the loot. Everybody who wasn't actually there—Floyd, Bonnie's mother, Mullins, et cetera—has their own version of how the trouble got started, but the heart of the argument was about whether the washerwoman should get an even cut the way Bonnie always does.

Floyd, who is no fan of Mary O'Dare, naturally says that his little brother is completely innocent and that what Clyde thinks he sees in the rearview mirror is really no more than Raymond trying to get her to shut up until he and Clyde can work it out later.

"Mary was still raisin' hell and you know they carried a sack around with what they called kitty money, expense money—each one of them throw so much money in there to pay for expenses, to pay for gasoline or food or anything; they reach in the sack and get it," says Floyd. "So Raymond just reached down and got the sack and got a handful of money and handed it to Mary, told her 'there, keep your mouth shut.'"

Mrs. Parker, who also detests Mary, says the trouble starts when Clyde catches Raymond taking more than his share and boils over when Mary O'Dare tries to convince Bonnie to poison Clyde and run off with the money. It's Bonnie, says her mother, who demands that Mary and Raymond leave.

"I hope they catch Raymond and string him right up in front of old lady Hamilton," says Emma.

Clyde flat out hates Mary O'Dare, to the point where he's talking occasionally with Methvin about the possibility of killing her. He's not going to do it, of course, but he's only half joking. He's mad as hell at both her and Raymond, which is not a situation anyone with sense wants to stay around for too long, and by the first week in March they're gone.

"When you wanted to get your prostitute sweetheart, I thought it O.K.,"
Clyde gets Bonnie to write in a letter to Raymond. "But when you were so
persistent about her going to town alone that idea wasn't so 'hot.' I thought
then and truthfully believe now that should she have gotten off without
Bonnie she would have 'spotted' us all. She hails from a 'rat' family, and you
couldn't expect better from her."

He's just warming up. "You exposed your hole card when you stole the
money from us on the Lancaster job. That's what I have my rear vision mirror for, to watch suspicious people. When I demanded a shakedown, you
offered such strange excuses for having the money on you I should have
killed you then."

She and Clyde know where to write to Raymond because, just as they
could have predicted, after about six weeks of high living with Mary O'Dare
he gets himself caught. They write because just before getting caught he
wrote a letter to the laws that wound up in all the papers, saying that Clyde
was the trigger-happy killer and he was just a fun-loving bank robber.
When Raymond is taken in at the end of April, he goes in his typical smart-
ass lamblike way, not even trying to put up a fight.

"I guess you know who you have caught," he says. "I'm Raymond
Hamilton, but I don't intend to give you any trouble. I'm just fresh out of
ammunition, money, whiskey and women. Let's go to jail."

Good old Ray, he's always at his best when he's in jail, wising off to the
guards and reporters. When they ask him if there's any truth to the rumors
about him and Clyde fighting over money and women, he just scoffs.

"We haven't split up because of any bad feeling," he says. "I decided in
Terre Haute about a month ago that I had some personal business to attend
to. I told Clyde I was going south for a while on personal business. He knew
what I meant. You know, once in a while a fellow in this racket has to get
out of action, go someplace where he can cool off for a while."

Mary's not with Raymond at the time he's caught, having been sent to
Amarillo when he ran out of money because she refused, as she says, "to
live on the highways with him like Bonnie Parker is doing with Barrow."

That's right, the washerwoman can't stand living on the road, but she
gets rounded up herself by Frank Hamer and some other Rangers. At one
point she says of Clyde and Bonnie, "They seemed like swell people" and, of
Bonnie, "Well, she dresses nicely." When she thinks it's safe to compare
notes with Jimmie Mullins while they're being transferred to jail together,
however, she's not so friendly.

"Mary O'Dare and I were talking the other night, April 26, while the
Rangers had us in a car about how dirty Clyde and Bonnie would let their

clothes and persons get," says Mullins. "She said while she and Raymond were with them up north around Terre Haute, Indiana, she and Raymond would break the ice on creeks to bathe their faces and hands, and brush their teeth, and Clyde and Bonnie would sit in the car and make fun of them."

Mary O'Dare notices something else about Bonnie that she tells both Mullins and the special agent from the FBI but that no one else in their circle talks much about. She says Bonnie is pregnant, six months or so by her guess.*

❀

"Let's take 'em," you say to Henry Methvin.

It's Easter morning, just about a month after Raymond and the washerwoman took off on their own and before they get arrested. You and Henry and Bonnie are just minding your own business parked on a side road near Grapevine, Texas. You're waiting for Joe Palmer, who is back with the gang but has hitched into Dallas to let your family know where you are. You've been sleeping in the back of the car, in fact, while Bonnie goofs around with this dumb rabbit she's taken in. Sonny Boy she calls him, and all you know about him is that he shits in the car. She wants to give him to her mother, though, and it's hard enough to be happy on the road, so if she wants a rabbit for a while, who cares. Methvin, big thick Methvin, is keeping watch on the road.

"It's the laws," Bonnie is saying as she shakes you awake. Two motorcycle cops who should have driven on by your side street have turned around and are coming back to see if you need help. You don't need help, and you don't need laws either. You need sleep, for crying out loud. But you're awake as soon as you hear her say "laws," and, standing up, you see that they're not coming after you with guns blazing or even drawn. They're just pulling up on their motorcycles nice and easy.

It's obvious these two cops have no idea who they're driving up on. One of them, H. D. Murphy, is barely out of training, on his first day on patrol. The other is twenty-six-year-old Edward Wheeler. He's wishing he could be spending Easter morning with his wife, whom he took over to her mother's that morning, saying that just because he has to work shouldn't mean she has to spend the holiday alone. They're both pretty green, these

---

* To this day, members of the Barrow and Parker families are adamant that Bonnie was not pregnant, and though there are several independent sources for the rumor, and Frank Hamer and the FBI both believed it to be the case, there's no way to confirm or disprove it.

two highway patrolmen, and with Methvin already with a shotgun in his hand and you armed as well, it's obvious too that you can get the drop on them, disarm them, and take them for a ride. Have a little fun with them, like that big police chief you and Fults took for a ride that time. Good old Ralph.

"Let's take 'em," you whisper to Henry.

Blam blam.

Goddamn if the kid doesn't let loose with that shotgun* and kill them both. He even goes right on over to one of them and puts a few more bullets in him after he's lying on the ground, just to be sure. Henry's kind of a killer at heart; word is what got him into Eastham in the first place was cutting the neck of some guy who picked him up hitchhiking. Cut his neck and took his money and car.

What's done is done, you know that as well as anyone, and you're the first to admit that you'll kill a cop if you need to. Or in this case, two cops. But goddamn, Methvin, that's not what you meant. For what it's worth— which isn't much—when you say "Let's take 'em" you mean take 'em for a ride. It doesn't matter what you meant, though, you know that. Nothing matters. You were there. Cops got killed. You did it. Case closed.

Not that you're crying for the dead laws; you're not. Not after they tried to ambush you not that far away from here that night when your old ma and Bonnie's family were around. They don't care who they might have killed, so why should you? Cops will say that you were there to meet up with Raymond to go rob a bank in Irving together. Then they'll say you were there to meet up and kill Raymond. They'll say that it was Bonnie who went over and put the bullets in the man on the ground, even though the only decent witnesses to the shooting told them clearly that it was the "taller of the two men" who did it, meaning big old dumb-ass Methvin. The cops will even come out and make a movie reenacting the idea of Bonnie doing all the killing and show it in the newsreels to try and turn the people against her. Cops!

You're not crying for them. What's done is done. It's just unfortunate that Dallas will be all heated up again. Hotter than a damn frying pan it'll be. So much for Easter visits. So much for getting rid of the stinking rabbit. There's nothing to do but get in the car and run like hell again up to Oklahoma. Here we go again.

❁

---

* Some sources say it was a BAR.

Bullets fired from an automobile of desperadoes near Grapevine Sunday blighted the romance of 20-year-old Marie Tullis of Alto, who was to have become the bride of Highway Patrolman H. D. Murphy, 23, on April 11.

Miss Tullis and Murphy became engaged a short while before the latter was assigned to duty in Fort Worth about a month ago. He had completed a training course at headquarters in Austin.

A furnished apartment here already had been rented to the couple. Murphy had selected it, a cozy home, where he planned to bring his bride in eleven days.

—*Dallas Morning News*

❁

"We are hunting Clyde Barrow and Bonnie Parker," says Frank Blake, the special agent in charge of the Dallas office of the FBI. "There is no doubt in our minds they did the killing. There is no couple in the Southwest—no couple in the whole nation—capable of a killing like that except Barrow and Bonnie."

Blake's got his entire office working on nothing but Clyde Barrow, which means primarily agents Winstead, Dowd, and himself. He's informed the Oklahoma City office to be on the watch, and Louisiana too. His boss, J. Edgar Hoover, is sending him messages. He's on a regular tear to get fingerprints for Bonnie, and refuses to put her on a wanted poster without them, which Blake can't understand since the presence of Bonnie is one of the most reliable ways to identify Clyde. After the killing of the highway patrolmen, though, Hoover cracks the whip a bit.

"Give every lead in your district thorough and vigorous attention," he helpfully suggests on April 5, in case the message isn't clear.

It's not all that different over at the Texas State Highway Patrol, whose chief, L. G. Phares, has put virtually his entire force on the job of tracking down the killers of their fallen comrades—some sixty officers, say the papers. His boss, Governor Ma Ferguson, announces a "dead or alive" award of five hundred dollars for Barrow, Hamilton, or "other persons who killed Highway Patrolmen E. B. Wheeler and H. D. Murphy." The Texas Rangers are taking up their own collection to raise a reward, and Phares is raising another one thousand dollars from his men. Phares also gets Governor Ferguson to assign one of his own men, Manny Gault, to work directly as Frank Hamer's partner.

With elections for governor and Dallas County sheriff, among other offices, coming up, politicians of all stripes and levels are getting in on the outrage. "The outlaw is in the saddle in Texas," says one candidate. "I voted for a reward 'dead or alive' in the legislature," says another, "and I particularly liked that 'dead' part of it."

Probably no one is feeling the heat more than Smoot Schmid, who's had his deputies Hinton and Alcorn working quietly on nothing but finding Clyde for months yet has nothing to show for it but a bungled ambush and some near misses. And those near misses are going to help a handful of law-and-order candidates hoping to win his job away from him come fall.

"Political heat was burning everyone," says Hinton.

Ever since the failed ambush at Sowers, Schmid has been cooperating a bit more with his colleagues. He's told the G-men about Alcorn's secret source close to the Barrow family, though he hasn't divulged who it is. Not all the tips are good—the New Orleans office gets sent on a wild-goose chase to Belle Chaney Springs, Louisiana, that turns up nothing. And the sheriff still rides around occasionally with Hinton and Alcorn hoping to get lucky, including one time where they almost manage to run Clyde off the road with a gravel truck. After the Belle Chaney incident, though, the sheriff seems to be done with his lone-cowboy fantasies regarding Clyde, and one of his deputies assures the FBI that the sheriff's office will be "cooperating fully from now on with all law enforcement agencies in this district."

In the immediate aftermath of the double murder of the motorcycle patrolmen at Grapevine, everyone with a badge of any sort in the entire Southwest is involved in the dragnet for Clyde, Bonnie, and a third man that some still think is Hamilton and some think correctly is Henry Methvin. They're certain Bonnie and Clyde were involved because witnesses saw a woman, and because the location of the killing was near a favorite Barrow family meeting place. There's also a whiskey bottle with fingerprints on it that are first identified as Clyde's but later turn out to be Methvin's. There's a cigar stub with small "tooth prints," which everyone assumes were made by Bonnie. It doesn't matter that most of their evidence is actually bogus; in this case, they're right.

"Hundreds hunting," scream the headlines. All the bridges across the Red River into Oklahoma are being guarded with roadblocks and checkpoints, though no one knows whether the blockades went up in time to stop Clyde and Bonnie and Henry from getting across. As the reward offers climb above two thousand dollars, there's no shortage of tips and leads: rumored sightings, unsigned letters, distant relatives, old girlfriends and employers to contact, old hideouts to search. They all come up dry.

"We don't know where he is," says one of Smoot's men. "I've driven, walked, and hunted until I'm about to drop. We've gone everywhere and done everything we can and we don't know where he is. He might be in Dallas or within ten miles of it and he might be a thousand miles away."

The answer comes at the end of the week, when two men and a blond woman gun down a town constable up in Commerce, Oklahoma, in the northeast corner of the state. It's definitely Bonnie and Clyde and whoever is with them, because they take the local chief of police for a twelve-hour joyride around southern Kansas.

❀

Bonnie lights a Camel and looks out the dirty car window at the strange, barren mountains of perfectly even gravel piled up by the Lost Trail Mine. Spoils, chat, trailings, tailings, whatever they are called—giant mountains of the stuff, piled there because all the money has been taken out of it already and sent to the banks. There are lead mines all over this corner of Oklahoma, and the landscape hardly looks real. It's like some version of hell, with seemingly endless dead dunes punctuated once in a while by machines and shafts that do nothing but make more of these gray poisonous dunes that can hardly be distinguished from the gray sky. It's been raining off and on pretty solidly since Easter, and all roads that aren't paved—that is, all the back roads that Clyde likes so much—are a total mess. The car is covered with mud, not just from driving, but mud smeared all over most of the windows to prevent the nosy from looking in. She blows smoke out of a crack in the window while Clyde and Henry settle in for a doze. It's a gray world except for her red dress and the red-hot tip of a morning smoke. Thank God for cigarettes.

That's the usual routine, anyway. Bonnie keeps watch while the car is parked and gets her sleep on the road. There's whiskey in the car, too, if she wants it, but it's pretty early in the morning for that. Around nine o'clock a cattle truck passes, with a man and a boy in the cab and couple of calves in the back.

"It was a kind of a raining, messy, sloppy morning," says the driver of the truck, Bill Cox. Cox thinks it's a bit odd to see the car parked there by the mine like that, because he's sure he saw the exact same Ford V-8 pass him going real fast about an hour before. He and his boy Fred were standing there trading for the cattle at the Laduke ranch when this fancy but incredibly muddy car had come flying out of nowhere down the lonely ranch road.

"Clyde waved at someone standing on the street there and the man waved back," says Henry Methvin. "I don't think Clyde knew the man; he just wanted to cut up."

Cox and Laduke do return Clyde's friendly wave, but now here's the same fellow who was in such a hurry parked in the middle of nowhere. So it's odd, Cox thinks. Odd enough that he doesn't stop to ask if there's anything he can do. Not with his boy in the car, anyway.

"I went on past him," he says, "and came on up to Commerce. We took this car's number and everything because I and Mr. Laduke and Fred, my boy, had talked about this car being suspicious."

Bonnie, Clyde, and Henry are still parked there by the mine when the Commerce town constable, Cal Campbell, and the chief of police, Percy Boyd, turn onto the road. Bill Cox stopped in to tell them about the strange car, and while the two lawmen agree it's odd, they're not all that alarmed; maybe the folks inside are just having car trouble and are waiting for the rain to let up a bit before going for help. So they pull right up, parking the nose of their car six or maybe ten feet from the nose of the Ford.

"I got out on my side of the car," says Chief Boyd. "Cal got out on his side."

Clyde is wide awake now, and as soon as he sees the two laws get out of their car he throws the Ford into reverse and backs away at high speed.*

Pow pow bang.

Constable Campbell starts running after the reversing car, firing his pistol. Campbell, who is sixty-one years old, has had no training as a peace officer and not much experience, either. "Dad had been a contractor until the Depression; then he lost everything," says his son James. "That's why he took that police job. It only paid about fifteen dollars a week, but it kept us eating. The only reason he had the job was because the people liked him. He sure wasn't a professional lawman."

Rata rata rata rat rat rata rata rata.

The answer, some seventy or eighty bullets in rapid succession from Clyde and Henry's BARs, is almost immediate. Police Chief Boyd isn't completely sure who really shot first, Campbell or someone from inside the car. One time he says Bonnie stuck a sawed-off shotgun out the window and that Clyde later chastised her for shooting too quickly. Another time he says, "I don't believe there would have been any shooting if Cal hadn't fired first."

Bang bang.

---

* Some sources say Bonnie was at the wheel at this time.

Boyd's firing his own pistol now, squeezing off a couple of rounds, one of which very nearly hits Clyde.

"He told me later that I almost got him and that he heard it zip close," says the police chief. Boyd is also a bit fuzzy on whether someone in the car started shooting out of the windows as they reversed at top speed or only after Clyde uncharacteristically lost control of the vehicle and it slipped off the side of the road into a ditch. Boyd does know, however, that he was hit by what he guesses was about the tenth bullet fired from Clyde and Henry, who jump out of the car as soon as it goes in the ditch and take turns unloading a clip of BAR bullets in the direction of him and Cal Campbell. Boyd is hit in the back of the head, just as he's turning to call to Campbell to get behind the car.

"When that bullet knocked me off my feet, I stayed down and, believe me, I almost dug into the dirt," he says. "I heard Cal groan. He was lying there beside the car."

Campbell doesn't groan for long. The bullet that hits him shreds his aorta and shatters his spine. He's dead within a minute.

Boyd, however, is not seriously injured. Clyde, operating with that strange calmness that comes over him when bullets are flying, sends Henry down the fifty yards or so to take Boyd prisoner. He, meanwhile, runs up to a nearby farmhouse to "borrow" a pickup truck to try to get their car out of the ditch. The road, which had seemed so deserted when they parked there, is starting to get busy. Several people have appeared out of nowhere—from the mine, from nearby houses, from cars—drawn to the murder scene by the sound of the gunfire and the sight of a man most of them know lying in a spreading pool of blood.

The pickup truck isn't heavy enough to get the car out. The rope breaks. Clyde looks at the gathered crowd of eight or ten men. He's in his bare feet, having been forced to get out of his car a little more rapidly than he generally likes, but he's holding an automatic rifle.

"Boys," he says, "one good man has been killed here and if we don't get this car out of the ditch there is liable to be some more killed."

It makes sense to everyone there and they all go down into the ditch and begin to push on the back of the car. All except Bonnie, that is, who stays in the passenger seat with a gun and a cigarette and her white rabbit.

"Well, that little fellow did all the commanding that was done," says William Hughes, who wandered down from his house up the way when he heard the *pop pop pop* of the guns. No one remembers Henry Methvin— tall, awkward, and afflicted with acne—saying a word.

Even with all the men behind it the car won't budge, but finally a good-sized truck comes along and Clyde commandeers it. Bonnie slides behind the steering wheel. The barefoot commandant gives the order, and with all hands pushing and the truck pulling, the car is out of the ditch. Then it's into the back seat for Chief Boyd and Henry Methvin and into the front for Clyde and they're away. Gone from the strange gray mounds of the Lost Trail Mine and north across the state line and then west, out to the spring green prairie farm country of southern Kansas.

Chief Boyd is pretty good company for a cop, as it turns out. When they read in the evening paper that Cal Campbell didn't make it, Clyde tells him he's sorry the old man was killed, that he was certain he was only wounded. He also denies that it was them who killed the two cops at Grapevine, though he's happy to talk about the Joplin battle. Mostly, though, Boyd and Bonnie talk. She tells him that her mother raises white rabbits, which leads him to believe that Sonny Boy must belong to Emma Parker.

"We have lots of friends in Texas," she says to him, though she won't elaborate on who they are or where Clyde is headed.

Once they are safely away from Commerce, Clyde pulls off the road at a secluded spot and Bonnie asks to take a look at Boyd's head wound. He lays his head down across Methvin's lap and Bonnie goes to work on it, cleaning and dressing the wound.

"She didn't have anything except some Mercurochrome and a tore-up shirt," says Methvin. That's nothing new; they've all had plenty of practice cleaning bullet holes, and Bonnie gets Boyd fixed up pretty quickly. He says later that he was never afraid of anything during his ride with the Barrow Gang except the possibility of running into other police.

They don't see any sign of the "army of peace officers" that the newspapers have reported are on their trail, and after ten hours together Clyde tells Boyd he might as well get out of the car. He says that he usually ties his hostages up but that he trusts Boyd to wait awhile before heading for a phone and calling the cops.

"You can tell the officers anything you want to," Clyde says to Boyd as he's getting out, "but be sure you tell them the truth. We would not have fired a shot if the old man had not come out of his car with his pistol."

Bonnie's got a last request for Boyd as well.

"Bonnie asked me to advise the public that she is not a cigar addict," says Boyd. "She said that all the rumors about her smoking cigars were the bunk."

CHAPTER 22

ON THE SPOT

This automobile was examined for latent fingerprints and two latent prints were photographed and lifted. Prints were also found on the rear vision mirror, which is being sent, together with the latent prints and photographs, to the Division Laboratory.

Found in the car was one .45 caliber automatic bullet, one fresh loaf of Jordan's sliced bread, one package of Bull Durham tobacco partly used, one Shreveport, Louisiana Journal dated April 8, 1934, one Fort Worth Star Telegram dated March 31, 1934 with headlines "Barrow in Texas Holdup," one woman's black turban hat, one pair pink step-ins, one woman's red cloth belt, one broken belt buckle, two price tags, no identification, two pairs men's socks, one flashlight (official Boy Scout flashlight with belt hook), two extra batteries, one pair tortoise shell goggles, brown lens, right lens missing; one blood soaked necktie, blue and white checked.

Also found in car was a head of cabbage and several partly chewed carrots, also evidences of a rabbit having been carried in the car.

—FBI DOCUMENT 26-4114-113

By the spring of 1934, clues are coming in from all over to Frank Hamer and the other principal lawmen on the case. The FBI gets reports of cars that have been stolen or recovered every few days and dutifully sends an agent over to inspect the car and interview the witnesses. Gas station holdups are checked out, bank jobs looked into. Various Parker and Barrow cousins all over the South and Southwest are located and interviewed. Scraps of paper collected on a roadside in Kansas are taped together; they appear to be in a woman's handwriting and include the words "the Ba . . . w Gang." All mail going to and from the Barrows and Parkers is traced. Henry and Cumie's phone is bugged. Alcorn and Hinton have their informants; the police have others. On the FBI payroll is "Informant B," who lives near the Barrow garage and keeps tabs on who comes and goes. The newspapers are full of sightings and rumors.

Even Lee Simmons, over at the prison system, is passing along tidbits that come to him through the grapevine. Some letters are intercepted going to Ted Rogers, Clyde's old buddy and the trigger man in the Bucher murder, suggesting that Clyde's working on a way to break him out of jail. Memos circulate about the potentials.

Even more valuable than abandoned cars and awestruck gas station attendants, by the end of April the laws have W. D. Jones, Raymond Hamilton, Jimmie Mullins, Hilton Bybee, and a couple of lesser associates locked up and talking. They also arrest Mary O'Dare, though she's out on bail almost immediately. It's Jones who points out that Clyde and Bonnie usually travel in roughly a circular pattern, always looping back to Dallas to see their families, a notion that sticks in Frank Hamer's head.

The problem with clues is that they invariably tell the laws where Bonnie and Clyde have been in the past, when what they need to know is where the bandits will be in the future. No one, not even Clyde, really knows that with any precision. The Dallas Police Department has a map on the wall with color-coded pins for every sighting and crime associated with the gang. They have life-sized cutout photographs of Bonnie and Clyde so the officers can familiarize themselves with their prey. But those are both essentially tools that, at best, will make the cops ready if they get lucky and run into Clyde and Bonnie by accident. Or if Cumie slips up and says something revealing over her telephone. Everyone in the hunt for Bonnie and Clyde knows what they have known for months: their only real hope is to get help from somebody close enough to "put them on the spot."

A surprisingly large number of people are willing to play that role. A lot of them are cranks and hopefuls, people who write letters to the various lawmen hoping to cash in on the rewards, maybe even get a little advance.

"Take my tip and I believe your troubles will be over with that pair of killers," they say. Each lead has to be run down and checked out, but often as not the local sheriff finds something along the lines of how the informant "stays drunk most of the time and when sober is unable to tell the truth about anything or give a connected story." Most leads are dead ends.

But not all the offers can be brushed off so easily; obviously, whoever it is that's talking to Bob Alcorn and Ted Hinton is serious, though whether he or she can produce another ambush opportunity remains in doubt. The Muckleroys have had enough of their wayward nephew and promise to contact the authorities if Clyde should ever turn up there again. There's also Bonnie's brother, Buster Parker. He tells Agent Winstead of the FBI that he "knows Clyde is going to get Bonnie killed, that he would rather know she was in a penitentiary than with Clyde." Winstead says Buster "promised that if he could learn of Clyde's whereabouts while separated from Bonnie, he will give that information."

The FBI and the State Highway Patrol also have a Barrow cousin from Waco, Bailey Tynes, on their payrolls. Tynes gets four dollars a day plus transportation to periodically go and live as a houseguest at the Barrow filling station and report back to Special Agent in Charge Frank Blake about what he hears. He's carrying on a flirtatious relationship with Marie Barrow as part of his cover. On April 23 Bailey Tynes is with Henry Barrow at the filling station when the old man gets drunk and says he and Cumie are worried sick that they haven't been able to get in touch with Clyde for a few weeks. Henry says that's why he's drinking so much these days. Henry also lets on that he thinks Clyde and Bonnie might be hiding on the land of some friends of Clyde's first girlfriend, Ebbie Williams, down near San Augustine, Texas, where he forgot to bring home that rental car so long ago.

"Clyde and Ebbie would have married but her folks objected," the drunk old man tells Tynes. It's interesting stuff, and of course it results in agents finding Ebbie Williams, who's since become a stenographer for a big Dallas department store. It doesn't produce Clyde and Bonnie, however, though Ebbie seems willing to cooperate should Clyde happen to try to reach her.

Clyde's other old love, Grace Donegan, is more interested in helping the laws. She tells Agent E. J. Dowd that Clyde rarely goes through Wichita Falls without trying to get in touch with her. She goes so far as to say he's something of a stalker, in fact, calling her sister and making up fake names and asking how to get in touch with Grace. Just a year ago, she tells Agent Dowd, Clyde tried to get her to leave her husband and go with him. That would have been around the time of the Joplin shoot-out, which doesn't really sound like Clyde. Grace says she doesn't know Bonnie.

"Grace Donegan insists that she can contact Clyde Barrow, who she claims is 'crazy' about her," says Agent Dowd. "To do so, all she has to do is to make a trip to Dallas, call on old lady Barrow, and stay with her for a while."

It sounds a bit too easy, and Agent Dowd has reason to be a bit circumspect about Donegan's claims. "Chief of Police Dick Morris advised me that Grace Donegan is well known to him, that she is classed as a dope head, but has never been arrested as such," Dowd writes in his memo to the Dallas office. "Grace Donegan at one time was considered a 'classy prostitute' who has never been known to solicit men on the streets, but has lived with men at Wichita Falls, that one of the lawyers at Wichita Falls, who was disbarred, and a number of criminals and underworld characters have been known to also live with her. Her husband has the reputation of being a 'dope head.'"

Grace Donegan isn't a perfect source, and at any rate she can't put any of her claims to work for the time being, as she is bedridden. (Chief Morris tells Agent Dowd that when Grace is not using morphine, she "goes out on parties and gets liquored up" to the point where he recently had to put her in the hospital.) Despite her flaws as a collaborator, though, both Dowd and Morris think she's got potential.

"Undoubtedly Grace Donegan appears to have been close to Clyde Barrow, his family and relatives, and might be used to good advantage as a confidential informant in this case," says Dowd. That is, he adds, "if arrangements can be made to pay her for her services."

The two women memorialized on Clyde's tattoos—Ebbie and Grace—aren't the only people from Clyde's preprison days to offer their services to the laws. One of the owners of the United Glass & Mirror Company, Patrick McCray, tells Agent Winstead and the Dallas police that Clyde has called a couple of times during the past few months. McCray is the one who vouched for Clyde when he was falsely charged with the murder at the beach down near Houston in 1930. Now, even though he's very nervous about his name getting out as an informer, McCray promises that "should he hear from Barrow by phone or otherwise, he will immediately notify the Dallas Division Office."

Even Aubrey Scalley, Clyde's buddy and protector from Eastham Farm, has let it be known that he will turn on Clyde if the price is right. He was actually one of the first to make the offer, way back in January. The day after the raid that liberated Hamilton but not himself, Scalley told a guard he could get in touch with Clyde and that "he can and will at any time 'put Clyde on the spot.'"

Simmons had him moved back to the main prison at Huntsville for further questioning from Frank Hamer and Agent Winstead of the FBI. They were interested but unimpressed.

"Very little dependence is placed in Scalley's statement that he could aid in the location of Barrow," says Winstead. "However, Mr. Simmons authorized him to write a letter to Mrs. Barrow and he would see that it was mailed."

❋

Mrs B[arrow] called Mrs P[arker] and said, "what are you doing?"

P said, "nothing how are you feeling?"

B said, "alright only I am mad as the devil."

P said, "what about?"

B said, "I just saw that stool pigeon Mary O'Dare go up to the Hamiltons' with Mildred" [Floyd's wife]. Said "she went to town and came back with her on the bus." Said "Mary had a suit case, guess she is going to stay a while."

P said, "are those people crazy?" Said "she is out there just to see what she can find out. She will have them all in jail in a week."

B said, "I don't care if they do get in jail if they don't have more sense than that." Said "she tried to get the kids caught when she was with them. And finally got Raymond caught." Said "she made the remark when she left C+B that she would get them caught before it was all over." Said "yes I know that she will." Said "she had better not show her face around [here] again if she wants to live and do well."

P said, "isn't that so."

B said, "I know she is going to be coming up here to use my phone."

P said, "if you let her come in your house I'll never come to see you again."

B said, "I've got a big iron here if she starts in my house I am going to hit her over the head with it." Said "I am not going to let that damn hussy set her foot in my house."

P said, "did they let Joe out?"

B said, "no they didn't."

P said, "well I'll just be damn."

P said, "I don't guess you know anything do you?"

B said, "no, not a thing."

—Dallas Police Department, Telephone Tap Log Barrow/
Parker Families

In a world full of potential rats who can get "the kids" killed on any given day, the people that Cumie and Henry Barrow and Emma Parker are most worried about in the spring of 1934 are Raymond Hamilton and his family. Ray's sister Maggie Farris has told them that her brother has become a "hop head and is using narcotics to excess." Their fear of Raymond and Mary O'Dare is only increased by the arrest of Hamilton on April 25. A potential death sentence will just make Raymond or one of his family even more likely to go yellow, to say nothing of Mary O'Dare, who is running around on bail.

They're a regular walking romance magazine, Mary and Raymond are, all over the Dallas newspapers morning and afternoon.

"When I get out of this trouble I'm going back to my husband and make him the kind of wife he wants me to be," Mary says when she's arrested. "I still think a lot of Raymond. I was attracted to him because of his promises to buy me lots of nice clothes and show me a good time. But I realize I don't love him. My husband has forgiven me for running off with Raymond and I am anxious to return to him."

This is too good, and the crime reporters in their trench coats and fedoras all rush right over to Smoot Schmid's office at the county courthouse. Schmid is so pleased to have caught Raymond that of course he'll let the prisoner be interviewed, and Raymond, in true form, obliges them with bombast.

"There is no such thing as a real friend anymore," he howls. "They will all double-cross you. Women cause men to become criminal. Then after you risk your life for them they generally are the cause of you getting caught. As long as you have money, people will pretend to be your friend. Then, when you go broke, they double-cross you."

Raymond also says, "I robbed a bank at Lewisville because Mary had sent me word she needed some money. I intended to get some money to her if I had gotten away."

On and on Raymond Hamilton's mouth goes, but all of the reporters notice that he actually looks quite hurt and saddened by the news that Mary O'Dare has dumped him and gone back to her husband. They ask him if he would have liked a chance to see Mary. He knows what they want. He knows what Mary wants.

"I would have given anything if I could," he answers.

"Yes," he says to another questioner. "I'm in love with her."

Sure enough, a few days later, Mary is telling the press, "I love Raymond and all that talk in the newspapers about me being through with him was bosh." She's going back to Wichita Falls to file for a divorce. "I love Raymond and he loves me. He's a swell guy. I have hopes that some way he may obtain his freedom again."

It's too much. The Barrows know that Clyde is not going to break Raymond Hamilton out of jail again, which leaves only one way for Raymond to conceivably get his freedom.

"We had better break away from that Hamilton bunch," Henry says to Cumie within earshot of cousin Bailey Tynes, the FBI mole. "Raymond is going to turn up and squeal."

It's a tricky situation, seeing as they're all neighbors and the kids grew up together. The Hamiltons are used to coming over and using the Barrows' phone, since they don't have one. Floyd is almost like one of their own, but Emma Parker now claims, "You know I've always said Floyd was just as bad as Raymond."

They've all been in the same wagon for so long—the Barrows, Hamiltons, and Parkers—but the ground is shifting. Clyde and Raymond are trading murderous letters in the press. These are not normal times in West Dallas. Blood and water are starting to separate, and Cumie, the center of the clan, is just about sick from stress.

"Mrs. P called B—talked to Marie," reports the Dallas police wiretap log from those days. "Asked if Mrs. B was still sick."

"Marie said 'yes she is in bed.' "

"P said 'ask her if a pint would cure her.' "

"Marie asked her and Mrs. B said 'yes she thought it would.' "

"P said 'tell her I'll come over and bring her one.' "

Not that Emma Parker is doing much better.

"We don't talk about her much around the house," says Billie Jean when asked about Bonnie. "Mother is taking all this pretty hard and we don't like to upset her. We've just got to keep our chins up."

Meanwhile, down at Smoot Schmid's county jail, Raymond Hamilton is full of his usual dramatic flip-flops.

"People have me all wrong. I'm not a killer," he says to a reporter. "I'd always give up at the showdown instead of fighting it out."

That same day, at a different time, he says to the same newspaper that

Clyde Barrow with his mother, Cumie Barrow, at
one of the last family gatherings before his death.
*(From the collections of the Texas/Dallas History and
Archives Division, Dallas Public Library.)*

his capture might have ended differently: "If I had a machine gun I would
have shot it out with them."

Cumie Barrow and Emma Parker are obsessive about the news at this
point, phoning regularly to ask if the other has heard the radio or read the
late edition. They get furious when the papers try to sell an extra edition
that has no real news in it. So they surely read this exchange between Hamilton and a reporter about putting Clyde on the spot:

"If you were a mind to, could you put the finger on Clyde for the
officers?" the reporter asks.

"That's the last thing I would ever think of doing if I could," Hamilton
replies. "But I couldn't do it. They move too fast."

Bonnie and Clyde's parents should take more comfort in Raymond's public statements than they do, because he is saying almost the same thing in private. "Almost" is the right way to put it: Raymond lets the laws know that he could do what they want him to, but that he's not the type to have the laws do his dirty work.

"Raymond stated that if he ever had an opportunity he would kill Clyde Barrow," says Winstead of the FBI. "That he, of course, knows how Barrow could be contacted but he would not divulge this information to any officer—even to save himself from the electric chair."

As for Floyd, poor old, good old, Floyd, bless his heart. Henry and Cumie should know better by now than to worry about Floyd. Of all the problem kids in West Dallas, Floyd never would have got into any trouble if he hadn't just been trying to help out. Floyd's not going to cave no matter how hard the cops try. After Mullins starts squealing and before Raymond is even caught, three Texas Rangers and a Dallas deputy sheriff round up Floyd and his father-in-law and whisk them away to a jail in Floresville, Texas. They leave them there for a week without filing any charges or telling anyone in the Hamilton family they have them in custody. Finally, a Dallas deputy sheriff named Denver Seale* comes in, along with an assistant prosecutor named Leonard King. King wants to talk with Floyd.

"Well, we have a lot of charges here against you, but if you play ball with us we'll play ball with you," he says. King and Seale say they know all about the raid on Eastham and the Lancaster bank job from talking to Mullins and others, but they have an offer they think Floyd might be interested in.

"I'm not going to ask you to help capture Raymond, but I want you to help us capture Clyde and Bonnie," King explains. "We'll dismiss all the charges against you, we won't bother you anymore in Dallas no matter what you do, and we'll give you five thousand dollars."

Floyd looks at the two men, astonished.

"Man, that's a lot a money," he says. "What you want to give me all that for?"

It turns out the two laws are freelancing.

"Well," says the assistant prosecutor, "Denver Seale wants to be sheriff of Dallas County and I want to be a judge and we feel if we can capture Bonnie and Clyde we can have the office just for asking."

"I don't care about making blood money," Floyd tells them. "I couldn't even set 'em up because you'd kill 'em. 'I know you may have to kill 'em . . .

---

* At other times, Floyd has said the deputy was Bill Decker, who did have aspirations to become sheriff. But it was Seale and King who later tried to frame Floyd (and Billie Jean Parker) for the Grapevine killings.

and if you did capture 'em you want to execute 'em anyway and it'd still be murder. So I don't want nothing to do with it."

Later, looking back, Floyd says, "They got up, stomped around, and said, You just haven't been in jail long enough. You'll wish you had played ball with us."

The Barrows needn't be so worried about Floyd and Raymond, not with their own cousin Bailey Tynes sitting right there in their kitchen with them. Tynes knows their obsession with the Hamiltons and has a plan.

"I might come up and stay a while during the Hamilton trial," he scribbles in a note to Special Agent Blake. "There will be lots of talk and I might hear something. Just one little slip one of them is going to make sooner or later that will deliver the goods. If I hear anything important I will phone you."

Bailey Tynes is dangerous. But even he's not one Clyde's mama should be lying awake worrying about. He's not the one Hamer, Alcorn, and the FBI are putting their chips on.

※

"I got my son out by the well for just a few minutes," says Henry Methvin's mother, Avie Methvin. "So we figured it out."

This isn't the first time Henry has come back to Louisiana with his new "friends" Bonnie and Clyde. He came home once before, right around the beginning of March, a little more than a month after he broke out of prison over in Texas. It's a shame, really, that he broke out when he did. At the time, Avie and her husband, Ivy, were working on getting their son some kind of parole. What with him being just a nineteen-year-old kid and all, they had high hopes; the family story says Ivy hitchhiked all the way to Austin only to be told there that Henry had just escaped with Clyde Barrow. After that, Henry's people hardly knew if he was dead or alive for weeks, until all of a sudden he drives up with Bonnie and Clyde.

That first visit Bonnie and Clyde don't even let him get out of the car. They just appear out of nowhere, say hello, and Henry gets to tell his family he's all right, and then Clyde hits the gas and they are gone. Clyde's problem isn't that he doesn't trust Henry's parents; he and Bonnie like Ivy and Avie Methvin well enough. What's more, with Dallas like a hornet's nest of cops that's permanently stirred up, sleepy little northwest Louisiana is looking pretty good. Clyde doesn't let Henry out of the car only because he doesn't trust the security situation where the Methvins are living. It's too busy, too full of nosy people, maybe too close to Shreveport. Rumors of their presence have been turning up in the Shreveport papers; Shreveport's hot.

By April, though, when Henry starts bringing Bonnie and Clyde around to visit a lot more often, none of that is a problem. Henry's parents are by no means wealthy, but they and one of Henry's brothers have now moved from Bossier to a couple of remote farms in nearby Bienville Parish, near Castor, Louisiana. There are lots of other Methvins in that corner of the woods, including Henry's uncle Iverson. Clyde, Bonnie, and Henry still keep on the move every couple of days, and even when stopped somewhere they rarely get out of the car for more than a few minutes. Still, with friends and adopted family around who are willing to have picnics and even occasionally dinner parties at out-of-the-way farmhouses, Bienville Parish is starting to feel as much like home as anywhere they've been in a long time.

Out of the way and out in the woods doesn't always mean out of sight, however. This is particularly true when people who never had any money start finding it.

"The Methvins lived in a very poverty type place," says H. M. Parnell, a neighbor from up in Gibsland, Louisiana. "They lived kind of in that swamp and like rural type people live like sharecroppers, and they did whatever they could do to gain whatever they wanted or needed. The people that I know disliked them very much. They were really crude and rude."

When people like the Methvins start driving nicer trucks and maybe moving onto new properties, neighbors take notice. Idle talk starts traveling, and pretty soon someone says something to the sheriff. On the evening of April 13, 1934, Agent L. A. Kindell of the New Orleans office of the FBI, the chief of police from Shreveport, and a couple of other unidentified lawmen come and pay a visit to Sheriff Henderson Jordan of Bienville Parish. Kindell is wondering about rumors that Clyde and Bonnie have been frequenting northwest Louisiana, and Jordan confirms that the word in the woods is that the famous outlaws are visiting the homes of various Methvins. Kindell pokes around some more and reports his findings to headquarters:

"Numerous contacts were made with informants in that vicinity and it was ascertained that Methvin's father and brother had recently moved to that section from near Bossier City, Louisiana; that both had shown signs of unusual and mysterious prosperity."* Kindell is fluent in the standard anonymous voice of the Bureau.

The current word is that Bonnie and Clyde have temporarily left the area, Kindell goes on, so he and his colleagues have decided against any kind of raid on the Methvins for the time being. Sheriff Jordan promises to

---

* Says Billie Jean Parker: "Clyde and Bonnie were so tired they wanted a place just to rest, so they bought this Henry Methvin's mother and father a little farm down in Loiusiana." The FBI also believes Clyde may have purchased property for the father of Hilton Bybee.

reach out to people who know Henry's parents to try to get a sense of where they stand in relation to their son's traveling companions. Kindell and his colleagues trust their new informants to let them know when their prey returns.

One man the career lawmen don't trust is Smoot Schmid. Everything that goes in his ear seems to come out of the mouth of Sheriff Ted Hughes of Shreveport, who, says Kindell, "invariably immediately gives all such information to the newspapers for publication." Kindell doesn't come right out and tell his superiors to cut the two elected big-city sheriffs out of the loop, but the implication is clear: there's a good chance of catching Clyde and Bonnie in Bienville Parish, but not if word gets out of the trap being set.

"Chief of Police Baser of Shreveport, Louisiana, was disgusted with the activities of Sheriff Hughes in this connection," says Kindell.

There's only one problem with cutting Smoot Schmid's office out: his deputies actually know what Clyde and Bonnie look like. Sure, there are pictures everywhere, even life-sized cutouts at Dallas police headquarters, but everyone involved knows the likely scenario is going to be an ambush of Clyde and Bonnie's car. No one among them wants to gun down the wrong short guy in a Ford with the wrong girl in a red dress beside him. If they get into the situation they're imagining—if they catch Bonnie and Clyde unawares—they're going to need Ted Hinton or Bob Alcorn, or both, to say, "Yeah, that's them."

Likewise Frank Hamer (who is almost certainly one of the unnamed lawmen at that first meeting in Bienville Parish with Henderson Jordan) brings more to the table than just his reputation as the "angel of death," though no doubt everyone's aware of the notches in his gun. They can all squeeze triggers, but Frank Hamer is the only one who has a sizable carrot in his arsenal as well. The Methvins, it appears, are getting plenty of money from Clyde and Bonnie. (Or somewhere else unknown.) Monetary rewards may not move them. But Hamer, through Commissioner Simmons of the prison system, can offer a pardon from the governor of Texas for Henry Methvin.

Agent Kindell is a discreet man. He doesn't say who the other lawmen are at that first meeting with Henderson Jordan. He does say that Hamer and Alcorn are there at a second meeting, on April 23, when Henderson Jordan takes them to Castor, Louisiana, to meet John Joyner.

"Joyner is a very good friend of the Methvin family, particularly with the old man," says Kindell. Joyner, who is hoping to get a piece of the reward money, is acting as a go-between with the Methvins, who do not want to risk being seen meeting with the lawmen in person. He tells the posse that he has already spoken with Ivy Methvin about the offer by the state of Texas to "wipe the slate clean" for Henry if the family will help get Clyde and Bonnie. The Methvins are open to the idea but are suspicious.

"Mr. Methvin and Mrs. Methvin told me it would have to be in writing," Joyner says, "that they wouldn't take their word for this but it would have to be in black and white."

Hamer assures everyone that won't be a problem. He leaves for Huntsville and Austin, to meet with Simmons and the governor. The plan is for him to return with the papers and give them to Joyner, who will then "show them to [Ivy] Methvin and advise him that the moment Barrow and Parker are 'apprehended' (the officers do not expect to take either alive), Henry Methvin will be a free man."

The third time the posse comes to Bienville Parish, just five days later, Ivy and Avie Methvin are ready to risk a face-to-face meeting. They want to get a look at who it is they're dealing with, because the way they see it they're putting their lives in these men's hands. Despite all the picnics and "mysterious prosperity," the truth is, the Methvins are scared to death of Bonnie and Clyde. One minute the two bandits are all smiles and friendliness, and the next minute one of them is coming into the house with an automatic rifle and telling Henry in no uncertain terms that his time with his ma and pa are up and they've got to be going.

"Barrow has threatened to kill the entire family if there is any treachery," Joyner explains to the lawmen.

That day, Hamer, Alcorn, Kindell, and Jordan make their way to a place in the woods about four miles from the Methvins' home. There, word comes that they may proceed on to the house, where Ivy and Avie are waiting. Henry's brothers, Cecil and Terrel, are also there. Hamer shows them the letter from Commissioner Simmons and Governor Ferguson but warns them that he can't promise anything about crimes Henry may have committed in other states or after the escape from Eastham. This complicates the family's thinking somewhat, and Ivy sends for his brother Iverson, Henry's uncle, for advice.

Once Iverson Methvin arrives, the family has a long debate on the pros and cons of the offer. It's a tense afternoon, with the lawmen sitting around in their suits and fedoras, smoking cigarettes and dropping hints that they're going to get Bonnie and Clyde one way or another and that if Henry happens to be with the pair when the shooting starts, well, there's no telling what might happen to him. The Methvins take the deal.

Ivy tells the officers that he thinks Joe Palmer is again with the group, and that he expects them all back in the neighborhood very soon. He knows this, he says, because Clyde asked him to go get Cumie Barrow and bring her out for a visit. He also says Clyde is more likely to go to Henry's brother Terrel's house than his own, because there are several good roads leading from that place, whereas Ivy's own farm is down at the end of a narrow track.

"The Methvins are in great fear of Barrow, and extremely anxious that Henry Methvin should be separated from him," Kindell reports. Henry has told his parents that he wants to get away from Clyde, only his family isn't sure but that the boy will "weaken in the pinch" and warn Clyde of the trap. Everyone agrees, therefore, that Henry Methvin should be the last to know.

"It should be stated that Henry Methvin will not be advised, for obvious reasons," says the report to FBI headquarters.

When the time comes, Avie or Ivy will try to get Henry aside for a moment or two, maybe out back, and explain the situation.

"Out at the well," says Avie. Clyde and Bonnie will be in their car in front, as usual, and she will get her boy to herself for one precious minute. She'll give him some of her own spine if she has to, but she'll make him do what he needs to do.

❉

Joe Palmer doesn't want to go back to Bienville Parish in the middle of May. He and Clyde and Bonnie and Henry have been on the road as usual. They rob a little bank up in Everly, Iowa, that nets seven hundred dollars from the till. There is nothing in the bank's safe, but seven hundred dollars is nothing to sneeze at, and with money in their pockets Henry starts talking about going home. Palmer, who gets a tight feeling whenever he thinks about heading back toward Louisiana, starts talking about going to the World's Fair up in Chicago.

"I was at Methvin's last April, last of April," Palmer says. "I would not come south and tried to get them not to come back south. They intended to go over there and do a little hunting and fishing on Black (or Bass) Lake. They talked about bathing suits."

Palmer refuses to go to Bienville Parish, so Clyde and Bonnie tell him they'll catch up with him down the road in one of the usual places. They drop him off near Joplin and turn south, taking Henry Methvin home for another visit.

A little fishing, a little swimming, some fun times with the Methvins— that sounds all right to Bonnie. Sounds good to Clyde, too. Maybe they can finally convince Ivy to go out to Dallas and pick up their mamas.

❋

"It's a snowball and you get on you can't stop, you know," says Ralph Fults. He's in jail, despite a half dozen efforts over the past eighteen months by Clyde and Bonnie to figure out a way to bust him out. "It's hard to quit, you know, when you get started, and later it's serious business. I know Clyde and Bonnie knew they didn't have long."

Ralph knows this because he knows Clyde and Bonnie as well as just about anyone outside their families. But also, Bonnie all but tells him so.

"I got a card from them two weeks before they got killed," he says. "All she said was she hoped she could see the flowers bloom again one more time . . . they knew the end was short. They didn't expect anything."

❋

Clyde and Bonnie are more relaxed when they show up in Bienville Parish in May. Or they're just plain deluded. Or resigned. In April they hardly got out of their car or came closer than a mile from anyone's house, even at the Methvins'. Now, for some reason, they're coming inside once in a while and eating at tables.

"We were in the house of my brother in law one night when they came. They were like any other guests," says Henry Methvin's sister-in-law Clemmie. Just like any other guests, that is, who come in and take a nap. "One of the things I remember Clyde saying was that they hadn't slept in a bed for months. They lay down in my niece's homemade bed, made by their grandfather."

Clemmie is pregnant with her first child, and nervous about miscarrying. She's anxious at first about the presence of her escaped con brother-in-law and his notorious companions, what with her own situation and her two little nieces in the house. But the evening goes well.

"I didn't really realize the danger we were all in," she says later. "If Sheriff Jordan hadn't held out, the Rangers and other law officers would have dropped a bomb on the house and two precious little girls would have lost their lives."

She's wrong about that, of course: Hamer, Alcorn, and the FBI agents have no interest in getting into a situation with Clyde if there are innocents around. Which isn't to say they're not a little miffed to find out about the dinner party only after it's over. "Clyde and Bonnie went to sleep in the house and slept until 3 a.m., having in their immediate possession only two pistols," says Agent R. Whitley, the head of the New Orleans office, in a letter to J. Edgar Hoover on May 14. "Various explanations were made as to why the officers were not advised, none of which are satisfactory to my mind."

Whitley realizes that the unmolested dinner and slumber party can work to the posse's benefit. "It's noteworthy," he says, "that Barrow appears to have implicit confidence in the Methvins as shown by the fact that he slept in their home without fear." That alone is the best thing the laws have going for them in their hunt. With that in mind, Whitley notes, "The Methvins were not questioned directly by me concerning their failure to report at the time for the reason that it is felt not advisable to antagonize them." The laws figure there will be another chance if they play their cards correctly.

Clyde and Bonnie are now going so far as to talk about renting or buying an abandoned home known locally as the John Cole place. Ivy Methvin's been over to talk to Otis Cole about the house, which hasn't been occupied for a couple of years but is otherwise in reasonably good shape. Clyde and Bonnie, on one of their quick trips to Dallas during these weeks, tell Emma and Cumie that the idea is that the family can come and use this place and Bonnie and Clyde can slip in at night for visits.

"He told his mother the last time he saw her that he was buying a fishing place in Louisiana," says old man Barrow. "Way out in a secluded spot where he wanted a comfortable house to move her to, as Clyde could not afford to go to an old vacant house when they wanted to sleep because that would attract too much attention."

Things are going to be good, Clyde and Bonnie tell their parents. There will be fishing and swimming. Relaxing. Clyde's even got himself a saxophone again; a person can play "Melancholy Baby" all night long out in those woods and no one will ever hear it.

In private, Bonnie's mother is not as optimistic about the scheme. "It would be the same old thing again," Emma Parker says about the place in Lousiana. "Secret meetings, signals, constant fear . . . but we let them plan."

Clyde's parents, meanwhile, are making another kind of plan during those first weeks of May.

"We are expecting Clyde to be killed at almost any time," Henry tells the Dallas undertaker who handled Buck's funeral. "And want you to be in readiness to handle [Clyde's] too."

❀

"The next time I saw them, they came to our house, just a week or two before the laws waylaid them," says Clemmie Methvin. "Bonnie was in the car drunk, and when she was drunk she couldn't walk. She had been burned badly in a car wreck running from the laws. Clyde carried her into the house."

"They ate supper. I remember I had cooked home-cured ham and corn bread. I don't remember what else, but when they left Bonnie wanted to take the corn bread with her."

Clemmie is still nervous about having Clyde and Bonnie around.

"As I look back now," she says, "the laws and the FBI were in the process of making a deal with my mother-in-law to turn them in."

But there's a piece of Clemmie that feels sorry for Bonnie, who, after all, is about the same age as she is but whose life couldn't be more different. What's more, Clemmie Methvin, who is within a couple of months of giving birth, is one of those who believes Bonnie is in the same situation.

"Bonnie would have had a baby the same time I became a mother," she says.

After the dinner, Clyde, Bonnie, and Henry hit the road again, but they promise to be back within a few days.

CHAPTER 23

THE END OF THE ROAD

"Now here is the present plan," says Agent Whitley of the New Orleans office of the FBI.

The idea is that Henry Methvin will convince Clyde and Bonnie to let him stay at home for a visit of a day or two, and the two of them will go off by themselves. When they return for him, the laws will be waiting. Or, failing that, once the three of them are back in Bienville Parish, Henry will find a way to get himself separated from the two of them. He'll then make his way home, where Bonnie and Clyde are certain to eventually appear to collect him.

"We expect to be waiting when Barrow appears," says Agent Whitley. "As you can see, we will have to work fast as Clyde may not remain away long before he returns to pick up Methvin. We will take up the watch and expect a climax."

The laws now are like cats who think they have found the mouse hole and are just waiting. Waiting. Waiting. Hamer's the point man.

"Immediately upon being advised by [Ivy] Methvin that Henry is at home, Sheriff Jordan will wire Hamer, who will be at either Shreveport or Monroe," says Whitley. "He does not intend to return to Texas feeling that the case has reached a critical point."

Frank Hamer is used to living in hotels. It's been a large part of his life as a Ranger for a long time now. The days of riding horses and sleeping on the range down by the border are long gone, and it's been trains, cars, sandwich shops, and hotels for decades. He and his partner, Manny Gault, are holing up in Shreveport at the New Inn, on Milam Street, waiting for the word. Sometimes Alcorn and Hinton are there, too. Sometimes Whitley or another of the G-men come through. But the point is to lie as low as possible, so as not to attract the attention of the publicity hound sheriff of Shreveport. Or, heaven forbid, the newspapers. They just lie low and wait for the telegram.

It's a bore, but Hamer hasn't been a lawman all these decades without developing the patience of an angler. Plus, he's got that feeling in his gut that it's getting close to the time. On May 11 he gets some stationery from the hotel and pens a letter to Blake at the Dallas office of the FBI, filling him in on Clyde and Bonnie's visit to Terrel Methvin's house, and other news from the front line.

"They told old man M they would see him soon," Hamer writes.

> They were in Dallas last sat night 5th trying to contact the old lady but joe had taken her and Billy to the old lady's sister's near Nacogdoches so they missed out but he left word that he would be back the latter part of the week. Their intentions are to get Billy [Billie Jean] for Henry.
>
> If the trap here fails I know what their places are and I will keep you posted. Bonnie as I told you before is in a delicate condition. I would suggest that a close watch be kept for their appearance about Sat. night. This they say will be the last try there for some time.
>
> I feel certain that we will sack the gang here.
>
> —Hamer

Hamer smells it coming.

❋

Henry Barrow is sitting at home at the filling station in Dallas with a neighbor when a Ford V-8 drives up carrying Clyde, Bonnie, and Henry Methvin.

"Mrs. Barrow had gone to East Texas and I was here tending the station," he says. "Clyde told me he wanted to talk to his mother and I told him she was not there but that I would go with him. I walked back and left some money with my neighbor to make change with. I asked him to tend the station until I came back."

As usual in these situations, Henry doesn't climb right into Clyde's car but lets his son drive off like any other customer. Only after a few minutes does Henry leave the filling station and walk around the corner to where the car is waiting. This time Clyde drives his father up to a secluded spot near the Western Heights Cemetery.

"When Clyde stopped the car, Methvin got out and walked back a piece to keep a lookout for us," says Henry. "Then Clyde took a searchlight and began going through several bags. He dug out some papers. They looked like legal documents. Clyde said they were papers on a farm he had bought in Louisiana for me and his mother. He also had some papers on a Ford V-8 passenger car and a truck.

"He told me he didn't know when they would get him and he wanted to fix those papers up for me and his mother. He looked through all his bags and a suitcase but could not find a fountain pen. Finally he said he would have to give them to me later, after he signed them.

"We sat there and talked, me and Clyde and Bonnie, until after one o'clock that morning. Clyde told me that he had moved Henry Methvin's father on the farm he had bought. He said they were the finest old couple he ever saw and that we could all meet down there every once in a while and have a good time fishing and hunting," Henry says.

"Finally, they called Henry back to the car and they took me back pretty close to the station and let me out. They drove on off with Clyde promising to bring the papers back later."

As they're pulling away Clyde says to his father, "Tell Mama that I have the papers and everything on that place and it will be ready in about two weeks."

Henry promises his son he'll do so, but as it turns out there's no point.

"That was the last time I ever saw my boy alive again," says Henry.

❋

Bonnie is happy she was able to finish that poem about her and Clyde and get it written out to give her mother the last time they were in Dallas. The ending is good, like a Jimmie Rodgers song, only without the yodeling. It's not a yodeling kind of story. It's more like one of the "famous recitations" from that collection of poems she used to have.

> They don't think they're too smart or desperate,
> They know that the law always wins;
> They've been shot at before,
> But they do not ignore
> That death is the wages of sin.

> Some day they'll go down together
> They'll bury them side by side
> To a few it'll be grief—
> To the law a relief—
> But it's death for Bonnie and Clyde.

Bonnie's relieved, as well, to have a conversation with her mother about the way she wants things after it's all over. Emma doesn't want to talk about it, but Bonnie insists.

"Why shouldn't we talk it over? It's coming—you know it—I know it—all of Texas knows it," Bonnie says.

It is an odd kind of visit, talking about buying houses in Louisiana and holding funerals in Texas, all within the course of a couple of hours on a side road somewhere. That's the kind of world she and Clyde live in: planning for everything and expecting nothing.

She tells Emma not to have a wake at a funeral home but just to bring her home for a single peaceful night before she's buried. They pore over pictures of her and Clyde, including the one of him holding her off the ground that will be famous someday. She looks beautiful, her cheek on his temple. He, in his three-piece suit with his hat in his hand and a Ford V-8 behind him, looks strong and proud.

"And another thing, Mama," she says to Emma. "When they kill us, don't ever say anything—ugly—about Clyde. Please promise me that."

Emma assures her daughter she will do as she asks, and Bonnie is happy about that, too.*

❉

Later, looking back, Henry Methvin says, "We went by home, that night—Clyde Barrow and Bonnie and myself—and I told my mother and my dad I would try to get away from them at Shreveport the next morning, and they would come down there looking for me."

He thinks it was the night of May 22, or maybe the 21st. "I talked to my mother and dad about it, and we left that morning and went to Shreveport," he says.

"What do you mean by 'we'?" someone asks him.

"Myself, Bonnie Parker, and Clyde Barrow," he answers.

"Go ahead," says the questioner.

"We got into Shreveport and they sent me after some sandwiches and while I was gone I had a chance to get away."

"Did you do that?"

"Yes, sir."

"What did you do?"

---

* Emma apparently didn't promise to bury them side by side as Bonnie's poem suggests. She did not permit it, supposedly saying that Clyde had Bonnie when she was alive but would not have her in death.

"I went back down to my brother's."

"Where does your brother live?"

"Down close to Castor, Louisiana."

Henry Methvin answers a few more questions about his return to Bienville Parish and about how he snuck out of the sandwich shop while Clyde and Bonnie were circling the block. He says he just left the sandwiches there on the counter and walked out the front door and up the street, doing his best to disappear into the morning crowds.

"Did you make any arrangements with your father to be out there at a certain place with a truck the next morning?" he's asked.

"No, sir."

"You didn't know there had ever been any arrangements made on May 21st, 22nd, or 23rd, 1934, to have that truck out there on the road?"

"Not at the time, for sure," he says.

"You didn't know anything about it until after it was all over?"

"I knew if Clyde and Bonnie went back down there, my mother and dad would have them to come back the next morning or some other time," says Henry Methvin. "They would come back down there to see if I had got home."

❉

"Well, about nine o'clock here they came. We saw them and got ready," says Prentis Oakley.

Oakley is Henderson Jordan's deputy, and he and Sheriff Jordan are there in the woods by the side of the Gibsland-Sailes road, about eight miles south of Gibsland. It's a bright Wednesday morning, May 23, 1934, and the other four members of the posse—Frank Hamer, Manny Gault, Ted Hinton, and Bob Alcorn—are there as well. They've been up most of the night, slapping mosquitoes and smoking cigarettes, and waiting. Just waiting and watching and swatting at bugs.*

Word finally came to Jordan after dark the night before from Ivy and Avie Methvin that Clyde and Bonnie had just come through looking for Henry. Clyde said he'd be back the following morning, Ivy told Jordan, who passed the word to Hamer and the rest. The word came too late, it turned out, for any of the FBI men to get there, but six men with BARs, shotguns, and handguns is really all they want or need. Late Tuesday night or in the early hours of Wednesday morning, the posse gathered as

---

* Later, when various members of the posse are asked about it, there will be a number of different stories about how long they lay in ambush, waiting for Clyde and Bonnie to appear. Hinton will say it was days. Hamer will say it was eighteen hours. The documents suggest it was half a night.

planned. They hid their cars in the woods and took up their positions in a spot of dense undergrowth at the top of a rise. They chose the spot because of the good cover, but also because it gave them clear views of the road in both directions.

Early in the morning, right before the dawn, old Ivy Methvin shows up with his log truck—the truck that some say Clyde paid for. He pulls over on the side of the road opposite from where the laws are hiding and gets out and removes a wheel off the rig to make it seem as if he's fixing it so that Clyde will slow down and stop. Ivy Methvin is not a happy man to be there, but he's made a deal for his son's liberty.

The sun rises, and Olin Jackson starts plowing his field not far away. Cars come by, and logging trucks. Bob Alcorn studies each one through binoculars as it appears, but none are carrying Clyde and Bonnie.

The sun rises higher, and at seven-thirty a school bus comes by. The driver, Dan Cole, stops and asks Ivy if he needs help. The old man shakes his head and says he's about done already, but thanks. About that time Methvin starts to have second thoughts. Every time a car comes by and it isn't Clyde and Bonnie, Methvin comes up from his truck and begs them to call off the ambush. But each time, they send him back down to his truck.

"That man was scared to death," says Prentis Oakley.

The sun climbs some more, but Bonnie and Clyde do not appear.

Until, finally, they do appear.

Through the binoculars, Bob Alcorn sees the tan Ford V-8 four-door sedan coming at them at top speed. They can hear the engine screaming and know it's got to be Clyde at the wheel. Alcorn announces it's the car they've been waiting for. The Ford is positively flying. It's them. Get ready. Will he stop? The car slows as planned.

"Bonnie and Clyde's car rolled up to the Methvins' truck and then stopped with the motor running," says Henderson Jordan. "As Methvin walked toward the car a pulpwood truck came into view. The car containing Bonnie and Clyde started to move forward and we opened fire. Prentis fired the first shot. We heard a scream like a panther come from the car."

"That's when we let them have it," says Oakley. "I was aiming right at Clyde Barrow's head when I shot."

"My BAR spits out twenty shots in an instant," says Ted Hinton.

"It was difficult to hear anything over the guns," says Jordan.

The six men of the posse are standing now and firing hundreds of bullets at the car as it slowly rolls away from them. They come out of the woods, still firing away. And then, all at once, there is silence.

"After a few moments the shooting stopped and the car rolled for a few feet and then went into a ditch," says Jordan. "I was certain no one could have lived through all those bullets, but we carefully approached the car."

Frank Hamer, who has seen more death than the rest of them combined, gets to the car, reaches in, and turns off the ignition. He opens the door.

"As inured as I am to slaughter of humans, I was sickened by the sight of Bonnie's body, nearly torn to pieces with bullets," he says. "Even though Bonnie was a despicable killer, I felt a sinking feeling at the pit of my stomach when I opened the door and saw her."

Henderson Jordan feels about the same. "I guess I will never forget the sight of that car," he says. "It looked like where hogs had been slaughtered."

The laws put their guns away.

❁

Bullets sound a lot louder when you're not pulling the trigger yourself, did you ever notice that? It's strange, too, how the sound seems to get to you later than the actual shove of the lead against and then through your body. If you haven't been shot you might not know how bullets kind of hit you like a fist and push you, knock you around. It's only later that you realize they've gone through you and out the other side. That's if you live; you realize there is a hole in you that is leaking like a rusted-out bucket.

It's like an echo, the way the sound gets there after the bullet, until one of them has gone through your brain and you don't hardly hear them normally at all. That's a good thing about bullets, you guess. *Rata rata . . .*

❁

A couple of different men in the posse claim that they personally shot the first bullet and that it went right through your head. It seems important to them to say that, but what they don't seem to see is that it doesn't really matter to you one way or the other whether it was the first, second, third, or fiftieth that kills you. And the same goes for Bonnie.

Poor beautiful Bonnie, your Bonnie girl, your melancholy baby, with her sandwich on her lap and a bullet through her head. Through her pretty jaw. Through about twenty-five or thirty places. Her hand is just about shot off. So is one of her breasts. You love Bonnie and you don't deserve her and you never have deserved her and you know you never will deserve her and now it's over. Only the thing is, she loved you, so maybe you do deserve her, right?

At last it's over.

Maybe you hear the first bullet fired, or the first ten, even. Or twenty. Or

all of them. Hundreds of bullets they fire. But after they finally stop shooting the car is just rolling slowly forward. Maybe you hear Bonnie scream,
right before she drops that sandwich on her lap. "Like a panther," the cops
say. She's no panther, though. They don't know anything about Bonnie. She's
leaning against you now, and you are leaning against the window of the
Ford. Let them shoot, you know how that feels too, to just hold that trigger
and let it rip and feel that *thump thump thump* of the recoil. The other
hundred and however many bullets, they're just an echo of something you
remember—

You remember Buck fighting chickens

And that tree by the deep water, that branch you could hang on as long
as you wanted to and then drop

You remember Bonnie drinking hot chocolate

You remember

You remember

Nothing.

Funny thing is, you can watch your own killing without anger—who
would have thought? The six lawmen are coming out of their hiding places
now, still firing their silent bullets into the car. What are they? Gone crazy?
The bullets go into your body and Bonnie's. God, you used to love those
guns. When did the cops get BARs?

So them laws finally got some decent guns, did they? About time they
took a lesson from old dead Clyde. But they don't seem to know how that
BAR will just pull your aim up, up, up, up toward the sky. There are bullets
in the trees on the other side of the road. Someone says that was Hinton
who shot the leaves out of the trees, but he himself says he got both of you
in his first four shots, which are right there close together through the door
of the car. Good old Ted Hinton; his mother ran the Western Union office
way back when you first came to Dallas from those hot cotton fields.

Ted Hinton is turning around now that the lead has stopped flying and
he's pulling out . . . what is that, a movie camera? Someone loaned it to
him, he says. Some friend of his said, "Ted, you're going to want to make a
movie of it if you actually get Clyde and Bonnie." So there he is, his gun
barrel still too hot to touch from all the shooting of bullets and he's already
shooting a movie of you and Bonnie all shot to shit in your car with all
your life's possessions laid out around you.

Look, there are your guns, two sawed-off shotguns, a couple of BARs,
propped against the trunk. Some of your pistols are lined up there, too.
There's Bonnie's notebook being rifled through by some lawman in a cheap

suit. There's her crocheted blanket hanging over the car door, her beauty cream and her perfume in her little suitcase. There are your license plates, a couple from each state—Texas, Kansas, Louisiana, Iowa, Indiana, Arkansas, Oklahoma, Missouri. There are your clothes tossed around on the ground in heaps. Your magazines and newspapers falling out the open car door. Your saxophone is leaning up there next to the guns. And of course there's the car itself, looking like a colander it's got so many holes in it.

There is your body leaning against the window now, blood coming out of your mouth. Bonnie's body is leaning on you. About the only sound is the *ticka ticka ticka ticka* of the movie camera. And as the sun heats things up, there's the sound of flies.

TICKA TICKA TICKA TICKA.

And then, people. There are people all around the car, now that word has trickled over to Arcadia and Gibsland that you and Bonnie are dead out here. This isn't a crowd like the mobs of thousands who will be there in Dallas when your pa comes up and takes your bodies back home. Down in Dallas, people you never knew will line up around the block for the thrill of filing past you lying there in a box. And you won't even be with Bonnie; Emma will see to that. She'll insist on separate funerals and separate graves in separate graveyards.

The crowds out here on the road in Louisiana aren't nearly as big as that, but there are still dozens of folks who arrive on the scene before the laws get back with a truck to tow the car into town with Bonnie still leaning against you in the front seat. When the towing starts it's like a parade, with the onlookers' cars tagging behind and hundreds along the side of the road here and there as they tow you into town. Schoolkids come running out of a school yard for a look at the shot-up vehicle; they crowd the street to the point where the driver of the tow has to stop and let them peer in at the two of you stiffening up in the front seat with flies buzzing around your heads.

At least the schoolchildren are too scared to be reaching in the windows like some of the adults do. Oh yeah, folks reach in and pull pieces of your clothes off, grab for souvenirs. One guy even gets his pocketknife out and is cutting at your ear. Even your stinking dead ear is famous now and the fellow wants it.

You would like to see him try that when you were alive. Ha! But there's nothing you can do about it now. And come to think of it, who cares? Hell, buddy, that doesn't even hurt, getting that ear cut off. Try chopping a toe off, or takin' the Texas bat on your backside with two fat trusties sitting on your head and feet. Try a half dozen bullets here and there over the years,

Clyde in the death car shortly after the ambush near Gibsland, Louisiana, on May 23, 1934. *(Missouri State Highway Patrol file photograph. Used with permission.)*

pulling them out yourself or getting Bonnie to pull them. Try a whole arsenal all at once. Try hearing Bonnie scream like a panther in the seat next to you.

You don't need that old ear—go ahead and take it, friend. Take Bonnie's jewelry, too. Sure, take those guns, Captain Hamer, they might be worth something someday. You don't need any of it now. You and Bonnie are around the corner and out of sight.

NOTES

As much as possible within the confines of nonfiction, I have tried to tell the story of Bonnie and Clyde in the voices of the participants. This strategy grew somewhat naturally out of the fact that most of the major players who ever had anything to do with the two outlaw lovers have at some point either written and published their own version of events, given testimony in court or signed a police confession, appeared in one of the multiple documentaries that have been created over the decades, or been interviewed and recorded by a relative, reporter, or other researcher. In the case of the FBI agents, they wrote reports in the clipped style of the Bureau.

In other words, there was a surprising plethora of "primary accounts."

Of course, every "primary source" has its own unique set of circumstances and qualifications. Floyd Hamilton, for instance, can reliably be counted on to tell things in a light that reflects positively on his little brother, Raymond. Blanche Barrow, similarly, is protective of Buck. In their own testimonies, W. D. Jones and Henry Methvin are likely to be asleep whenever someone gets shot. The many newspaper interviews both at the time of the events and decades later are filtered through the reporters' questions, transcriptions, and interpretations, as well as the norms of the day and the vagaries of journalistic honesty. It also bears saying that many of the subjects are criminals—sometimes on trial, sometimes reformed, sometimes wary of revenge from their fellow outlaws, but in all cases generally accustomed to telling different versions of the truth at different times of their lives.

The effect of the passage of time on sources' memories is tricky to judge. Time might be assumed to make recollections fuzzier, but in the case of those on the criminal side of the line, one senses that they get more honest as time passes and the fear of prosecution or retribution fades. Thus W. D. Jones is asleep at all the hot moments in his sworn testimony in 1933 but is wide awake in his tell-all in *Playboy* magazine in 1968. (If a generalization must be made about the lawmen, it would be that their individual roles seem to grow with the passage of time: see Lee Simmons and Ted Hinton.) In 1967, after the enormously influential Warren Beatty–Faye Dunaway movie came out, an entire new crop of interviews with minor and major participants in the story appeared in the local papers of towns where shoot-outs or other crimes had taken place. The movie, written by Robert Benton and David Newman, clearly affected both the decision of editors to track down aging witnesses and those witnesses' remembrances. The subliminal effect of the film on popular perception—including this author's—of Bonnie and Clyde cannot be underestimated.

One volume of eyewitness testimony deserves special comment, both because it's impossible to write about Bonnie and Clyde without making significant use of it and because its provenance is somewhat problematic. The book originally came out under the title *Fugitives*, but most copies are titled *The True Story of Bonnie and Clyde: As Told by Bonnie's Mother and Clyde's sister, Mrs. Emma Parker and Mrs. Nell Barrow Cowan*. True to its subtitle, the main contributors to the book are Emma Parker and Nell Barrow (with sizable sections from "cousin Bess"). It's divided into sections that purport to be by the various family members and includes the text of letters and poems. It's well worth reading for anyone interested in the story, and many of the smallest details are corroborated in other sources. But there is no easy way to discern where the hand of Jan Fortune—the professional writer who "compiled, arranged, and edited" the book—starts and stops. Also, while *Fugitives* does not attempt to gloss over the crimes of Clyde and Bonnie, it's worth remembering that it was created shortly after their death but while Blanche Barrow was still in prison, and some have suggested a noticeable slant toward encouraging leniency toward Blanche in the telling. In the specific notes below, quotes from this source will identify first the relative who is the source of the story, followed by the name Fortune and a page number.

My inclination is to take eyewitness accounts, including those in *Fugitives*, at face value, and I have avoided getting into long discussions about veracity within the main text. Two liberties I have taken with material that appears inside quotation marks bear mentioning. First: occasionally when a witness says someone else said something to them, I have chosen to just use the portion attributed to the second person and present it as a quote rather than stumble repeatedly over such constructions as "so-and-so says he said." In the notes below, such quotes will be identified first by the name of the person who is quoting another person, and by where that interview might be found. For instance if I quote something that Emma Parker says Bonnie said to her, the note will read "per Emma Parker" and then give the source. In all cases, where several consecutive quotes come from the same source, I have simply listed the first, followed by "etc."

The second liberty is with the punctuation and spelling of quotes, which may differ in the text of this book from some other versions of the same quotes. In many cases I worked with recordings of interviews done by others, so the punctuation of those quotes is mine to start with. In those cases, I have listed the source as simply the name of the audio or video recording. In one very important written source, Blanche Barrow's memoir, virtually all of the punctuation in the published version, *My Life with Bonnie and Clyde*, was added by the editor, John Neal Phillips. This is because Blanche wrote it almost entirely without punctuation or paragraph breaks, and while I think Phillips did a typically magnificent job with *My Life with Bonnie and Clyde*, in a few places I removed some of his punctuation to preserve a little more of what seemed to me the stream-of-consciousness flow of Blanche's thoughts.

The work of John Neal Phillips deserves special mention. There have been many, many books written on Bonnie and Clyde before this one, and there will no doubt be others to follow. Phillips's work, in his biography of Ralph Fults, *Running with Bonnie and Clyde*, and in his editor's afterword to Blanche Barrow's memoir, stands as a sort of baseline of good scholarship and clear writing. While I eventually tracked down the same, similar, or other primary sources for much of the material in Philips's books, I would be remiss not to acknowledge that my work would have been immensely more difficult (or impossible) without the groundwork and archival work done by him. The other two secondary sources worthy of special attention are James R. Knight and Jonathan Davis's *Bonnie and Clyde: A Twenty-First-Century Update* and *On the Trail of Bonnie and Clyde: Then and Now*, edited by Winston Ramsey. Many other secondary sources are listed in the bibliography and the chapter notes below.

One final note: many of the newspaper stories I used were found not in actual microfilms or archives but in clippings folders at various libraries and museums around the Southwest. Many of the Dallas news stories were found in Smoot Schmid's scrapbooks at the Dallas Public Library. Similarly, Harry McCormick's scrapbook contained many stories from Houston. In most of these cases the page numbers of the stories were not preserved and the dates were handwritten in by either the original clipper or some later researcher. It was not possible for me to hunt down every story in an original archive and verify the date and find the page number, so in the notes below I have simply given the name of the publication and the date. In a few cases only the dateline of the story is available, and I've noted it as such. A similar problem exists at the other end of the technological spectrum, with sources reprinted in electronic media (see W. D. Jones's *Playboy* tell-all); where the page numbers have been dropped I have simply listed the source. Specific inquiries regarding sources can be directed to me at www.schneiderbooks.com.

Epigraphs:
vii "I'm going to tell the truth": Hoover, xviii.
vii "People only live happily": Barrow, 3.

Chapter 1: Eastham
The story of Bonnie and Clyde's spectacular raid on the prison farm at Eastham was all over the Texas newspapers in January 1934. More details of the planning and execution came to light in Mullins's confession to the FBI and in the testimony given by him and others at Palmer's and Hamilton's trials for the murder of the guard Major Crowson. (Page numbers are tricky in transcripts, as some records have multiple documents, each numbered separately.) Floyd Hamilton also offered some details in various interviews, and Simmons included an extended interview with Palmer in his book. For more information about life at Eastham, see Fulsom, Brown, Good, and the *Houston Press* stories cited in the notes to chapters 10 through 12.

1 "Let's don't be sad": per Nell Barrow in Fortune, 122.
4 "Eighteen, Boss,": etc.: Fulsom, 47.
4 "Goes to bed with you": Fulsom, 17.
4 "Can to can't": Good, 26.
5 "See nothing": Earl Small in Fulsom, 6.
5 "I'm Clyde Barrow's buddy": *Houston Press*, 1/17/1934.
6 "were asking for trouble": *Houston Press*, 1/18/1934.
6 "Mr. Simmons said": *Houston Press*, 1/22/1934.
7 "no duty except to stay": Simmons, 115.
7 "a crack shot with both revolver": Simmons, 117.
7 "It was about 7:15": *Joe Palmer v. Texas*, 31.
7 "Yes, it is": ibid.
7 "It all happened so quickly": *Houston Press*, 1/17/1934.
8 "Throw up your hands": *Joe Palmer v. Texas*, 42.
8 "Don't move": Simmons, 166.
8 "He didn't give us time": *Houston Press*, 1/17/1934.
8 "My God": *Joe Palmer v. Texas*, 24, 41.
8 "They both screamed": *Raymond Hamilton v. Texas*, TCCA 17227, 66.
8 "Give us something else": *Joe Palmer v. Texas*, 11.
8 "Let 'em have it": per Emma Parker in Fortune, 156.
8 "Clyde started to shooting": *Raymond Hamilton v. Texas*, TCCA 17227, 26. (Mullins's name is spelled several different ways in different sources. I've used the spelling from the court transcripts—"Mullins"—throughout this book.)

8   "I might as well bought an overcoat": per Emma Parker in Fortune, 155.
9   "I never left": *Raymond Hamilton v. Texas*, TCCA 17227, 69.
9   "The first man to raise his head": paraphrased by Simmons, 116.
9   "After Joe Palmer shot me": *Joe Palmer v. Texas*, 31.
9   "It wasn't necessary": *Dallas Evening Journal*, 5/4/1935.
10 "Nobody but Raymond": per Joe Palmer in Simmons, 166.
10 "We don't want that old boy": per Lorraine Joyner letter in Texas Prison Museum files.
10 "Yes we do": ibid.
10 "Shut your damn mouth": per Joe Palmer in Simmons, 167.
11 "Guess four of us": ibid.
11 "Nobody but Raymond": per Joe Palmer in Simmons, 166.
11 "You've got to get off the ground": *Ralph Fults Tells His Story*.
11 "Get in, son": interview with Lorraine Joyner.
11 "Everybody hang on": per Emma Parker in Fortune, 156.
11 "I went to Governor": Simmons, 126–27.

Chapter 2: Telico, Texas

In re-creating the early days of the Barrow family a writer is necessarily (and somewhat un-
comfortably) reliant on the stories told by various family members in Fortune. Very helpful for
understanding the life of poor Texas farmers of the time is Rebecca Sharpless's fine study *Fertile
Ground, Narrow Choices*. The archive of the *Dallas Morning News* was also very helpful for articles on topics ranging from cockfights to cockroaches. Utley and Harris and Sadler were useful on the rise in Mexican migration.

13 "In many country homes": *Dallas Morning News*, 1/3/1909.
13 "last Indian to surrender": www.statemuseum.arizona.edu.
13 "made a rapid swelling": *Dallas Morning News*, 3/24/1909.
15 "We didn't have any Mexicans": Sharpless, 182.
16 "My dad [was] a tenant farmer": *Dallas Morning News*, 5/29/1978.
16 "A million and one farmers": *Dallas Morning News*, 6/29/1910.
18 "Way back yonder": Sharpless, 121.
18 "Rarely ever had enough" and "I suppose": Nell Barrow in Fortune, 24.
19 "My daddy": Sharpless, 181.
19 "Clyde loved guns": Nell Barrow in Fortune, 26.
19 "It was up to me": ibid., 27.
20 "I didn't go to do it": ibid., 24.
21 "The younger cock" and related quotes: *Dallas Morning News*, 5/9/1926.
22 "Cheese it!": *Dallas Morning News*, 5/9/1926.
22 "Buck had one problem": Boots Hinton, interviewed 5/21/2007.
22 "was always getting chickens," etc.: Nell Barrow in Fortune, 28.
23 "Farmers have kept": *Dallas Morning News*, 1/3/1909.
24 A "Ranger conviction": Utley, 5.
24 "You are hot-footing it": Utley, 73.
25 "He couldn't farm": *Dallas Morning News*, 5/29/1978.

Chapter 3: Cement City

Ken Holmes of Southwestern Historical Inc. was an invaluable guide to West Dallas and the
various places where Cement City used to be, as were the staff members of the Dallas Public Library Texas history collection, who brought me maps and miscellaneous unpublished
papers on the founding of the cement plant and other events of the time. Troup's study of
early Hispanic communities in Dallas was also useful, as was Davidson's history of the cement company.

26 "The following industries": Rowena Centennial, 4.
27 "The only knocks": Skinner, 59.
27 "where it would do": Emma Parker in Fortune, 44.
27 "The old stock ranches," "this county is as good," etc.: Rowena Centennial, 5.
27 "After he completed the job": Ballinger Ledger, 12/7/1973.
28 "Here lies our liberty": Rowena Centennial, 6.
28 "Nigger don't let the sun": sundry interviews in Rowena, Texas, 7/4/2007.
28 "Outside of church activities" and "He's a Devil": Emma Parker in Fortune, 43.
29 "To the west": Dallas Morning News, 12/19/1920.
31 "The Invisible Empire," etc.: Dallas Morning News, 5/22/1921.
31 "Brazilian Gypsies" and related quotes: Dallas Morning News, 1/05/1918.
31 "The iron hand": Dallas Morning News, 1/9/1918.
32 "So many Chinamen": Dallas Morning News, 11/19/1909.
32 "When Bonnie was six": Emma Parker in Fortune, 44.
32 "When a passing neighbor": cousin Bess in Fortune, 48.
32 "This went on night": cousin Bess in Fortune, 47.
33 "She had musical": The Truth About Bonnie and Clyde.
33 "Bonnie was so outraged": Emma Parker in Fortune, 45.
34 "I knew Bonnie real well": Bonnie & Clyde and Me!
34 "Yeah she acted," etc.: The Truth About Bonnie and Clyde.
34 "Cement City won," etc.: Dallas Morning News, 3/28/1922.
35 "Death seemed to cling": Hamilton, Public Enemy, 28.
36 "On March 22": Dallas Morning News, 3/14/1926.
36 "When Bonnie loved": cousin Bess in Fortune, 49.
36 "unusual act," etc.: Dallas Morning News, 1/3/1926.
36 "is said to be": Dallas Morning News, 6/13/1926.
37 "Naturally, I didn't want": Emma Parker in Fortune, 49.

Chapter 4: Under the Viaduct
38 "There are seventy-five": Dallas Evening Journal, 5/3/1935. (Note: this article on the camp is from a few years later than the scene portrayed.)
38 "I first saw Clyde": Jones, "Riding with Bonnie and Clyde."
39 "I've traveled pretty": Dallas Evening Journal, 5/3/1935.
40 "Their daddy didn't": Hamilton, True Story, 2.
40 "Money was tight": Remembering Bonnie and Clyde.
41 "I got a job": Bonnie & Clyde and Me!
41 "I bought him a service": Dallas Morning News, 5/29/1978.
42 "Clyde was kind of": Bonnie & Clyde and Me!
43 "You see, I moved": ibid.
43 "My wife said": Bonnie & Clyde and Me!
43 "or over by the fence": Hamilton, True Story, 2.
43 "One of Clyde's problems": Dallas Morning News, 5/29/1978.
43 "He didn't take part": Hamilton, True Story, 2.
43 "But still": Bonnie & Clyde and Me!
43 "Neither of us ever liked school": Nell Barrow in Fortune, 27.
44 "All the time, Clyde": Dallas Morning News, 5/26/1996.
44 "I found a job": Nell in Fortune, 29.
45 "Clyde was one of the": Dallas Morning News, 5/29/1978.
45 "Clyde still wanted": Nell Barrow in Fortune, 30.

Chapter 5: West Dallas

Once again, most of the anecdotes about Clyde's and Bonnie's early love affairs come from the various accounts in Fortune. There are also, however, interesting tidbits in the FBI documents, as agents later tracked down Clyde's old lovers and interviewed them. The Dallas papers, of course, are rich sources for day-to-day life in the city, as are the early chapters of Hinton and Gatewood.

46   "Juvenile bicycle thieves": *Dallas Morning News,* 3/16/1922.
46   "My brothers didn't": *Dallas Morning News,* 5/23/1981.
46   the Royal Order of the Fleas, etc.: Miller, 60–70.
47   "Living in the West Dallas": *Dallas Morning News,* 5/23/1981.
47   "They were in scrapes": Hinton, 8.
47   "Buck did fight": *Dallas Morning News,* 5/26/1996.
48   "practically raised me": Hinton, 1.
48   "The other street urchins": Hinton, 3.
48   "Buck and Clyde got": *Dallas Morning News,* 5/29/1978.
48   "Clyde was a": *Remembering Bonnie and Clyde.*
48   "There was a time": *Dallas Morning News,* 2/19/1919.
49   "Clyde, you should": Nell Barrow in Fortune, 32.
49   "It's easier to run": per Nell Barrow in Fortune, 32.
51   "Watch for a Nichols Bros.": *Dallas Morning News,* 12/13/1931.
51   "was just a kid," etc.: Phillips, *Running,* 49.
51   "After Clyde": *Remembering Bonnie and Clyde.*
52   "They could also let": undated clip entitled "Desperado" by Neil Hoey in the Bonnie and Clyde File at the Texas Prison Museum.
52   "Bonnie was very": *Dallas Daily Times Herald Magazine,* 2/12/1967.
52   "It really became a joke": Emma Parker in Fortune, 49.
52   "That suited them": ibid., 50.
53   "He treats you like": ibid., 55.
53   "He was an alcoholic": *Dallas Daily Times Herald,* 9/16/1979.
53   "I want him back": per Emma Parker in Fortune, 55.
53   "Dear Diary" and other diary entries: Fortune, 51ff.
55   "It looks sort of dirty": per Emma Parker in Fortune, 56.
55   "There were lots of scenes": Nell Barrow in Fortune, 37–38.
55   "Prices of Stocks": *Dallas Morning News,* 10/29/1929.
56   "She was perky": Hinton, 8.
56   "Photographs made with the little": Hinton, xiii.
56   "Several of the men my age": Hinton, 8.
56   "could turn heads": Hinton, xiii.
57   "They were very much in love": *Remembering Bonnie and Clyde.*
57   "Bonnie was in love": *The Truth About Bonnie and Clyde.*
58   "I knew there was something": Emma Parker in Fortune, 58.

Chapter 6: Root Square, Houston

59   "Life was desperate enough": *Dallas Daily Times Herald,* 7/27/1984.
60   "It was a bad situation": *Ralph Fults Tells His Story.*
60   "Well, I guess at an early": *Remembering Bonnie and Clyde.*
60   "Clyde was just a": *Dallas Dispatch,* 5/25/1934.
61   "He was a little": *Houston Press,* 4/28/1934 (dateline).
61   "I was sitting": *Houston Press,* 7/3/1929.
61   "There's been an explosion": *Houston Press,* 7/3/1929.

61 "Let's get away," etc.: *Houston Press,* 4/1/1930.
62 "Clyde tired of petty": *Dallas Dispatch,* 5/25/1934.
62 "I graduated from picking": *Houston Press,* 3/26/1930.
62 "Say, that boy Frenchy": *Houston Press,* 3/31/1930.
62 "I have from time to time": *Dallas Morning News,* 4/15/1933.
63 "We'll hit the ground running," etc.: *Dallas Dispatch,* 4/30/1934.
64 "Gosh, Mama" and following quotes: Nell in Fortune, 39–42.
65 "My brothers' trouble": *Dallas Morning News,* 5/26/1996.
66 "My son met Willie Turner": *Waco News-Tribune,* 3/28/1930.
67 "Turner is a Wacoan": *Waco News-Tribune,* 3/12/1930.
67 "and his companions": *Waco Sunday Tribune-Herald,* 3/2/1930.
68 "Clyde was a good boy": *Waco News-Tribune,* 3/12/1930.
69 "If you've got any rabbit": per Emma Parker in Fortune, 58.

Chapter 7: Waco
70 "I met his old gal Sadie": Jimmie Rodgers, from "In the Jailhouse Now."
71 "My crookedness," etc.: in letters to his parents, 1/12/1930, 1/16/1930, and 2/24/1930, reprinted in Knight, 28.
72 "I was so blue": undated letter to Clyde in Fortune, 61–62.
73 "Honey, I sure wish": letter to Clyde, 2/14/1930, in Fortune, 59.
74 "She began going out": Emma Parker in Fortune, 59.
74 "I liked Bonnie": *Remembering Bonnie and Clyde.*
75 "an all-day automobile": *Waco News-Tribune,* 3/17/1930.
75 "After he had been involved": *Waco News-Tribune,* 3/12/1930.
76 "One riot, one Ranger": Utley, 1.
76 "A colored man": Alyn, 156–57.
76 "That negro may": *Dallas Morning News,* 1/04/1922; "negro" was lowercased in the article, according to the newspaper's practice at the time.
76 "He ruined my health" and "An affecting scene": *Dallas Morning News,* 2/25/1922.
77 "It's high time," etc.: *Waco Times-Herald,* 1/3/1922, and *Dallas Morning News,* 1/4/1922.
78 "for kidnapping my little girl": *Waco News-Tribune,* 3/4/1930.
78 "Sugar, when you do": letter to Clyde, 2/14/1930, in Fortune, 59.
79 "Dear I know": undated letter to Clyde, in Fortune, 63.
79 "And honey": letter to Clyde, 3/3/1930, in Fortune, 67.
79 "I will sentence them": *Waco News-Tribune,* 3/6/1930.
80 "A note addressed to": ibid.
80 "to do the best that": letter to his parents, 1/12/1930, in Knight, 28.
82 "Mother thought I'd" and following quotes: *Blanche Barrow: A Voice from the Past.*
82 "I did not know": Barrow, 8.
82 "That's Buck": per Marie Barrow in Knight, 30.
82 "When Buck escaped": Barrow, xxx.

Chapter 8: Middletown, Ohio
83 "Jailer Glenn Wright": *Waco News-Tribune,* 3/26/1930.
84 "The first thing she'll do": *Houston Press,* 7/2/1930.
85 "Darling," she asks him: letter to Clyde, 2/23/1930, in Fortune, 64.
85 "One of the boys": letter to Clyde, 2/14/1930, in Fortune, 60.
85 "someone told Bud": letter to Clyde, 2/23/1930, in Fortune, 65.
85 "Dear, promise me": undated letter to Clyde, in Fortune, 62.
85 "Frank says": ibid.

86 "You didn't act": letter to Clyde, 3/3/1930, in Fortune, 67.
86 "I want you to be": undated letter to Clyde, in Fortune, 63.
86 "You're the sweetest baby": Phillips, *Running*, 48.
87 "I was never so scared": cousin Mary in Fortune, 68.
88 "If William Turner": *Waco Sunday Tribune-Herald*, 3/9/1930.
88 "A burglary": ibid.
88 "He wasn't a bad boy": cousin Mary in Fortune, 69.
89 "It is better to be beaten": *Waco News-Tribune*, 3/12/1930.
89 "Stick 'em up," says Abernathy, etc.: ibid.
91 "Had I known about" and "Bonnie was a dramatist": Emma Parker in Fortune, 71.
93 "We didn't have time," etc.: *Waco Times-Herald*, 3/23/1930.
95 "Their car was full": ibid.
95 "WILLIAM TURNER ALIAS": *Waco Times-Herald*, 3/18/1930.
95 "Just a fellow" and "I had the gun": *Waco Times-Herald*, 3/23/1930.
97 "When they brought me": ibid.
97 "I don't know": *Waco Times-Herald*, 3/19/1930.

Chapter 9: Waco, Again
98 "Mrs. Barrow and a young woman": *Waco News-Tribune*, 3/28/1930.
98 at "schoolboy Barrow": *Waco News-Tribune*, 3/12/1930.
98 "Waco's Dumbbell Bandits": *Waco Times-Herald*, 3/23/30.
98 "Baby Thugs Captured" and "Dumbbells?": *Waco News-Tribune*, 3/19/1930.
98 "They're just as bad": *Waco Times-Herald*, 3/24/1930.
99 "Well, boy": ibid.
99 "third-floor strong box": *Waco Times-Herald*, 3/27/1930.
100 "This information": *Houston Press*, 3/25/1930.
100 "Three weeks after": ibid.
101 "Horse feathers," etc.: *Waco News-Tribune*, 3/26/1930.
103 "Jail Break Plot Fails": *Waco News-Tribune*, 3/27/1930.
104 "The investigation of 1925": Simmons, 55.
104 "The following barbarous": Texas State Senate, Stenographic Report, 14.
104 "This was done" and other quotes from Mills: Brown, 138ff.
105 "We are afraid": *Houston Press*, 3/5/1930.
105 "What is the Prison Board": *Dallas Morning News*, 3/6/1930.
105 "Listen, Mr. Paddock," etc.: *Waco News-Tribune*, 3/27/1930.
106 "It was foolish": *Waco News-Tribune*, 3/28/1930.
106 "Barrow was among": *Houston Chronicle*, 3/26/1930.
107 "Clyde never drank," etc.: *Waco News-Tribune*, 3/28/1930.
107 "It was not until the filing": *Houston Press*, 3/31/1930.
107 "Just when will the case," etc.: *Houston Chronicle*, 3/26/1930.
108 "My accusers ought": *Houston Chronicle*, 3/29/1930.
108 "I have spent half": *Houston Chronicle*, 3/30/1930.
108 "the pistol that boy": *Houston Chronicle*, 3/28/1930.
108 "I didn't want": *Jimmie Arnold v. The State of Texas*, 34.
109 "He knows me intimately": ibid., 11, 33.
109 "Friends?": *Houston Chronicle*, 3/29/1930.
109 "I was afraid": *Houston Press*, 3/31/1930.
110 "Jimmie went toward": *Houston Chronicle*, 3/31/1930.
110 "I may be a fool": *Houston Press*, 4/3/1930.
110 "You can't frame": *Houston Press*, 3/31/1930.
110 "I cried the other night": *Houston Chronicle*, 3/29/1930.

111   "They just thought": *Waco News-Tribune*, 3/26/1930.
111   "Now honey," etc.: letter to Bonnie, 4/19/1930, in Fortune, 72.

Chapter 10: Huntsville, Texas
113   "The condition of the": *Houston Press*, 4/9/1930.
113   "I suppose Uncle Bud": Simmons, 179.
113   "chain-bus": Brown, 62.
113   "Black Mariah," "Black Bessie": Boettcher, 20.
114   "The customary crowd": Simmons, 181.
114   "Boys, get ready": Mills, 4.
114   "walked around and gazed": Brown, 64.
114   "Roast him!," etc.: *Houston Press*, 5/10/1930 and 5/14/1930.
116   "Mr. Russell is one of the finest": Mills, 5.
116   "was a sincere friend": Good, 22.
116   "If I had a dog": *Dallas Morning News*, 1/30/1930.
117   "The conditions which": Simmons, 66.
117   "You've got to watch": *Houston Press*, 4/28/1930.
117   "the usual crowd": *Houston Press*, 9/19/1930.
117   "No one who never," etc.: *Houston Press*, 9/20/1930.
118   "We kept up with Bonnie": *Remembering Bonnie and Clyde*.
119   "Bonnie was inconsolable": Emma Parker in Fortune, 74.

Chapter 11: Burnin' Hell
In addition to the various record books and reports at the Texas State Archives and the re-
markable series of prison exposés that appeared the *Houston Press* in September 1930, I am
indebted, in this section, to Brown's *Texas Gulag*. Also worth mentioning are Fulsom's
Prison Stories, McConal's *Over the Wall*, and Sandra Rogers's unpublished interviews at the
Texas Prison Museum. As the notes below attest, the recorded interview *Ralph Fults Tells
His Story with Bonnie and Clyde* was a great resource, especially when paired with Phillips's
biography of Fults for context.

120   "The slave camps": Simmons, 67.
120   "a slave of the state": Phillips, *Running*, 26.
120   "Everywhere was filth": Simmons, 67.
121   "that hellhole": Phillips, "Raid" (online edition).
121   "twenty lashes reg strap" and similar quotes: Texas State Prison System, Conduct Reg-
      ister. The details of inmates' appearances are from the Convict Record.
121   "not over two": Texas State Senate, "Report of the Senate Committee," 1915, 14.
121   "putting bodies on stretchers": Texas State Senate, Stenographic Report, 1925, 14.
121   "We whipped": Simmons, viii.
121   "He made Smith pull": Brown, 37.
121   "We laid him on his stomach": Brown, 138.
122   "the Bones' OK": *Houston Press*, 9/19/1930.
122   "I've never heard": *Houston Press*, 9/29/1930.
122   "Sometime they soaked": *Ralph Fults Tells His Story*.
123   "Building Tender": McConal, 90.
123   "They carried dirk knives": Brown, 187.
124   "They all married": *Ralph Fults Tells His Story*.
124   "Then the boy": Brown, 181.
125   "She was a thoroughly normal": Emma Parker in Fortune, 74.

125   "At that time": *Bonnie & Clyde and Me!*
125   "Twenty-two, Boss": Fulsom, 47.
125   "The men had lined up": *Houston Press,* 10/6/1930.
126   "We worked in the cotton": Carey, 49.
126   "A good boy": *Fort Worth Star-Telegram,* updated clip by Janice Johnston in Rev. Phil
       McClendan's clipping collection.
127   "Dear Sir": Collection of Texas Prison Museum, file on Joe Palmer.
127   "Once I visited him": Nell Barrow in Fortune, 77.
127   "A horse stepped on me": *Houston Press,* 10/6/1930.
128   "If you escaped": *Ralph Fults Tells His Story.*
128   "While I was on the Eastham": *Dallas Daily Times Herald,* 6/1/1934.
128   "He gave us enough": *Houston Press,* 1/17/1934.
129   "So I got that on my mind," etc.: *Ralph Fults Tells His Story.*
129   "Every now and then": McConal, 74.
130   "not only to prevent": *Houston Post,* 1/3/1937.
130   "They let the packs go": McConal, 76.
130   "The hounds dragged": *Houston Press.* (This article, by Harry McCormick, ran under
       the headline "Convict, Forced to Leap Among Bloodhounds, Dies from Bites." I found
       it clipped and glued into McCormick's unpublished personal scrapbook. Unfortu-
       nately, he did not include the dateline of the story and I was unable to locate it in the
       unindexed microfilms of the paper.)
131   "I got out at two o'clock": *Ralph Fults Tells His Story.*
131   "He was just what you call": ibid.
131   "I'd escaped": ibid.
132   "At Camp Two": Simmons, 67.
132   "While Clyde and I," etc.: Phillips and Fults, 11.
133   "He was an awful sensitive": *Dallas Daily Times Herald,* 7/5/91.
133   "Yeah, I wasn't as bitter," etc.: *Ralph Fults Tells His Story.*
134   "Clyde and myself": *Remembering Bonnie and Clyde.*
134   "We had a way to get word": *Ralph Fults Tells His Story.*
135   "Sugar, mother": letter to Bonnie, 12/21/1930, in Fortune, 76.
135   "Why, honey": letter to Bonnie, 12/11/1930, in Fortune, 74.
135   "He loved his mother": *Remembering Bonnie and Clyde.*
136   "I was very worried": Barrow, 11.
136   "run from place to place," etc.: ibid., 8.
137   "Buck, we felt": Nell Barrow in Fortune, 78.
137   "He depended on Mama": *Dallas Morning News,* 5/26/1996.
137   "We were sure Clyde": Barrow, 11.

Chapter 12: The Tank

Though it's now a common assertion among students of Bonnie and Clyde that Barrow was
raped at Eastham by Ed Crowder, I was unable to find any direct, quotable assertion of the
event by a witness. This is not surprising, of course, given the nature of the crime. The main
source for the story appears to be Ralph Fults, who was interviewed numerous times before
his death by the Bonnie and Clyde scholar John Neal Phillips. In his 1996 biography of
Fults, Phillips says Crowder "had been preying on Barrow, beating him and sodomizing
him repeatedly" (p. 53). In his 2004 notes to Blanche Barrow's memoir he backtracks somewhat, saying, "Crowder raped Clyde Barrow at least once" (p. 207). That Clyde did the
killing seems incontrovertible; even the FBI found out about it: "Clyde beat Bob [*sic*] Crowder to death with an iron bar inside of the barracks at Eastham Farm" (Doc. 26-4114-2).

138   "We looked at him": *Houston Press*, 3/17/1926.
138   "Sure, I robbed": *Houston Press*, 3/23/1926.
139   "I had to break laws": *Houston Press*, 4/16/1926.
139   "he saw a 'lifer' ": Nell Barrow in Fortune, 77.
140   "pink-faced kid": *Dallas Morning News*, 12/21/1967.
140   "It was a stool": *Bonnie & Clyde and Me!*
140   "One of the men": *Houston Press*, 10/30/1931.
141   "It was he who slugged": *Houston Press*, 1/17/1932.
141   "We gave the Huntsville": Nell Barrow in Fortune, 78.
141   "Warden Waid was very kind," etc.: Barrow, 9.
143   "They would stick their foot": Boettcher, 3.
143   "Fourteen men cut," etc.: *Ralph Fults Tells His Story*.
144   "Now can I lay in?": Fulsom, 41.
144   "Dr. Veazey was the doctor": Boettcher, 2.
144   "Between letting a few": *Houston Press* (undated clipping in McCormick's personal
        scrapbook).
145   "He did this": *Bonnie & Clyde and Me!*
145   "couldn't keep up": Jones, "Riding with Bonnie and Clyde."
145   "He did it so he would be sent": Barrow, 11.

Chapter 13: Back in Business
146   "I was more relieved": Emma Parker in Fortune, 76.
147   "I had a good girl": per Nell Barrow in Fortune, 78.
147   "nobody but bootleggers," etc.: Nell Barrow in Fortune, 78.
148   "Shucks": per Emma Parker in Fortune, 79.
149   "When he got out": Hamilton, *True Story*, 2.
149   "Clyde had this buddy": *Dallas Daily Times Herald*, 9/16/1979.
149   "Maybe you'd get to," etc.: Emma Parker in Fortune, 80.
149   "My mother . . . my mother, um": *The Truth About Bonnie and Clyde*.
150   "I am lonesome": letter to Cumie Barrow in Knight, 42.
150   "Sis, I nearly died": per Nell Barrow in Fortune, 80.
150   "He just seemed": *Remembering Bonnie and Clyde*.
150   "When he went": Nell Barrow in Fortune, 77.
150   "I don't know": *Remembering Bonnie and Clyde*.
151   "Clyde was restless": Nell Barrow in Fortune, 86.
151   "He changed": *Ralph Fults Tells His Story*.
151   "I loved his people": Barrow, 23.
151   "He was this tall": Barrow, 193.
152   "You showed up": Phillips and Fults, 13.
152   "I heard him tell his mother": *Ralph Fults Tells His Story*.
152   "I'll never go back": Phillips and Fults, 13.
152   "So we formed the gang": *Dallas Daily Times Herald*, 9/16/1979.
152   "He kept coming," etc.: *Ralph Fults Tells His Story*.
153   "You better not lose": Phillips, *Running*, 64.
153   "He had that sawed-off": Jones, "Riding with Bonnie and Clyde."
153   "we're going to crack," etc.: *Dallas Morning News*, 3/25/1932.
154   "The corrupt police": Phillips and Fults, 13.
154   "We was stealing them": *Dallas Daily Times Herald*, 9/16/1979.
154   "He was the complete": Jones, "Riding with Bonnie and Clyde."
155   "You know robbin' ": *Bonnie & Clyde and Me!*
155   "Ninety percent": *Ralph Fults Tells His Story*.

155   "Clyde always believed": Jones, "Riding with Bonnie and Clyde."
155   "When we used the sawed-off": *Ralph Fults Tells His Story.*

Chapter 14: Fun While It Lasted
157   "I'm a pistol packin' papa," etc.: Jimmie Rodgers, "Pistol Packin' Papa."
157   "We recruited ex-cons": *Remembering Bonnie and Clyde.*
158   "We had about twelve": *Ralph Fults Tells His Story.*
159   "Could happen to anybody," etc.: ibid.
161   "In a few days": *Dallas Morning News,* 4/16/1932.
161   "Will you all do me a favor," etc.: *Ralph Fults Tells His Story.*
163   "Bonnie told me": Emma Parker in Fortune, 81.
163   "Course the original gang": *Remembering Bonnie and Clyde.*
164   "She had every record": *The Truth About Bonnie and Clyde.*
165   "Think we'll have any trouble," etc.: Phillips and Fults, 20.
166   "I saw some good guns," etc.: *Ralph Fults Tells His Story.*
166   "Clyde was about": Jones, "Riding with Bonnie and Clyde."
167   "known for its pitching": *Dallas Morning News,* 4/20/1932.
167   "Finally, a posse," etc.: *Ralph Fults Tells His Story.*
167   "I'm going to try": per Ralph Fults, ibid.
168   "I believe to my soul": Jimmie Rodgers, "Blue Yodel No. 11."
168   "Once or twice Bonnie": cousin Bess in Fortune, 47.
169   "If you don't give up," etc.: *Ralph Fults Tells His Story.*
169   "I remember my momma": Ramsey, 48.
170   "I told Bonnie": *Ralph Fults Tells His Story.*
171   "Yeah, that's the guy," etc.: ibid.
172   "I was too big": *Dallas Daily Times Herald,* 7/5/1991.
172   "Only a mother can," etc.: Emma Parker in Fortune, 81.
173   "Bonnie was in": *Bonnie & Clyde and Me!*
173   "I took the rap": Fortune, 83. (There is some reason to believe this poem may not have
       been written in its finished form as early as Emma Parker suggests in Fortune. In par-
       ticular the reference to "this island out here in the bay" is problematic, as Alcatraz did
       not become a federal penitentiary until 1934.)

Chapter 15: The Beginning of the Road
177   "No, Sis," etc.: per Nell Barrow in Fortune, 87.
177   "Clyde told me," etc.: *Bonnie & Clyde and Me!*
179   "Clyde just come," etc.: ibid.
181   "I'm through": per Emma Parker in Fortune, 89.
181   "Well, they wanted": *The Truth About Bonnie and Clyde.*
181   "they are known": *Dallas Dispatch,* 1/26/1932.
181   "Bonnie and Clyde are in love": *Dallas Daily Times Herald,* 7/26/1933.
183   "I was at the front," etc.: *Dallas Daily Times Herald,* 1/26/1933.
183   "Where's the money": *Dallas Morning News,* 8/2/1932. (See also various articles on
       Hamilton's subsequent trial in Smoot Schmid's scrapbook dated 1/26/1933.)
183   "Listen over the radio": per Emma Parker in Fortune, 91.
184   "I didn't mention Clyde": Emma Parker in Fortune, 90.
184   "We were just big": *Atoka Indian Citizen,* 6/24/1992.
185   "They had an outside": undated statement by Duke Ellis in Confederate Museum,
       Atoka, Oklahoma.
185   "It was a typical": Atoka County Historical Society, 170.
185   "One man had a brand-new": *Atoka Indian Citizen,* 6/24/1992.

185 "It was great fun": undated statement by Duke Ellis.
186 "Atoka County was full": *Atoka County Times* (undated clipping in file of Confederate Museum, Atoka).
186 "Of course they were drinking": *Atoka Indian Citizen*, 6/24/1992.
186 "I never saw him take a drink": *Dallas Daily Times Herald*, 7/26/1933.
186 "Clyde was pretty smart": *Dallas Daily Times Herald Magazine*, 2/2/1967.
186 "Come sweetheart mine": "Melancholy Baby," lyrics by Nelson and Watson.
186 "Clyde Barrow and Ray Hamilton": *Atoka County Times*, 3/14/1968.
187 "Gene will go with me": *Atoka County Times*, 3/21/1968.
187 "Consider yourselves": *Coalgate Record Register*, 8/11/1932.
187 "Drop it": *Atoka County Times*, 3/21/1968.
187 "I don't know," etc.: per Nell Barrow in Fortune, 96.
187 "I didn't see the shooting," etc.: *Atoka County Times*, 3/14/1968.
188 "I guess I was the last": *Atoka Indian Citizen*, 6/24/1992.
188 "They gunned my father," etc.: *Chicago Daily News* (undated clip in Joplin Public Library file).
189 "For about five minutes," etc.: undated statement of Duke Ellis in Confederate Museum, Atoka.
189 "Ed was in front of me," etc.: *Atoka County Times*, 3/14/1968.
190 "Dear Friends": *Indian Citizen-Democrat*, 8/18/1932.
191 "It was about twelve o'clock," etc.: *Atoka County Times*, 3/28/1968.
192 "he never answered the door": *Roseburg Douglas County News-Review*, 11/21/2003.
192 "We were again sitting": Emma Parker in Fortune, 94.
193 "They gained definite": *Dallas Morning News*, 8/9/1932.
193 "Positive identification": *Indian Citizen-Democrat*, 8/11/1932.
193 "cooped up," etc.: *Dallas Morning News*, 8/9/1932.
193 "I guess I used," etc.: per Nell Barrow in Fortune, 96.
194 "Bonnie realized": Emma Parker in Fortune, 91.
194 "After they killed": *Bonnie & Clyde and Me!*
194 "They wanted to be married": *The Truth About Bonnie and Clyde.*
194 "Clyde just wanted to stay alive": Jones, "Riding with Bonnie and Clyde."
195 "I was irrigating," etc.: Ramsey, 66.
196 "a couple of boys": per Floyd Hamilton (who wasn't there), *Bonnie & Clyde and Me!*
196 "Stick 'em up": *San Antonio Express*, 8/16/1932.
196 "I started to reach": statement of Joe Johns, 8/17/1932, reprinted in Ramsey, 68.
196 "We're ready to drive": *San Antonio Express*, 8/16/1932.
196 "Shut up," etc.: Ramsey, 68.
198 Honey: *Dallas Morning News*, 8/16/1932.
198 "No, Sheriff," etc.: Ramsey, 68.

Chapter 16: Merry Christmas and a Happy New Year
199 "I know Clyde Barrow": Jones, Voluntary Statement.
199 "Course Ray never did": *Bonnie & Clyde and Me!*
199 "Right after the escape": Nell Barrow in Fortune, 100.
201 "the description of the girl": *Dallas Morning News*, 8/16/1932.
202 "After staying in Michigan": Nell Barrow in Fortune, 100.
202 "Young man, you can't do that": Ramsey, 75.
203 "The bandit whose photo": *Sherman Daily Democrat*, 10/12/1932.
203 "He told me": *Bonnie & Clyde and Me!*
203 "They just hung it on us": per Nell Barrow in Fortune, 101.

203 "I knew it was him": Ramsey, 74.
204 "He is a thoroughly": wanted poster, Dallas Municipal Archives.
204 "In those days, Joplin": Missouri State Highway Patrol, 23.
205 "Leave him alone!," etc.: *Carthage Evening Press,* 11/30/1932.
206 "We had a shooting scrape": *Joplin Globe,* 4/18/1933.
206 "well dressed" and "less than 500": *Carthage Evening Press,* 11/30/1932.
206 "The thief": Nell Barrow in Fortune, 102.
206 "I wisht you'd put that gun": Nell Barrow in Fortune, 103.
207 "Clyde was telling me": *Bonnie & Clyde and Me!*
207 "I want to see my mama": per Nell Barrow in Fortune, 101.
207 "How we got and they got": *The Truth About Bonnie and Clyde.*
207 "L.C., usually": *Remembering Bonnie and Clyde.*
208 "I've got a big pot": Dallas Police Department, "Telephone Tap Log of Barrow/Parker Families," p. 42.
208 "But it wasn't no big": *Remembering Bonnie and Clyde.*
208 "He come around there": *Dallas Morning News,* 5/26/1996.
208 "We had a half gallon": Jones, Voluntary Statement.
209 "All the girls thought": *Remembering Bonnie and Clyde.*
210 "He told quite a few": *Remembering Bonnie and Clyde.*
210 "I was pretty drunk": Jones, Voluntary Statement.
210 "Clyde Barrow and Bonnie": Jones, Voluntary Statement.
210 "Clyde was wanted," etc.: Jones, "Riding with Bonnie and Clyde."
210 "He hung around up and down": *Remembering Bonnie and Clyde.*
211 "some girl that Raymond": *Bonnie & Clyde and Me!*
211 "Clyde Barrow and Pretty Boy": FBI document 26-4114-42.
211 "RAYMOND HAMILTON ARRESTED": Telegram, 12/9/32, Dallas Municipal Archives.
211 "I'll wait my chance": *Dallas Daily Times Herald,* 1/16/1934.
212 "Clyde suggested to me": Jones, Voluntary Statement.
212 "I went. I know now," etc.: Jones, "Riding with Bonnie and Clyde."
212 "That's my boy's car!," etc.: ibid.
214 "Didn't let me out": Jones, Voluntary Statement.
214 "Clyde gave him fair": *Joplin News Herald* (AP), 4/14/1968.
215 "Say, don't I know you?": Underwood, 22.
215 "Don't worry about": Hinton, 5.
215 "I aways felt—sick inside": per Nell Barrow in Fortune, 108.
216 "I was about half drunk": Jones, Voluntary Statement.
216 "I let her have it": per Nell Barrow in Fortune, 107.
217 "I crawled over," etc.: Jones, Voluntary Statement.
218 "As far as I know": Jones, "Riding with Bonnie and Clyde."
218 "Hold on there": *Dallas Morning News,* 1/8/1933.
218 "Then the shot": Jones, Voluntary Statement.
218 "He was known to friends," etc.: *Dallas Morning News,* 1/8/1933.

Chapter 17: Joplin, Missouri
219 "Clyde Barrow, will o' the": *Dallas Evening Journal,* 2/27/1933.
220 "He believed in," etc.: Jones, "Riding with Bonnie and Clyde."
222 "You've read the story": Fortune, 167.
222 "Run, run, run": Jones, "Riding with Bonnie and Clyde."
222 "Dallas police": *Dallas Morning News,* 2/28/1933.
223 "She stated she had no": FBI documents 26-4114-17, 26-3068-8.

223   "She did not know": memo to Doug Walsh, Dallas Municipal Archives.
224   "After thinking over," etc.: FBI document 26-4114-17.
224   "should they put," etc.: FBI document 26-4114-28.
224   "Clyde Barrow is wanted," etc.: FBI document 26-4114-17.
225   "The Federal Bureau": FBI document 26-4114-244.
225   "The room was still dark," etc.: Barrow, 20.
226   "I personally was instrumental": FBI document 26-4114-90.
226   "I used to dream": per Nell Barrow, in Fortune, 111.
226   "Blanche, you know": Barrow, 27.
226   "You fool around": Nell Barrow in Fortune, 112.
226   "Buck got out": *Dallas Daily Times Herald,* 7/23/1933.
226   "We had not been in bed," etc.: Barrow, Appendix A, 200 (see also pp. 24ff).
228   "He will shoot to kill," etc.: Barrow, 32ff.
229   "The morning they left": *Dallas Daily Times Herald,* 7/23/1933.
229   "They do a lot of lovemaking": *Dallas Daily Times Herald,* 4/20/1934.
230   "One time she did," etc.: Jones, "Riding with Bonnie and Clyde."
232   "If I felt": Barrow, 30.
232   "You don't need to be afraid": unidentified clipping in Joplin Public Library file, head-
       lined "Newton County Coroner Names Barrows as Slayers."
233   "We used to laugh": Barrow, 42.
233   "He was never more than" and footnote: Jones, "Riding with Bonnie and Clyde."
233   "Those people are always": Barrow, 45.
234   "Clyde could hardly get Bonnie," etc.: Barrow, 42ff.
235   "It was April 13," etc.: Missouri State Highway Patrol, 19.
235   "They lived there with their curtains": *Joplin Globe,* 4/14/1933.
235   "We decided that Grammer": Missouri State Highway Patrol, 20.
236   "They kept arguing": Barrow, 48.
236   "I never knew him": *Dallas Daily Times Herald,* 4/20/1934. (The third portion of this
       quote, beginning with "He slaps her," is not in quotation marks in the article.)
236   "All of us had the jitters": Barrow, 49.
236   "While the others": Missouri State Highway Patrol, 20.
236   "Oh Lordy": Barrow, 51.
237   "Step on it," etc.: Missouri State Highway Patrol, 20ff.
238   "But I know I didn't," etc.: per Nell Barrow in Fortune, 113.
239   "Blanche, they shot me": Barrow, 52.
239   "Leave everything": Phillips, *Running,* 128.
239   "Get in the car," etc.: per Nell Barrow in Fortune, 112.
239   "I started to push," etc.: Barrow, 54.
240   "For God's sake," etc.: Bonnie Parker in Fortune, 114.
240   "We seemed to almost jump": Barrow, 56.
240   "DeGraff and I": Missouri State Highway Patrol, 21.
240   "Missouri State Highway Patrol": Archives, Missouri State Highway Patrol.
241   "On a table": Missouri State Highway Patrol, 21.
241   "He was on the porch": undated clipping in Joplin Public Library, headlined "The
       Story 'Bonnie and Clyde' Ignores."
242   "Special Agent in Charge": FBI document 264114-57.
242   "When I came to next": Jones, Voluntary Statement.
242   "I think I must": Barrow, 56.
243   "My belly ached," etc.: Jones, "Riding with Bonnie and Clyde."
243   "Bonnie and Clyde said": Barrow, 58.

Chapter 18: The Middle of the Road

244 "We didn't go": Jones, Voluntary Statement.

244 "I lost all track": Barrow, 59.

244 "I do not know what filling stations": FBI document 26-4114-90.

244 "I'd get the chair," etc.: Nell Barrow in Fortune, 122.

244 "We never had": FBI document 26-4114-90.

245 "One woman was a blonde," etc.: FBI document 26-4114-121.

245 "Jesse James Next?": *Dallas Morning News*, 1/20/1933.

245 "the clamor was growing": Hinton, 50.

246 "In all modesty": Hinton, 49.

246 "Bob Alcorn and I": Hinton, 39.

246 "In my opinion," etc.: *Dallas Morning News*, 4/15/1933.

247 "hole large enough to put": Missouri State Highway Patrol, 22.

247 "I had my car," etc.: *Dallas Morning News*, 3/18/1968.

248 "The man said something": Barrow, 61.

248 "Mr. Darby was still": Aswell, 8.

248 "The back seat": *Dallas Morning News*, 3/18/1968.

248 "He was drinking," etc.: Aswell, 8.

248 "If W.D. had left": Barrow, 61.

249 "Once Bonnie whined": *Dallas Morning News*, 3/18/1968.

249 "She was dirty": Aswell, 10.

249 "She asked me to describe": *Dallas Morning News*, 3/18/1968.

249 "got to liking them": Carver, 61.

250 "I know we're going to," etc.: *Dallas Morning News*, 3/18/1968.

250 "I thought that they," etc.: Aswell, 9.

250 "The bandit car": *Pharos-Tribune*, 5/12/1933.

250 "When we drove": Barrow, 63.

250 "I would say that": FBI document 26-4114-90.

251 "We had to laugh": Barrow, 80.

251 "Put 'em up": *Pharos-Tribune*, 5/12/1933.

251 "Why, honey": Nell Barrow in Fortune, 121.

251 "Those who saw the bandits": *Pharos-Tribune*, 5/12/1933.

252 "As the woman driver," etc.: *Okabena Press*, May 25, 1933.

252 "Bonnie said": Barrow, 68.

253 "She was going to shoot": Barrow, 72.

253 "Let's don't be sad": per Nell Barrow in Fortune, 122.

253 "Mama, we've": *Dallas Daily Times Herald Magazine*, 2/2/1967.

253 "They talked about everything": Barrow, 80.

253 "They were afraid": *Dallas Morning News*, 5/23/1981.

253 "We traveled so fast": Barrow, 65.

254 "The car caught fire," etc.: Jones, "Riding with Bonnie and Clyde."

255 "Can't afford it": *New York Times*, 6/11/1933.

255 "She had dirt and sand": Ramsey, 133.

255 "What can we do," etc.: statement of Marshall Paul Hardy, reprinted in Ramsey, 134.

258 "He set them in the back": Jones, "Riding with Bonnie and Clyde."

258 "Did you coppers," etc.: Ramsey, 137.

258 "We set there a few": Jones, Voluntary Statement.

259 "Then we saw Clyde": Barrow, 95.

259 "What we gonna do," etc.: Ramsey, 140. (In his statement, Hardy consistently misidentifies W.D. as Buck, and in the source this quote is attributed to the latter.)

259   "Buck was all for killing": Jones, "Riding with Bonnie and Clyde."
259   "What would you do," etc.: Ramsey, 140.
260   "Bonnie was a mass": Barrow, 95.
260   "When she was so bad": Jones, "Riding with Bonnie and Clyde."
260   "it took $9 a day": Billie Jean Parker in *Dallas Daily Times Herald Magazine*, 2/2/1967.
260   "Dope," etc.: Barrow, 98.
261   "I went to Bonnie": Smoot Schmid scrapbook, 11/28/1933.
261   "I was confused": Hinton, 54.
261   "Bonnie's leg, all the muscle," etc.: *The Truth About Bonnie and Clyde.*
262   "Don't get excited," etc.: Barrow, 101.
262   "One's ankle": *The Truth About Bonnie and Clyde.*
262   "Oh, Daddy, are you hurt," etc.: Barrow, 103.
262   "We had to leave": *The Truth About Bonnie and Clyde.*
263   "Bonnie never got over": Jones, "Riding with Bonnie and Clyde."
263   "She and W.D. had become": Barrow, 106.
263   "So the lady had been back," etc.: *The Truth About Bonnie and Clyde.*

Chapter 19: Platte City
265   "They couldn't keep two": Barrow, 104.
265   "These three subjects": FBI document 26-4114-73.
266   "brought back so many": Jones, Voluntary Statement.
266   "More guns and ammunition": Barrow, 107.
266   "Clyde wouldn't fight fair": Barrow, 71.
266   "Clyde dominated all them": Jones, "Riding with Bonnie and Clyde."
267   "Just get the food," etc.: Barrow, 111ff.
268   "We had no two-way," etc.: Missouri State Highway Patrol, 27.
269   "Then I jumped": Barrow, 116.
269   "The sheriff. Open up!": Missouri State Highway Patrol, 29.
269   "Tell them the men," etc.: Barrow, 117.
269   "let's give them some gas": FBI document 26-4114-90.
270   "That's the law," etc.: Jones, Voluntary Statement.
270   "I saw my father stumble," etc.: Kansas City Star, 12/21/1967.
270   "Baxter staggered," etc.: Missouri State Highway Patrol, 29.
271   "My husband used a Brownie": FBI document 26-4114-90.
271   "The armoured car," etc.: FBI document 26-4114-90.
271   "The car that seemed," etc.: Barrow, 118–19.
272   "When they did": Missouri State Highway Patrol, 30.
272   "It seems to me": FBI document 26-4114-90.
272   "They've killed Buck": Barrow, 119.
272   "When we opened the [garage]": Jones, Voluntary Statement.
272   "The hail of bullets": Missouri State Highway Patrol, 30.
273   "They can't survive": *Dallas Daily Times Herald*, 7/20/1933.
273   "May God spare," etc.: *Dallas Daily Times Herald*, 7/23/1933.
274   "We ran for a long while": Jones, Voluntary Statement.
274   "Most everything was wet," etc.: Barrow, 122ff.
276   "Buck wasn't out": Jones, Voluntary Statement.
276   "I could have screamed": Barrow, 128.
276   "Officers became suspicious," etc.: *Stuart Herald*, 7/28/1933.
277   "I was roasting": Jones, Voluntary Statement.
277   "Look out!": Barrow, 129.
277   "Shooting was going on": Jones, Voluntary Statement.

277   "Clyde, I'm shot," etc.: Barrow, 129.
277   "Clyde was yelling," etc.: Jones, Voluntary Statement.
278   "Let's run": Barrow, 129.
278   "Clyde decided": Jones, Voluntary Statement.
278   "Come on," etc.: Barrow, 129–30.
279   "They got him this trip," etc.: Bonnie Parker in Fortune, 140.
279   "didn't intend to," etc.: Jones, "Riding with Bonnie and Clyde."
280   "W.D. already had the gun": Barrow, 285, note 20.
280   "There they are," etc.: Barrow, 132.
280   "She got up from back," etc.: *Remembering Bonnie and Clyde*.
282   "I never knew if Buck was mad," etc.: Barrow, 136ff.
282   "Are you all right," etc.: Bonnie Parker in Fortune, 140.
282   "I was carrying her": Jones, "Riding with Bonnie and Clyde."
283   "We had three cars," etc.: Ramsey, 175.
283   "We didn't have nothing": Jones, "Riding with Bonnie and Clyde."

Chapter 20: Sowers
284   "How can they avoid": *Dallas Daily Times Herald,* 7/26/1933.
284   "I just know," etc.: *Dallas Morning News,* 7/25/1933.
285   "The fact is": Hinton, 80.
286   "Mother Barrow," etc.: unidentified clipping headlined "Mother Barrow Awaits Word" in Smoot Schmid's scrapbooks, Dallas Public Library.
286   "Kind Sir Chief of Detectives": copies of letters found in collection of Reverend Phillip McClendon, current owner of the Joplin shoot-out apartment. Presumably they are originally from the archives of the Joplin Police Department.
287   "W.D. told us": Barrow, 126.
287   "We was wearing": Jones, "Riding with Bonnie and Clyde."
287   "We traveled all around": Jones, Voluntary Statement.
288   "The robbing and killing": Jones, "Riding with Bonnie and Clyde."
288   "I drove on up": Jones, Voluntary Statement.
288   "I'd had enough": Jones, "Riding with Bonnie and Clyde."
288   "Scars on body": FBI document 26-4114-144.
289   "We lived in little": Bonnie Parker in Fortune, 142.
289   *The Most Wonderful*: Bonnie's copy was found in an abandoned car after the shoot-out at Sowers. The snippets of poems are from the *The Most Wonderful Collection of Famous Recitations Ever Written.*
290   "There's lots of untruths": Knight, 159.
291   "We felt that the end": Bonnie Parker in Fortune, 142.
291   "Bonnie was still unable": Emma Parker in Fortune, 145.
292   "I remember that several": *The Truth About Bonnie and Clyde.*
292   "The Irving News": *Irving News,* 1/12/1934.
293   "Sheriff Fondles": *Dallas Dispatch,* 8/25/1933.
293   "The kidnapped": *Dallas Evening Journal,* 9/4/1933.
293   "Sheriff's Office 'Hot' ": *Dallas Dispatch,* 9/1/1933.
293   "It would be completely": Hinton, 104.
293   "There couldn't have been": Hinton, 99.
294   "From Irving": Knight, 159.
294   "God, I'm glad": Hinton, 102.
294   "We have trailed": *Dallas Morning News,* 11/23/33.
295   "Alcorn failed to convince": Hinton, 104.
295   "He stated he would," etc.: FBI document, 26-4114-120.

296   "We had met Clyde": *Remembering Bonnie and Clyde.*
296   "We usually met them," etc.: *The Truth About Bonnie and Clyde.*
296   "We saw his lights": *Remembering Bonnie and Clyde.*
296   "They got about a car's": *The Truth About Bonnie and Clyde.*
296   "It was just fire": *Remembering Bonnie and Clyde.*
297   "Bonnie was shooting": Hinton, 105.
297   "Alcorn winked": Hinton, 109.
297   "It won't be nice": *Temple Daily Telegram,* 11/24/1933.
297   "Barrow has vanished," etc.: *Temple Daily Telegram,* ibid.
297   "I don't know how," etc.: *The Truth About Bonnie and Clyde.*
297   "Clyde said that one": FBI document 26-4114-171.
297   "and she was": FBI document 26-4114-145.

Chapter 21: Eastham, Again
299   "Even the prison grapevine": *Houston Press,* 1/17/1934.
300   "I put it up to Clyde": FBI document 26-4114-171.
300   "She clapped her hands": *Bonnie & Clyde and Me!*
300   "The only thing to do": FBI document 26-4114-64.
300   "I can't admit that," etc.: *Bonnie & Clyde and Me!*
301   "Come on, son": *Interview with Lorraine Joyner.*
301   "Clyde was driving": *Raymond Hamilton v. Texas,* TCCA 17227, 25.
301   "Did you hear," etc.: *Bonnie & Clyde and Me!*
302   "They all talked about," etc.: FBI document 26-4114-64.
302   "I was supposed to get": *Joe Palmer v. Texas,* 16.
302   "Billie Parker was": FBI document 26-4114-171.
302   "sure enough money," etc.: FBI document 26-4114-72.
303   "I was in the back": *Dallas Morning Herald,* 6/18/1934.
303   "because I had called": Simmons, 167.
303   "Clyde maybe was": Simmons, 146.
304   "take Clyde and Bonnie": Simmons, 127.
304   "angel of death": Johnson, 174.
304   "How many men," etc.: *Dallas Evening Journal,* 6/7/1934.
304   "No matter how long," etc.: Simmons, 128.
305   "The Dallas underworld": *Dallas Dispatch,* 1/18/1934.
306   "If a policeman": Knight, 102.
307   "I think it's just dreadful": *Dallas Evening Journal,* 4/13/1934.
307   "Not many people": *Dallas Morning Herald,* 6/18/1934.
307   "I always figured": Jones, "Riding with Bonnie and Clyde."
308   "I didn't love Gene": *Dallas Morning News,* 4/27/1934.
308   "Long as I had": *Dallas Daily Times Herald,* 4/26/1934.
309   "I never saw two," etc.: *Dallas Morning News,* 2/28/1934.
309   "Mary was still raisin' ": *Bonnie & Clyde and Me!*
309   "I hope they catch Raymond": Dallas Police Department, "Telephone Tap Log Barrow/Parker Families," p. 19.
310   "When you wanted," etc.: *Dallas Dispatch,* 5/28/34.
310   "I guess you know," etc.: *Dallas Daily Times Herald,* 4/26/1934.
310   "They seemed like swell": *Dallas Morning News,* 4/27/1934.
310   "Mary O'Dare and I": FBI document 26-4114-171.
311   "Let's take 'em": *Bonnie & Clyde and Me!*
311   "It's the laws": per Emma Parker in Fortune, 161.
313   "Bullets fired from": *Dallas Morning News,* 4/2/1934.

313   "We are hunting": *Dallas Dispatch,* 4/2/1934.
313   "Give every lead": FBI document 26-4114-96.
313   "dead or alive," etc.: *Dallas Dispatch,* 4/2/1934.
314   "Political heat": Hinton, 133.
314   "cooperating fully": FBI document 26-4114-10.
314   "tooth prints": Associated Press report, 4/2/1934.
314   "Hundreds hunting": Smoot Schmid's scrapbook, 4/5/1934.
315   "We don't know where": *Dallas Dispatch,* 4/3/1934.
315   "It was a kind": *Methvin v. State.*
315   "Clyde waved": *Miami Daily News Record,* 9/18/1934.
316   "I went on past": *Methvin v. State.*
316   "I got out on": ibid.
316   "I don't believe": *Miami Daily News Record,* 4/8/1934.
317   "He told me later": *Joplin News Herald,* 4/7/1934.
317   "When that bullet": *Miami Daily News Record,* 4/8/1934.
317   "one good man," etc.: *Methvin v. State.*
318   "We have lots of friends": FBI document 26-4114-152.
318   "She didn't have anything": *Methvin v. State.*
318   "army of peace officers": *Dallas Morning News,* 4/7/1934
318   "You can tell the officers": FBI document 26-4114-152.
318   "Bonnie asked me to advise": *Miami Daily News Record,* 4/8/1934.

Chapter 22: On the Spot
319   "This automobile": FBI document 26-4114-113.
320   "Informant B": FBI document 26-4114-62.
320   "put them on the spot": Simmons, 166.
321   "Take my tip": FBI document 26-4114-127.
321   "stays drunk": FBI document 26-4114-184.
321   "knows Clyde": FBI document 26-4114-156.
321   "Clyde and Ebbie": FBI document 26-4114-61.
322   "Grace Donegan insists," etc.: FBI document 26-4114-66.
322   "should he hear": FBI document 26-4114-81.
322   "he can and will," etc.: FBI document 26-4114-176.
323   "Mrs. B[arrow] called": Dallas Police Department, "Telephone Tap Log Barrow/
        Parker Families," p. 56.
324   "hop head and": FBI document 26-4114-61.
324   "When I get out," etc.: *Dallas Dispatch,* 4/27/1934.
324   "There is no such": *Dallas Evening Journal,* 4/26/1934.
325   "I love Raymond": *Dallas Daily Times Herald,* 4/26/1934.
325   "We had better break": FBI document 26-4114-61.
325   "You know I've always," etc.: Dallas Police Department, "Telephone Tap Log Barrow/
        Parker Families," p. 19.
325   "Mrs. P called B": ibid.
325   "We don't talk": *Dallas Evening Journal,* 4/13/1934.
325   "People have me all": *Dallas Morning News,* 4/26/1934.
326   "If you were a mind": *Dallas Daily Times Herald,* 4/26/1934.
327   "Raymond stated": FBI document 26-4114-81.
327   "Well, we have a lot," etc.: *Bonnie & Clyde, and Me!*
328   "I might come up": FBI document 26-4114-78.
328   "I got my son out": *Methvin v. State.*
329   "The Methvins": *Rembembering Bonnie and Clyde.*

329   "Numerous contacts," etc.: FBI document 26-4114-141.
330   "Joyner is a very good," etc.: FBI document 26-4114-157.
331   "Mr. Methvin and Mrs. Methvin": *Methvin v. State.*
331   "show them to [Ivy] . . . Barrow has threatened": FBI document 26-4114-157.
332   "The Methvins are in," etc.: FBI document 26-4114-166.
332   "Out at the well": *Methvin v. State.*
332   "I was at Methvin's": Simmons, 165.
333   "It's a snowball," etc.: *Ralph Fults Tells His Story.*
333   "We were in the house," etc.: statement of Clemmie Methvin in archives of the Texas Prison Museum, Huntsville.
333   "Clyde and Bonnie went," etc.: FBI document 26-4114-196.
334   "He told his mother": *Shreveport Journal,* 5/29/1934.
334   "It would be the same": Emma Parker in Fortune, 165.
334   "We are expecting": *Shreveport Times,* 5/29/1934.
334   "The next time I saw," etc.: statement of Clemmie Methvin in archives of the Texas Prison Museum, Huntsville.

Chapter 23: The End of the Road

336   "Now here is the present plan," etc.: FBI document 26-4114-196.
337   "They told old man M": FBI document 26-4114-82.
337   "Mrs. Barrow had gone": *Dallas Daily Times Herald,* 6/3/1934.
338   "They don't think": Knight, 159.
339   "Why shouldn't we talk," etc.: Emma Parker in Fortune, 166.
339   "We went by home," etc.: *Methvin v. State.*
340   "Well, about nine," etc.: Aswell, 24.
341   "Bonnie and Clyde's car": *The Death of Bonnie and Clyde.*
341   "That's when we let": Aswell, 24.
342   "As inured as I am": *Shreveport Times,* 5/24/1934.
342   "I guess I will never": *The Death of Bonnie and Clyde.*
343   "Ted, you're going to want": Boots Hinton, interviewed 5/21/2007.

SOURCES

Newspapers and Magazines

Atoka County Times
Atoka Indian Citizen
Ballinger Ledger
Bienville Democrat
Carthage Evening Press
Chicago Daily News
The Chicago Daily Tribune
The Coalgate Courier
The Coalgate Record Register
Commerce News
Daily Current-Argus
Dallas Daily Times Herald
The Dallas Dispatch
Dallas Evening Journal
The Dallas Morning News
Dallas Times Herald Magazine
Denton Record-Chronicle
Des Moines Tribune
The Echo (Texas prison system)
Electra News
Electra Star
Enid Morning News
Fort Dodge Messenger and Chronicle
Fort Smith Southwest American
Fort Worth Star-Telegram
Grand Prairie Texan
Hillsboro Evening Mirror
Houston Chronicle
The Houston Post-Dispatch (and Houston
    Post)

The Houston Press
The Huntsville Item
Indian Citizen-Democrat
Irving News
The Joplin Globe
Joplin News Herald
Journal of the North Louisiana Historical
    Association
The Kansas City Star
Kaufman Daily Herald
The Landmark
McKinney Courier-Gazette
Miami Daily News Record
Middletown Journal
New York Sunday News
The New York Times
News-Leader
Okabena Press
Pharos-Tribune
Playboy
Ranger Telegram
Rembrandt Pilot Tribune
Roseburg Douglas County News-Review
The Ruston Daily Leader
The San Angelo Standard-Times
San Antonio Express
Sherman Daily Democrat
Shreveport Journal
Shreveport Times
Stone County News-Oracle

The Stuart Herald   Waco Sunday Tribune-Herald
Temple Daily Telegram   Waco Times-Herald
Time   Wichita Daily Times
Waco News-Tribune   Wichita Falls Record-News

Recorded Interviews and Documentaries

Blanche Barrow: A Voice from the Past. Debborah Moss, 2006.
Bonnie and Clyde Film Special. Southwestern Historical Inc.
The Death of Bonnie and Clyde. Doug Libert, 2005. Southwestern Historical Inc.
Interview with Lorraine Joyner. Data Becker Corp. 2005. (Southwestern Historical Inc.)
Bonnie & Clyde and Me! The Floyd Hamilton Story. Minneapolis, Greatapes, 2000.
Ralph Fults Tells His Story with Bonnie and Clyde. Southwestern Historical Inc.
Remembering Bonnie and Clyde. Video documentary. St. Louis: Turquoise Film/Video
    Productions, 1994.
The Truth About Bonnie and Clyde as Told by Billie Jean Parker. Interview by Jud Collins.
    RCA Victor sound recording, LSP 3967, 1968.

Unpublished Materials and Public Documents

There are hundreds of miscellaneous documents (individual mug shots, police reports, escape reports, wanted posters) in the files on the Barrow/Parker gang at the Dallas Public Library, the Texas Prison Museum, the Texas Ranger Museum, the Dallas Municipal Archives,
the Texas State Archives, and on the walls of the Bonnie and Clyde Ambush Museum in Gibsland, Louisiana. The annotated list below contains some of the most important to the writing of this book and/or those that might not be found in general files on Bonnie and Clyde.

Boettcher, Hazel Hamilton. Interviewed by Sandra Rogers, Texas Prison Museum, unpub-
    lished.
Cullum Jones v. State. TCCA case 10327.
Dallas Police Department. "Telephone Tap Log Barrow/Parker Families," Texas/Dallas
    History and Archives Division, Dallas Public Library.
Dallas Public Library. Texas/Dallas History and Archives Division, Cement City Collection.
FBI files, United States Department of Justice. (Note: document numbers are at best a
    rough guide as some numbers appear on more than one document.)
Governors' Papers. Ross S. Sterling, Texas State Prison System, Texas State Archives.
Hilton Bybee v. Texas. TCCA case 15484.
Jimmie Arnold v. The State of Texas. TCCA case 13597.
Joe Palmer v. Texas (Eastham break). TCCA case 17260.
Jones, W. D., Voluntary Statement B71, Dallas County Sheriff's Department. November 18,
    1933. Dallas Municipal Archives.
McCormick, Harry. Personal scrapbook. Collection of Anne Wright Williams.
Methvin v. State. Oklahoma Criminal Court of Appeals, No. A9060.
Methvin, Clemmie. Handwritten statement in files of Texas Prison Museum, Huntsville, Texas.
Miller, Haskell. "Boys' Gangs in Dallas." Master's thesis, Southern Methodist University,
    1933. Dallas Public Library.
Raymond Hamilton v. Texas (Bucher). TCCA case 16396.
Raymond Hamilton v. Texas (Eastham break). TCCA case 17227.
Raymond Hamilton v. Texas (Neuhoff). TCCA case 16318.
Raymond Hamilton v. Texas (robbery). TCCA case 16227.
Raymond Hamilton v. Texas (robbery). TCCA case 16317.
Schmid, Smoot. Scrapbooks. Dallas Public Library. (Some of the microfilm rolls appear to
    be Ted Hinton's scrapbook.)

Texas State Prison System. Annual Reports 1929, 1930, 1931, Texas State Archives.

Texas State Prison System. Clemency Report, 1931–32, Texas State Archives, Austin.

Texas State Prison System. Complaints 2/12/1931 to 9/15/1932, Texas State Archives.

Texas State Prison System. Conduct Register, Texas State Archives, Austin. (Contains prison assignments and official punishments of prisoners in Texas prison system.)

Texas State Prison System. Convict Register, Texas State Archives, Austin. (Contains names, ages, sentences, and descriptions of convicts in the Texas prison system.)

Texas State Prison System. Escape Record, Texas State Archives. (Contains names and dates of escapees from the Texas prison system.)

Texas State Prison System. General 2/16/1932 to 3/28/1932, Texas State Archives.

Texas State Prison System. Report of the Texas Prison Centralization Commission, 1929, Texas State Archives.

Texas State Prison System. Report on Inspection of State Prison System, 1933, Texas State Archives.

Texas State Senate. Stenographic Report of Testimony [in the] Penitentiary Investigation, March 5, 1925, Texas State Archives.

Texas State Senate. Report of the Senate Committee Investigating the Affairs of the Prison System of Texas, 1915.

United States Census Records, 1910, 1920, 1930. Dallas Public Library.

United States of America vs. Mary Pitts, alias Mary O'Dare et al. (harboring trial). USDC, Northern District of Texas, No. 8250, Cr.

Books and published materials

The list below contains only those books and articles specifically quoted in the text of this book or that were particularly valuable. I have not included many general works on the Depression, gangland life, the FBI, Texas geography, and the like that would serve to make the list longer but were not, in the end, uniquely useful. (See also my comments on specific books at the beginning of the notes section.)

Alyn, Glen. *I Say for Me a Parable.* New York: Norton, 1993.

Aswell, Thomas E. *The Story of Bonnie and Clyde, from the Pages of the Ruston Daily Leader.* Ruston, LA: Ruston Daily Leader, 1968.

Atoka County Historical Society, ed. *Tales of Atoka County Heritage.* Atoka, OK: Atoka County Historical Society, 1987.

Baker, Eugene, ed. *Blanche Barrow, the Last Victim of Bonnie and Clyde: Prison Letters from 1933 to 1936.* Waco: Texian Press, 2001.

Barrow, Blanche Caldwell. *My Life with Bonnie and Clyde.* Edited by John Neal Phillips. Norman, OK: University of Oklahoma Press, 2004.

Brown, Gary. *Texas Gulag: The Chain Gang Years, 1875–1925.* Plano, TX: Republic of Texas Press, 2002.

Carey, Mary. *How Long Must I Hide.* Austin: Eakin Press, 1984.

Carver, Carolyn. "A Day with Bonnie and Clyde." *North Louisiana Historical Association Journal* (Winter 1971), pp. 59–62.

Davidson, Sidney A. *General Portland Inc.: The Dallas Plant Story.* Undated company publication from the collection of Ken Holmes Jr. Dallas: Southwestern Historical Inc.

Fortune, Jan I., ed. *The True Story of Bonnie and Clyde: As Told by Bonnie's Mother and Clyde's Sister, Mrs. Emma Parker and Mrs. Nell Barrow Cowan.* New York: Signet Books, 1968.

Fulsom, Louise Adams. *Prison Stories: The Old Days.* Published by the author, 1998.

Gatewood, Jim. *Decker: A Biography of Sheriff Bill Decker of Dallas County.* Garland, TX: Mullaney, 1999.

Good, Milt. *Twelve Years in a Texas Prison.* Lawrence: Regents Press of Kansas, n.d.

Hamilton, Floyd. *Public Enemy Number One.* Dallas: Acclaimed Books, 1978.

————, as told to Chaplain Ray. *The True Story of Floyd Hamilton: Public Enemy No. 1.* Dallas: Chaplain Ray International Prison Ministry, n.d.

Harris, Charles H. III, and Louis R. Sadler. *The Texas Rangers and the Mexican Revolution: The Bloodiest Decade, 1910–1920.* Albuquerque: University of New Mexico Press, 2004.

Hendricks, George D. "Texas Folk Similes." *Western Folklore,* vol. 19, no. 4. (October 1960), pp. 245–62.

Hinton, Ted, as told to Larry Grove. *Ambush: The Real Story of Bonnie and Clyde.* Dallas: Southwestern Historical Publications, 1979.

Holmes, Maxine, and Gerald Saxon, eds. *The WPA Dallas Guide and History.* Dallas: Dallas Public Library, 1992.

Hoover, J. Edgar. *Persons in Hiding.* Boston: Little, Brown and Co.

Hounschell, Jim. *Lawmen and Outlaws: 116 Years in Joplin History.* Joplin, MO: Joplin Historical Society, 1993.

Johnson, Benjamin Heber. *Revolution in Texas: How a Forgotten Rebellion and Its Bloody Suppression Turned Mexicans into Americans.* New Haven: Yale, 2003.

Jones, W. D. "Riding with Bonnie and Clyde." *Playboy* (November 1968), pp. 151–65. (The online reprint I used did not have page numbers.)

Knight, James R., with Jonathan Davis. *Bonnie and Clyde: A Twenty-First-Century Update.* Austin: Eakin Press, 2003.

McConal, Patrick. *Over the Wall: The Men Behind the 1934 Death House Escape.* Austin: Eakin Press, 2000.

Mills, Bill. *25 Years Behind Prison Bars.* Giddings, TX: Wilson's Selective Publications, 1990.

Missouri State Highway Patrol. *To Serve and Protect: A Collection of Memories.* Jefferson City: Missouri State Highway Patrol, 2006.

Phillips, John Neal. "Raid on Eastham." *American History,* vol. 35, no. 4 (October 2000), pp. 54–64.

————. *Running with Bonnie and Clyde: The Ten Fast Years of Ralph Fults.* Norman: University of Oklahoma Press, 1996.

————, and Ralph Fults. "The Man Who Ran with Bonnie and Clyde." *Dallas Life Magazine* (*Dallas Morning News*), June 10, 1984.

Ramsey, Winston G., ed. *On the Trail of Bonnie and Clyde, Then and Now.* London: Battle of Britain International, 2003.

Rowena Centennial Committee, ed. *Rowena Centennial.* Ballinger, TX: Ballinger Printing and Graphics, 1998.

Sharpless, Rebecca. *Fertile Ground, Narrow Choices: Women on Texas Cotton Farms, 1900–1940.* Chapel Hill: University of North Carolina, 1999.

Simmons, Lee. *Assignment Huntsville: Memoirs of a Texas Prison Official.* Austin: University of Texas Press, 1957.

Skinner, A. E. *Rowena Country.* Wichita Falls: Nortex Offset Publications, 1973.

Troup, Alexander. *Beginnings and Evolution of the Mexican-American Hispanic Communities in Dallas County: People, Places and Folklore.* Dallas: Alexander M. Troup & Associates, 1998.

Underwood, Sid. *Depression Desperado: The Chronicle of Raymond Hamilton.* Austin: Eakin Press, 1995.

Utley, Robert M. *Lone Star Lawmen: The Second Century of the Texas Rangers.* New York: Oxford, 2007.

Walker, Donald R. *Penology for Profit: A History of the Texas Prison System, 1867–1912.* College Station: Texas A&M Press, 1988.

Webb, Walter Prescott. *The Texas Rangers: A Century of Frontier Defense.* 1935. Reprint, Austin: University of Texas Press, 1977.

ACKNOWLEDGMENTS

First of all, I want to thank the Joplin, Missouri, police department for holding its fire and allowing me to put my pants on. It was the middle of the night and I had been asleep in the very bedroom that Clyde and Bonnie shared in the little second-floor apartment in Joplin where the epic gun battle between the gang and members of the Missouri State Highway Patrol took place in 1933. This is a true story, I assure you, and I am extremely grateful to the Reverend Phil McClendan of Joplin for offering to let me stay for free in the apartment for a few nights while I researched the shoot-out. The McClendans have restored the apartment to roughly how it appeared in the 1930s, but their neighbors have prevented them from renting out the place as a bed and breakfast. It was these neighbors who decided at 2:00 A.M. that my trusty Mini Cooper, which had been parked in front of the apartment all afternoon, must in fact be the getaway vehicle of a dangerous intruder.

Was I dreaming, or was someone really banging loudly on the door, down at the bottom of the stairs? I stumbled to the windows overlooking the street below—the ones that Buck had fired from—and a half dozen uniformed men shined very bright flashlights in my face and demanded I come down and open the door. This was something new. Like Blanche at the Red Crown, I politely asked them to let me get dressed and pulled on some jeans and went down and let them in. We had a good laugh eventually, the laws and I, and they said, yes, they'd like to see the place they'd always heard about. We looked at the closet over the stairs where Clyde stored his BARs, and the kitchen where Bonnie sat at the table and wrote her poetry. They couldn't have been friendlier, or more professional, and they apologized for waking me up when in fact it was a highlight of my trip. So thanks to Joplin Police Department, to the McClendans, and to their neighbors, too. I'm not superstitious, but I couldn't help thinking as I dozed off that Bonnie might have made that call for my amusement: I won't soon forget that evening.

As in the past, I could not have written this book without the inspiration and assistance of my editor, Jack Macrae, whose idea it was to look into Bonnie and Clyde in the first place. Jack's associate, Supurna Banerjee, has also been unflagging in her support of the project, as well as wise in her many suggestions along the way. The copy editor, Bonnie Thompson, also deserves a particular mention for going over the manuscript with a fine-tooth comb. Wherever she put her blue pencil down, and I don't think she missed a single page, the book was improved. To the rest of Henry Holt, and to my agent David Kuhn, I am also grateful.

To my family I owe somewhat more than gratitude. My wife, Nina Bramhall, and our son, Natty Schneider, lived with me day in and out throughout the process. That itself is support enough, but Nina also read early drafts and her comments were the perfect blend of encouragement and subtle direction. As always my mother, Pat Schneider, and my father, Peter Schneider, were invaluable readers as were my sister Bethany Schneider and Kib and Tess Bramhall. Thanks also to Tony Omer and Al Miller.

The list of helpful people in Texas, Oklahoma, Missouri, Louisiana, Arkansas, Ohio, New Mexico, and elsewhere is long, even without the many librarians and archivists along the way whose names I do not know. Particular thanks go to Ken Holmes of Southwest Historical Inc. and to Ted "Boots" Hinton of the Bonnie and Clyde Ambush Museum in Gibsland, Louisiana. I've already mentioned John Neal Phillips's important scholarship on the subject, but he was also personally generous with his advice and encyclopedic in his knowledge. Others who provided invaluable help were Laura Saegert, Tony Black, and Bill Simmons at the Texas State Library and Archives; Debbie Lopes at the FBI; John Slate at the Dallas Municipal Archives; Cheryl Cobb, Sergeant Casey, and Lori Marble at the Missouri State Highway Patrol; Michelle Lyons at the Texas Department of Criminal Justice, who, among other things, arranged for me to visit the old buildings at the Eastham prison farm in the pleasant company of Assistant Warden Gregg Oliver; Sandy Rogers and Jim Willett at the Texas Prison Museum in Huntsville; Rachel Barnett at the Texas Ranger Hall of Fame in Waco; Yvonne Weeks and Christopher Wiseman at the Joplin Museum; Barbara Rust at the National Archives–Southwest Region; Mark Tate at the Lubbock Public Library; Joyce Meeks at the Electra Public Library; Beth Andresen and the rest of the staff at the Texas/Dallas History and Archives Division of the Dallas Public Library.

There is also a lengthy list of people who are not employed by archives and museums but who nonetheless were generous with their extensive knowledge and their family lore or were just plain friendly and encouraging along the way. The list includes but is not limited to Tom Methvin, who knows everything Methvin; Robert Brunson (who was one of the last to see Bonnie and Clyde alive) and his daughter Bobbie Bruce; Olin Jackson and Calip Jackson of Gibsland; Rhea Leen Linder; Buddy Williams; Rick Raye; Linda Harryman and Pat Harryman; Ted and Karron Prince; Pam and Robert Hubbard; Ernest Barron and Jim Balzaretti in Huntsville; Joe Williams; John Davis; Diane Carson; Sharon Marsh and Shirley Best were helpful on finer points of Barrow genealogy; Rick Williams in Middletown, Ohio; Pat Lange, who introduced me to just about every resident of Rowena, Texas, at the Fourth of July town barbeque; Jeaneta Isom Morris; Kenneth Williams and Mr. and Mrs. Jones of Telico; and Ms. Morris's cousin Nedra Pilant in San Antonio. A special thanks to my friend Dr. Dan Lane of San Antonio, who introduced me to his marvelous cousin Anne Wright Williams and her husband, Joe Williams. Anne was a great friend and colleague at the *Dallas Morning News* of the late Harry McCormick, the great muckraker and confidant of the imprisoned, and loaned me the newspaperman's personal scrapbook.

I am grateful to my cousins Richard and Cinnamon Manley, who lent me a bedroom when I was in Dallas. Loren, Jeanine, Gus, and Rafaela Demerath did the same thing for me when I was in Shreveport. Raffi even moved out of her bedroom for a few days so her dad's old high school buddy didn't have to sleep on the couch. Thanks!

INDEX

Page numbers in *italics* refer to illustrations.

ABOUT THE AUTHOR

PAUL SCHNEIDER is the author of the critically acclaimed *Brutal Journey*; the highly praised and successful *The Adirondacks*, a *New York Times Book Review* Notable Book; and *The Enduring Shore*. He lives with his wife and son in Massachusetts. Find out more at www.schneiderbooks .com.